Military and society
in post-Soviet Russia

MANCHESTER
1824

Manchester University Press

Military
and society in
post-Soviet Russia

edited by
Stephen L. Webber
and Jennifer G. Mathers

Manchester University Press
Manchester and New York

distributed exclusively in the USA by Palgrave

Published by Manchester University Press
Oxford Road, Manchester M13 9NR, UK
and Room 400, 175 Fifth Avenue, New York, NY 10010, USA
www.manchesteruniversitypress.co.uk

Distributed exclusively in the USA by
Palgrave, 175 Fifth Avenue, New York,
NY 10010, USA

Distributed exclusively in Canada by
UBC Press, University of British Columbia, 2029 West Mall,
Vancouver, BC, Canada V6T 1Z2

British Library Cataloguing-in-Publication Data
A catalogue record for this book is available from the British Library

Library of Congress Cataloging-in-Publication Data applied for

ISBN   0 7190 6149 0   *hardback*
EAN   978 0 7190 6149 3

First published 2006

14 13 12 11 10 09 08 07 06   10 9 8 7 6 5 4 3 2 1

Typeset in Sabon by
D R Bungay Associates, Burghfield, Berks
Printed in Great Britain
by CPI, Bath

Contents

Contents

Part III Citizenship, identity and the challenges of the society–military relationship

List of tables

Notes on contributors

Mikhail A. Alexseev is Assistant Professor of Political Science at San Diego State University. His publications include *Without Warning: Threat Assessment, Intelligence and Global Struggle*; and (as editor) *Center–Periphery Conflict in Post-Soviet Russia: A Federation Imperiled*.

Pavel K. Baev, a Senior Research Fellow at the Peace Research Institute Oslo, is the editor of the journal *Security Dialogue*. His publications include *The Russian Army in a Time of Troubles*.

Julian Cooper is Deputy Director and Professor of Russian Economic Studies at the Centre for Russian and East European Studies, University of Birmingham. He is the author of *The Soviet Defence Industry: Conversion and Reform* and the co-editor of *The Technological Level of Soviet Industry*; *Industrial Innovation in the Soviet Union*; and *Technical Progress and Soviet Economic Development*.

David Gillespie is a Reader in Russian in the Department of European Studies and Modern Languages at the University of Bath, where he has taught since 1985, having spent five years in Moscow and Leningrad. He has published widely on post-war Soviet literature and film, and his book *Russian Cinema* was published in 2002.

Lev Gudkov headed the Department of Social and Political Studies at the All-Russian Centre for the Study of Public Opinion until 2003, and now works as a senior analyst at the Analytical Centre of Iurii Levada (following the takeover of the All-Russian Centre by the Russian Government), teaching also at the Russian State Humanities' University in Moscow. A well-known Russian commentator on political and social affairs, he is a frequent contributor to the Russian press and has many publications in Russia on a wide range of sociological topics.

Jennifer G. Mathers is a Senior Lecturer in the Department of International Politics at the University of Wales, Aberystwyth. She is co-editor of the journal

Minerva: Women and War and the author of: *The Russian Nuclear Shield from Stalin to Yeltsin*; 'Outside politics? Civil–military relations during a period of reform', in Anne C. Aldis and Roger N. McDermott (eds) *Russian Military Reform 1992–2002*; 'Reform and the Russian military', in Theo Farrell and Terry Terriff (eds) *The Sources of Military Change: Culture, Politics, Technology.*

Bettina Renz is a PhD student at the Centre for Russian and East European Studies, University of Birmingham, and where between July 2002 and December 2003 she was employed as research fellow on the Economic and Social Research Council-funded project 'Securitisation in contemporary Russia'. She graduated from the University of Edinburgh in 1998 with an MA in Russian and gained an MSc by research at the same university in 1999, with a dissertation on 'The representation of political figures in the commercial Russian press'.

Elisabeth Sieca-Kozlowski, who has a doctorate in sociology, is a freelance researcher and editor of *Post-Soviet Armies Newsletter* (www.psan.org), an internet publication dedicated to the study of post-Soviet armies. In partnership with A. Toumarkine she wrote *Géopolitique de la Mer Noire*, Karthala, 2000. She is Chief Editor of the *Journal of Power Institutions in Post-Soviet Societies*, an electronic journal (www.pipss.org) of social sciences dedicated to the structures and forces that make up the security systems in Commonwealth of Independent States (CIS) countries. With Joris van Bladel she is currently writing a book on the crisis of the Russian military.

Stephen L. Webber is a Senior Lecturer at the Centre for Russian and East European Studies, European Research Institute, University of Birmingham. His publications include *School, Reform and Society in the New Russia* and (as co-editor with I. Liikanen) *Education and Civic Culture in Postcommunist Countries.* He recently completed a major project on society-military relations in Russia, Germany and the United Kingdom, and is co-authoring a book on the findings.

Valerie Zawilski gained her PhD at the University of Toronto, and she is now an Assistant Professor of Sociology at Trent University in Peterborough, Ontario, Canada. She has several written books and articles about Russian nationalism in the Soviet and post-Soviet eras, as well as the plight of soldiers and civilians living and working in conflict zones such as Chechnia, Bosnia and Kosovo. From 2001 to 2003, Dr Zawilski worked for the Belgian military as a research advisor on civilian–military relations in peace-support operations in Kosovo.

Alina Zilberman is currently completing her PhD at the European Research Institute, University of Birmingham. Her research and publications focus on the linkage between public opinion and foreign and security policy decision-making.

Foreword

At a time when Russia is no longer front-page news, this volume is a timely reminder of why we would be most unwise to neglect unfolding events in that country. To judge by current press coverage, Russia today is 'normal', 'just like us', 'stable'. Stable it may be, but as President Putin entered his new term of office with overwhelming popular support, Russia seemed to be steadily moving away from European democratic values.

In addressing military–society relations in much broader terms than usual, the authors of this volume have gone a long way towards explaining the many failed military reform initiatives of the previous decade. The fact is that the armed forces have for so long played a large role in Russian and Soviet society that military reform cannot be achieved without a corresponding degree of social reform.

Russia is in real need of strong and effective armed forces and security forces. But the forces Russia currently has are far from ideally suited to the security threats that the country actually faces. By putting the issue of armed forces and society in a holistic context – something that more conventional studies of civil–military relations, democratic control and military reform do not do – this work gives us a greater insight into both the human aspects of the Russian military and the more obscure recesses of Russian society.

For those of us who work with Russians and who think it important to engage Russia and the Russian military in fruitful collaboration, this book valuably affords us an unusually comprehensive understanding of the complexities of the civil–military debate within a society which is still in the throes of an intense transition towards a yet unknown destination.

Christopher Donnelly
Senior Fellow, Defence Academy of the United Kingdom

Acknowledgements

We express our sincere thanks to the Royal Military Academy, Brussels, for hosting a workshop in February 2002 at which the papers on which this volume is based were discussed. We thank also the Press and Information Office of the North Atlantic Treaty Organisation, The University of Wales, Aberystwyth and the University of Birmingham for co-sponsoring this event. We are grateful to an anonymous reviewer for helpful comments and to the staff at Manchester University Press, who have offered great support and shown enormous patience waiting for the manuscript to be completed.

Note on transliteration

With the exception of certain terms (such as *Politburo*) and individuals' names (such as Yeltsin, Tolstoy, Trotsky), for which the most commonly used spellings have been adopted, the Library of Congress system of transliteration from the Cyrillic alphabet has been used throughout this volume.

Abbreviations

ABM	anti-ballistic missile
ARA	*Antimilitaristskaia Radikal'naia Assotsiatsiia* (Anti-Militarist Radical Association)
AS	*Arkhiv samizdata* (*Samizdat* Archive)
BBC	British Broadcasting Corporation
BICC	Bonn International Centre for Conversion
CAC	Cossack Affairs Council
CAST	Centre for the Analysis of Strategies and Technologies
CC CPSU	Central Committee of the Communist Party of the Soviet Union
CFSP	Common foreign and security policy of the European Union
CIRF	Commission on International Religious Freedom
CIS	Commonwealth of Independent States
CPSU	Communist Party of the Soviet Union
CSIS	Center for Strategic and International Studies
CSM	Committee of Soldiers' Mothers (*Komitet soldatskikh materei*)
DACOWITS	US Defense Advisory Committee on Women in the Services
DDA	Development and Disarmament Agency
DTRA	US Defense Threat Reduction Agency
ETA	Basque separatist organisation
FBIS	Foreign Broadcast Information Service
FOM	*Fond Obshchestvennogo Mneniia* (Public Opinion Foundation)
FSB	*Federal'naia Sluzhba Bezopasnosti* (Federal Security Service)
GDP	gross domestic product
GNP	gross national product
Gosplan	*Gosudarstvennyi Komitet Planirovaniia* (Committee of State Planning)

GRU	*Glavnoe Razvedovatel'noe Upravlenie*
	(Main Military Intelligence Directorate)
GULAG	*Glavnoe Upravlenie Ispravitel'no-trudovykh Lagerei*
	(Labour Camps Directorate)
ICBM	intercontinental ballistic missile
ILO	International Labour Organisation
IMEMO	*Institut Mirovoi Ekomoniki i Mezhdunarodnykh Otnoshenii*
	(Institute of World Economy and International Relations)
IPB	International Peace Bureau
IRA	Irish Republican Army
KGB	*Komitet Gosudarstvennoi Bezopasnosti*
	(Committee of State Security)
MChS	*Ministerstvo po chrezvychainnym situatsiiam*
	(Ministry of Emergency Situations)
MEP	Member of the European parliament
MGIMO	*Moskovskii Gosudarstvennyi Institut Mezhdunarodnykh Otnoshenii*
	(Moscow State Institute of International Relations)
MIC	military–industrial complex
MID	*Ministerstvo inostrannykh del*
	(Ministry of Foreign Affairs)
Minfin	*Ministerstvo finansov Rossiiskoi Federatsii*
	(Ministry of Finance of the Russian Federation)
Minoborony	*Ministerstvo oborony Rossiiskoi Federatsii*
	(Ministry of Defence of the Russian Federation)
MN	*Moskovskie novosti* (*Moscow News* newspaper)
MOD	Russian Ministry of Defence
MVD	*Ministerstvo vnutrennykh del*
	(Ministry of the Interior/Internal Affairs)
NATO	North Atlantic Treaty Organisation
NCO	non-commissioned officer
NGO	non-governmental organisation
NKVD	*Narodnyi Kommissariat Vnutrennykh Del*
	(People's Commissariat for Internal Affairs)
NTV	Russian television channel
NVP	*nachal'naia voennaia podgotovka*
	(basic military training)
OMON	*Otriad Militsii Osobogo Naznacheniia*
	(Ministry of Internal Affairs Special Purpose Militia Unit)
OPEC	Organisation of Petroleum-Exporting Countries
OSCE	Organisation for Security and Cooperation in Europe
OTEI	*Otdel Tekhnicheskogo Ekonomicheskogo Issledovaniia*
	(Department of Technical–Economic Research of the Institute of World Economy and International Relations)

OVS	*Osnovy voennoi sluzhby* (foundation studies for military service)
PONARS	Program on New Approaches to Russian Security (based in the Center for Strategic and International Studies, Washington, DC)
R&D	research and development
RAN	*Rossiiskaia Akademiia Nauk* (Russian Academy of Sciences)
RASU	*Rossiiskoe Agentstvo po Sistemam Upravleniia* (Russian Agency for Control Systems)
RF	*Rossiiskaia Federatsiia* (Russian Federation)
RFE	Radio Free Europe
RL	Radio Liberty
RSFSR	*Rossiiskaia Sovetskaia Federativnaia Sotsialisticheskaia Respublika* (Russian Soviet Federated Socialist Republic)
SAIC	Science Applications International Corporation
SIPRI	Stockholm International Peace Research Institute
SMI	society–military interface
SMO	Soldiers' Mothers Organisation
SOBR	*Spetsial'naia Organizatsiia Bystrogo Reagirovaniia* (Special Rapid Reaction Unit)
SPS	*Soiuz Pravykh Sil* (Union of Right Forces – Russian political party)
TsNIIEiK	*Tsentral'nyi nauchno-issledovatel'skii institut ekonomiki i konversii voennogo proizvodstva* (Central Research Institute for the Economics and Conversion of Military Production)
TSV–PK	*Teleinformatsionnaia set' voenno–promyshlennoi kommissii* (Information Agency for the Military–Industrial Commission)
TV6	Russian television channel
UN	United Nations
USSR	Union of Soviet Socialist Republics
WPS	*What the Papers Say*
WREI	US Women's Research and Education Institute
VPK	*Voenno–promyshlennaia kommissia* (Military–Industrial Commission)
VTsIOM	*Vse-Rossiiskii Tsentr po Izucheniiu Obschestvennogo Mneniia* (All-Russian Centre for the Study of Public Opinion)
WTO	World Trade Organisation

Glossary of Russian terms

afgantsy (pl.); *afganets* (sing.)
Refers to people (or a male in the singular) from Afghanistan; also used in Russian popular discourse to refer to a Soviet/Russian veteran or veterans of the 1979–89 Afghanistan War

ataman
A title used for Cossack chiefs elected to lead military units or villages

apparat
The bureaucracy, or 'apparatus', of the USSR or Soviet State

boeviki (pl.); *boevik* (sing.)
Literally 'fighter(s)', used to refer to Chechen soldiers fighting against Russian federal forces

chechentsy (pl.); *chechenets* (sing.)
Refers to people (or a male in the singular) from Chechnia; also used in Russian popular discourse to refer to a Russian veteran or veterans of the conflicts in Chechnia which began in 1994

Chekist
A general, if pejorative, term for those who used to be employed in the Soviet State's security operations – the KGB, GRU, MVD, FSB, etc.; from *Cheka*, the agency established by Dzerzhinsky under Lenin (see also *siloviki*)

dedovshchina
Form of hazing and brutality inflicted by senior conscripts (*dedy; ded* [sing.]) in the Soviet and Russian armed forces on junior conscripts

Duma
Russian Parliament

glasnost'
Literally 'openness' or 'publicity', refers to the policy of the Gorbachev leadership of permitting greater press freedoms

kolkhoz
kollektivnoe khoziaistvo or collective farm

Komsomol
  Young Communist organisation
kontraktniki (pl); *kontraktnik* (sing.)
  Professional military personnel (the term refers to the fact that they sign a contract of service on enlistment)
krai
  Soviet and Russian administrative–territorial unit
molokh
  A term meaning 'monster', used to refer to the Soviet military-industrial complex
neustavnye otnosheniia (pl.)
  Literally 'relations not in compliance with the military code' (*ustav*), used in reference to the informal patterns of relations among military personnel, including the practice of *dedovshchina*
nomenklatura
  The political elite of the Soviet Union who occupied privileged positions in the Communist Party or the Soviet State
oblasti (pl); *oblast'* (sing.)
  Soviet and Russian administrative–territorial unit(s)
okrug
  Soviet and Russian administrative–territorial unit
perestroika
  Literally 'reconstruction', used to refer to the policy initiatives of the Gorbachev leadership aimed at revitalising Soviet politics, society and the economy
politburo
  The 'Political Bureau' of the Communist Party's Central Committee during the Soviet period, comprising the most powerful political figures
Rosoboroneksport
  Literally 'Russian defence export', the Russian State's arms' export agency
samizdat
  Literally 'self-publishing', used to refer to dissident works which were reproduced and circulated clandestinely during the Soviet period
siloviki (pl.); *silovik* (sing.)
  Usually refers to senior current or former representatives of the 'power ministries' (*silovye ministerstva*), such as the MOD, MVD, FB, and so on. The term has become more frequently used during President Putin's tenure in office.
Soiuzmol
  Association of Youth Organisations (in post-Soviet Russia), modelled on the *Komsomol*
Spetsnaz
  Special forces

voennyi okrug
> military district (Soviet and Russian military administrative–territorial unit)

voenruk (voennyi rukovoditel')
> Military instructor (usually a retired officer or NCO) responsible for the delivery of basic military training in a secondary school (Soviet and post-Soviet periods)

voiska
> Forces (e.g. Soviet forces–*voiska*–were withdrawn from Afghanistan)

vydvizhenets
> Person promoted above his abilities

zachistki (pl.); *zachistka* (sing.)
> Literally 'cleansing'; refers to operations of the Russian federal forces during the Chechen wars (1994–96; 1999–2003) to remove Chechen fighters and sympathisers from an area

zashchitnik rodiny/otechestva
> defender of the motherland/fatherland; a term frequently used in official and popular discourse with reference to military personnel

zemliachestvo
> Used in reference to groups of soldiers from the same region or from the same ethnic community

Stephen L. Webber

Introduction:
the society–military interface in Russia

Why society–military relations?

For those who grew up during the Cold War, in the West and East, an abiding image of the strength of the Union of Soviet Socialist Republics (USSR) was provided by the military parades which took place in honour of the Great October Socialist Revolution and Victory Day. The rows of missile launchers and tanks rumbling across Red Square in Moscow served to reinforce the perception of the threat that the Soviet Union posed, and in the USSR were presented as a symbol of the country's might and international standing. Then, from 1990 until 1996, no military parade at all took place on Red Square, until President Boris Yeltsin reintroduced the event, following requests from war veterans.[1] The reinstated parades now tend to be a much more modest affair, with no military hardware rolled out at all,[2] and they are afforded a much lower profile in the media and in society at large.

What does this tell us? On the surface, at least, it would appear to indicate the extent to which the status and influence of the military have declined on the domestic and international stages, an impression reinforced by the myriad accounts in Western and Russian analysis which demonstrate the severity of the social problems endemic in the military, the degree of corruption found at all levels in military structures, the effects of considerable reductions in expenditure on defence, and the rapid and large-scale downsizing of the military after 1990.[3] Some analysts, on the other hand, point to the role that the military sphere has appeared to play in political life (including the use of armed force to resolve political disputes), which has given rise to:

- speculation about the likelihood of a military coup taking place;[4]
- the supposed securitisation of the political hierarchy, with President Vladimir Putin's appointment of figures from the military and security agencies to key political posts;[5] and
- what some have labelled the potential re-militarisation of society through the introduction of military-based patriotic education schemes.[6]

These apparently contradictory trends – of a perceived simultaneous decline and increase in influence – are actually quite logical products of the ongoing process of readjustment in which military and society have been engaged in Russia since 1985. Such a large and powerful institution as the Soviet armed forces was bound to have a major part to play in the reshaping of Russian society, as both an object and subject of change, even without the political, economic and social crises that Russia has had to contend with or the various armed conflicts that Russia has engaged in both inside and outside its borders. The story of the Russian military since 1991 is a complex and important one, which has continued to grip the attention of academic and policy analysts in Russia and abroad.

In the field of Russian civil–military relations, the principal focus has been on the elite-level politico-military interaction, with a considerable number of studies – some subtle and accurate, others sensational – devoted to the questions of the establishment of civilian and democratic control over the armed forces, and the degree to which the military engages in, or aspires to, intervention in the political life of the country. This is indeed an issue of great import, and the works produced by such authors as Brian Taylor[7] and the debate seen in the analytical community can be said to have made a considerable contribution to our understanding of this key policy arena in Russia. Further valuable work has been conducted by such authors as Pavel Baev[8] and Dale Herspring[9] on the nature of change in Russia's military institutions themselves as they have grappled with the imperatives of reform, the challenges of downsizing, the opportunities and the costs they have faced in the wars in Chechnia, and how these factors have affected the military's relations with the political sphere.[10] Much attention has also been paid to the role of Soldiers' Mothers Organisations (SMOs), which have been the subject of many studies in Russia and the West, often from a gender-studies perspective and/or as an example of civic culture and the development of social action in Russia.[11] The related issue of military service and the problem of brutality among service personnel, including the phenomenon of *dedovshchina*[12] and associated deaths of service personnel on peacetime duty,[13] have been frequent topics of analysis and discussion in academic, media and policy arenas, although the related issue of massive human rights' abuses by Russian forces against the civilian population and opposition fighters in the wars in Chechnia has received far less attention and discussion in Russia.[14] A good deal of analysis has also been produced in the media and by academics in Russia and the West about problems of corruption in the military, issues relating to secrecy and the freedom of access to information, and other topics.

Much important work has been produced, therefore. However, as a rule, the various levels and aspects of the Russian society–military relationship continue to be treated separately, as discrete entities, rather than as relatable strata.[15] (This is also a feature – and weakness – of many studies of society–military relations conducted on other countries.) In order to gain a comprehensive insight into the nature of the relationship between society and the military we need to adopt a holistic approach, tying together the diverse elements of the society–military nexus – from high politics and military reform to the portrayal of the military and warfare in rock music, and the reshaping of gender relations in Russia as the country moves towards a professional and smaller military. In other words, 'society–military relations' refers to *all* aspects of the interface between civilian society and the military sphere, in the political, economic, social, symbolic and cultural realms. It is our aim in this volume to bring together a sample of the range of subjects and approaches covered in the field of society–military studies, to allow the reader to gain a broad sense of the relationship between them, the ways in which events at the grass roots impact on policy-making, how policy initiatives are received by society and how developments in the society–military sphere can be seen to reflect, and affect, trends in Russian society as a whole.

A growing number of Russian policy-makers and advisers acknowledge that understanding and responding to the societal context is a key consideration in the formulation of policy decisions in today's Russia,[16] although the ways in which state institutions interact with the societal sphere may nevertheless reflect a desire to impose a top–down dynamic in policy formulation and implementation. As Webber and Zilberman show in chapter 7, while the agenda of the States' institutions may at times appear to be dominant and neglectful of societal views (or seeming even to regard them as illegitimate), the implementation of policies is subject to intense mediation and renegotiation at the societal level, resulting in significant effects, both open and hidden, on policy outcomes (including failure of implementation) that policy-makers cannot ignore and to which they have to respond. There are still many in the policy-making community in Russia, and indeed in the analytical and academic communities in Russia and the West, who tend either to downplay the significance of societal response to policy-making in Russia, or to ignore it altogether. This scepticism about the role played by the societal sphere (e.g. with regard to the linkage between public opinion and policy-making) echoes that often heard, even today, with regard to advanced Western democracies such as the USA, with some analysts holding still to such claims as the alleged ignorance of the public in the sphere of foreign and security policy (and hence people's inability to offer reasoned opinions) or perceptions of the ways in which governments attempt to manipulate public opinion. However, while such considerations do indeed reflect something of the reality, the societal sphere is more complex than they suggest. As is shown conclusively by the extensive literature on this subject – conducted mainly on the USA by such authors as Douglas Foyle,[17] Ole Holsti,[18] Lawrence Jacobs,[19] Benjamin Page[20] and Robert Shapiro[21] – public opinion and other elements of the societal response to policies cannot be so easily dismissed or ignored in the analysis of policy-making and policy implementation.

Any attempt, then, to analyse policy-level developments that does not refer to the societal response to such developments cannot provide a full or accurate picture – and in the case of Russia, where there is always a gulf between official rhetoric, laws, policy and doctrine and what actually transpires on the ground, this is particularly important. Indeed, a small number of authors, such as Charlotte Wagnsson[22] and William Zimmerman,[23] have addressed the issue of the relationship between public opinion and policy-making and policy implementation in the foreign, security and defence spheres in the Russian case, and their work demonstrates the value that such studies bring to our understanding of post-Soviet Russia.

We can illustrate the importance of synthesising the study of policy-level matters with the way in which they are received and responded to by society at large, by referring to a number of examples from Russia's recent experience. For most of the Soviet period, the military and security spheres were taboo areas, with public debate on the issues tightly monitored, controlled and restricted. Information regarding the USSR's involvement in conflicts during the Cold War was passed on to the Soviet public in very small doses and with very heavy bias towards *positive* news (e.g. from 1979 to 1984 the conflict in Afghanistan was afforded very little attention in the Soviet media, and when it was referred to not as a war but as an internationalist operation in support of socialism, with news about casualties suffered almost completely suppressed until a groundbreaking article in the widely read newspaper *Komsomol'skaia pravda* in 1984). A similar veil of secrecy surrounded the enormity of the Soviet State's expenditure on defence and the military–industrial complex, the creation and maintenance of 'closed cities', Soviet mobilisation plans – in short, all aspects of the country's military activities.

Soviet citizens knew the boundaries beyond which discussion of the military sphere could not go, and kept within them, although this does not mean that no attention was given to understanding the societal response to policies by the policy-makers in the USSR. Indeed, considerable efforts were made in this sphere in particular, but also in all other policy arenas, to monitor public responses – e.g. through KGB (*Komitet Gosudarstvennoi Bezopasnosti* or Committee of State Security) channels of observation and information-gathering via informants and other means; analysis of letters to newspapers; reports on questions raised at party meetings, etc..[24] Further, the attempted monopolisation of information available to the public,[25] and the active suppression of dissenting voices and activities, belie the authorities' obsession with seeking to control public opinion, and their apprehension with regard to the public's potential response were people to find out the actual facts about, say, casualties of the Afghanistan campaign.

This latent societal power, and the possibility for citizens to occupy their legitimate place in the policy-making arena, surfaced under Mikhail

Gorbachev's policies of *perestroika* and *glasnost'*, which revolutionised the sphere of society–military relations.[26] As a wave of information about the war in Afghanistan, the social problems of the armed forces, the extent of the military budget and other issues hit the headlines in the late 1980s, with the media becoming increasingly daring and unrestrained in its criticism, the military sphere became a symbolic arena for the scrutiny of the nature of the Soviet system itself. The public, the media and politicians on all sides, in addition to various factions within the armed forces themselves, engaged in a far-reaching and at times emotional debate, and this played a significant part both in the reshaping of the society–military interface and in the drama of the final years of the Soviet system as a whole.

In the post-Soviet period the debate has been seen by some analysts as less intense and meaningful (see chapter 1 by Lev Gudkov, this volume), with some even pointing to what they see as a restoration of the *status quo ante*. I would maintain, however, that the debate *has* continued in political, military, media and public circles, and that the public's *ownership*[27] of or influence in the military and security spheres is now immeasurably more powerful and tangible than it was even during the Gorbachev period – even if this is not always recognised by those taking part in the debate, who perhaps already take it for granted. It is the nature of the debate that we need to study, to identify whose voices are most prominent and effective, who sets the agenda for the debate, who does not choose to participate in the debate and why, and the implications and effects of the debate. The experience of Russia since 1991 provides many examples of the complexity of the debate, of the ways in which it has opened up and of its ongoing limitations. For instance, what some saw as the retrograde reaction of the Soviet police state, as state and military officials attempted to cover up the truth and prevent information from being released in the aftermath of the sinking of the *Kursk* nuclear-powered submarine in August 2000, was soon shown to be unfeasible in the new societal conditions of post-Soviet Russia, where the Government and the navy had to comply with the demands of the public and media for information to be disclosed and for appropriate action to be taken.[28] In the case of NATO (North Atlantic Treaty Organisation) enlargement and the first Chechen war (1994–96), as Charlotte Wagnsson shows convincingly,[29] the attempts by Russia's political and military elites to securitise the issue met with failure, as they were not accepted by the public. The role of public opinion with regard to the conflicts in Chechnia (as both an indicator of support for and opposition to the conflicts at various stages) has been instrumental in its effect on decision-making (as Mikhail Alexseev demonstrates in chapter 4), and, indeed, to the political fortunes of Boris Yeltsin and Vladimir Putin.

In the sphere of military reform, societal attitudes and responses to policy initiatives can again be seen to have played a key role, particularly in relation to the proposed shift to professional armed forces: both President

Yeltsin (in a 1996 electoral pledge)[30] and President Putin (e.g. in assuring the public that professionalisation will lead to the solution of the problems of brutality among personnel)[31] have engaged with the population on these issues, a reflection of the potent nature of this issue in Russian society.[32] As Bettina Renz shows (chapter 2 in this volume), Russian military elites have constantly expressed deep disquiet about the nature and extent of media criticism of the armed forces. While Renz presents convincing evidence of the way in which the media has come under tighter restrictions and self-imposed restraint during the Putin era, societal pressure on the military is nevertheless being exercised with increasing effectiveness. Witness the episode in early 2004, when public pressure for an explanation of events surrounding the ill-treatment and neglect of conscripts en route to Magadan *oblast'*, when they were kept for an inordinately long time in freezing conditions, leading to several deaths among and serious ill effects on many conscripts. The reaction among the public, and statements made by military officials and, indeed, by President Putin himself, reflected in the extensive media coverage of the event, were seen to contribute to the precipitous setting up of an investigation, which quickly led to a senior general being charged.[33]

In other words, while the instincts of some in Russia's defence and security apparatus may still be rooted in the more secretive approaches of the Soviet era, and while their attempts to continue to deny the public access to information may be successful in the short term, it has increasingly become the case that the changed nature of Russian society has meant that such practices have sooner or later been rendered untenable, and ground has had to be given to society's demands. This, after all, is a test of the degree of democratic accountability – a notion which is only now developing in Russia, but which is tested frequently over security and defence issues in many countries, including those seen to be established democracies. The tendency to cover up is a reflex action of institutions worldwide, in democracies as well as authoritarian regimes. There are many examples of cases in the UK, the USA and elsewhere of the closed military organisation – which deals, after all, with matters of national security on which it may quite justifiably adopt a secretive stance, but which also wishes to project an image of a successful, powerful institution that does not make mistakes – attempting to avoid disclosure of information that it fears may harm its reputation or compromise its activities. If these attempts are perceived by society to be illegitimate, and it is deemed that this information should be made available to the public realm, then the measure of a society's will and means to ensure that the public is informed can tell us much about the degree of accountability and transparency operating in that society. In Russia's case, there is no doubt that the country has come a long way since Soviet times, even if (as is the case in certain more established democracies, after all) such advances need to be consolidated and taken further.

These examples from the crucially important area of the societal debate on the military and security demonstrate convincingly the need for a more holistic approach, and one which will be embedded in a comparative context, in order to allow us to evaluate the extent to which developments and trends in Russia can be seen to be similar to or different from those elsewhere.

Our use of the term 'society–military', rather than 'civil–military', reflects our view that the field of civil–military relations internationally has tended, in its relatively short history, to focus too heavily on the more visible issues of politico-military interaction or on the nature of the military organisation and its culture, consequently giving less attention to wider aspects of the interface between societal and military spheres. This is not surprising, given that many specialists in the field are by discipline political scientists, whose focus can be seen to reflect their primary interest; similarly, military sociologists have often placed the military institution at the centre of their attention. Meanwhile, mainstream sociology has not, as a discipline, tended to afford the study of the military's relations with society as much attention as was warranted by the enormous influence that the military and warfare have had on the world. The start of the post Cold-War era might be seen to have added weight and momentum to what Martin Shaw labelled the shift to 'post-military societies',[34] with downsizing of militaries the norm among the former ideological adversaries. The bloody conflicts seen since 1991, however, and the international reaction to the terrorist threat that the events of 11 September 2001 highlighted, mean that the military sphere will undoubtedly remain a core feature of Western and other societies for the foreseeable future, but probably within a reshaped relationship with society that reflects their respective new roles and the changes that have occurred within the domestic and international political, economic and social contexts in recent years. There remains, therefore, a strong imperative to deepen our understanding of the society–military relationship. How will notions of citizenship, which in many countries have had a long-standing connection with the military, be affected by the transition, seen across Europe, towards professional armed forces, and by the diminishing degree of contact between the public and the military? How will trends in societal development continue to impact on military culture? Will society consider as legitimate the new roles and actions in which the military is engaged? Will it support the levels of expenditure on the military sphere that military leaders request? Will the military continue to be seen as the means of solving or deterring problems across the security spectrum or will other agencies take over? Will the military institution's level of political influence decline?

These are all issues that are relevant for Russia's society and its military today. If we are to understand fully the nature of citizenship, identity, gender relations and other key aspects of Russian society and culture, and if we are to be able to appreciate the challenges and the possibilities presented to Russia's political, military and commercial sectors at the federal and regional levels as society–military relations are redefined, then we must understand the roles and the level of the influence that the military has had, and is set to have, in Russia. This volume contributes to that process of developing a clearer understanding of these issues. The volume's contributors represent various disciplines (political science, sociology, cultural studies, security studies, economics), and include Russian experts as well as Western analysts of Russian affairs. We specifically did not attempt to recruit *edinomyshlenniki* (like-minded thinkers); thus the reader will find that there are internal disputes between the contributors on a good number of issues. This is an important point, as it reflects the contested nature of the subject itself. The topics covered by the contributors provide an effective cross-section of the field, showing the diversity of society's relations with the military sphere. Contributors were free to define 'military' for them-selves – as agreed during the group discussion at the workshop in which the original chapter drafts were discussed. There is awareness, of course, that the term 'military' can be applied to a wide range of organisations in Russia, far beyond the limited scope of the branches of the armed forces overseen by the Ministry of Defence (MOD). Indeed, it is vital that we understand the roles and cultures of these various forces, which range from the border forces of the Federal Security Service (*Federal'naia Sluzhba Bezopasnosti* – FSB, the KGB successor organisation), the forces of the Ministry of Emergency Situations (*Ministerstvo po chrezvychainnym situat-siiam* – MChS), the forces of the Interior Ministry (*Ministerstvo vnutren-nykh del* – MVD), and so on. Insufficient attention has been paid to these and other institutions in Russia which have a military or paramilitary func-tion, a deficiency now starting to be addressed by the analytical community. In this volume, however, the accent is on society and its relations with the military sphere writ large, with contributors referring to issues that map across distinct institutional divides.

Revisiting notions of *militarism* and *militarisation*

A key theme which is addressed implicitly or explicitly in all chapters is that of the notions of militarism and militarisation and their relevance to the study of Russian society–military relations (and, in connection with this, the subject of the two wars in Chechnia that have taken place since 1994 serves as an impor-tant *leitmotif* in almost all chapters). Militarisation and militarism are con-tested notions that have been hotly debated at the conceptual level,[35] although, as Martin Shaw notes in his seminal work on the subject *Post-Military Society* (1991), in which he calls for a sociological approach that would take greater account of the meaning of those notions in the societal sphere to be embedded more fully into the study of these issues, the two terms have been used by analysts often without a satisfactory attempt to achieve precise definition and distinction between the two notions. [36] Lack of conceptual clarity is exacerbated by the fact that both terms have also been a constant feature, until recently at least, in the popular discourse of the modern era, and both carry a heavy ideological charge, principally expressed through the terms' negative connotations. The underlying ideologically driven antipathy towards militarism and militarisation are clearly present in, for instance, the work of Marxist writers (including Marx himself), feminist writers on women, war and the military,[37] and pacifist (anti-militarist) writers,[38] and the same theme was also used frequently by either side during the Cold War to describe the stance of the other side as 'militaristic' and by extension a threat to security. This tendency to load the terms with negative associations is also very much present in their popular use by the media and the broader public, at least in European and North American societies.[39]

The lack of conceptual clarity – itself the result, in part at least, of the relative paucity of scholarly debate on what one might think would be a subject of primary concern to academics and the broader public, given the central role played by war and the military establishment in societal development – leads, then, to variation in the interpretation and employment of the terms. Militarisation, for instance, can often be used to indicate a perceived over-emphasis on military dominance in one sphere or more of society (e.g. the militarisation of the economy, of the socialising of youth, of women,[40] of politics, and 'militarisation' as arms' build-up and war preparation). The process is depicted often as an extreme condition, associated with aggressive regimes based on military strength (e.g. Nazi Germany) or times of increased international tension in which authoritarian and democratic regimes alike aim to increase their military potential (e.g. the arms races that took place prior to the First World War and during the Cold War). In the interpretation provided by Andrew Ross, it can also be a process that leads to *militarism* as a mindset inclined towards the employment of violent military means to achieve ends.[41] In other interpretations, however, militarism is not seen as a causal product of militarisation; rather the latter is viewed as a sub-element of the former. Stanislav Andreski, in his classic work *Military Organisation and Society*, suggested that we unpack the notion to identify four elements of militarism:

- *militocracy* (the presence of an undue influence of the military over civilian authorities);
- *militancy* (the presence of an aggressive, presumably military based foreign policy);
- *militolatory* (the presence of an ideology that promotes military values); and
- *militarisation*, which in Andreski's application refers to the subjugation of society to meet the needs of the military.[42]

This gives the reader a sense of the lack of conceptual clarity and consensus inherent in this subject. Shaw's work does take us much closer to providing a more adequate and universally applicable definitional statement, and one which is crucially fixed in a sociological understanding. The post-military society hypothesis provides a challenging starting point for reflecting on the nature of the society–military relationship since the end of the Cold War, based on the perception and anticipation that the level of militarisation internationally would continue to decrease substantially after 1991, with force reductions and falling expenditure on defence the norm in Western societies, accompanied by the redefinition of military missions in line with changes in the ways we define security itself.[43] It is clear, of course, that further reconceptualisation is required in the wake of the regional and ethnic conflicts seen around the world in the last decade and a half,[44] the aftermath of 11 September 2001, and changing perceptions of and responses to security challenges.[45] Indeed, particular attention has been paid by such authors as Michael Mann to what some see as the renewed emphasis on militarism and militarisation in the case of the USA, the global 'hyperpower'.[46] Do such events and developments disprove the post-military thesis or do they highlight the fact that Western societies are both moving towards a post-military status (e.g. as seen through the decreasing level of direct involvement of the population with the military organisation) while simultaneously retaining, even increasing, their military capacity (see, for instance, calls for the EU to develop its own military forces)? What are the implications held by this for maintaining societal and political scrutiny over the military sphere? And how do such developments in Western societies relate to developments in other parts of the world, where war and insecurity remain as constant or frequent features of life?

These are questions to be addressed elsewhere. For the purposes of this volume I propose that we adopt a working interpretation of *militarism* and *militarisation* that attempts to divest the terms of their ideological baggage and avoids separating them into causal pairings or sub-components of one another, but which sees them as interrelated notions in a dynamic, symbiotic environment (in which they may affect one another or exist independently), and which is then located in the broader context of the social domain, whether this be at a sub-national (e.g. Northern Ireland, Chechnia), national, transnational (e.g. the EU) or global level. In this, *militarism* can be seen as an ideational concept (rather than a more narrowly defined ideological one), which refers to the nature of beliefs and worldviews. If we then place this on a continuum, we can identify extreme militarism at one end of the scale and extreme antimilitarism/pacifism at the other. *Militarisation* is also placed on a continuum, with total militarisation (e.g. the full mobilisation of the citizenry for war) at one end and total demilitarisation (e.g. complete disarmament) at the other. It relates, for example, to social practices and to policy-making, and refers to any aspect of a society or polity which contains a military-related element, such as expenditure on defence, conscription into the armed forces or playing war games in the playground. In contrast to many traditional interpretations, militarisation is not a linear process, but rather a constantly fluctuating dynamic.

If we were to study militarism and militarisation in isolation, then such a proposed approach would possibly be counter-productive, for this would reveal, for instance, that almost all, if not all without exception, industrialised nations can be perceived to be militarised to some degree at least (with neutral states such as Switzerland in some respects more militarised than non-neutral states with large armed forces). If, however, the focus is the study of the relationship between societal and military spheres writ large, a broader context in which the proposed (redefined) notions of militarism and militarisation form sub-components and can be analysed as such, this will allow us to achieve a more comprehensive understanding of the nature of society–military relations as a whole, since the ideological and emotional charges contained within much of the writing on militarism and militarisation are reduced, and their meanings will be more clearly visible. In turn, this enriched understanding of society–military relations will allow us to develop a more complete awareness of the nature of militarism and militarisation.[47]

The society–military interface model

Having deconstructed the notions of militarism and militarisation in the manner suggested above, we can proceed to suggest an analytical model to be employed in order to examine the nature of society–military relations. These relations can be mapped within the analytical construct of what we can term a 'society–military interface (SMI) model', which we describe as an arena that embraces all aspects of the interaction of individual citizens and society at large with the military sphere (from the abstract–symbolic to the discrete–personal levels), and in which practices and policies related to society–military relations are subject to continual mediation and renegotiation. By placing them within this model we aquire the ability to discriminate, compare and evaluate the various sub-components of society–military relations. We can also employ this model to locate the level of significance and influence of the society–military relationship within broader societal and political contexts, whether at a sub-national, a national or an international level.

In this SMI model, then, the elements of militarism and militarisation are reconstructed to provide a tool with which we can effectively assess their dynamics and outcomes in the context of the broader societal setting (i.e. what impact they have had in society large, how long-lasting has their effect been, how have various trends in militarisation related to one another?). Indeed, we can also employ the model for predictive purposes: e.g. in

chapter 7 of this volume Webber and Zilberman argue that the reintroduction of basic military training (*nachal'naia voennaia podgotovka* – NVP) in
Russian schools is not likely to lead to the militarisation of youth, as some
have warned (see also the reference to the study of NVP in the Soviet period
in the following section). This relates to a key aspect of the model, as it is
essential that we understand the ways in which militarism and militarisation
operate through analysis of the reception and reaction to 'events' in this
sphere among the audiences involved. For example, the prospects for
success of any attempt (from wherever this emanates) to impose militaristic
ideas, or mobilise a nation through militarisation, or other related issues,
depend in the end on the degree to which these goals can be achieved (in the
short and long-terms), either through consensus or coercion. In this way, it
can be seen to operate according to a similar logic to that contained within
the notion of 'securitisation' put forward by Ole Waever and Barry Buzan of
the 'Copenhagen School',[48] although an attempt to 'militarise' is, I would
suggest, likely to be more complex in its features than a securitisation
attempt, for instance when it is used alongside a call for mobilisation of the
military and call-up of civilians for possible engagement in combat.

Militarism, militarisation and the society–military relationship: the cases of the USSR and Russia

Returning to the aims of this volume, it has not been the brief of chapter
contributors to engage directly in this discussion and relate their case studies
to the proposed revision of these notions. Rather it will be the readers' task
to carry their own interpretations forward using the analysis of the range of
aspects of the Russian society–military relationship presented here. It is
worthwhile, however, in light of the above discussion to revisit the debates
that have taken place on the extent to which the USSR and now Russia can
be regarded as militaristic and militarised, to develop a better understanding
of the society–military relationship in that country.

The nature of militarism and militarisation (of society, the economy, the
political spheres etc.) in the USSR provoked a considerable debate among
Western analysts, with a range of valuable contributions made by such writers as Ulrich Albrecht,[49] Timothy Colton,[50] Egbert Jahn,[51] William Odom,[52]
Richard Pipes,[53] Dmitrii Simes[54] and David Stone.[55] The analysis was then
extended in such works as Ellen Jones's *Red Army and Society*[56] and
Andrew Cockburn's *The Threat: Inside the Soviet Military Machine*[57] to an
exploration of the broader society–military relationship in the USSR
(although the emphasis tended to remain on the military establishment, as a
reflection perhaps of the political imperatives that lay behind such studies),
and also to comparative studies of the nature of militarism and militarisation in communist countries,[58] and of the militarisation seen in the
East–West arms race.[59] These scholars put forward important hypotheses

based on informed analysis, though their task was extremely difficult as they had to study the subject from afar, using only very limited information on what was, after all, an area shrouded in secrecy and disinformation, factors that rendered any conclusions on these matters necessarily tentative and qualified, as it was impossible to test them. By the late Soviet period it became relatively more feasible, on some issues, to provide subtle analysis through mapping policy initiatives against their societal reception – with the introduction of *glasnost'* expanding such opportunities considerably. The West German scholar Friedrich Kuebart, for instance, in his 1987 study of the impact of the introduction of NVP, was able to show that what Odom, writing in 1976, had suggested was a policy that could lead to the militarisation of Soviet youth[60] needed to be set against the evidence which showed that in many cases, for a variety of reasons, secondary schools had not implemented the policy effectively.[61]

The restrictions faced by Western scholars, however, pale into insignificance when compared to those that smothered any inkling of a meaningful, open, societal debate in the USSR until the late 1980s. Soviet scholars either steered well clear of the military sphere as a subject for study or, if they did venture into this sphere, would take enormous care to ensure that their analyses coincided tightly with the *official* line, until the debate opened up during *perestroika*, as referred to above. One of the most important aspects of the legacy of this situation is its effect on the development of a more informed and mature debate in the post-Soviet period: the very limited tradition of academic scholarship and specialist media coverage, the inexperience of the new generation of politicians and economists – and, indeed, of Russian society as a whole – in engaging in open debate in this field is still having an impact today.[62] Further, the heavy veil of secrecy, accompanied by disinformation and intimidation, which surrounded the Soviet military and security establishments has – as one might expect – continued into the post-Soviet period, rendering attempts to engage in research on the Russian military organisation problematic. Restrictions apply to foreign researchers, but also to Russian researchers, including those from within the military organisation itself. Indeed, at times researchers have encountered problems with the state authorities in Russia, even when using data obtained through publicly available sources, problems which have led to long-term imprisonment.

Of course, it is accepted that any military organisation needs to be able to impose a reasonable degree of secrecy with regard to discussion of its activities, but the key requirement in a democracy is that this should be conducted within the parameters of what is permitted by law, and be accountable to scrutiny by civilian authorities. The examples referred to above surely indicate an unacceptable state of affairs in a country which claims to be based on democratic values and respect for civil liberties. It furthermore serves as a strong disincentive to those who would conduct research in this field. At the same time – and seemingly paradoxically, yet quite understandably in fact – the breakdown in systemic cohesion and the growing openness of Russian society as a whole have eroded such secretive and anti-democratic practices, with the result that, in some cases, Russian military figures have felt themselves either able or compelled to play a very active part in public debate on military issues, indeed over and beyond the degree to which their counterparts in the established democracies of the UK, the USA and elsewhere can be seen to be playing. At one international seminar in Moscow, for instance, I observed a colonel from the MVD forces openly criticising a very senior Russian politician, who was present, for being a 'hawk' and opposing democratic reform of the armed forces – surely a scene unlikely to be encountered in the stable environment of either an established democracy or an established authoritarian regime. As another example, there is the well-known case of a serving army officer in the Leningrad military district whose apartment became known in the 1990s as a 'safe house' for conscripts running away from problems of brutality they had encountered in their military units.[63] The military authorities tolerated his open insubordination towards the military organisation – which would inevitably have led to severe disciplinary measures against him in both functioning democratic and authoritarian military organisations – perhaps as a resigned acceptance that it could itself not deal effectively with such problems. There are many more examples of the stretching of the boundaries of military tolerance towards the actions of its personnel, signs of the degree of fragmentation of the identity of the Russian military organisation that has occurred in recent years, a fragmentation the significance – indeed, even the presence – of which has been given far too little attention by observers within Russia and abroad. The Russian military organisation is far from being the monolithic entity that it is still perceived to be in some quarters.

This stretching of the boundaries has also taken place through the engagement of Russian citizens – both civilian and military – in academic discussion, passively (e.g. as interview respondents) and actively, as researchers, authors of academic and media publications, and through participation in social movements working on military-related issues, thus countering and serving to undermine the attempts made by those within the Russian military and state establishment who would try desperately to cling on to the secretive practices of the past and stifle public debate. This public debate is very much alive as a component of the development of civic culture in Russia, as is convincingly shown by Alexseev, Webber and Zilberman and Zawilski, in their respective analyses (chapters 4, 7 and 9) of the influence that the general public and social movements can be seen to have in the military sphere, and indeed implicitly in all chapters of this volume, this debate having developed and evolved very rapidly in scale and scope in the last twenty years. The genie is out of the bottle to stay, I would contest, for the stakes for Russian society are too high to allow the debate to be smothered.

The military subject remains very much a salient one for Russian society as a whole (as opinion polls, and my own research among Russian citizens, demonstrate). In comparison to many Western societies, where there is a (perhaps complacent) perception that civil– and society–military relations are less problematic, Russian society has been engaged (as a survey of the Russian press will demonstrate) in what at times has been an intense and emotionally charged debate on the future of its military, and has also been reflecting on its military past, since the introduction of Gorbachev's reforms.[64] This volume, then, seeks to make a contribution to this debate, by attempting to locate Russia's position on the trajectory along all three axes of the SMI model proposed above, i.e. providing an assessment of the nature and degree of militarism and militarisation in Russia today, and mapping this against the dynamics of the SMI. The outcome of this assessment holds great import for Russia's relations with the outside world, and for the development of Russian society.

Part I: military as symbol, image and text

In the three chapters of this first section, contributors explore the symbolic–interpretative level of the society–military relationship, to examine the meanings contained within this relationship, and the ways the relationship is constructed and portrayed. This is a fascinating aspect of the cultural identity of any society in which the military institution, military values or war have played a significant role in shaping that country's fortunes. In the symbolic–interpretative realm, we can refer to such diverse yet closely interrelated issues as the:

- extent to which a culture of militarism is promoted as an ideology and the degree to which the audience (e.g. citizens) subscribe to such messages;
- ways in which military symbols and values are portrayed, received and replicated in a society (e.g. statues, parades, Remembrance Day);[65]
- extent to and manner in which military-related themes are represented in the mass media, through cinema, theatre, literature, visual arts and other cultural practices (such as the playing of war games in the playground[66]) and the impact that they can be said to have on an individual's identity (e.g. in terms of citizenship, gender,[67] etc.); and
- ways in which a country's military past can be seen to interact on a symbolic level with its present (e.g. compare the 'victory cultures' of the UK and the USA[68] with the 'defeat' cultures of Japan and Germany, post-1945).

Each of these areas is extremely complex and difficult to analyse – not least because this has tended to be an emotive sphere, connected to the fundamental core values of a society (and indeed to issues of life and death), but it has also been a sphere that has been treated as taboo, to some extent at least, something that has restricted the scope and depth of societal debates in this subject. These issues, then, comprise multiple layers of attitudes, values and practices, sometimes seemingly in opposition to each other. If we look at the case of Great Britain prior to the First World War, we can note the degree of public support for the policy of building up the strength of the Royal Navy, as a symbol of the power of the country and as a response to perceived threats, on the one hand, but also as a policy which meant that conscription to bolster the number of soldiers in the army was not introduced. Thus while society favoured what can regarded as a militaristic arms build-up, one part of the motivation was connected to what is a fundamentally anti-militaristic position, of individual citizens wanting to retain their status as civilians. If we take the issue of symbolical representation, we can also reveal a multi-layered complex. The reader may, for instance, wish to conduct the exercise of surveying the number of statues and monuments that are dedicated to wartime exploits in his or her own country's capital city. However, the fact that military symbols are present will not necessarily result in the militarisation of consciousness among the public – if the symbol of Nelson's Column in London, the showing of 'war films' on television, or the use of military and war-related terminology in everyday speech to refer to non-military issues are not perceived to represent military values or be related to military issues, then we can hypothesise that reference to them does not, in fact, reflect an active militarisation of consciousness (although this point would be contested by those who argue that even at an unnoticed, even subliminal, level such symbols represent an ongoing influence on the identity of citizens).

Russia, like the UK, is a country in which the military and warfare have played a huge part in the development of nation and society, and in which the symbolic importance of the military institution is still very much evident today. Thus, memories of the sacrifices necessitated by the Second World War (Great Patriotic War) and other conflicts, and perceptions of Russia's standing as an international power on the basis of its military strength, still resonate. As polls demonstrate, the Great Patriotic War figures highly in the citizenship identity of many Russians today, even among the younger generation (as demonstrated by the findings of my research among Russian youth on perceptions of security and citizenship).[69] The war is often portrayed as a symbol not just of survival and victory, but also of enormous collective effort and suffering, and as perhaps the key achievement of Soviet State and society. (It should be noted, however, as the eminent Russian sociologist Boris Grushin points out, that in 1963, the war featured much lower in the collective public consciousness, as indicated in a survey conducted among the readership of the newspaper *Komsomol'skaia pravda*, in which 6,425 respondents participated.[70] We can note that it was later, during the

Brezhnev period (1964–82), that the status of the Great Patriotic War was elevated by an increased emphasis in the mass media and other sources, including a mythologising of events and exploits.)

In chapter 1 Lev Gudkov addresses such issues, comparing the experience of the Soviet period with developments since 1991. Gudkov is a well-known public opinion analyst in Russia, having worked until 2003 in the famous All-Russian Centre for the Study of Public Opinion (*Vse-Rossiiskii Tsentr po Izucheniiu Obschestvennogo Mneniia* – VTsIOM) when that institution was controversially taken over by the Russian Government, with the result that the core staff, including Gudkov and the centre's director, Iurii Levada, left to form an independent centre.[71] In this chapter, Gudkov analyses the role the military has played as an instrument of socialisation, the ways in which Soviet society was mobilised using values and rhetoric adopted from the military sphere, and how a process of demobilisation has occurred since the fall of communism. He argues that despite – or, perhaps we could speculate, because of – the decline of the military in real terms since the end of the Cold War, there has been a consistent effort on the part of the military, supported by the State, to retain its influence on society. Nevertheless, these attempts, according to Gudkov, are ultimately in vain, as can be inferred from his conclusion, because the values being promoted by the military are too far out of step with the needs and aspirations of contemporary Russian society.

The increasing readiness of the mass media in many countries in recent years to adopt a critical stance in coverage of the armed forces has played a key role both in taking the societal debate forward and in influencing the extent of change within the military organisation itself, including, for example, the expansion of recruitment of previously under-represented groups in the military.[72] In the USSR in the late 1980s, as was mentioned above, the media debate on the military (with criticism of the war in Afghanistan, and social problems such as *dedovshchina*) acquired a much broader significance as the military sphere became one in which to criticise the Soviet system as a whole. In the 1990s and beyond, partly reflecting the turbulence seen in Russia's broadcast and print media in general, coverage of military issues has followed various trends. On the one hand, critical accounts of key problems has continued (for example, on problems concerning military service and *dedovshchina*, corruption, the poor conditions faced by military personnel and their families, and indeed the stance adopted on the first Chechen campaign by significant elements in the media), journalists at times displaying heroism in the face of life-threatening consequences of their pursuit of a story, sometimes showing a lack of responsibility and professional ethics in their manipulation of the facts. On the other hand, the State, especially since Putin's election as president, has made various attempts at controlling the ways in which the media operates (thus affecting the ways in which it portrays the military sphere), through the imposition of direct and indirect restrictions on the media and attempts to control the public debate, and through actively promoting a positive image of the military.[73] There have been a number of high-profile clashes between the media and military–state establishments (e.g. those involving Andrei Babitskii,[74] Dmitrii Kholodov,[75] Grigorii Pas'ko[76] and Anna Politkovskaia[77]) which have added further intensity to the public debate.

In chapter 2 Bettina Renz draws on a content analysis of a sample of Russian newspapers' coverage of the specific issue of *dedovshchina* and on her interviews conducted among Russian military journalists and other experts to provide an empirically informed examination of the nature of this relationship and give an assessment of the extent to which the media has been able and willing to perform a watchdog role in both the Yeltsin and Putin periods. Renz concludes that 'the media–military relationship ... has been one of mutual distrust and hostility ... The liberal-oriented media's ability to perform efficiently as a part of the system of civilian control has been stifled, and the prospects for the development of democratic society–military relations ... have furthermore decreased'. Just how far the consequences of this worrying situation will impact on the public's perception of the military sphere remains to be seen, however: the Russian public, after all, has a longstanding tradition of not accepting blindly what it is told by either the State or the media.

The representation of the military theme in the worlds of art, literature, music, film and other creative forms has received relatively little attention from the academic community, yet it provides a crucially important insight into the ways in which the powerful symbols of the military and of warfare are presented and received in a society. Democratic and authoritarian societies alike have seen their fair share of the military and war employed for the purposes of glorification, of the promotion of patriotic sentiment, of celebration of or nostalgia for a country's military power and wartime achievements. In a democratic society such as the USA, however, they can also be used to provide a platform for open protest, as in the case of Bruce Springsteen's treatment of the Vietnam War as a theme in his songwriting; and as a means of societal introspection, as seen in the many US films purging the 'shame' of the Vietnam conflict and depicting its impact on US society (although, it has to be said, far fewer films deal with the impact the war had on the Vietnamese people).

In an authoritarian regime, censorship and control of the cultural sphere by the State restricts the scope for *alternative* interpretations, of course, with the officially endorsed representation of the military and conflict used more often than not in a black-and-white manner, its emphasis on military heroism used to bolster the legitimacy of the State and the ruling ideology. This was of course true in the case of the USSR, although there were pockets of opportunity for writers, film directors and other creative artists to develop alternative representations, notably during the Khrushchev 'Thaw', such as the film *Ballada o soldate* (Ballad of a Soldier) and then, more substantially and lastingly, after the process of *glasnost'* had begun under Gorbachev (such as the protest songs against the war in Afghanistan by Viktor Tsoi and his group KINO and the bard Aleksandr Rozenbaum; and the depiction in the short story 'Sto dnei do prikaza' ('A hundred days to go until demob') by Iurii Poliakov in the journal *Iunost'* in 1987.

In chapter 3, on the portrayal of war in post-Soviet films, David Gillespie provides a wide-ranging and fascinating analysis of the very different depictions of such events as the wars in Chechnia, demonstrating how these films can be seen to reflect the emotional tensions present in Russian society as a whole towards these conflicts, and also placing his examination in the broader comparative context of the war-film genre at the international level. Gillespie argues convincingly that whereas the war films produced during the Yeltsin period were 'thoughtful and provocative … and provide a sad commentary on the disempowerment of the State, once a mighty global player', since the arrival of Putin as president, war films have found 'a new hardness and clarity of focus', expressed through an emphasis on Russian military prowess and the virtue of patriotism, with the 'self-doubting male [of the films of the 1990s] … replaced by testosterone-fuelled competing masculinities'. Thus the film medium mirrors the shift along our continuum of militarism and militarisation that can also be noted in the State's efforts to promote patriotic sentiment through education, enacted in the cultural sphere through, for example, state sponsorship of patriotic war films. (In this there is a parallel with the USA in the aftermath of the terrorist attacks of 11 September 2001, when the US authorities engaged in dialogue with Hollywood film producers over the proclaimed need for films of a patriotic nature.)

Part II: the political and economic interfaces with the military sphere

As was mentioned earlier, the political aspect of the society–military interface has traditionally been the key focus for analysts of civil–military relations, with the result that in its application to the Soviet and Russian cases elite-level interaction between the military and political leaders, as well as the political role that the military can be perceived to play, have received a considerable amount of attention from Russian and Western scholars. In addition to the examples of works in the field cited above, we can also add mention of the contributions of (on the Soviet period) Andrei Kokoshin (former deputy minister of defence of the Russian Federation [*Rossiishaia Federatsia* – RF]),[78] Roman Kolkowicz[79] and Timothy Colton, and, on the post-Soviet period, Viktor Baranets,[80] Iurii Deriugin,[81] Robert Barylski,[82] David Betz,[83] Michael Desch,[84] and V. Serebriannikov.[85] Authors of the better works are able to combine appropriately adapted theoretical approaches with methodologically sound research and an understanding of the cultural contexts of contemporary Russia. In the less sophisticated works, we can see the Russian case being judged against ideals of democratic control that have never been obtained anywhere in the world, but for failing to reach such norms the Russian military and political leadership are castigated; or in which the spectre of a military coup (not seen in Russia since the failed attempt of 1991) is raised, accompanied by warnings of the dire consequences for Russian democracy – yet without adequate explanation of why such a coup has failed to materialise. For instance, the simplistic formulaic approach adopted by some commentators calling for civilian control over the military as a sure-fire guarantee of democratic accountability fails to recognise the damage done by the administration of President Yeltsin (a civilian leader) in its manipulation of the military for political purposes.

Despite the relative abundance of literature, both good and bad, on the political sphere of the society–military relationship, there are still gaps in the coverage which have to be filled if we are to develop a rounded understanding of this complex issue. Further, it is, to reiterate the point, essential that such analysis relates to the broader parameters of the society–military relationship – something which all too many of the existing sources on Russian civil–military relations do inadequately. In part II Mikhail Alexseev and Pavel Baev, two well-known Russian specialists who have long standing experience of working in the West, deal with two crucially important factors: respectively, the nature of the conflict in Chechnia, analysed through the application of 'audience costs' theory, and the regional dimension of military reform. In chapter 4 Alexseev uses the conflicts in Chechnia as a case study to examine the political imperatives of seeking public accountability and securing the integrity of the Russian State. The inherent tension within these aims is referred to by Alexseev as the 'transitional democracy dilemma'. After a careful analysis of the Russian State's handling of the Chechen crises, Alexseev concludes that 'the lesson for civil–military relations is that the more acutely the political leaders feel the state-building imperative, the less they need formal, rule-based oversight of the military by democratic institutions within society'. This indeed holds worrying portents, although in the development of Russian democracy in the years to come a crucial factor will perhaps be played by Russia's closer interaction with foreign governments and its integration with international institutions. Baev (chapter 5) conducts a telling examination of the interrelationship between the trajectories of military reform and regionalism in Russia under Yeltsin and Putin. He assesses the manner in which the Russian military's status as a 'presidential institution' evolved during the 1990s and beyond, and how the process of regionalisation occurred as the military perceived its ties and influence with the centre to be in decline in Yeltsin's later years. Baev then demonstrates how the Putin administration set about reversing this process, using the second war in Chechnia as a tool to achieve this, as well as his regional policy (including the setting-up of the seven 'federal districts' headed by presidential envoys), and then concludes with an exploration of three possible scenarios for the future of Russia and the implications these hold for military reform.

The question of the economic factor in society–military relations has not received the degree of attention it deserves (although within this area the specific issue of the restructuring of the Russian military–industrial complex (MIC) has been the subject of much research and publication).[86] However, gaining control over the Soviet MIC and reining in the exorbitant expenditure on defence was obviously a key priority for the post-Soviet Russian Government as it entered a phase of economic shock therapy, followed by rapid privatisation and the rush towards the market economy. The ensuing squeeze on funding has added to the severe challenge faced by the armed forces as they have struggled to respond to the demands of wide-scale military reform and downsizing,[87] compounded further by a backdrop of political instability and a lack of commitment to the implementation of reform among key political and military incumbents.[88] Meanwhile, the conflicts in Chechnia have provided a huge financial drain on the State and the military, in addition to the human costs incurred.[89]

Another key issue in the economic sphere relates to the heated and protracted debate (begun in 1989 in the USSR's newly elected Congress of People's Deputies) over the move to professional armed forces in Russia, with the claims and counter-claims that this would prove less or more expensive than a conscript-based military, echoing the similarly vacuous discussions on this theme seen in other countries that have weighed up, or made, the move from a conscript to an *all-volunteer* force.[90] The fact is that the Russian economy stands to gain from the transition to a professional military, as young men will be freed from the prospect of conscription. In many cases, conscript service has had little to do with military training and duty, and much to do – as the International Labour Organisation (ILO) has argued – with the employment of conscripts as 'grey' labour, with conscripts paid a pittance yet required to contribute to the economy through work in, for example, construction or agriculture, both legally and semi-legally (through having to work for their base commander, the local general, etc.)[91] In other cases, those who have sought to evade military service have often done so by opting out of mainstream society, thus denying themselves the opportunity to develop professionally, and denying the economy, their skills. Furthermore, many former conscripts face real difficulties in resuming their education or professional training as a result of the physical and mental effects of their military service (a common claim made by higher-education students who have had to serve, for instance, is that they have lost two years of their life). On the other hand, it is certainly the case that for a contingent of the conscript population the military does offer an opportunity for upward mobility and the chance to gain professional skills. But this positive aspect is outweighed considerably by the negative factors mentioned here. As Russia now, in 2004, finally moves towards professionalisation, there will be considerable consequences not just for its military but also its society and its economy.

In chapter 6, Julian Cooper, who has studied the Soviet and Russian defence economy for many years, provides a detailed examination of the contours of the economic dimension of the society–military relationship. He makes an in-depth assessment of the extent to which the Soviet and Russian economies can be said to have been demilitarised since the late 1980s, and of the key issue of public accountability and transparency of military budgets, with additional analysis of the economics of military reform, the establishment of civilian expertise and engagement in military economic policy, and the degree to which Russia can be seen to be adhering to international commitments in making available accurate and comprehensive data on military expenditure and sales of military equipment. He concludes with an examination of the obstacles that still exist (or have been revived) and stand in the way of transparency and the development of an appropriate level of civilian control in this area.

This is a most convincing analysis, although we could also add that the fact that the Ministry of Finance (*Minfin*) has for the most part been able, throughout the Yeltsin and Putin periods, to resist the quite enormous pressure emanating from the MOD and the other 'power ministries' for expenditure to be increased substantially. This represents in real terms a very significant step in the establishment of effective civilian control over the defence and security sectors, continuing the clamp-down on spending begun under Gorbachev. This has proceeded, it is true to say, in the absence of an adequate legal basis and set of procedures for assuring civilian control over the military sector (much work still needs to be done in setting up adequate parliamentary scrutiny, for instance),[92] but the net result of the long-term restriction on defence expenditure has sent a powerful, tangible and symbolic message to the military itself, and indeed to Russian society as a whole.

Part III: citizenship, identity and the challenges of the society–military relationship

In the development of Russia's civic identity following the collapse of the USSR, the military sphere and the nature of society–military relations would provide a case against which to evaluate, for example, the strength of civic culture and civil society, or the extent to which notions of democratic citizenship, individual rights and tolerance towards others have evolved. It would also, given the strong association that the military organisation in Russia – in common with militaries throughout the world – has with national and state identity, be a forum for debate over the vexed issue of

Russian identity, questions of patriotism, duty and allegiance, and over Russia's standing in the world.

Here, then, the focus is on the ways in which individuals relate to and engage with the military organisation as an institution and as a symbol or more abstractly with the notions of militarism and militarisation. This brings me back to the central importance, referred to frequently above, of examining the societal reception of and interaction with the military, without focusing heavily or even exclusively on developments at the policy and institutional levels, if we are to be able to render valid and meaningful the society–military interface model.

In chapter 7, on the relationship between citizenship and the military sphere, Stephen Webber and Alina Zilberman take the post-military society hypothesis of Martin Shaw as the starting point of an investigation of the changing notions of citizenship in Russia and their impact on the society–military relationship and of how, in turn, notions of citizenship have been affected by changes in the military sphere. Drawing on the findings of Webber's comparative research project and on public opinion poll data, they examine the citizenship aspect of military service, including the reception among young people of official discourse linking military service with notions of duty and patriotism, and debates surrounding alternative service and the transition to professional forces, together with the likely impact of such developments on citizenship identity. They then broaden the scope of analysis to study the extent to which citizens have a sense of 'ownership' in the military policy arena. They argue that despite respondents' overwhelming feeling that such a sense of ownership was at best negligible, the mass evasion of military service seen in recent years and the clear effects this has had on defence policy in Russia are illustrative of an unconscious social movement (drawing on the work of Beck and other sociologists)[93] and of the impact that the citizenry can have in the society–military relationship.

In chapter 8, Jennifer Mathers continues the treatment of the citizenship theme through her detailed consideration of women soldiers in the armed forces, in which she employs a theoretically driven comparative approach to highlight the broader societal significance of the major increase since 1991 in the number of women serving in the Russian military. She draws on three frameworks developed in Western studies of change within military organisations: the postmodern military concept discussed earlier in this chapter; the liberal feminist perspective; and the anti-militarist feminist perspective, in order to guage the extent to which these approaches are applicable to the Russian case. This is a ground-breaking piece of work on an under-studied aspect of Russian society–military relations, and Mathers demonstrates through her empirically informed analysis that the use of these concepts does indeed provide a useful model, if not a comprehensive one: 'while these Western frameworks help to highlight certain features of women's military service in Russia, none of them places much emphasis on understanding the motivations and experiences of women soldiers'. She goes on to relate that many Russian female personnel appear to have signed up for short-term pragmatic reasons, which, Mathers argues, are 'matched by the short-term and pragmatic nature of the MOD's motives for allowing large numbers of women to enter the armed forces: namely the pressing need to make up the shortfall in (male) personnel'. This may well signify, Mathers concludes, that the commitment to gender integration will not be long-term.

On the issue of military service itself, unforeseen difficulties have meant that it was not possible to include the planned contribution to this volume of a chapter on this subject, which was to have focused on the debate over professionalisation. The reader is advised to refer to other works by the intended author, Joris van Bladel, who has conducted a comprehensive theoretically driven study of this issue, supported by extensive empirical findings.[94] The themes of military service and professionalisation are, however, dealt with in some depth in a number of the contributions to this volume (see chapters 1, 2 and 7–10).

In the development of social movements (or, as they were labelled then, *neformal'nye ob"edineniia*, informal associations) in the late 1980s, military-related issues figured prominently, from the creation of the first SMO, through the development of a network of *afgantsy* (veterans of the war in Afghanistan)[95] and, indeed, the representation of reform-minded military officers such as Vladimir Lopatin, lobbying for a transition to professional armed forces as deputies in the Congress of People's Deputies. In the post-Soviet period the SMOs and *afgantsy* groups have continued to operate, joined in the 1990s by veterans groups from the Chechen conflicts (*chechentsy*), by human rights groups working on military issues (such as Memorial),[96] protest groups such as the Anti-Militarist Radical Association (*Antimilitaristskaia Radikal'naia Assotsiatsiia* – ARA),[97] and by the All-Russian Movement in Support of the Army, the Defence Industry and Military Science (*Vse-Rossiiskoe Dvizhenie v Podderzhku Armii, Voennoi Promyshlennosti i Voennoi Nauki*), established by General Lev Rokhlin in 1997, and which subsequently came to be used as an electoral *bloc* under the leadership of Viktor Iliukhin, chair of the *Duma's* Committee on Security. The activities of these and other groups clearly form an important constituent of the societal debate on military issues in Russia, and deserve further investigation from the academic community.

Turning to the question of SMOs, in particular, it may be that we are so accustomed now, by 2004, to seeing them play so influential and high-profile a role in Russia, with military and political authorities engaging in dialogue with them, indeed, inviting them at times to take part in policy debates, that we can forget just what an achievement it is that they have acquired this status. For female-based groups, operating on a sensitive and highly charged subject such as the protection of the rights of conscripts, and taking on the might of the military establishment in what is still very much a male-dominated society, the odds, surely, were stacked against their chances of being heard in the first place, let alone influencing policy in this area. Yet over the years the SMOs, in particular the Moscow-based CSM, have consistently made their voices heard and have made a major contribution to effecting change in the sphere of military service, calling first for students to be exempted from the draft during the final stage of the war in Afghanistan, then more broadly in highlighting the severe problems faced by conscripts during their military service, and throughout the post-Soviet period in challenging the State's position on conscription and ensuring that this question remained high on the agenda of the media and the public in Russia. It is quite remarkable, I would contest, that military unit commanders have regularly come to accept the presence of SMO activists on their bases in order to work towards the resolution of conscripts' problems.[98]

In chapter 9, following a review of these achievements in which she places them in the context of the development of Russia's civil society, Valerie Zawilski addresses the specific issue of the role that soldiers' mothers have played in relation to the conflicts in Chechnia. Using the frame-analysis approach to the study of social movements, Zawilski examines the social and political origins of the 'motherist' identity of the Committee of Soldiers' Mothers (*Komitet soldatskikh materei*, CSM)[99] as a feminine organisation (comparing them with the 'mother activism' seen during the *Intifada* in Palestine, by the Mothers of the Plaza de Mayo in Argentina, by the Mothers' Front of Sri Lanka, and other groups). Zawilski focuses on the nature of the influence that the CSM brought to bear on public opinion in Russia (and abroad) during the conflicts in Chechnia. In an amazing episode in 1995, 'Russian television showed images of the soldiers' mothers braving bombs and artillery to pull their sons out of what they believed to be a pointless war', having made a highly publicised march down to the battle-fields of Chechnia. Zawilski notes that 'the key role that the Russian and international media played in supporting their campaign during the 1994–96 conflict was absent during the second Chechen war. SMOs have been marginalised in Russian society, and though they have held demonstrations and publicly protested against the second war, there has been little public interest in or support for their cause.'

Nevertheless, despite such relative loss of direct influence during the second war in Chechnia, the SMOs have retained a high profile in the Russian political scene, playing a part alongside other Russian non-governmental organisations (NGOs) in the controversial Civic Forum (*Grazhdanskii Forum*) initiative of the Putin Government, and voicing their opinions on military reform, patriotic education and other issues. It will be interesting to see how such civil society groups develop as Russia moves towards professional armed forces, which they have been advocating for so long – it is likely, I would suggest, that the problems of protecting the human rights of service personnel will persist even in a professional military. In such professional militaries as those in the UK and the USA, after all, interest groups have been instrumental in calling for, and eventually having an impact on, change in the culture of the military organisation: see, for instance, the heated debates and substantial changes with regard to the recruitment and deployment of female personnel (as discussed by Jennifer Mathers in chapter 8), the rights of gay personnel,[100] the recruitment of ethnic minorities[101] and other issues in which the military has come to effect change in order to reflect developments in society.[102]

In all the chapters of part III, the question of *identity* is a central theme, reflecting both its key role in the development of post-Soviet Russian society, where the debate over identity issues has been highly contested and dynamic, and its importance to any examination of society–military relations, whatever the country. Young people in particular have been bombarded with myriad competing claims for their identity as individuals and as members of large groups and communities, a situation that contrasts with the ideological monopoly that the Communist Party of the USSR attempted to impose. (Contrary to the assumption of many outside observers, the Soviet population never really subscribed to this ideology in a submissive and complete manner.) Within the official and societal rhetoric on military service, for example, young men are still being told that they need to serve in the military in order to become a 'real man', while in the attempts by the authorities to revive notions of patriotism and its linkage with military service the Russian Orthodox Church has become ever more closely involved with the Russian armed forces.[103] The question is, of course, whether such messages can be seen to resonate with their intended audience among the Russian population and especially among the young. The evidence provided by numerous opinion polls, confirmed in the qualitative research conducted in my project, and seen graphically in the continued mass evasion of military service by young men, suggests that while there may be a certain amount of superficial resonance with calls for a revival of patriotic spirit (e.g. though *liubov' k rodine*, or love of the Motherland), this often remains at the level of an 'empty signifier',[104] with young people setting their priorities on a more individual agenda,[105] points which Webber and Zilberman take up in chapter 7.

In the final chapter of the volume, Elisabeth Sieca-Kozlowski takes up this identity theme with a well-documented and detailed case study of the integration of the Cossacks into the Russian armed forces. Placing this analysis within the broader context of Russia's search for a post-Soviet identity, she assesses the risks which, she argues, this integration held for the Russian army as an institution, given the implications for inter-ethnic relations and the challenges to the chain of command, and the prospects for the development of regional military identities (on this, see also chapter 5, by Pavel Baev). She goes on to examine the part that might be played by Cossack groups in the military training of Russian youth, and the ways in which the Cossack movement interacts with issues of nationalistic patriotism.

Conclusion

The case of the Cossacks provides another test for Russian society's capacity to absorb and tolerate the activities of minority groups, including those which seek to play an active political role. On a broader scale, this case, as with the subjects covered in all the chapters of this volume, illustrates the nature of the challenges facing Russia in its redefining of the society–military relationship, as the practices of the past intermingle with competing visions of identity, the priorities of the State, regions, individuals and groups, and the relative importance of the military sector in comparison to the need to focus on such concerns as economic development, social welfare, education, the more effective integration of Russia with the international community. It is clear that Russia's societal debate over the military sphere will remain a dynamic, disputed and extremely important aspect of that country's development in the years ahead.

Notes

1 '9 maia na Krasnoi ploshchadi snova proidet voennyi parad', *Izvestiia* (4 October 1996), p. 3.
2 'Den' pobedy. Po Krasnoi ploshchadi so shtandartom', *Trud* (4 April 2002), p. 2.
3 See, for example, A. Aldis and R. McDermott (eds) *Russian Military Reform, 1992–2002* (London: Frank Cass, 2003).
4 See, for example, S. Simonsen, 'Marching to a different drum? Political orientations and nationalism in Russia's armed forces', *Journal of Communist Studies and Transition Politics*, 17:1 (2001), 43–64; B. Taylor, 'Russia's passive army: rethinking military coups', *Comparative Political Studies*, 34:8 (2001), 924–52.
5 O. Kryshtanovskaya and S. White, 'Putin's militocracy', *Post Soviet Affairs*, 19:4 (2003) 289–306. This claim, that representatives of the security and military establishments (*siloviki*) have been taking over the Russian political scene, has gained popularity among a sizeable contingent in the analytical community, yet the argument put forward here and elsewhere by Kryshtanovskaya and White and others writing on the subject is at times extremely tenuous and speculative, with selective use of case examples employed to back up their claims, and a lack of attention to the key issue of placing such developments in their broader societal contexts. This is not to deny that the topic is a valid one, for it surely is; the point is rather that the study of such complex and politically charged and contentious issues needs to be conducted according to a rigorous methological approach. The use of the term 'militocracy' by Kryshtanovskaya and White is not defined, with no reference to the term's introduction and definition by Stanislav Andreski, in his classic work *Military Organization and Society* (London: Routledge and Kegan Paul, 1968).

6 V. Sperling, 'The last refuge of a scoundrel: patriotism, militarism and the Russian national idea', *Nations and Nationalism*, 9:2 (2003), 235–53.

7 B. Taylor, *Politics and the Russian Army: Civil–Military Relations, 1689–2000* (Cambridge: Cambridge University Press, 2003).

8 P. Baev, *The Russian Army in a Time of Troubles* (London: Sage, 1996).

9 D. Herspring, *Russian Civil–Military Relations* (Bloomington: Indiana University Press, 1996).

10 See, for example, B. Nygren and Y. Fedorov (eds) *Russian Military Reform and Russia's New Security Environment* (Stockholm: National Defence College, 2003).

11 A. Caiazza, *Mothers and Soldiers: Gender, Citizenship, and Civil Society in Contemporary Russia* (London: Routledge, 2002); B. Vallance, 'Russia's mothers: voices of change', *Minerva: Quarterly Report on Women and the Military*, 18:3–4 (2000), 109–28.

12 *Dedovshchina* is the term principally used to refer to the hazing, or bullying, of junior conscripts by more senior conscripts. There are various theories on the likely origin of the problem, which acquired ever greater proportions in the 1980s and 1990s, in the flux that accompanied the collapse of the Soviet system and the crises that came with Russia's transition. Some trace its roots to the Second World War, others to the reform of military service of 1967, which led to greater numbers of conscript non-commissioned officers (NCOs) being asked to take on responsibilities formerly assumed by professional NCOs and commissioned junior officers. An early attempt to study the problem was made by Colonel Iurii Deriugin of the Red Army's sociological research unit. In an interview in 1997, Deriugin (then retired) told me that he had taken his report on the very worrying signs that the problem was expanding to the Soviet General Staff in the mid-1970s, but had seen his report dismissed out of hand, while being told to desist from this research, since such a problem 'could not exist in the glorious Red Army that had been victorious in the struggle against the Fascist invader [Nazi Germany].' The General Staff should have listened. It is not possible to state with certainty how widespread the problem has been, as its severity and rate varies from unit to unit, although it is accurate to say that it has been observed to be widespread, even among elite units (such as the Kremlin Guard). In its extreme form, it can lead to permanent (and severe) physical and mental trauma being suffered by victims, with death as a result of beatings and other violence also a frequent occurrence. The military authorities have struggled to deal with the problem (and have at times been accused by some of not just allowing the practice to happen, but of encouraging it). The authorities have been negligent and have often preferred to turn a blind eye to, rather than confront, the issue, although recently there have been more concerted attempts to tackle it through the military prosecutors' office and other means. At the time of writing, however, and probably for some time to come, it remains one of the key issues in the societal debate on the military in Russia. On this issue see, for example, K. Bannikov, *Antropologiia ekstremal'nykh grupp: dominantnye otnosheniia sredi voennosluzhashchikh srochnoi sluzhby* (Moscow: Institut etnologii i antropologii RAN, 2002); N. Gross, 'Youth and the army in the USSR in the 1980s', *Soviet Studies*, 42:3 (1990), 481–98; A. Kostinskii, 'Ocherki dedovshchiny', *Indeks*, 19 (2003), available online: www.index.org/ru. See also the detailed reports

provided by human rights groups such as Memorial (Russia), SMOs in Russia, Amnesty International, Human Rights Watch.

13 V. Marchenko, *Takaia armiia: Narusheniia prav cheloveka v vooruzhennykh silakh* (Moscow: Norma, 1995). Marchenko headed the NGO *Pravo materi*, or Mothers' Right, which assisted parents of conscripts who had lost their lives while on peacetime duty to investigate the causes of their deaths.

14 On this issue, see S. Cornell, 'International reactions to massive human rights violations: the case of Chechnya', *Europe–Asia Studies*, 51:1 (1999), 85–101, as well as numerous reports by Western and Russian human rights organisations, the Council of Europe, etc. The estimates of the number of civilian deaths in the two wars vary widely, but run into many tens of thousands at least. There are many factors that may explain the paucity of public debate in Russia on the issue of civilian casualties and the problems of refugees, ranging from a desire on the part of some in the population to turn a blind eye to the conflict, from a feeling either of helplessness or of indifference, to sentiments of prejudice against the Chechen ethnic group (although many thousands of Russian inhabitants of Chechnia have also been killed as a result of the actions of the federal forces). As with any country that has been engaged in such a conflict which has entailed so much destruction, if Russia is truly to become a tolerant democratic society, then it must surely summon the courage to face these issues and demand that the interests of those who have suffered in Chechnia on all sides, combatants and civilians, be afforded the priority treatment they deserve – something that was not the case in the turbulent period following the end of the Soviet campaign in Afghanistan, for instance. It is to be hoped that the reconstruction efforts and relative stability now seen in Chechnia in 2004 will allow for such developments to occur. With regard to societal self-reflection on the legitimacy or otherwise of the actions of Russian forces in Chechnia, the recent trial of Colonel Iu. Budanov, who was sentenced in 2003 to ten years' imprisonment for the abduction, rape and murder of a captured Chechen female sniper, gained a great deal of media attention in Russia and abroad, although this is one of a series of convictions by Russian courts of service personnel who had been accused of murdering civilians in Chechnia ('Kak sudili voennykh za ubiistva chechentsev', *Kommersant Daily* (4 April 2004), p. 6). This remains a long way from the demands of human rights groups for the Russian military and political authorities to be called to account for the systematic abuse of human rights through the use of filtration camps and other mechanisms, but it does perhaps represent a move towards a more open societal debate. See also David Gillespie's discussion of the treatment of the Chechen wars in Russian cinematography in chapter 3 of this volume.

15 For examples of works which, on the contrary, do provide a more synthetic approach that combines analysis of various aspects of the Society–Military interface, see: F. Daucé, *L'Etat, l'armée et le citoyen en russie postsoviétique* (Paris: L'Harmattan, 2001); G. Honneland and A.-K. Jorgensen, *Integration versus Autonomy: Civil–Military Relations on the Kola Peninsula* (London: Ashgate, 1999).

16 Interviews with Russian policy-makers and advisers, conducted by S. Webber and A. Zilberman (2002–4).

17 D. Foyle, *Counting the Public In: Presidents, Public Opinion and Foreign Policy* (New York: Columbia University Press, 1999); D. Foyle, 'Foreign policy analysis

and globalization: public opinion, world opinion, and the individual',
International Studies Review, 5:2 (2003), 163–70.

18 O. Holsti, *Public Opinion and American Foreign Policy* (Ann Arbor: University
of Michigan Press, 1996); O. Holsti, 'Public opinion and foreign policy analysis:
where we were, are, and should strive to be', in M. Brecher and F. Harvey (eds)
*Conflict, Security, Foreign Policy, and International Political Economy: Past
Paths and Future Directions in International Studies* (Ann Arbor: University of
Michigan Press, 2002), pp. 72–90.

19 L. Jacobs, 'Manipulators and manipulation: public opinion in a representative
democracy', *Journal of Health Politics, Policy and Law*, 26:6 (2001), 1361–73;
L. Jacobs, 'The recoil effect: public opinion and policymaking in the US and
Britain', *Comparative Politics*, 24:2 (1992), 199–217.

20 B. Page, 'Democratic responsiveness? Untangling the links between public
opinion and policy', *PS: Political Science and Politics*, 27:1 (1994), 25–9.

21 L. Jacobs and R. Shapiro, *Politicians Don't Pander: Political Manipulation and
the Loss of Democratic Responsiveness* (Chicago, IL: University of Chicago
Press, 2000); B. Page and R. Shapiro, *The Rational Public* (Chicago, IL:
University of Chicago Press, 1992).

22 C. Wagnsson, *Russian Political Language and Public Opinion on the West,
NATO and Chechnya: Securitization Theory Reconsidered* (Stockholm:
University of Stockholm, 2000).

23 W. Zimmerman, *The Russian People and Foreign Policy: Russian Elite and Mass
Perspectives, 1993–2000* (Princeton, NJ: Princeton University Press, 2002).

24 Information elicited in interviews conducted by Webber and Zilberman with
policy-makers, pollsters and academic analysts. On the activities of the KGB and
other organs in monitoring public responses, see, for example, V. Shlapentokh, *A
Normal Totalitarian Society: How the Soviet Union Functioned and How it
Collapsed* (Armonk: M.E. Sharpe, 2001).

25 For a detailed overview of the nature of state propaganda techniques and the use
of the mass media to purvey the official line, see, for example, A. Inkeles, *Public
Opinion in Soviet Russia: A Study in Mass Persuasion* (Cambridge, MA:
Harvard University Press, 1950).

26 D. Holloway, 'State, society and the military under Gorbachev', *International
Security*, 4:3 (1989–90), 5–24.

27 The notion of *ownership* in the field of military and security issues is being developed by S. Webber on the basis of his research findings

28 See S. Webber and J. van Bladel, 'Russia's past or future?' *World Today*, 56:10
(2000), 4–7.

29 Wagnsson, *Russian Political Language*, chapters 4 and 5.

30 An account of this event is provided by Aleksandr Oslon, the director of the Public
Opinion Foundation (*Fond Obshchestvennogo Mneniia* – FOM), who was at
that time a member of Yeltsin's election team, in B. Doktorov, A. Oslon and E.
Petrenko, *Epokha El'tsina: mneniia rossiian* (Moscow: FOM, 2002) pp. 370–1.

31 'Putin schitaet, chto professionalizatsiia armii pomozhet razreshit' problemu
dedovshchiny', available online (accessed 18 December 2003).

32 On this point see also S. Webber, 'Public attitudes towards the armed forces in
Russia: do they count?' in S. Cimbala (ed.) *The Russian Military into the Twenty-
First Century* (London: Frank Cass, 2001), pp. 153–78.

33 Iu. Taratuta and O. Guseva, 'Rassledovanie: FSB proigrala spor Minoborony. Komanduiushchii pogranotriada otvetit za zamerzshikh novobrantsev', *Kommersant Daily* (9 February 2004), p. 7.

34 See M. Shaw, *Post-Military Society: Militarism, Demilitarization and War at the End of the Twentieth Century* (London: Polity Press, 1991). Shaw puts forward a challenging and convincing argument, drawing our attention to just how deep the military factor has been in societal development, and the implications held by a reduction in its influence. See the application of his hypotheses to the research conducted by Webber, outlined in chapter 7 of this volume.

35 On the debates see, for example: S. Andreski, *Military Organization and Society* (London: Routledge and Kegan Paul, 1968); V. Berghahn, *Militarism: The History of an International Debate, 1861–1979* (Leamington Spa: Berg Publishers, 1981); M. Edmonds, *Armed Services and Society* (Leicester: Leicester University Press, 1988); J. Gillis (ed.) *The Militarization of the Western World* (Newark: Rutgers University Press, 1989); M. Mann, 'Authoritarian and liberal militarism: a contribution from comparative and historical sociology', in S. Smith, K. Booth and M. Zalewski (eds) *International Theory: Positivism and Beyond* (Cambridge: Cambridge University Press, 1996), pp. 221–39; P. Regan, *Organizing Societies for War: The Process and Consequences of Societal Militarization* (Westport, CT: Greenwood Press, 1994); K. Skjelsback, 'Militarism, its dimensions and corollaries: an attempt at conceptual clarification', *Journal of Peace Research*, 16:3 (1979), 213–29.

36 Shaw, *Post-Military Society*.

37 See, for example, J. Elshtain and S. Tobias (eds) *Women, Militarism and War* (New York: Rowman & Littlefield, 1989).

38 See, for example, the classic work by Karl Liebknecht, after the publication of which the author was put on trial and found guilty of high treason by the German authorities in 1907: K. Liebknecht, *Militarism and Anti-Militarism* (Glasgow: Socialist Labour Press, 1917).

39 The terms 'militarisation' and 'militarised' definitely carried negative connotations among the Russian and German respondents (aged 15–30) in the research project I conducted with a colleague from the University of Birmingham between 1998–2002. This is a result, we speculate, both of a hang-over from the ways in which these terms were employed during the Cold War to criticise the policies of the 'other side' and of the negative connotations such terms carry internally, within a society, particularly in one such as Germany where the collective emphasis of state and societal stances on military issues has been to reduce the influence of the military on society and to increase the influence of society on the military. This active stance provides evidence, I would contest, of one aspect of the development of a *post-military society*; among the respondents in the UK, another, more passive, feature can be observed: the vast majority seemed never before to have encountered the terms 'militarisation' and 'militarised'.

40 C. Enloe, *Does Khaki Become You? The Militarisation of Women's Lives* (London: Pluto, 1983).

41 A. Ross, 'Dimensions of militarisation in the third world', *Armed Forces and Society*, 13:4 (1987), 561–78.

42 Andreski, *Military Organization and Society*

43 Shaw, *Post-Military Society.*
44 See, for example, discussion of the impact on women of the ongoing legacy of Cold War militarisation, set against other issues connected with development and environmental problems, in J. Turpin and L. Lorentzen (eds) *The Gendered New World Order: Militarism, Development and the Environment* (London: Routledge, 1996).
45 See, for example, Martin Shaw's development of the notion of 'risk-transfer militarism' in M. Shaw, 'Risk-transfer militarism and the legitimacy of war after Iraq', available online: (accessed 2004).
46 M. Mann, *Incoherent Empire* (London: Verso Books, 2003); see also Chalmers Johnston's discussion of US militarism in C. Johnston, *The Sorrows of Empire: Militarism, Secrecy, and the End of the Republic* (New York: Metropolitan Books, 2004).
47 It should be stated that while certain factors can be assessed more or less objectively (e.g. the level of national expenditure on defence, the size of the armed forces, the proportion of the population serving in the armed forces), for the most part any assessment will remain at the level of perception and analysis of behaviour and practice.
48 See, for example, B. Buzan, O. Waever and J. de Wilde, *Security: A New Framework for Analysis* (London: Lynne Rienner, 1998). The securitisation concept offers a useful starting point as an analytical tool, although to date there has been relatively little satisfactory empirical testing of the concept by the academic community.
49 U. Albrecht, 'Red militarism', *Journal of Peace Research*, 17:2 (1980), 135–49.
50 T. Colton, *Commissars, Commanders, and Civilian Authority: The Structure of Soviet Military Politics* (Cambridge, MA: Harvard University Press, 1979).
51 E. Jahn, 'The role of the armaments complex in Soviet society (Is there a Soviet military industrial complex?)', *Journal of Peace Research*, 12:3 (1975), 179–94.
52 W. Odom, 'The "militarization" of Soviet society', *Problems of Communism*, 25:5 (1976), 34–51
53 R. Pipes, 'Militarism and the Soviet State', *Daedalus*, 109:4 (1980), 1–12.
54 D. Simes, 'The military and militarism in Soviet society', *International Security*, 6:3 (1981–82), 123–43.
55 D. Stone, *Hammer and Rifle: The Militarization of the Soviet Union, 1926–1933* (Lawrence: University of Kansas Press, 2000).
56 E. Jones, *Red Army and Society: A Sociology of the Soviet Military* (Boston, MA: Allen & Unwin, 1985).
57 A. Cockburn, *The Threat: Inside the Soviet Military Machine* (London: Random House, 1984).
58 E. Jahn, *Kommunismus – und was dann? Zur Bürokratisierung und Militarisierung des Systems der Nationalstaaten* (Hamburg: Rowohlt, 1974).
59 T. Cusack and M. Ward, 'Military spending in the United States, Soviet Union, and the People's Republic of China', *Journal of Conflict Resolution*, 25:3 (1981), 429–69; C. Gray, 'The urge to compete: rationales for arms racing', *World Politics*, 26:2 (1974), 207–33.
60 Odom, 'The "militarization" of Soviet society'.

61 F. Kuebart, 'Patriotische Wehrerziehung in der Sowjetunion', in H. Adomeit, H.-H. Hoehmann and G. Wagenlehner (eds) *Die Sowjetunion als Militärmacht* (Stuttgart: Kohlhammer, 1987), pp. 90–114.
62 On the development of the field of military sociology in Russia, see V. Dobrenkov, *Sotsiologiia v Rossii: voennaia sotsiologiia* (Moscow: Mezhdunarodnyi Universitet Biznesa i Upravleniia, 2002).
63 Information related to Webber during interviews with Russian respondents, 1999–2000.
64 See, for example, the range of articles on this subject published in the journal *Neprikosnovennyi zapas,* available online: www.nz-online.ru.
65 For a study of the ways in which Soviet era monuments (including *Park Pobedy* – Victory Park – in Moscow) have been represented since 1991, see B. Forest and J. Johnson, 'Unravelling the threads of history: Soviet-era monuments and post-soviet national identity in Moscow', *Annals of the Association of American Geographers*, 92:3 (2002), 524–47.
66 See, for example, P. Regan, 'War toys, war movies and the militarization of the United States, 1900–85', *Journal of Peace Research*, 31:1 (1994), 45–58.
67 See, for example, Cynthia Enloe's wide-ranging examination of what she regards as the influence of militaristic values on women's lives in C. Enloe, *Maneuvers: The International Politics of Militarizing Women's Lives* (Berkeley: University of California Press, 2000).
68 T. Engelhardt, *The End of Victory Culture: Cold War America and the Disillusioning of a Generation* (Boston: University of Massachusetts Press, 1998).
69 This research is principally drawn from the Economic and Social Research Council (UK) project 'Youth Perceptions of Security and Citizenship in Russia, Germany and the United Kingdom', conducted by S. Webber and K. Longhurst, University of Birmingham, between 1998 and 2002. see www.crees.bham.ac.uk/research/cmil/index.htm for further details.
70 B. Grushin, *Chetyre zhizni Rossii: v zerkale oprosov obshchestvennogo mneniia. Epokha Khrushcheva* (Moscow: Progress-Traditsiia, 2001), pp. 403–4. The Great Patriotic War was named by only 2.7 per cent of respondents when asked to identify the most important event of the twentieth century (compared with 39.2 per cent of respondents who named the Great October Socialist Revolution). The results might be said to reflect the readership profile of *Komsomol'skaia pravda*: 97 per cent of respondents were aged under 30, and the majority were urban dwellers.
71 Details of the new centre can be found at www.levada.ru.
72 See, for example, the analyses of contemporary society–military relations in Western and post-communist societies in: P. Feaver and R. Kohn (eds) *Soldiers and Civilians: The Civil–Military Gap and American National Security* (Cambridge, MA: Belfer Centre for Science and International Affairs, 2001); J. Kuhlmann and J. Callaghan (eds) *Military and Society in 21st Century Europe* (New Brunswick: Transaction Publishers, 2000); C. Moskos, J. Williams and D. Segal (eds), *The Postmodern Military: Armed Forces after the Cold War* (Oxford: Oxford University Press, 2000).
73 For a survey of this field, see M. Pogorelyi and I. Safranchuk (eds) *Contemporary Russian Military Journalism: Experience, Problems, Perspectives* (Moscow: Gendalf, 2002).

74 E. Loriia, 'Babitskii ostaetsia s sudimost'iu', *Novye izvestiia* (14 December 2000), p. 2.

75 The case of the journalist Dmitrii Kholodov, who was killed by a car bomb in 1994 while investigating a story of corruption allegedly involving the higher echelons of the military organisation (possibly, as rumours abounded, including the then minister of defence Pavel Grachev), led to a protracted and controversial court case (which still had not been concluded by 2004) in which several former military personnel were accused of his murder. Grachev himself gave evidence in the trial, maintaining his complete innocence, while allegations abounded that he had been directly involved in a conspiracy to murder Kholodov. On this story see V. Demchenko, 'Pavel Grachev vystupil svidetelem po delu Dmitriia Kholodova', *Izvestiia* (26 March 2004), p. 3; Iu. Mikhailina, 'Smert' slova: Tysiacha sudebnykh oshibok v dele Dmitriia Kholodova', *Gazeta* (27 May 2003), p. 3; S. Rogozhkin and O. Ruban (eds) *Dmitrii kholodov. Vzryv: khronika ubiistva zhurnalista* (Moscow: Eksim, 1998).

76 A. Chernyshev, 'Delo Pas'ko: Protsess. Grigorii Pas'ko perestal platit' v "obshchak" i vyshel na svobodu', *Kommersant Daily* (24 January 2003), p. 5.

77 A. Politkovskaia, *A Dirty War: A Russian Reporter in Chechnya* (London: Harvill Press, 2001).

78 A. Kokoshin, *Armiia i politika: sovetskaia voenno–politicheskaia i voenno–strategicheskaia mysl', 1918–1991 gody* (Moscow: Mezhdunarodnye otnosheniia, 1995).

79 R. Kolkowicz, *The Soviet Military and the Communist Party* (Princeton, NJ: Princeton University Press, 1967).

80 V. Baranets, *El'tsin i ego generaly: zapiski polkovnika genshtaba* (Moscow: Sovershenno sekretno, 1997); V. Baranets, *Poteriannaia armiia: zapiski polkovnika Genshtaba* (Moscow: Sovershenno sekretno, 1998).

81 Iu. Deriugin and V. Serebriannikov, *Armiia Rossii: sostoianie i perspektivy vykhoda iz krizisa. Sotsial'no-politicheskii srez sovremennogo voennogo sotsiuma* (Moscow: Institute of Socio-Political Research, 1998).

82 R. Barylski, *The Soldier in Russian Politics: Duty, Dictatorship and Democracy under Gorbachev and Yeltsin* (London: Transaction Publishers, 1998).

83 D. Betz, *Civil–Military Relations in Russia and Eastern Europe* (London: RoutledgeCurzon, 2004).

84 M. Desch, *Civilian Control of the Military: The Changing Security Environment* (London: Johns Hopkins University Press, 1999).

85 V. Serebriannikov, *Bezopasnost' Rossii i armiia* (Moscow: Institute of Socio-Political Research, 1995).

86 See, for example, V. Pimenov, 'O napravleniiakh strategii reformirovaniia oboronno-promyshlennogo kompleksa', *Politiia*, 2 (2001), 89–98.

87 V. Tsymbal, 'Ekonomicheskie aspekty voennoi reformy v sovremennoi Rossii', *Politiia*, 2 (2001), 82–8.

88 See, for example, P. Baev, 'The Russian armed forces: failed reform attempts and creeping regionalization', in D. Betz and J. Löwenhardt (eds) *Army and State in Postcommunist Europe* (London: Frank Cass, 2001), pp. 23–42.

89 On the difficulties faced by Russian journalists, politicians and others in ascertaining the financial costs of the wars in Chechnia, see, for example, I. Andreev,

'Biudzhet voiny: Zachistka finansov', *Novaia gazeta* (23 January 2003), pp. 2–3. In the spring of 2004, in the lead-up to the presidential elections, the Ministry of Economic Development (under Minister German Gref) published figures stating that to 2003 some 40 billion roubles had been spent on the restoration of Chechnia. The total accurate figure for military expenditure had still not been made available by 2004, although experts estimated that some 8 billion US dollars had been spent (V. Sukhov, 'Peizazh posle bitvy: Ko vtorym vyboram Vladimira Putina Chechniu ne bombiat, a vosstanavlivaiut', *Vremia novostei* (18 February 2004), p. 6).

90 The myth that a professional military is more expensive is examined by M. Borodin, 'Tochka zreniia: Dva mifa o voennoi reforme', *Sankt-Peterburgskie vedomosti* (6 May 2003), p. 4.

91 In addition to the work of the ILO, the issue of the use of conscripts as grey labour has been investigated in comparative terms by the European Council of Conscripts Organisations.

92 Y. Ivanov. 'Legal, political and budgetary aspects of civilian control of the military in Russia', in Betz and Löwenhardt, *Army and State in Postcommunist Europe*, pp. 11–22.

93 See, for example, U. Beck, *Risk Society: Towards a New Modernity* (London: Sage, 1992).

94 See, for example, J. van Bladel, 'Russian soldiers in the barracks – a portrait of a subculture', in A. Aldis and R. McDermott (eds) *Russian Military Reform, 1992–2002* (London: Frank Cass, 2003), pp. 60–72.

95 For coverage of this issue see M. Galeotti, *Afghanistan: The Soviet Union's Last War* (London: Frank Cass, 1998).

96 See www.memo.ru.

97 See www.ara.ru/index.html.

98 This can be seen as another sign of the fragmented identity of the Russian military and as an open admission, perhaps, of its inability to solve such problems by itself. However, I would contest that it can be seen also as a more pragmatic approach to the relationship between the military and civilian society, which might be appropriately introduced into the more closed (by dint of being more effectively organised) traditional military cultures of such countries as the UK, where social problems faced by personnel are more often than not dealt with internally, without reference to the support that could otherwise be offered by outside agencies.

99 The committee was later renamed as the Union of Committees of Soldiers' Mothers, to reflect the leading role that the Moscow committee has played in the network of such committees found across Russia (see www.ucsmr.ru). A separate organisation, the Soldiers' Mothers of Saint Petersburg (*Soldatskie materi Sankt-Peterburga*) has also been very active in this field (see www.soldiersmothers.spb.org).

100 T. Barkawi , C. Dandeker, M. Wells-Petry and E. Kier, 'Rights and fights: sexual orientation and military effectiveness', *International Security*, 24:1 (1999), 181–201.

101 C. Dandeker and D. Mason, 'The British armed services and the participation of minority ethnic communities: from equal opportunities to diversity?' *Sociological Review*, 49:2 (2001), 219–35.

102 J. Van Der Meulen and J. Soeters (eds) *Managing Diversity in Armed Forces: Experiences from Nine Countries* (Tilberg: Tilberg University Press, 1999).

103 B. Lukichev and A. Protopopov, 'Vzaimodeistvie armii i tserkvi', *NG Religii* (22 September 1999).

104 An empty signifier holds a vague or varying meaning, thus reducing the degree of congruence of meaning among its interpreters. See, for example, the application of this concept to the presentation of Marxist–Leninist ideology in the Soviet Union in R. Walker, 'Marxism–Leninism as discourse: the politics of the empty signifier and the double bind', *British Journal of Political Science*, 19:2 (1989), 161–89.

105 On Russian young people's attitudes to politics, see F. Markowitz, 'Not nationalists: Russian teenagers' soulful a-politics', *Europe–Asia Studies*, 51:7 (1999), 1183–99.

I

Military as symbol, image and text

1 *Lev Gudkov*

The army as an institutional model[1]

Translated from the Russian by Jennifer G. Mathers

The army in a mobilised society

One of the reasons for the extreme slowness of Russia's integration into the international community in comparison to other East European states is the specific role which the army plays in the socio-political life of the country. The usual explanations (such as Russia's imperial past and authoritarian traditions, and its leaders' claims to great power status) are completely justified, but are too general to permit an understanding of the concrete mechanisms of conservatism. There is a paradox lurking here for the foreign observer: the weakness and disintegration of the contemporary Russian army and its low combat effectiveness (which became apparent in the course of both Chechen campaigns and was confirmed by press reports of frequent catastrophe and failures of military technologies), do not in any way influence its political role, its significance in society and the people's trust in it. This paradox may arise from false comparisons between a Soviet-type army and armed forces in Western democratic countries.

The functions of the Soviet armed forces were never limited to the task of defence from foreign aggression.[2] Indeed, it is precisely because of the retention of its other functions, which are not directly related to defence and national security, that it continues to exist in a form which is almost unchanged since the Soviet period. In this chapter the word 'army' is used in its broad sense, referring to the command of different forces but also meaning, first and foremost, the top brass in the MOD. The army, then, remains not only the most important tool of power, in the sense of providing support for a certain political course, but also a source of government personnel. The army provides many members of the staff of the national leaders and the leadership of the middle layer of government (regional, branch, institutional, etc.), and in recent years even the deputy corps at various levels. It is this latter factor that makes the army an extremely important mechanism of social control for the country's top political leadership. It is the ability to influence the choice and selection of personnel that determines the army's role in internal political contests, and also ensures the preservation of those values and norms which allow the army to be a symbolic model of identification for society.

The cult of the army in the USSR took shape at the very beginning of the 1930s, although at this time there was little likelihood that another state would attack the USSR. The creation of a powerful army was one of the policies developed by Stalin to strengthen the regime. In order to achieve the final suppression of opposition in the country (after Trotsky had been removed from power and sent into exile), it was necessary to remove any external threat to the regime.[3] The ideological justification for strengthening the repressive regime became the thesis of the inevitability of imminent world war. This thesis was accepted by society and became one of the main elements of national identification, being preserved up to the present day.[4] The issue was not about whether there was a fatal inevitability of a new (second) world war , but about the very social system constructed around the army and repressive institutions, which was legitimised by the search for 'enemies' within the country and paranoid ideas of an imminent military clash. Such a conflict, which was seen as a precondition of the confrontation between 'socialism' and 'capitalism', would arise sooner or later. Prewar Soviet propaganda assumed that the USSR would be drawn first into small local conflicts and then into large wars.[5] An army which was developed for such purposes would be unlikely to meet the criteria of sufficient defence.

For the top political leadership, control of the army was the most important factor in the internal political struggles of the *nomenklatura*, and the participation of state security structures has made the difference at critical moments. If we consider only the postwar period, the military and security services played a key role in the following:

- the removal of Lavrentii Beriia and the confirmation of the collective leadership of Nikita Khrushchev;
- Khrushchev's removal as a result of the leadership plot in 1964;
- the Gorbachev period in 1990–91;
- Yeltsin's leadership in 1993; and
- Putin's presidency in the events of the summer and autumn 1999 in the North Caucasus.

As far as the population was concerned, from the very birth of the Soviet regime the army (together with the 'internal forces': the People's Commissariat of Internal Affairs (*Narodnyi Kommissariat Vnutrennykh Del'*) or NKVD, the MVD, the KGB, the FSB) was an instrument of punitive policy and was used in that capacity in relation to the most diverse social groups (such as rebellious industrial workers, restless peasants, prisoners of the Labour Camps Directorate or GULAG (*Glavnoe Upravlenie Ispravitel'no-trudovykh Lagerei*), or whole provinces with mainly non-Russian populations (Cossacks,

Ukrainians, the Baltic nations, the nationalities of the Caucasus and Central Asia), to say nothing of the so-called 'repressed peoples' – Chechens, Ingush, Crimean Tatars, and others. One should not suppose that the use of the army against the civilian population was characteristic only of the period when the totalitarian regime was being formed (1920–40): it was more or less a constant feature, and any aggravation of a situation immediately prompted an appeal to the army – for example, in 1957 in the Caucasus and in Abkhazia; in 1985 in Kazakhstan; in 1988–91 in Central Asia (Kirgizia, Uzbekistan, Tadzhikistan), again in the Caucausus (in Azerbaijan and Armenia), in Moldova, Lithuania, Latvia and other places.

But if the army's internal use had been limited to repression, the system could not have functioned for so long. Instead the army became the most important institution of social and ideological processing of the population and the channel of social mobility for huge masses of people who had been deprived of their rights by the State. Right up until the 1970s military service opened up possibilities for inhabitants of the countryside, those without passports and therefore with no legal basis for escape from a situation of serfdom dependent on the *kolkhoz*, and also for young people from provincial cities and lower-class city dwellers to receive a professional education and to improve their social status. For the agrarian population, especially the villages, ravaged by collectivisation, which barely survived the famine of the 1930s and 1940s, military service represented a highly attractive occupation, and a military career was extremely prestigious. This combination of the threat of repression for the whole population and the opportunity of careers and social mobility for selected individuals who demonstrated special loyalty to the system became a very effective method for the integration of society.

The significance of the army as an institution of socialisation is determined by the coincidence of two factors. First, an enormous contingent of the population, dominated by peasants, were brought into the modern era as a result of their service in the army. These were people not only in Russia but also in other regions annexed to the empire who, in essence, had not yet emerged from the limitations of a traditional way of life. Second, this army was the channel for the creation of a specific type of mass society: a totalitarian one. The army was one of the very few models of social relations in Soviet society which clearly and definitely demonstrated the fundamental principles of socialism. The transfer of army forms of organisation of life into *civilian* relations and institutions (both foreign and domestic) implied the possibility, and even the necessity, of similar conformities.

Soviet power took shape in the context of military defeat in the First World War and the failure of a state which could not manage the powerful tensions between an extremely archaic patrimonial bureaucracy and a rapidly developing capitalist economy. The bankruptcy of the social and state formations of the old regime and the exaggerations of communist propaganda meant that, for a long time, any institutions which safeguarded the normal functioning of society and the economy were discredited in Russia. The Soviet regime went beyond simply preserving the fundamental aspects of militarisation which were necessary for the functioning of a war industry on such a scale. Instead the Soviet regime repeatedly strengthened these characteristics of a military-mobilised society (such as a planned economy subordinated to simplified and oversimplified military aims, repressive legal proceedings, a hierarchical and unaccountable power structure, censorship, and forced labour), making its readiness for mobilisation one of the legitimising principles of power. Thus the entire organisation of the social system was built 'from the top down' as a rigidly hierarchical coordination of different levels of control and administration.

Mobilising structures did not simply penetrate the depths of civilian life, they ran through its most important spheres and placed the latter under their control. Hundreds of books have been written about the military–industrial character of the Soviet economy and the priorities of the military–industrial complex.[6] It is known that each civilian factory had its own mobilisation plans, which detailed the enterprise's immediate shift to output for military production in the event of war – and very often it was precisely the need to be prepared for immediate military production that impeded a factory's optimisation or modernisation of production technology and the range of products it could make. But it is possible nevertheless to discuss the total influence of the military on society without even touching on the economy. First and foremost there was the universality of military obligations: almost all young men were obliged to spend 2–3 years in compulsory service. Those with higher education received officers' ranks 'in reserve', and once every few years they would go on 'exercises' (1- or 2-month long courses or programmes of military training and higher qualifications). If from 1960 to the mid-1970s between 45 and 60 per cent of men of conscription age served in the army, then today the army manages to take in no more than 10 per cent of those called up. Military training has practically died – there is no money for it in the state coffers.

For the Communist Party of the USSR (CPSU) the army became a model of mass control, and its pattern was intended for use in a wide variety of circumstances. A significant feature of this form of organisation is the indivisibility of its fundamental authority: solidarity and passion combined with rigid compulsion; the peremptoriness of command and the lack of an alternative to subordination. The army presented itself as the model of an optimal social structure and a simple pattern of mass administration which could be understood by all, based on: a rigid hierarchy; centralised repressive control; a monopoly on the means of coercion; weak functional differentiation; discipline; the suppression of individual autonomy and freedom; and the absence of diverse sources of information. Thanks to this it was possible for the army rationally to ensure that its needs were met even above and beyond those of defence and security. In this way a model of the Soviet military organisation was developed which was applicable to all aspects of Soviet life.

At the same time, as is known, one can never ensure a stable structure of social relations using force alone. For this it was necessary to ensure a mobilised and repressed society, with a consolidated image of the 'enemy', living in a chronic state of a 'fortress under siege'. Therefore the army, as a state organisation of violence, embodied the main values of Soviet society and the mechanisms of collective identity. If modern Western societies were formed through the institutionalisation of such values as individual autonomy, the coexistence of different beliefs and religions, freedom and the necessity of representation (in the market, in Parliament, in a multiparty system, in the independent courts, and so on), then Soviet society with all its apparent ideological messianism and revolutionary expansionism was constructed from the beginning as deeply conservative and intolerant of innovations and alternative values. Conservatism underpinned the very principle ('socialist gene') of the vertical construction of society, as multilevelled systems of social control and power determined the forms of social behaviour which were necessary and acceptable. It is precisely for this reason that the Soviet system had no social mechanisms for the formal transfer of power from one leader to the next or open discussions about the direction of future development, or indeed about any other political programmes. This was not a defect of the system but its principal feature.

Militarism was not so much a *technical* basis for resolving ideological or political tasks (for example, the creation of dominance over any spheres of influence accessible for expansion, such as the countries of Eastern Europe and the Third World) as much as the ideal construction of Soviet society, towards which the CSPU's economic leadership and *apparat* were constantly striving.[7] The issue is not whether the expansionist programme ('the construction of socialist society in other countries') was successful or not, for while success could confirm the legitimate character of the regime, failure would not always undermine it. The issue instead was about the very constitution of society.

The expanse of totalitarian propaganda revealed two key metaphors: 'the construction of a new society' and 'the front'. Both meanings form a single semantic complex: the construction of a future society (undoubtedly a model for 'all countries' and people of 'good will') takes place in extreme conditions of open and secret wars of external and internal class enemies. Those 'socialist regimes' are in a situation of hostile encirclement, inside a 'ring of enemy countries'.[8] The significance of the metaphors of 'the enemy' and 'the hostile encirclement of countries of socialism' lay in the legitimisation of a new socialist order, with an important structural element played by the army and the security services as institutions of uninterrupted and systematic terror. Force was affirmed as a necessary condition for the mass

motivation to work and towards obedience in the thesis of the Central
Committee of the Workers' and Peasants' Party (the Bolsheviks) 'On the
mobilisation of the industrial proletariat, the labour obligation, the militarisation of the economy and the use of military units for economic necessi-
ties', written by Lev Trotsky in 1920. Trotsky asserted:

> Since the army is the most important experience of mass Soviet organisation,
> its methods and manuals should be (with all necessary changes) transferred
> into the field of labour organisation for immediate use ... The tools of state
> coercion are its armed forces. Consequently, an element of militarisation of
> labour to some extent, in some form or other, is an inevitable characteristic of
> a transition economy based on a common labour obligation.[9]

Military–state rhetoric subordinated and put aside the task, in the revolutionary phraseology, of 'the uncompromising struggle of workers against
the world bourgeoisie'. The initial ideological position of 'construction in
conditions of actual war' was used by Stalin and his colleagues in 1924 in
the course of the internal CPSU struggle with Trotsky. Stalin used the thesis
of 'the possibility of building a fully socialist society in a single country', but
under one condition: the conduct of the accelerated military–industrialisa-
tion of that country. (Since there were no other sources of finance for this
project, its realisation became possible only at the price of the systematic
lowering of living standards to the minimum necessary for physical survival
– the development of an *apparat* for coercion and propaganda could be
reconciled with similar conditions.) This programme ('building socialism in
one country') meant more than a break with all previous theories of socialism and socialist movements in Europe: it went further and turned any
opponents of Stalin into enemies of the CPSU and the USSR. Moreover, by
implication it proposed the restoration of features of empire such as the
complex of great powers, colonial expansionism, the superiority of Russians
over other peoples, isolationism and so on. From the mid-1930s the revolutionary rhetoric of empire was supplanted by the introduction of corresponding attributes and rituals of the tsarist period. The replacement of
legitimising legends of power went on almost in parallel with the replacement of cadres and the purges during the Great Terror.

Both the tsarist and Soviet regimes, in large measure, depended on the
mobilisation of a society which was constantly roused by the expectation of
war, lived through war and prepared for new war. Military victories traditionally served as a justification or, at least, a strong argument for the
preservation of a despotically paternalistic society. In imperial Russia this
was the military–police dictatorship. In the Soviet period, military tension
supported the ideology of a confrontation between the USSR and the rest of
the world (expressed in traditional anti-Westernism, the 'besieged fortress'
syndrome and isolationism). For two centuries rare victories strengthened

these foundations, while hard defeats in the Crimean, Russo-Japanese and Afghan wars shattered them. Military success in this system of ideas was associated, in the first instance, with the price of 'great power' status. It could also be interpreted as a significant component of a symbolic whole, of the organic social order on which Russian statehood was based. In this respect an actual victory is unnecessary: the very cultivated ideological value of victory became functionally significant.

These values, including military ideas and virtues – heroism, loyalty, readiness for self-sacrifice, courage, obedience, steadfastness, fortitude – comprise the most important background of the semantics of Soviet power. It is precisely this power which is the source of corresponding definitions. Anti-Westernism (anti-modernism) and the ideology of the 'special path' made up a single complex composed of several components: the first is the military–police regime, or the commanding vertical in the constitution of society; the second is horizontal mass solidarity, in other words social uniformity and controllability from the point of view of those with power.

The first period of Soviet history (up to the beginning of the 1940s) provided the rhetoric of 'class' or civil war (1918–22). The second period of Soviet history (from the Cold War to *perestroika*) was dominated by the 'Great Patriotic War' (not the Second World War, but 'patriotic'). Victory in that conflict became, in the popular consciousness, a pivotal event for all of Russian history.[10] The triumph of 1945 not only provided a justification for all the horror of the Stalinist terror, the mass famine during collectivisation and the chronic poverty of daily life in the Soviet period, but substantiated the necessity of similar sacrifices. It made natural, among other things: an atmosphere of fear; the expectation of repression; a police regime of suspicion towards everyone; watchfulness; xenophobia; readiness to repel any conceivable aggression. Victory in that war also legitimised the strengthening military and ideological opposition of 'socialism' to 'capitalism'.

The 'Cold War' of two world social systems turned into the rivalry of two superpowers, with the USSR presented as the centre of the communist world, the epitome of progress and social justice, while the USA was portrayed as the essence of everything alien, such as modernity, wealth, exploitation and racial inequality. This ideological depiction of reality governed the entire period from the 1950s through the 1970s, gradually conceding its place to Brezhnev's rhetoric of 'international *détente*' and Gorbachev's *perestroika*. To a certain extent it is preserved even in the present day, but in the place of the confrontation between the USSR and the USA we now see a different kind of phobia and paranoid suspicion in relation to Western countries, NATO, anti-Americanism, and so on.[11]

The socio-cultural meaning of this organisation of society was not that 'communist Russia' (or the USSR) brought to the world the light of a certain 'higher revolutionary truth' embodied in a kind of Marxist ideological mission of freeing the working man from exploitation, national oppression, colonialism, and so on. These ideological aspirations (at least, from the 1930s) did not have any sort of concrete demonstration. The documents of the communist leadership did not contain anything principled, 'religious' or dogmatic; instead, they presented themselves as the legalisation of the actual interests and tasks of radically changing current politics – from the universalism of the processes of world revolution and the export of socialism to the national supremacy of Russians over other peoples and the desirability of complete isolationism. The self-preservation of the *nomenklatura* (the fundamental corporate motive for the actions of the USSR's highest leadership) presupposed not simply the interpretation of any events of the outer or inner world as the confrontation of *ours* and *theirs*, enemies and allies, but gave rise to the method of organising reality along the principle of irremovable confrontation, imputing motives of hostility towards the Soviets to everyone who is not on *our* side.

A similar type of socio-political culture presupposes that any positive national characteristics are not independent and self-sufficient, but represent that which is dependent on imagined traits of the *enemy*. In other words, the collective self-identification as Soviet (Russian) is constructed as a scheme of opposition, as a negative and dependent identity: we are good not because we possess rare merits (national wealth, a high standard of living, developed industry, a healthy population, culture, and so on) but because the enemy is bad – worse than we are. From this 'our worthiness appears only in extreme situations – wars, ordeals, difficulties overcome, struggles'.

Therefore the army and the police have become central state institutions, symbolically revealing the fundamental values of the entire 'collective', especially the priority of common interests over individual interests and the importance of preserving the whole. In this way Soviet (and to some extent post-Soviet) society differs from modern society in the West, where other public institutions (economic, political, scientific, artistic, sporting, public welfare, and so on) provide the means of integrating the entire instrument of the system of symbolic communications and exchange.

In Soviet times it was senseless to ask oneself 'How much does this tank or ballistic missile cost?' since there was no way of establishing an approximate correspondence between social spending and the price of demand. The proportions could not be established in relation to human spiritual needs and requirements, since resources were managed according to the influence of groups in the *nomenklatura* and top leadership. On the contrary, the level of consumption and living standards grew out of 'planning norms', 'according to the residual principle', that is, as the minimum expenditures necessary in order to preserve the structure of the State and the priorities of the military–industrial complex. In the late Soviet period economists tried to calculate the burden of military–industrial production in the USSR, determining, for example, that the cost of the *Buran* programme (an unpiloted multi-use spaceship, the Soviet version of the US space shuttle) was approximately equivalent to a decade-long programme of housing construction in the USSR.[12] But no one asked the Soviet people whether they were prepared to sacrifice their living conditions for the sake of achievements in the space race with the USA. The system of values and priorities was arranged from the top down, without alternatives, and was not subject to discussion.

The imperatives of universal mobilisation became the principles for the organisation of daily life – they determined employment opportunities, conditions of study in institutions of higher education, the parameters of social mobility (the freedom to change jobs) and the right to property. They also set the limits for what was permitted in terms of individual conduct, and for the types of relationship which individuals could have, both with higher 'authority' and with their families, close friends, work colleagues, and so on, which acted to limit the repressive influence coming 'from above'. In other words, the idea that the country was located within 'a circle of enemies' corresponded to the notion of 'order in the country' (in effect a rigid and repressive regime of organising life), a social correlate of 'defence consciousness'. Both of these factors – together with the mobilisation imperatives of 'threat from without' and the popular perception of power as a source of protection, social defence, the distribution of blessings, and the repository of justice and equality – are interdependent and support each other.

The army in post-Soviet Russia: preserving the system

The collapse of the USSR, which took many by surprise, revealed among other things a more powerful deficit of understanding about the nature of the late totalitarian society. The events of the end of 1991, according to most commentaries, were proclaimed 'democratic revolutions' against the totalitarian regime.[13] They generated a mass of hopes about the chances for the rapid integration of Russia within the association of 'developed' countries. However, after several years, the euphoria within the country vanished and was replaced by a much more sceptical interpretation of the nature of post-communist society.

The collapse of the totalitarian regime led to the suspension of modernising processes of the Soviet type (military–industrial modernisation) and to conditions of chronic socio-political instability and rapidly developing regressive nationalism (sometimes even religious fundamentalism), with very strong elements of neotraditionalism. It later led to the appearance of a post-totalitarian semi-authoritarian regime, based on the situational, or accidental, composition of social forces or corporate interests and supported by the ideology of anti-Westernism or some sort of local version of *special* (religious or secular national) socialism.

Internal mechanisms preserving the role of the military

The Soviet super-centralised state system, which lacked institutionalised mechanisms for the representation of various group interests and therefore also for regulated changes of power, could not endure the internal pressure created by the processes of decentralisation and development. Publicly or privately the slogan 'democratisation' became only the external expression of real popular dissatisfaction, on which republican ethno-nationalist or religious cliques and groups of provincial *nomenklatura* (which had little chance of promotion in the old party–state gerontocracy) based their desire for emancipation from the federal centre.

It was the elevated character of the struggle for power, together with the continued alienation of the population from politics itself and the extreme immaturity of the structures of civil society, which explain the relatively peaceful character of the collapse of the state political system and, more-over, created the sense of powerful popular, social movements in deep trans-formative processes. But already the consolidation of the redistribution of power and the conservation of a new established order immediately required a demonstration of military force, a strengthening of the role of the army and the special services as an instrument of the restoration of the control of central power over the ongoing strengthening of the weakened *vertical* social order.

The influence of the communist revolt after the lengthy confrontation between the Russian Soviet Federated Socialist Republic (*Rossiiskaia Sovetskaia Federativnaia Sotsialisticheskaia Respublika* or RSFSR) Supreme Soviet and the president of Russia in the summer and autumn of 1993 occurred with the direct participation of the army. The result of this, evidently, was a rise in the influence of the generals and the special services (the successors of the USSR's KGB), both in Boris Yeltsin's immediate circle and in other social institutions with some influence on policy decisions – in the Government, Parliament, the Security Council, and so on – and the weakening, therefore, and exclusion from the leadership of more liberal and pro-Western 'young reformers'. After the adoption of the new constitution, the Russian Parliament played a less significant socio-political role, losing a number of important legal monitoring functions. At the same time, senior military officials gained great influence over policy, which the president considered as a reward for their direct support for his personal power and a guarantee of its stabilisation.

The direct consequences of this were visible by the end of 1994 with the first Chechen war and a change in the orientation of Russia's foreign policy. New figures of speech appeared in the political rhetoric, revealing a transi-tion from declarations about the necessity of integration with the Western world (in a more populist and therefore also more influential version – betrayal 'by the democrats' of the national interests of Russia and the sur-render of the country to Western capitalism) through moderate opposition, and then to anti-Western hysteria, including calls to erect barriers against the expansion of NATO to the east. Various kinds of phobias were thus exploited, from 'the defence of the national interests of Russia' to assertions of a direct threat to its security, amid accusations that the Western countries were striving to colonise Russia. In addition, a steady stream of information presented the policy of reform in the country as the realisation of a long-standing plot by Western circles against 'Great Russia'. These tactics turned out to be very productive, since in the popular consciousness the acute economic crisis and the falling standards of living were closely connected with the market and democratic changes. The policy of isolationism was strengthened, the anti-liberal mood in the country grew and nostalgia for the Soviet past increased. The weaker Boris Yeltsin became, physically and politically, the more significant was the role of the military – or, more precisely, 'those who wield force', including also the Presidential Guard headed by A. Korzhakov, who actively interfered in political life.

A closed circle formed. Reforms which were begun but not completed constituted a source of social tension and a crisis of power, and thus represented a potential threat to social stability. The removal of these threats, in the opinion of the highest leadership, could be done only by strengthening the force structures (the MVD, the army, the FSB) and, correspondingly, by dismissing those cadres who could relatively consistently and happily complete the reforms and achieve positive results (namely, improving the economy and raising the material level of life for the population). It was precisely in these years (1994–97) that the MVD was granted enormous material–financial means, there was an increase in the personnel and a reorganisation of the armed units of the internal forces, and the structures of state security were reactivated and partly rehabilitated.

The start of the Chechen war became the first and most significant attempt undertaken by the 'force *bloc*' to preserve the collapsing structure of a mobilised and repressive state, and to ensure for itself the popular support of Russian society.[14] War in this event was only a means of consolidating society around the symbolic axes of power, of retaining and reproducing an institutional system, in particular of selecting for the higher echelons of power a certain personality type, and of mechanisms for redistributing financial resources. The Chechen war is an artificial problem in the sense that it was initiated by the most sclerotic structures of power in response to the weakening of their political and administrative capabilities. It would not, however, have become a national problem if these formations, which represent the preservation of the spirit of the Soviet regime (that is, the force ministries and the special services – the army, state security, the MVD, the Ministry for Nationality Affairs and the Security Council), had not presented a local conflict as a threat to the entire state machine and received popular support. In other words, they succeeded in converting technical questions of policy into symbols.

The issue is neither the natural inclination of the Chechens towards banditry nor their vindictiveness, but that it is impossible for Russian power to find a mutually advantageous form for its relations with the Chechen leadership and the inhabitants of the Republic. The processes of decentralisation and the collapse of the totalitarian regime were not conditioned by a new recognition of human values, a new social and cultural quality of Russia, which could be connected with *democracy*, the claims to various individual rights, freedoms and so on. Instead these processes came as the result of the sluggishness inherent in the Soviet regime and the impossibility of reproducing the old relationship between the State and its subordinates. The declarations which resounded in capital cities around the world about the end of the dictatorship of the CPSU and the KGB, about the great future of a free and democratic Russia, did not in principle affect the system of internal violence on which the Soviet State's structure was supported. (The collapse of the communist system is not the same as the formation of democracy. In this sense, changes in one level of the system or in one institutional sub-system do not mean the transformation of all of its other links and parts.)

During eight years of war Russia's generals have gained unprecedented political influence. Only in conditions when central power is chronically weak could the military's decisions and acts of coercion be represented both to the political leadership and to society as a whole as the most simple and effective in the circumstances.[15] The Russian military was able to turn to advantage even its defeat, by accusing the politicians of 'tying their hands', of not giving them the chance to destroy completely the vanguard of the Chechen resistance. (In reality such a 'final solution' could have taken only one form – the supreme leadership sanctioning the military to carry out the genocide of the Chechen ethnic group, or 'the transformation of the territory of Chechnia into the Gobi desert', as General Aleksandr Rutskoi requested.)

In this context Vladimir Putin, formerly the head of the FSB, came to power. In order to understand the mechanisms of the consolidation of Russian society it is unimportant whether the FSB initiated the introduction of Shamil' Basaev's Chechen units into Dagestan and terrorist acts (explosions in high-rise apartment buildings) in Russian cities with the aim of destabilising the situation in the country, creating the atmosphere of fear and mistrust necessary to justify an authoritarian-style administration.[16] In and of itself the rise to power in Russia of such a figure as Putin – previously practically unknown, without a distinctive political programme of his own, on whom any political forces and groups could project something of their own mood – meant only that Putin is a *vydvizhenets*, a person promoted above his abilities, a creature of those whose power lies in the structures of the state administration or which depends on the state sector of the economy.

As the analysis of the results of a VTsIOM opinion poll demonstrates, the phenomenon of the president's popularity is in no way connected with the results of his political actions.[17] Nor is it related to the personal qualities of Putin himself, who spent a long time as a middle-ranking bureaucrat and then a short time as the head of the FSB[18] without revealing any charismatic leadership qualities. The issue, rather, lies in whether this figure can live up to his popular socio-political expectations, in correspondence with which he was 'identified' as the man who was 'needed' at that place and time.

Today the influence of the military on political life takes several forms. The highest level of political leadership – the inner circle of the president – consists almost exclusively of former KGB officers, army leaders and retired generals. Out of the 7 representatives of the president in the federal districts, 5 are former generals or Chekists. High-ranking officers who support the Putin administration go into politics either as governors or as *Duma* deputies, on party lists, with the use of administrative resources in the regions. As a rule, they chair key *Duma* committees (on defence, security, and so on). Less noted are the processes by which military personnel and former employees of the special services penetrate the financial–economic structures of large corporations and the coercion of the leaders of large enterprises, the so-called 'oligarchs', who finance the party of power and the election campaigns in the provinces.[19]

The strengthening of the special services and the military has not gone unnoticed in Russian society, although it does not provoke the appropriate negative reaction, namely opposition. On the contrary, it reflects popular disappointment in the character and results of reform in society and the economy, the discrediting of state power as a whole, nostalgia for the Soviet past and representations of the army as the embodiment of national symbols and values.

Among the various social and political institutions, popular trust remains only in:

- the president himself (as the personification of popular expectations and the representation of national aspirations);
- the church as a symbol of the unity of the nation and a surrogate for personal morals;
- the army and the FSB.

Indices of popular trust in institutions in a survey conducted in March 2003 were divided in the following way: the president (+52); the Church (+24), the army (+4), organs of state security (+1). All the rest – the press, television and other means of mass information, the Government, local power, the courts, the public prosecutor, the militia, Parliament, political parties and trades unions – are in the field of complete mistrust.[20]

Table 1.1 Which social forces (or which groups' interests) does President Putin represent?[a]

	February 2001	March 2002	March 2003	March 2004
'The forces of power': the special services, the army, the MVD	28	36	33	44
'The oligarchs': bankers and entrepreneurs	18	18	25	29
'The family': Boris Yeltsin's inner circle	22	22	21	28
'The middle class'	18	23	23	27
'Ordinary people': office workers, manual labourers, farmers	25	18	17	21
The state bureaucracy	13	19	23	21
Directors of industry, heads of large enterprises	10	16	18	17
The cultural and scientific elite	6	9	7	11
Russian society as a whole	8	11	10	9

Note [a] As a percentage of the number of those polled, N = 1,600

Such a condition of popular consciousness could mean only one thing: a residual syndrome of fear is preserved in society, which reflects its mobilised condition. The high status of the army and the special services is an indication of the absence of change, or, in other words, the preservation of an uncontrolled position of power. From a certain point of view what provokes this fear (or, more precisely, how it is explained psychologically, how the condition of popular anxiety is rationalised) – whether it is the threat of Chechen terrorism or the danger of world war – is unimportant. The level of these or other fears in the social consciousness is dependent on external circumstances. For example, the fear of a world war sharply increased after the events of 11 September 2001, during the NATO bombing of Yugoslavia in the spring of 1999, and during the Iraq war and the overthrow of Saddam Hussein's regime in 2003. By contrast, a wave of hysterical aggression towards Chechnia tends to rise after extraordinary terror acts in Russian cities, for example in 1999 after explosions in Moscow and Volgodonsk, in the autumn of 2002 after the seizure of the *Teatr na Dubrovke* in Moscow, and so on.[21]

The reproduction of 'defensive consciousness': Russia and NATO
The popular suspicion and hostility in relation to NATO (as a military organisation of Western countries commanded by the USA) remains a very noticeable factor of political consolidation: 40 per cent of those questioned in the March 2003 survey referred to above said that the policy of NATO

expansion to the east threatens the security of Russia (14 per cent of respondents said that, on the contrary, it strengthens Russia's security and another 25 per cent believes that it 'does not have an important influence' on the status of Russia). Precisely because there is no real basis for Russia's fear of NATO, those fears should be regarded as a perversion of Russia's own long history of institutional aggression. However, that very aggression (or residual militarism) is in a state of 'semi-collapse'. The more specific the formulation of the question, the further it moves from the traditional clichés of Soviet propaganda and the more measured the reaction of the Russian population. For example, the responses to the question 'Does NATO now present a threat to Russia?' break down as follows: only 32 per cent of respondents said 'yes', while 49 per cent said 'no'. Over the last 5–6 years, in answer to similar questions about similar circumstances ('Is there a threat to Russia from Western countries? Does Russia threaten the countries of the West?'), VTsIOM sociologists received sharply differing answers. The percentage of people who agreed that 'there is no threat to Russia from the West' was 27–9 per cent (58–9 per cent of those who believed that there is such a basis [correlation = 0.5]), and the number of those who said that 'Russia should fear the West' was more than twice as great as those opposed (2:1, or 58–60 per cent versus 27–30 per cent).

Over the past 6–7 years Russians' attitude to the entry of the former countries of the socialist camp into NATO is chiefly negative (the correlation of poll opinion = 0.4) and practically unchanged if you do not consider the negligible growth of those indifferent to this question (from 22–30 per cent). The very same question, but related to the former republics of the USSR (Ukraine, Georgia, and others), provokes forceful emotions of a negative kind: those respondents expressing an unfavourable view on this issue over the past several years has grown from 41 per cent to 48 per cent.

As far as Russians are concerned, the preferred scenario for the relationship between Russia and NATO is 'regulated cooperation', the establishment of 'partner-like relations' with the North Atlantic bloc (in the course of the last several years 28 per cent expressed themselves in favour of this) or 'the non-participation of Russia in any military *blocs*' (27–8 per cent in favour). Extreme opinions ('the entry of Russia into NATO' or 'the creation of a defensive union of the RF) with other countries against NATO') were supported by insignificant groups of Russians (10 and 18 per cent, respectively). In other words, the dominant view is that relations with NATO should be restrained and distanced. It is unfavourable towards the North Atlantic alliance but not aggressive.[22]

The process of 'demobilisation' and post-traumatic syndrome
At the beginning of the 1990s, with the destruction of everything connected with the whole system of totalitarian institutions of supreme power – the alliance of the Central Committee (CC) of the CPSU, the Government, the

KGB, the MOD, *Gosplan* (the state economic planning agency) and the industrial ministries – a strange situation arose: society was in fact living through a state of demobilisation, a weariness of the chronic readiness for war, marked by a clear disinclination to be involved in any military conflict, even one with the very highest aims. Public opinion polls after Afghanistan (and also the dramatic and negative experience of the use of the army for political purposes in the Baltics, in Central Asia and in the Caucasus) demonstrated opposition to the involvement of the Russian Army in any hot spots, whether civil war in Tajikistan or ethnic conflicts in Yugoslavia. According to VTsIOM, from 55 to 60 per cent of those questioned during this period opposed the sending of armed units to hot spots or to Russia's borders to carry out any military tasks, and this included the military police. A single exception was made for the former republics of the USSR, when ethnic confrontation there threatened to turn into mass slaughter. But that was the only exception. In any other circumstances public opinion refuses to give government the right to use force for purposes not connected with the defence of the border of Russia itself (this was true for the beginning of the first Chechen war and the entire time of its conduct). Therefore even the return of armed units from the countries of the former socialist camp (Germany, Hungary, Czechoslovakia), despite all expectations, did not provoke among the population of the former empire any appreciable reactions, especially condemnation or opposition.[23]

Although both the structure and the function of the army have remained the same – the defence of uncontrolled power, ensuring the reproduction of the previous social structure – attitudes towards military service in society have changed sharply. In answer to the question 'Would you like your son (brother, husband or other close relative) to serve in the army now?' fewer than 30 per cent of men and only 15 per cent of women said 'yes'. Among young men of conscription age it was 14 per cent. VTsIOM research conducted over 1992–2002 shows that the military is striving to propagandise 'army' values and virtues in both schools and institutions of higher education, but the latter are seeking a guaranteed deferral of military service for school pupils at the age of 18. This division acquires a social character: the better-educated parents and those oriented towards the education of their children are striving to ensure a career for them without military service; parents without education more often agree with the perspective of the draft. The army, as the officials of the military themselves say, is becoming a 'worker–peasant army', for which contingent, army service is frequently an alternative to prison.[24] Almost three quarters of young people (72 per cent) are in favour of the shift to a contract basis for the army (only 17 per cent of those in this group favour the preservation of conscription). In contrast, most older people (51 per cent) support the continuation of universal military service and the staffing of the army via conscription. To a great extent the failure of the federal forces in Chechnia has inclined society against service in the armed forces: in 2001 84 per cent of Russians agreed that Russia needs a professional army on a contract basis.

At the same time the population has sharply and repeatedly rejected the very notion that in a crisis situation 'the army should take control of the country in its own hands' (85 per cent disagreed with this statement, 15 per cent agreed).

One could say that Russian society today is living sluggishly through the current phase of a post-traumatic syndrome (first described as 'Vietnam syndrome'). [25] In Russia it became known to so-called *afgantsy*, soldiers who had served in the war in Afghanistan, and later to those who fought in Chechnia. Its characteristics include:

- the inability to have normal social relations;
- little interest in one's partner;
- the predominance of negative ideas about others, and, correspondingly, the impossibility of making long-term plans for the future;
- a chronic psychopathic condition, expressing itself as alternating states of apathy and aggression;
- a high level of anxiety and phobias;
- extremely high levels of alcoholism and suicide (in recent years Russia has gone to second place in the world, behind Lithuania, for the number of suicides – 41 in 100,000 inhabitants[26]).

In the post-Soviet period militarism (as an ideology, an economic structure or as characteristic bellicosity, expansionism of the popular mood) has practically vanished. It remains only in inert forms in the institutional organisations of daily life, such as mass obedience, complexes of national inferiority or injury, an awareness of the irreversible disintegration of the army, popular national–political attenuation, the unavoidable consequence of a situation of chronic long-term mobilisation.[27] This in no way contradicts the fact of periodic explosions of nationalist anti-USA hysteria, diffuse and aimless fears of the threat of a new world war, terrorism, the fear of being drawn into a new military adventure through the will of those in power. But psychological demobilisation, or diffused social nationalist aggression, signifies a change not so much in the institutional structures as in the patterns of mass identity.

The reason for the stability of the mobilised repressive syndrome lies in the fact that, in spite of the disintegration of the army and the militaristic complex, these institutions have not been replaced. The preservation of the old institutional system hinders the rise of other conceptions of the army and the military's relations with society, preventing a review of other institutional models, paralysing the very possibility of a conception of the armed forces, as the fate of all discussions about military reform demonstrate.[28] The interests of the bloated corps of generals is today one of the chief reasons for Russia's internal political paralysis, the absence of significant changes and the failures of modernisation which have already occurred in the post-communist period. These high-ranking officers oppose any changes and put all their efforts towards conserving what is, in essence, still Soviet military doctrine – one which will provoke wars and crisis situations – in order to preserve the financial and staffing structure of the army. But it would be incorrect to think that only generals, the officer corps or enterprises in the military–industrial system are interested in maintaining the current model of relations between the army and society. The readiness of the majority of Russians to approve an increase in military spending is proof of this, in spite of the rather deplorable condition of the state budget.[29] Those questioned in VTsIOM polls said that it is not the model of the army which is bad, but the current conditions of its implementation. Among the various ills of the army about which they were questioned, the majority (43 per cent) named social problems as the most significant: low wages; the absence of housing for officers; poor social conditions and nutrition of soldiers, and so on. The low level of combat readiness was identified by 20 per cent, and only 35 per cent indicated the senselessness and danger of service in the army itself for the current conscript soldiers (forced service, the war in Chechnia, *dedovshchina*, the conscription of students into the army), and so on. Nevertheless 55–60 per cent of those questioned in 2000–1 believed that the army could defend them in the event of a real military threat from other states.

The sluggish discussions about reform of the army (that is, the preservation of a conscript army versus the shift to a professional army through service by contract) conceals the absence of a military doctrine in the new 'democratic' Russia. This means that any attempt to reconsider the role of the military will run into the fierce and aggressive opposition of the generals and that they will propose only variations of Soviet conceptions of the armed forces, left over from the Cold War. In other words, the reform of the army is not a problem simply of the transformation and modernisation of the armed forces, but the fate of the entire totalitarian order which preserves the structure of a mobilised–repressive society. Yet this in its turn, means that the link between the army and the power structures strengthens the process of the disintegration of the army, which does not have truly military functions and tasks, and has lost its military spirit and discipline. The situation in Chechnia, where regular units were turned into bands of marauders, extortionists and aggressors, vividly demonstrates precisely this.

At present the Russian Army as a military machine presents itself as disintegrating, demoralised and disoriented, comprised of the remnants of a previously mighty, privileged and exclusive corporation, which was united in the awareness of its exclusivity, necessity and authority in society, supported by social and material goods, and integrated by a model of its organisation and a clear image of 'the enemy'. Burdened by the survivals of a 'great power' ideology and by its imperial traditions, today's Russian Army is not in a position to overcome the institutional inertia of the Cold War period. In particular, the Russian Army is burdened by an enormous quantity of ageing weapons, intended for military operations based chiefly on the experience of the Second World War, together with strategic nuclear missiles, formerly the chief means of argument in the confrontation between the West and the communist world, but now completely unnecessary, a navy which has become incapacitated in current conditions, long-range aviation, and so on. The possession of this antiquated arsenal has an extremely oppressive effect on the contemporary development of Russia.

Notes

1 Other works by Lev Gudkov on this theme include: 'Armiia v postsovetskoi Rossii', *Indeks*, 19 (2003), available online: http://index.org.ru/journal/19/gudkov19.html; and *Negativnaia identichnost'* (Moscow: NLO, 2003).

2 The latter were not even priorities which came out of the actual correlation of forces and material resources for corresponding tasks by the armed forces, but official patriotic rhetoric. The catastrophic experience of the first months of 1941 is more convincing evidence of all of this, although it is possible to come to these conclusions by investigating the character of the Finnish campaign of 1939–40 or the intervention of Soviet forces into Czechoslovakia in 1968 or, in its own way, the obvious failure of the military in the current Chechen war.

3 After the acute crisis of 1927, when the Soviet Government believed that the country was on the brink of war, it was decided that coerced military–industrial modernisation was a necessity. The collectivisation of agriculture (as a source of finance) was one attempt at its realisation, but there were also the development of the enormous punitive apparatus of the secret police, the system of total social control and propaganda. The preparation of society for war was one of the triggers and conditions of social consolidation.

4 In June 2001 47 per cent of the Russians questioned believed that war was inevitable at the end of the 1930s. (Here, as in other cases, when VTsIOM conducts these regular opinion polls, they are carried out according to a representative selection of all Russians, $N = 1,600$.)

5 It is important to emphasise that a generational change took place at the beginning of the 1930s. Gradually the influence of people who had lived through two wars – the world war and the civil war – was lost. Communist power in Russia, as in other totalitarian countries, gambled on the young, on the generation of 'Soviet people', born in the years of the Bolshevik Revolution and civil war, who were contemporaries of the regime, and who had no other models for collective socialisation.

6 The well-known scholar of the Soviet system V. Zaslavsky described the USSR as 'a military industrial society', and modernisation in the USSR as 'militarist modernisation': see 'The Soviet system and the Soviet Union: causes of collapse', in K. Barkey and M. von Hagen (eds), *After Empire* (Boulder, CO: Westview Press, 1997), and *Storia del sistema sovietico: L'Ascesa, la stabilita, il crollo* (Roma: Carocci, 2001).

7 On this point see M. Sapper, 'Diffuznaia voinstvennost', *Neprikosnovennyi zapas*, 1 (1999), 10–21.

8 Remnants of this way of thinking today reveal themselves in the shape of amorphous and diffuse religious phobias, in a suspicion of Western countries, especially the USA, in the conviction that the West wants to colonise Russia, to appropriate its natural wealth, to humiliate Russia, and so on. Similar opinions are shared by 50–60 per cent of the population. Moreover, with Putin's accession to power, this projected hostility has only strengthened. In answer to the question 'Do you agree that Russia always provoked hostile feelings in other states?' 42 per cent answered positively in November 1994, while in April 2000 66 per cent agreed: *Obshchestvennoe mnenie 2000* (Moscow: VTsIOM, 2000), p. 86.

9 L. Trotsky, 'Kak vooruzhalas revoliutsiia (na voennoi rabote)', in L. Trotsky, *K Istorii Russkoi revoliutsii* (Moscow: Politizdat, 1990), pp. 155–6.

10 L. Gudkov, 'Pobeda v voine: k sotsiologii odnogo natsional'nogo simvola', *Monitoring obshchestvennogo mneniia*, 5 (1997), 12–19.

11 L. Gudkov, 'Otnoshenie k SShA v Rossii i problema antiamerikanizma', *Monitoring obshchestvennogo mneniia*, 2 (2002), 32–48; Iu. Levada, 'Otlozhennyi Armageddon? God posle 11 sentiabria 2001', *Monitoring obshchestvennogo mneniia*, 5 (2002), 7–18.

12 Information which I can neither prove nor disprove from one of the engineer–economists who worked in a closed scientific space research institute in the military–industrial complex in the early 1980s.

13 See, for example, I. Starodubovskaia and V. Mau, *Velikie revoliutsii: ot Kromvella do Putina* (Moscow: Vagrius, 2001).

14 Once again I will emphasise that this series of events followed two unsuccessful attempts at the restoration of previous systems – the August coup of 1991 and the confrontation of Yeltsin and the RSFSR Supreme Soviet in October 1993, which turned into an armed rebellion and was suppressed by Yeltsin with the help of the elite units of the army and special services loyal to him.

15 Essentially, herein lies the logic of the collapse of the post-Soviet system, forcing individual subjects (that is, political leaders or parties, social groups or institutional sub-systems) to come running to move simple, traditionally worked-out, solutions. It could even be called a process of relative social 'primitivisation' (*primitivizatsiia* in the original Russian – trans.] in the sense that the models of action and examples used for resolving these conflicts are borrowed from ideological and cultural resources of the preceding phase of the social condition.

16 The FSB would not disown the suspicions which arose from time to time that it was a participant in these raids by Chechen separatists or even that it provoked them so that, through an artificial aggravation of the situation in the country, it would get the chance to introduce a state of emergency. But the fact that it was Putin who was the leader of the FSB at this time, who therefore possessed corresponding information and the means of control over the situation in the region and in the country as a whole, allows us to understand those mechanisms used by the groups which brought him to power according to a scenario well known since 1934 (that is, the murder of Kirov).

17 In the economic sphere the results of its activity are estimated predominantly negatively: 65 per cent polled in July 2000 and 62 per cent in November 2002 believed this. The number who believed that Putin had not achieved 'any success'

or his actions were 'completely unsuccessful' rose over this period from 67 per cent to 74 per cent concerning military operations in Chechnia. Negative views also prevail concerning the struggle to combat corruption, crime, and so on. The only area where the president achieved notable successes, in the opinion of the respondents, was in foreign policy, where Putin was able to defend the interests of Russia and protect its authority as a great power in the world: see *Obshchestvennoe mnenie 2002*. For material on 1989–2002 see *VTsIOM Annual*, (2002), 51–64.

18 In the course of regular monthly VTsIOM polls in 2000 (that is, soon after Putin came to power) respondents were asked: 'Does Putin's long career in the FSB make you uneasy?', with 75–9 per cent of Russians answering 'no' (only 17 per cent in January compared to 22 per cent in October 2000 gave the opposite answer). Considerably more disquiet was expressed in connection with issues surrounding Yeltsin (this circumstance was indicated by 48 per cent of those polled), the absence from his administration of any political programme (66 per cent) or that he got bogged down in the Chechen war (80 per cent).

19 In this respect the most recent and sharpest conflict between the *siloviki* and the Russian company Iukos is especially interesting. Formerly this appeared to be an investigation by the prosecutor-general of a breach of economic activity of one of its daughter firms. In fact, the issue was about attempts by one of the clans of the 'Petersburg Chekists', who came to power with Putin and comprised an influential wing in his administration, to ensure for themselves stable positions in politics and the economy until after 2008, that is, when Putin steps down from the post of president.

20 VTsIOM poll, representative of the general Russian population, N = 2,100 people, March 2003.

21 *Monitoring obshchestvennogo mneniia*, 4 (2003), 65.

22 The entry of Russia into NATO was supported by 35 per cent, while 47 per cent opposed it (N = 1,600, March 2003).

23 Characteristically, in the first years of reform the army would remain apolitical and neutral. Even the division of powers within the armed forces themselves was in part furthered by this, with the dismissal of many generals from the Soviet era opening up the possibility of career growth for middle- and upper-ranking officers.

24 *Obshchestvennoe mnenie 2002* (Mooscow: VTsIOM, 2002), p. 120.

25 More than a million young conscripts have passed through the wars in Chechnia since 1994. Their experience is, in any event, being interpreted by a society which is undergoing an acute identity crisis.

26 See the electronic version of Demoscope, 5 (20 January–5 February 2001): www.demoscope.rrrru/weekly/005terna00001.php.

27 Iu. Levada, 'Problema emotsional'nogo balansa obshchestva', *Ot mnenii k ponimaniiu* (Moscow: Moscow School of Political Research, 2000), pp. 359–90.

28 The polls showed a very high level of support for the idea of reform of the army and its shift to a contract basis, and initially the introduction of alternative civilian service. But the terms of a general version of the law on alternative service which was adopted caused public opinion to turn against it. This version of the law did not simply double the length of alternative service, but

placed conscientious objectors in what are known to be most difficult conditions, in fact making them serve a 'sentence' for rejecting the army.

29 In January 2002 54 per cent of those polled agreed with the statement 'Russia
should in future increase expenditure on defence, perhaps even at the expense of
other items in the budget', 31 per cent were opposed and 15 per cent found it difficult to answer this question (the number polled = 1,600). A year later, in February
2003, public opinion about what should be done to improve the situation in the
army was divided as follows: 39 per cent believed it necessary to maintain the current size of the army and increase funding from the budget for its maintenance; 24
per cent said that the size of the army should be reduced but that expenditure on
its maintenance should be increased; the remainder believed that the optimal
decision was either a reduction in the size of the armed forces (and also while
maintaining the current defence budget – 17 per cent) or a reduction in the size
and the budget (9 per cent).

2 *Bettina Renz*

Media–military relations in post-Soviet Russia: who is the watchdog?

The failure of the Russian armed forces both to introduce a significant level of structural reform since 1989 and to accept even a rudimentary system of civilian control is often explained, at least partially, by the military leadership's resistance to change. Equally, military conservatism tends to be perceived as inhibiting media access to the armed forces in post-Soviet Russia and as the main driving force in the creation of a media–military relationship that is generally characterised by mutual mistrust and hostility. Although many Russian journalists covering military affairs see it as a part of their professional duty to engender a certain degree of civilian control over the armed forces, their ability effectively to perform such a watchdog role has been severely limited and has even been decreasing in recent years. Instead of attributing the blame for this state of affairs mainly to the military leadership, however, I argue that limitations on the watchdog function of the Russian media are not predominantly the result of the military's conservatism and its hostile attitude towards the media: such limitations owe more to the attitude of post-Soviet Russia's civilian masters who have determined the structural framework within which the media–military relationship is acted out.

A note on theory and method

The available body of theoretical work concerning media–military relations in the West tends to concentrate on times of war and the results of involvement in armed conflict. The aftermath of the Vietnam War was especially influential in this respect, as it became conventional wisdom to assume that 'it was lost because of a betrayal of the United States (US) fighting forces by the media'.[1] The reactions of Western governments to the media's perceived influence on the outcome of the war in Vietnam gave rise to a large number of works on media–military relations concerning subsequent major and minor armed conflicts.[2] The focus of this literature on situations of armed conflict can be explained by the fact that while the problem of direct state censorship and regulation of the media in Western liberal–capitalist states in times other than war has mostly been resolved, it resurfaces as an issue for debate in times of war and involvement in armed conflict.

Likewise, in the Russian case, discussions of media–military relations in the post-Soviet era have focused predominantly on differences in information policy during the first and second Chechen campaigns.[3] In this chapter I seek to expand the analysis of media–military relations in post-Soviet Russia beyond situations of war and armed conflict for two reasons. First, issues of press freedom and state censorship in post-Soviet Russia are still a major area for debate, and not only in times of war. Second, in contrast to the mainstream Western press, where media coverage of military themes appears to address predominantly the defence industry, the military budget and involvement in armed conflicts, Russian newspapers regularly cover issues concerning the armed forces' problems and activities beyond the scope of their fighting missions. These issues include social problems affecting military personnel, problematic aspects of conscription, crime in barracks and corruption within the military. From an analysis of Russian newspapers, it seems that the coverage of these issues is the *main* peacetime reason for the military's hostility towards the press.

The emphasis in this chapter is on establishing the extent to which the Russian press can, during peacetime, be perceived to have fulfilled the role of a watchdog over the military establishment for the first decade of post-Soviet rule. The term 'watchdog' (or also 'fourth estate') is often used to describe the desirable function of the press in democratic states,[4] and here is to be understood as involving two obligations: first, the press ought to perform a surveillance of the socio-economic environment, reporting events likely to impinge on the welfare of citizens; second, the press is expected to provide mechanisms for holding state officials to account for their exercise of power.[5]

Furthermore, the absence of state censorship is imperative in order to enable the press to fulfil this function effectively, and the understanding of the press as watchdog must be shared by journalists and state officials alike. The analysis which follows addresses two determinants for the effectiveness of the press as watchdog: the military and the political leadership. It is acknowledged that the journalists' role in this relationship is also an important one, and that role will be addressed, albeit relatively briefly. In doing so, it is not my intention to portray the journalists as the 'defenders of democracy', hounded by the 'undemocratic' military and civilian leaderships. It should not be overlooked, for instance, that a large proportion of the Russian defence journalists writing for mainstream newspapers come from a military background and so, as might be expected, are critical of 'civilians', especially women, writing about military affairs. It is my aim in this chapter to show how the actions and reactions of the post-Soviet military and civilian leaderships, respectively, have limited the post-Soviet Russian media's performance of a 'watchdog' role over the armed forces.

Before proceeding to the analysis, certain analytical tools and approaches need to be clarified. First, in using the term 'military' the emphasis will be on the army as the numerically dominant arm of service, but naturally 'military' will refer to the other services as well. Second, the term 'military leadership' will refer to officers who hold the rank of general – that is, the most influential, higher echelon, elements. Third, the term 'media' will refer to the press. Although it is acknowledged that Russian broadcast media, as in the West, reach a considerably wider audience, preference in this analysis of media coverage will be given to the print media. Since the closure of the commercially owned channel TV-6 in January 2002, the entirety of Russian national television has become state-owned and lacks the variety of opinion generated in the newspaper market by the views of different owners and by contrasting ideological orientations. The broader conclusions offered at the end of this chapter, however, are applicable to the entire mass media, including the broadcast media. Fourth, in terms of defining the military leadership's 'hostility' towards the media, and in order to illustrate the key aspects of the media–military relationship in post-Soviet Russia, the focus will be on the newspaper coverage of a particular problem concerning the armed forces. This is the tradition according to which new conscripts are bullied, or 'hazed', by older comrades, in some cases resulting in serious injury to and even the death of conscripts. This practice, commonly known as *dedovshchina* in Russia, (see the definition of this term in the Introduction to this volume), is used as an analytical tool in examining the media–military relationship in post-Soviet Russia. It is in areas like these that it is desirable for the press to act as watchdog over the armed forces in peacetime and to inform society about the conditions of service life, as *dedovshchina* immediately affects the welfare of Russian citizens. The coverage of *dedovshchina* was examined in four newspapers during the years 1996, 1997, 2000 and 2001 in order to analyse the changing relationship between the military and the print media under the governments of Presidents Boris Yeltsin and Vladimir Putin. The newspapers *Krasnaia zvezda* (published by the MOD) and *Rossiiskaia gazeta* (published by the Russian Government) were chosen to represent the official line of the armed forces and of the civilian leadership, respectively. *Izvestiia* and *Komsomol'skaia pravda* were chosen as widely read examples of the independent and liberal-oriented press; they are also important because, as one general put it, 'they form public opinion'.[6] Findings of this newspaper analysis are supplemented by material from interviews with Russian defence journalists conducted by the author in 2001 and 2002.

The military's role in Russian media–military relations: barking at the 'watchdog'

The relationship between the military and the press in post-Soviet Russia could be described as one of mutual mistrust and hostility. This attitude originated in the rapid and fundamental transformation of the Soviet press monolith at the end of the 1980s. Prior to *perestroika*, the Soviet press was entirely state-owned and had a function in sharp contrast to that of the press in Western liberal–capitalist states where it is perceived to perform the function of a 'fourth estate', mediating between the State and society, or as a 'watchdog', guarding the work of state institutions. A central component of this function is that of an *informer*, alerting the public and politicians to certain problems, tendencies or events in order to provoke a reaction and subsequent solution to the problem. A major task of the media's role as a watchdog is to voice criticism and elevate perceived problems to the public agenda, without glossing them over to uphold a certain image of a state actor, institution, etc. As a result, media reporting is sometimes perceived as overemphasising the negative and as being overly pessimistic.[7]

In contrast, the function of the Soviet press was that of a *teacher*, 'educating the public in the "right" way, and acting as the [Communist P]arty's publicist',[8] as opposed to merely informing the public. While not entirely absent from Soviet press coverage, criticism was allowed only in accordance with party policy. 'Sensationalist' news – reporting accidents or crimes – were deplored as a threat to the national interest, and a general preference was apparent for emphasising the positive.[9] Criticism of the military was a taboo.[10] In the words of Viktor Baranets, a prominent Russian military correspondent, 'in [the USSR] there was one rule until 1991: the army is a "sacred cow", and one is allowed to criticise it only with the permission of the CC CPSU [Central Committee of the Communist Party of the Soviet Union]'.[11] Each Soviet publication acted as the official mouthpiece for a state institution (*Pravda* for the CC CPSU, *Izvestiia* for the Supreme Soviet, *Komsomol'skaia pravda* for the Young Communists, or *Komsomol*, etc.) or represented the interests of a professional or other group. The armed forces, as one of the Soviet State's largest institutions, boasted approximately 15 central periodicals, 24 regional army and navy newspapers, plus a large number of divisional publications, some of which had print-runs of up to 8 million.[12] When the Soviet press monolith began to crumble with the introduction of the Law on the Press in 1990, which allowed the publication of non-state-owned newspapers, the popularity of state-sponsored and specialist newspapers – including those of the military – quickly diminished[13] and the newspaper market became organised along the usual central/regional and broadsheet/tabloid press divide. Military affairs remained an important issue in the press, but were now covered in publications appealing to a general audience, and were no longer necessarily geared towards expressing the interests of the military organisation. Many journalists were eager to prove their new independent credentials by voicing loud criticism about the State and its organs, including the military.

Given the specific function of the Soviet media and the fact that the military previously had been treated as a sacrosanct institution in its *own* newspapers, the military establishment in the Soviet era was unaccustomed to criticism and outside analysis of its affairs. An antagonistic relationship between the military and the press grew from the beginning of *perestroika*. The military's attitude towards the media and its reaction to criticism remained fraught throughout the 1990s. Major General Vladimir Zolotarev, head of the MOD's Institute of Military History since 1993, wrote in 2001 that 'the mass media continue to distribute anti-patriotic propaganda and to blacken the heroic image of the soldiers that fought in the years of the Great Patriotic War and in the subsequent military conflicts involving the Soviet and then Russian army'.[14] One authoritative representative of the official military press confirmed that Zolotarev's view continues to represent the attitude of many Russian generals today and is principally responsible for the tense media–military relationship in post-Soviet Russia.[15]

One especially sore point concerning Russia's media–military relationship has been the press coverage of *dedovshchina*. This phenomenon has acquired notoriety beyond Russia's borders and has been actively discussed in the Western media as a major problem facing the contemporary Russian armed forces.[16] An analysis of the MOD's official newspaper *Krasnaia zvezda* during the years 1996–97 and 2000–1 revealed that out of 82 articles which mention *dedovshchina*, 26 are directly or indirectly critical of coverage of the issue by the Russian mainstream media. In 1997, for instance, one author wrote the following: 'Permanent accusations made by dilettantes rain down on the army about "mass *dedovshchina*" and "systematic assaults", and this has already resulted in a genetic allergy of the officers.'[17] The tendency of some military representatives to interpret mainstream press criticism of *dedovshchina* and other problems of the armed forces as malicious and incompetent assaults on the military was still apparent in 2000. A writer in *Krasnaia zvezda* commented: 'Publications about the Russian armed forces … basically discuss only negative events occurring in the armed collectives, that is, the violation of the rules of conduct between military personnel and its consequences.'[18]

The military's criticism of journalistic conduct in discussing problems facing the armed forces, however, does not indicate a desire simply to cover up existing problems. On the contrary, none of the eighty-two articles mentioning *dedovshchina* in *Krasnaia zvezda* deny the existence of the problem. Some even feature statistical information that is not exactly flattering to the military: 'This year, cases of nonstatutory relations[19] were 6.5 per cent higher than last year.'[20] Another article reveals: 'In the ten months since the beginning of 1997, about 10,000 crimes were registered in the armed forces, as a result of which 3,000 personnel were hurt and 520 died. A total of thirty-two died from nonstatutory relations. More than 1,000 soldiers suffered from *dedovshchina*. About 300 servicemen committed suicide.'[21] Twelve of the articles give accounts of official and legal measures taken against *dedovshchina* and discuss their effectiveness.

According to military commentators, *civilian* journalists are to blame, not for discussing *dedovshchina*, but for taking a biased and destructive approach to the issue. In the eyes of military commentators, reports of *dedovshchina* in the mainstream press are counter-productive, because no solutions are offered. Journalists are also accused of reducing the military's problems down to the existence of *dedovshchina*, and of representing it as symptomatic of a greater malaise. One colonel-general, for instance, commented:

> Unfortunately there are many [newspapers with an anti-army outlook] and they form public opinion. The press – I do not mean *Krasnaia zvezda*, of course – is painting a repulsive picture of the army. Despite the fact that there are shortcomings in the army – and serious ones – the majority of publications are far from objective. This *dedovshchina*, for example. It is not a mass phenomenon.[22]

In the eyes of the military, this type of coverage of military affairs 'disorients society as to the real situation in the military',[23] because negative factors are emphasised while positive points are ignored. Reports of *dedovshchina* are seen as scare stories that are damaging to the army's image in society and lead to an unwillingness to serve among prospective conscripts. In response, in the four years covered by this analysis, *Krasnaia zvezda* published eleven columns of letters, mainly written by enthusiastic conscripts and soldiers' mothers, asserting that although they had been afraid of *dedovshchina* initially because of the way it is presented to society, it did not turn out to be a problem in reality. The author of one of these letters remarks: 'Today everybody is afraid of *dedovshchina*, although there are only rumours about it.'[24] Another conscript writes in an enthusiastic account of his military service: 'Initially I was afraid of going to the army, because of *dedovshchina*, about which one hears so much in civilian life.'[25] Journalists are criticised also for the way in which they apportion blame. They are asked, in regard to *dedovshchina*: 'Are the generals and officers to blame for everything?'[26] To counteract these accusations, 18 of the 82 articles from *Krasnaia zvezda* present the general 'moral decay' of post-Soviet Russian society and the consequent low standard of conscript material as the main reason for *dedovshchina*. The blame is not the army's: '*Dedovshchina* as a problem is not restricted to the army. It is a result of Russian society's social illness.'[27]

In order to put the military's criticism of the media into context, the coverage of *dedovshchina* in two independent civilian newspapers was also analysed. There is no evidence to support the accusation made by *Krasnaia zvezda* and by other military commentators that reports in these publications blame the problem exclusively on the generals and officers. During the same time period of 1996–97 and 2000–1, the popular tabloid *Komsomol'skaia pravda*[28] published nineteen articles that mentioned *dedovshchina*. Not one of those 19 articles so much as implied that the military alone was to blame for the practice of *dedovshchina*; indeed only two articles criticise the military leadership for attempting to hide or ignore the problem. In the broadsheet *Izvestiia*, 6 articles out of 31 referring to *dedovshchina* attribute a degree of the blame for the problem to the current military leadership. However, the vast majority of articles in the two civilian newspapers are either factual, reporting cases of *dedovshchina* officially investigated by the military prosecutor, or are openly sympathetic to the military and see the reality of such problems in the armed forces as symptomatic of the moral decay of society as a whole.

How, then, can the Russian military's hostility to the media be explained? A closer look at the military's expressions of dissatisfaction with the representation in mainstream media outlets of problems facing the armed forces reveals that its criticism is not aimed at the press *per se*, but specifically at *liberal*-oriented publications. This is evident in the following passage quoted from *Krasnaia zvezda*: 'The military has already got used to articles that are completely "stigmatising" the army and are written with some sick sort of emphasis ... Today for a lot of Russian "liberal" newspapers any attack on the army is a godsend.'[29] In contrast, the approach of the communist and patriotic press is compatible with the military's preferred coverage of military affairs. This is, first, because a basic feature of the communist and patriotic ideology emphasises the traditions and historical roots of the Russian armed forces and it therefore displays a generally positive disposition towards the military as an institution; second, also as a result of this ideological perspective, the communist and patriotic press does not view its function as that of a 'watchdog'. One military correspondent of a patriotic newspaper confirmed that his attitude towards the representation of military affairs by liberal-oriented newspapers is very similar to that of military commentators discussed above:

> The majority of civilian newspapers give their military departments to people who fear the army and live with stereotypes ... Journalists have three words that they associate with the army: '*dedovshchina*', 'stupidity' and 'to death'. That's all. They do not know anything else, and the majority of publications are on this level.'[30]

The military leadership's exaggeratedly suspicious attitude towards liberal elements in the press can be explained by the fact that its understanding of the function of newspapers is fundamentally incompatible with that of many journalists with a liberal outlook in the post-Soviet period. Many of the latter perceive it to be their professional responsibility to inform the public about existing problems in order to provoke a reaction and eventual solution to the problem. Vitalii Dymarskii, the deputy editor-in-chief of *Rossiiskaia gazeta*, made this clear:

In Soviet times ... you often heard the idea that we need to write positive material. But this is not what the mass media are for. The press is an institution that signals to those in power and to society that some sort of a problem exists. And if today all mass media outlets unequivocally proclaim that, let's say, *dedovshchina* exists, then of course there might be a military leader [who] will say 'What are you doing? Only one soldier has been beaten up, it is not a mass phenomenon! A mass phenomenon is taking place on the parade ground where everybody marches and is excellently trained. The mass media do not write about this!'... But I do not think that the mass media are exaggerating. Quite the opposite – they need to exaggerate, because otherwise they will not get rid of the problem.[31]

In contrast, the military leadership continues to perceive negative information and criticism as counter-productive, and believes that the main task of the press is to educate the public in the *right* way. One general wrote, for instance:

If we want to see a strong Russia that is flourishing in the 21st century and is able to defend the national interest, we need a strong army. The creation of such an army and to strengthen its authority is the task of the whole of society. This includes the mass media and film-makers, who can become a factor in the formation of spirituality and the patriotic ideals of individuals.[32]

These contradictory views concerning the proper function of the press – exemplified by the reporting of the *dedovshchina* problem – have created tension in the media–military relationship in post-Soviet Russia. Feeling hounded by the liberal press, the military became defensive towards the media at large. Given the broad discussion of the *dedovshchina* problem in *Krasnaia zvezda*, the Russian military's hostility to the press cannot be interpreted as its leadership's desire to deny the *existence* of the problem. However, it fails to appreciate the view of liberal-oriented journalists that 'problems require criticism' in order to initiate the process of their solution, and thus they disagree with the specific way in which the armed forces' problems are reported in the mainstream media. For the military representatives quoted above, 'criticism creates problems' and the performance of the liberal press is perceived as counterproductive to the interests and effectiveness of their institution – as a guardian of the State.

The civilian leadership's role in Russian media–military relations: handling the watchdog

Although the military leadership has retained a consistently conservative and even hostile attitude towards the press throughout the post-Soviet era, this phenomenon is by no means unique to the Russian case. It has become a commonplace in civil–military relations theory that any 'military that does not like journalists is normal'.[33] Furthermore, such a relationship does not exist in a vacuum. Perhaps the single most important role in shaping the media–military relationship is played by a state's civilian leadership. It does so by providing the structural framework within which the media–military relationship is acted out. In an ideal case scenario, the democratically elected political leadership of a state should determine the degree of access to information concerning the military organisation which is granted to the press. To enable the media to participate in the system of civilian control over the armed forces, the political leadership must also ensure that such a degree of access is respected by the military leadership. Ideally, it should be in the interest of a democratic civilian leadership to ensure that the media *can* perform a watchdog function over the State's institutions, including the military, and it should equally have an oversight function that dilutes media–military antagonism. The civilian leadership in post-Soviet Russia, however, has not fulfilled this role. There are two factors in particular relating to civilian oversight that have been especially influential in regulating the degree to which the press has been able to act as a watchdog: first, the quality of civil–military relations or, more specifically, executive–military relations over the past decade of post-Soviet rule; second, the civilian leadership's information policies and handling of media affairs on a more general level. In terms of both executive–military relations and information policies it is necessary to point out the contrast between the differing approaches pursued by Yeltsin and Putin, because politics in post-Soviet Russia has been dominated by the power of the executive.

Throughout the presidency of Boris Yeltsin, the relationship between the civilian leadership and the armed forces' leadership was one of mutual mistrust, for a number of reasons.[34] An expression of, as well as a reason for, this negative relationship was the fact that Yeltsin did not refrain from publicly criticising the military leadership in several respects. For example, he openly expressed his concern about *dedovshchina* and other criminal activities in the armed forces, portraying them as problems specific to the military, much to the disdain of the military leadership. In one of his speeches Yeltsin asserted the following: 'I especially want to speak about the moral climate in the army. Corruption is disintegrating the officer corps like rust. Another ugly phenomenon, the trade of weapons from army arsenals, cannot be stopped. *Dedovshchina* cannot be eliminated among the private staff. Elementary order must be established in the army!'[35]

That such criticism of the military was considered as generally acceptable by the Yeltsin administration is apparent in the coverage of military affairs during this period in the official newspaper of the Russian Government, *Rossiiskaia gazeta*.[36] The coverage of *dedovshchina* in this publication during Yeltsin's presidency is largely reminiscent of the 'problems-require-criticism' coverage in liberal newspapers condemned by the military leadership. In some cases *Rossiiskaia gazeta*'s coverage points to the military command as being at least partly to blame for the existence of the problem: 'It is impossible to get rid of the terrible forms of *dedovshchina* in the brigade. About 550 soldiers are on the run today. Many decided to make this step because of the unbearable conditions under which they have to serve: hunger, cold, assaults and humiliation not only from older conscripts, but also from officers.'[37]

In contrast to Yeltsin, it was one of President Vladimir Putin's first priorities to create an agreeable relationship with the armed forces' leadership.[38] An attempt to return the military leadership to the power base of the civilian government appears to be a part of the wider ideological and political changes introduced by Putin, which emphasise patriotism and the recreation of a strong and integrated state.[39] Although the civil–military relationship since Putin's accession in early 2000 has not been without flaws,[40] the mutual understanding between the civilian and military sides has been immeasurably more pronounced than at any point in the Yeltsin era. Improvements in the civil–military relationship under Putin can be put down not least to his public treatment of military affairs, which seems diametrically opposed to the outbursts of criticism voiced by Yeltsin that so displeased the military leadership. One American analyst wrote that 'the most important step taken by Putin is the most intangible one: through his expressions of strong support for military needs, his patriotic rhetoric ... he has made the military feel important again'.[41] Many of the remarks made by Putin about the Russian armed forces echo the military leadership's reproach of the liberal media's 'problems-require-criticism' approach discussed above, as the following statement by Putin confirms: 'Recent months have revealed that all the talk about the disintegration and reduction of the army's fighting capacity is an outright lie. This attitude towards the army is wrong and disrespectful. We do not have to be ashamed of our soldiers, officers and paratroopers'.[42]

This change in the official line concerning the armed forces is also apparent in the coverage of military affairs in the Government's official newspaper, *Rossiiskaia gazeta*.[43] In looking again at the example of *dedovshchina*, after Putin's accession to the presidency coverage of the issue that was critical of the military in this newspaper decreased and it came to resemble *Krasnaia zvezda*'s 'criticism-creates-problems' approach. While the problem is not denied, blame is placed on the general moral state of society and consequent poor quality of conscript material:

> When people speak about morals in the army and assert that it is riddled with *dedovshchina* they, of course, are not thinking about the educational standard of those serving in the army ... An uneducated person does not understand the power of the word, but decides everything with his fists ... And the army has been blamed for all of this. But is it really to blame?[44]

Although neither *Komsomol'skaia pravda* nor *Izvestiia* was especially critical of the military in their coverage of *dedovshchina* during the Yeltsin era, any such criticism all but ceased in 2000 and 2001. The former limited its coverage to reporting cases of *dedovshchina* that were officially registered by the military prosecutor, and the only article targeting blame at internal military circumstances in the latter takes the form of a reader's letter that was, furthermore, written by a long-serving soldier.[45] The contrasting positions of the two presidents *vis-à-vis* the military set the tone for the coverage of military affairs in the media for their respective periods in power. Each president specified the degree of criticism acceptable concerning the country's armed forces in line with his own relationship with the military leadership.

Having said that, a change in the civil–military relationship of a democratic state as such naturally should not automatically bring about a change in the coverage of military affairs on the part of the country's media. In order to understand why the Russian media appear less free to criticise the military under the leadership of Vladimir Putin than they were under his predecessor, and why this is significant, it is necessary to take a closer look at the information policies and the handling of media affairs by the respective presidents.

Differences in Yeltsin's and Putin's handling of media affairs cannot be explained simply by the democratic credentials of each president. On the one hand, many liberal-minded journalists are sure that their working conditions are more restrictive under Putin than they had been under his predecessor.[46] However, many of them also agree that the freer conditions under president Yeltsin were due largely to the generally unstructured handling of information policy within an emerging democratic framework, to which politicians of the early post-Soviet era were simply unaccustomed. Military correspondents, in particular, concede that within this void of rules and standards the early post-Soviet press contributed to the military's negative attitude to the press today. One such journalist noted: 'During Yeltsin's rule there was no control over the press at all, and it tried to gain dividends by criticising the army.'[47] Another stated:

> If we look at the beginning of the 1990s when the Soviet army was transformed into the Russian army, and the mass media were able to criticise the army ... the army simply started to lose on the informational front ... At that time there really was an attack on the army. The press criticised everything and called officers – all officers – dogs ... These were really hard times.[48]

The lack of a well-worked-out information policy in the initial years of the post-Soviet era was especially apparent during the first Chechen campaign that started in 1994. This experience constitutes an especially painful chapter in the media–military relationship in post-Soviet Russia. In the words of one journalist 'there was no censorship as such during the first Chechen war. There were only some attempts to put pressure on the press.'[49] At the start of the second Chechen war, the State's authorities, guided by Putin as prime minister, took care not to repeat this mistake by introducing a number of strict guidelines. While these measures by the Russian authorities often tend to be interpreted in the West as a clampdown on press freedom,[50] it is fair to point out that similar restrictions on the media are the rule rather than an exception during times of war and armed conflict.

Differences in the respective Governments' official handling of media affairs during *peacetime* are far more useful in explaining the changes in press coverage of military-related issues in post-Soviet Russia. Although it is a common assumption, especially in the West, that the Russian mass media underwent a period of unprecedented freedom under Yeltsin, this conclusion requires a decree of modification. The first indicator that Yeltsin's attitude towards a free press was far from that of a champion of liberal democracy came only one day after the coup attempt in August 1991, when all newspapers that had supported the coup were closed down by presidential decree.[51] Similarly, during the conflict between the president and the legislature in October 1993, Yeltsin committed a plain breach of the Media Law of June 1990 when he temporarily banned some twenty publications that were loyal to the communist opposition. *Pravda* and *Sovetskaia Rossiia*, for instance, were effectively prevented from publishing until the elections in December 1995 had taken place.[52] In contrast, liberal-minded and pro-Western newspapers were largely unaffected by these attempts to stifle the press under Yeltsin's leadership[53] because the President was both indebted to, and dependent on, these publications. In October 1993, and again during the election campaigns in 1993, 1995 and 1996, they helped to ensure his victory by adopting a strongly partisan pro-Government stance. Given the choice between temporary self-censorship and the threat of a communist resurgence, which would inevitably have signalled the end of their existence, these publications chose the former and backed Yeltsin.[54] As a consequence, liberal newspapers were allowed to flourish despite the fact that their 'problems-requires-criticism' approach was by no means limited to the military, but was often displayed in radical criticism of the president himself.

The combination of this relatively free working environment for the liberal press, with the problematical executive–military relationship under Yeltsin led on the one hand to increased tensions in the media–military relationship; while on the other, liberal-minded media were able to fulfil their watchdog function over the armed forces, despite the military's discontent with the press. *Komsomol'skaia pravda*, for instance, published an article in 1997 about extensive problems with *dedovshchina* and other criminal activities in an elite military unit.[55] The following day it reported:

> [A]t a press conference yesterday, Iurii Demin (chief military prosecutor) remarked that the article in *Komsomolka* [the shortened version of the title *Komsomol'skaia pravda*] is playing an important role in the unfolding war of the prosecution against nonstatutory relations in the army.[56]

Similarly, *Izvestiia* reported in the same year that, as a result of one of its articles about problems with *dedovshchina* and other criminal activities in the MVD's 101st brigade, 'the MVD rapidly started to bring order to the units. The Minister of Internal Affairs, Anatolii Kulikov, personally inspected the 101st brigade in Stavropol'.'[57] It is vital to point out, however, that Yeltsin's acceptance of, and responsiveness to, criticism concerning the military did not mean that he wholeheartedly embraced the idea of the press as a watchdog, guarding the activities of *all* state officials and state organs. Reminiscent of the Soviet era, the press under Yeltsin was allowed to act as watchdog over the armed forces only because this fitted with his personal political agenda.

Since the accession to the presidency of Vladimir Putin, media outlets that had acquired the image of being especially independent and pro-Western have lost a considerable degree of their influence. The most noted events in this respect were the closures of the independent television channels NTV in April 2001 and TV-6 in January 2002. The newspaper market was also affected, with the closure of *Segodnia* and the replacement of the editor-in-chief of *Nezavisimaia gazeta* Vitalii Tret'iakov, after which the newspaper displayed a noticeably pro-Putin stance. In addition, military correspondents of independent newspapers have asserted that their ability to effectively criticise problems in the armed forces is considerably reduced under President Putin. This is because the Government's official line is to ignore criticism of the armed forces, which is perceived to run counter to its attempts to build a generally more positive relationship with the military leadership. While liberal journalists in post-Soviet Russia clearly continue to embrace the watchdog function of the press, and thus see themselves as a part of the system of civilian control, they assert that their efforts are no longer effective under the Putin presidency. One military correspondent noted:

> When I write today that nuclear materials are being sold on Red Square, not even the FSB gives me a call. There is total apathy today. And I see that this apathy is making the press completely powerless. You understand, in order to build democracy, those in power have to react to what is written in the press, but they could not care less! … They like a press that draws people's attention away from political and economic processes … This is the essence of a so-called loyal press.

As for what this means for the coverage of military affairs, he continued:

If you follow my publications attentively, you have probably noticed that today I either write about investigations concerning the *Kursk* [the nuclear-powered submarine lost in August 2000], about Afghanistan, some tactical–technological data, or about threats facing Russia ... I have not analysed what is going on in the General Staff for a long time ... I say 'I', but I am a typical representative of opposition military journalism, who wants to tell those in power the truth about what is moving the higher military leadership, but I do not have the right to do so.[58]

The editor-in-chief of another independent newspaper specialising in the coverage of military affairs complained about the political leadership's unresponsive behaviour when his publication attempted to start a public discussion about civilian control over the armed forces in Russia: 'We are trying to do something. Only recently a discussion was started on the pages of our newspapers. ...But practically no politician supports these things.'[59]

Conclusions

The media–military relationship during the first decade of post-Soviet rule in Russia has been one of mutual mistrust and hostility, though this applies more specifically to the relationship between the military leadership and the liberal-minded press. This can be explained by the incompatibility of the military and journalistic understandings of the function of the press: while journalists working for liberal-minded newspapers have largely embraced the idea of a watchdog press, the military leadership continues by and large to view the media as an *educator*. The military's discontent with criticism in the liberal-minded media is therefore inevitable, but the delivery of such criticism is fundamental to what these journalists understand as their professional duty. It was also pointed out, however, that tensions in the media–military relationship are by no means limited to the RF, but that the ability of the State's media to perform a watchdog role and to contribute to the system of civilian control over the armed forces is dependent largely on the attitude of the civilian leadership in this respect.

While the Yeltsin administration's handling of information policies was by no means flawlessly 'democratic', the combination of his critical attitude to the military leadership and his dependence on the liberal media facilitated the latter, to some extent, in fulfilling their watchdog function and in contributing effectively to civilian control over the armed forces. Because it was the result of fortuitous circumstances rather than the civilian leadership's wholehearted embrace of the watchdog role of the press, the media's function as a means of exercising civilian control over the armed forces was evidently fragile. The Putin Government is not responsive to criticism of the armed forces, as this is perceived to run counter to its attempt to build a generally more positive relationship with the military leadership. This Government is not dependent for its popularity on the support of the liberal media, which, as a result and despite their continued wish to do so, have less licence to perform a watchdog function concerning military affairs. This plays into the hands of the conservative military under Putin. A military commentator affirmed this after Putin's election to the presidency: 'thanks to the competent policy of the country's leadership in regard to the mass media ... the popularity of the military in the country has been boosted'.[60] Furthermore, the Putin Government is displaying clear signs of agreement with the military leadership over the function of the press. In January 2002, it was reported that the Department of Education in the MOD was drawing up plans in conjunction with the Ministry of Culture to raise the profile of the military in society through patriotic media and cultural programmes and to 'develop in Russians a feeling of patriotism, pride in their country and contribution to world civilisation'.[61] Furthermore, in March 2002 the Ministry of the Media announced a plan to spend 16 million dollars on 'military–patriotic' media projects with the purpose of 'stimulat[ing] the interests of the mass media in military–patriotic education'.[62] These efforts, reminiscent of a bygone age, express the military's understanding of the mass-media as an *educator*, and they appear to be shared and actively endorsed by the civilian Government under the leadership of President Putin. While this inevitably will make the media–military relationship less tense, the liberal-minded media's efficient performance as a part of the system of civilian control has been hampered, and the prospects for the development of democratic society–military relations in post-Soviet Russia have furthermore receded.

Notes

1 S. Badsey, 'The influence of the media on recent British military operations', in I. Steward and S. Carruthers (eds) *War, Culture and the Media: Representations of the Military in 20th Century Britain* (Trowbridge: Flick Books, 1996), p. 10.
2 See, for instance, H. Smith (ed.) *The Media and the Gulf War* (Washington, DC: Seven Locks Press, 1992); W. Bennett and D. Paletz (eds) *Taken by Storm: The Media, Public Opinion, and U.S. Foreign Policy in the Gulf War* (Chicago, IL: University of Chicago Press, 1994); B. Rolston (ed.) *War and Words: The Northern Ireland Media Reader* (Belfast: Beyond the Pale Publications, 1996); Steward and Carruthers (eds) *War, Culture and the Media*; W. M. Hammond, *Reporting Vietnam: Media and Military at War* (Lawrence: University Press of Kansas, 1998).
3 See, for instance, G. Herd, 'The "counter-terrorist operation" in Chechnya: "information warfare" aspects', *Journal of Slavic Military Studies*, 13:4 (2000), 57–83; O. Panfilov and A. Simonov, *Informatsionnaia voina v Chechne: Fakty, dokumenty, svidetel'stva. noiabr' 1994–sentiabr' 1996* (Moscow: Prava Cheloveka, 1997).
4 J. Lichtenberg, 'Foundations and limits of freedom of the press', in J. Lichtenberg (ed.) *Democracy and the Mass Media* (Cambridge: Cambridge University Press, 1990), p. 105.

5 M. Gurevich and J. Blumler, 'Political communications systems and democratic values', in D. Graber (ed.) *Media Power in Politics* (Washington, DC: CQ Press, 1994), p. 26.

6 'General Polkovnik Petr Gorchakov: Ia veren "Zvezdochke" vsiu zhizn', *Krasnaia zvezda* (18 December 1997). Although the scope of my discussion cannot extend to evaluating the effect of media coverage on the readership, the press remains an important source of information about the military and must therefore be classified as relevant: according to a survey conducted in 1998, the print media are the major source of information about military affairs for 35 per cent of the respondents (see *Formirovanie voisk Rossii. Tekushchii moment: Obzor dinamiki obshchestvennogo mneniia v 1996–2001 g. v materialakh FOM, VTsIOM, ARPI*, available online: http://college.biysk.secna.ru/mil/veo-club/history/Complekt/nowRussia1.htm).

7 J. Hartley, *Understanding News* (Bungay: Richard Clay, 1982), p. 39.

8 J. Murray, *The Russian Press from Brezhnev to Yeltsin: Behind the Paper Curtain* (Aldershot: Edward Elgar, 1994), p. 88.

9 M. Hopkins, *Mass Media in the Soviet Union* (New York: Pegasus, 1970), p. 121.

10 E. Mickiewicz, *Changing Channels: Television and the Struggle for Power in Russia* (Oxford: Oxford University Press, 1997), p. 56.

11 Viktor Baranets, military correspondent of *Komsomol'skaia pravda*, interviewed by the author, Moscow, January 2002.

12 'Voennaia pechat': Reforma davno nazrela', *Nezavisimoe voennoe obozrenie* (16 March 2001).

13 The flagship of the official military press, the MOD's mouthpiece *Krasnaia zvezda*, for instance, decreased its print-run to 80,000 at the end of 2001. Vadim Saranov, military correspondent of the weekly *Versiia*, furthermore asserted in an interview that the 'real print-run' of *Krasnaia zvezda* is a mere 2,500, which is the number of *voluntary* subscriptions by individuals after obligatory subscriptions to battalions, educational institutions, etc., are deducted. Attempts were made after the demise of the USSR to establish independent or unofficial military publi- cations, but neither of these attempts has been particularly successful. Such attempts were *Shchit Rossii, Armiia Rossii, Georgii Pobedonosets, Sluzhba, Nezavisimoe voennoe obozrenie*, the last of which was the most successful, with a print-run of 29,320 at the end of 2001 (see 'Tochka zreniia: Reforma nuzhna, no ne s kommercheskim uklonom', *Krasnaia zvezda* [28 March 2001]).

14 V. A. Zolotarev, *Voennaia bezopasnost' gosudarstva Rossiiskogo* (Moscow: Kuchkovo Pole, 2001), p. 299.

15 Interview conducted by the author, Moscow, November 2001.

16 A programme entitled 'Soldat', containing explicit footage of *dedovshchina* filmed in Russian military units, was aired on the UK's Channel 4 in August 2001.

17 'S nog na golovu', *Krasnaia zvezda* (22 January 1997).

18 'Ne ostavit' shansa dezertiram', *Krasnaia zvezda* (29 July 2000).

19 Editor's note: non-statutory relations (*neustavnye otnosheniia*) is the euphemism used within the Russian armed forces to refer to relations between personnel which run counter to the standards laid down in the military codes of behaviour or are not covered by the code, and includes the practice of *dedovshchina*.

20 'Vse ta zhe "*dedovshchina*": novaia stadiia staroi bolezni', *Krasnaia zvezda* (9 January 1997).

21 'Prava voennosluzhashchego ne pustoi zvuk', *Krasnaia zvezda* (18 December 1997).

22 'General-polkovnik Petr Gorchakov'.

23 *Ibid.*

24 'Riadovoi Naumov pogib spasaia komandira', *Krasnaia zvezda* (11 February 1997).

25 'Chitatel'skaia pochta sentiabria: Drug, tovarishch i brat', *Krasnaia zvezda* (7 October 1997).

26 'Replika: Otkroveniia "s dushkom"', *Krasnaia zvezda* (6 March 2001).

27 'Rossiia i mir', *Krasnaia zvezda* (22 November 1997).

28 Data from January 1996–October 1997 are unavailable.

29 'Amputatsiia sovesti, ili kak "Obshchaia gazeta" "otrezala" soldatu nogi', *Krasnaia zvezda* (10 December 1997).

30 Vladislav Shurygin, military correspondent of *Zavtra*, interviewed by the author, Moscow, December 2001.

31 Interview conducted by the author, Moscow, December 2001.

32 'Chitatel' negoduet: Vystrel v idealy', *Krasnaia zvezda* (16 February 2001).

33 T. A. Thrall, *War in the Media Age* (Cresskill: Hampton Press, 2000), pp. 6–7.

34 Most importantly, concerning civil–military conflicts over the use of the armed forces in the constitutional crisis of October 1993 and the first Chechen campaign that was started in September 1994.

35 From the speech by Boris Yeltsin given at the appointment of Defence Minister Rodionov, reported in *Krasnaia zvezda* (19 July 1996). The same newspaper reported Yeltsin's State of the Nation Address in which he stated: 'I will talk some more about the situation in the armed forces. There are more than enough problems there. Among them are very serious ones, such as *dedovshchina* and theft among the commanders' (1 March 1997).

36 Data from October 1997 to July 1999.

37 'Esli vyzhivet, to invalidom Sindrom chechenskoi voiny i segodnia kalechit soldatskie sud'by', *Rossiiskaia gazeta* (6 November 1997). See also 'Otvetnaia Mera': 'Not only insolent "*dedy*" [older conscripts] are involved in nonstatutory relations, but also officers, commanders of units and platoons and their deputies', *Rossiiskaia gazeta* (14 July 1998).

38 See, for instance, B. Taylor, 'Putin and the military: how long will the honeymoon last?' *PONARS Memo 116* (April 2000), available online: www.fas.harvard.edu/~ponars/POLICY%20MEMOS/Taylor116.html.

39 See, for instance, A. Tuminez, 'Russian Nationalism and Vladimir Putin's Russia', *PONARS Memo 151* (April 2000) available online: www.fas.harvard.edu/~ponars/POLICY%20MEMOS/Tuminez151.html.

40 There have been repeated rumours about the military leadership's discontent with the current minister of defence, Sergei Ivanov, an ally of Vladimir Putin, who is the first defence minister in post-Soviet Russia without a background in the armed forces.

41 Taylor, 'Putin and the military'.

42 Presidential speech concerning the social provision of military personnel (22 February 2000), online: http://194.226.159/events/9.html. Similarly: 'Not long ago it was said that the army is in a state of degradation and that we cannot expect any outstanding results in the military sphere … Life itself showed that

[this claim] is a lie ... All nationwide television channels are broadcasting this meeting live to the whole country. I am asking not only those in this hall, but also those watching and listening, to rise and remember our heroes in a minute of silence' (from a presidential address to the Federation Council of the RF (3 April 2001), available online: http://194.226.80.159/pressa/2001040301.html).

43 Data from 2000 to 2001.

44 'Moskovskie Maugli berut v ruki avtomaty', *Rossiiskaia gazeta* (3 August 2001); see also the article 'Sbezhavshaia diviziia': 'Unfortunately the intellectual and moral potential of conscripts coming to the army has left much to be desired in the past years. And this is a serious problem for our army ... It is not a secret that the Russian army is suffering from absolutely the same symptoms as society as a whole'. *Rossiiskaia gazeta* (1 July 2001)

45 'CHITATEL' – SOAVTOR', *Izvestiia* (10 October 2001)

46 This fact was communicated to the author by journalists from *Nezavisimaia gazeta*, *Segodnia*, *Komsomol'skaia pravda* and *Versiia* in interviews conducted in Moscow between November 2001 and January 2002.

47 Viktor Baranets, military correspondent of *Komsomol'skaia pravda*, interviewed by the author, Moscow, January 2002.

48 Vadim Saranov, military correspondent of *Versiia*, interviewed by the author Moscow, January 2002.

49 Igor Malashenko quoted in 'Media coverage of the chechen war: then and now', transcript of weekly analytical programme on the media 'Chetvertaia Vlast'' (22 January 2000), available online: www.internews.ru/crisis/mediacoverage.html.

50 See, for instance, Radio Liberty report 'Press freedom changing in the post-communist world' (28 March 2002) available online: www.rferl.org/welcome/english/releases/2002/03/85-280302.html.

51 B. McNair, *Glasnost, Perestroika and the Soviet Media* (London: Routledge, 1991).

52 D. Wedgwood-Benn, 'The Russian media in post-Soviet conditions', *Europe–Asia Studies*, 48:3 (1996), 471–9.

53 During the October 1993 crisis, two articles from the liberal daily *Nezavisimaia gazeta* and one from *Segodnia* were reportedly excised by the censors as well: see Murray, *The Russian Press from Brezhnev to Yeltsin*, p. 19.

54 *Ibid.*, pp. 472–3; K. Tanaev, 'The Russian media and the 1993 elections: familiar problems and inadequate solutions', in Y. Lange and A. Palmer (eds) *Media and Elections. A Handbook* (Strasbourg: European Institute for the Media, Tacis Services DGI, European Commission, 1995), p. 47; L. Belin, 'Politicization and self-censorship in the Russian media', (Radio Free Europe–Radio Liberty, 1997), available online www.rferl.org/nca/special/rumediapaper/introduction.html.

55 'Vo mordoboi idut odni 'stariki': "Dzerzhinka" – elitnaia diviziia, proshedshaia parady i Chechniiu – stala poligonom izdevatel'stv nad molodymi soldatami', *Komsomol'skaia pravda* (4 November 1997).

56 'V mordoboi idut odni "stariki"', *Komsomol'skaia pravda* (5 November 1997).

57 101-ia brigada bol'she voevat' ne budet', *Izvestiia* (25 December 1997).

58 Viktor Baranets, military correspondent of *Komsomol'skaia pravda*, interviewed by the author, Moscow, January 2002.

59 Vadim Solov'ev, editor-in-chief of *Nezavisimoe voennoe obozrenie*, interviewed by the author, Moscow, November 2001.

60 M. Zelenkov, 'Maintenance of morale in the military', *Military Thought* (November 2000), online edition: www.findarticles.com/cf_0/m0JAP/6_9 /72703609/p1/article.jhtml?term=Zelenkov.

61 'Military enlisting artists', *Moscow Tribune* (25–27 January 2002); see also 'Military arms itself with TV, radio and film', *Moscow Times* (25–27 January 2002).

62 *RFE–RL* (Radio Free Europe – Radio Liberty) *Newsline* (21 March 2002), online: www.rferl.org/newsline/2002/03/210302.asp.

Confronting imperialism: the ambivalence of war in post-Soviet film

The war film as genre

The war film has been a staple ingredient of Soviet and post-Soviet cinema. Russia's twentieth-century capacity for waging war gave cinema much fertile soil, be it the First World War, the civil war, the Great Patriotic War, the Afghan War of 1979–89 and the more recent Chechen conflicts. Films about the civil war, such as the Vasil'ev brothers' *Chapaev* (1934), helped define the genre and also established the charismatic Bolshevik leader as a revolutionary hero, a figure to be emulated in later films such as Dovzhenko's *Shchors* (1939) and Aleksandr Faintsimmer's *Kotovskii* (1942). In films about the Great Patriotic War, the enemy is painted, if he is depicted at all, in unbelievably black colours. Victory is achieved by the soldiers' total and selfless devotion to the cause.

War films reveal the shifting ideological priorities of the times in which they are made. Mikhail Chiaureli's *The Fall of Berlin* (1949) recounts in heroic style the struggle of the USSR against the merciless fascist invader, but the film is also a hymn to the seemingly superhuman abilities of Stalin as military leader and the epicentre of post-war civilisation. Grigorii Chukhrai's *Ballad of a Soldier* (1960), made during the 'thaw' years, removes the heroic gloss from victory and concentrates more on the human cost of the war, the pain of loss and inconsolable grief. Films of the 'stagnation' period, such as Aleksei German's *Trial on the Road* (1971) and Larisa Shepit'ko's *The Ascent* (1976), explored questions of collaboration and moral integrity, with CPSU priorities and values exposed as at best false, at worst treacherous. It is interesting to note that black-and-white certainties persist even in post-Soviet times: both Mikhail Ptashuk's *In August 1944* (2000) and Nikolai Lebedev's *The Star* (2002) remain old-fashioned in their unequivocal depiction of good Soviet soldiers and bad Germans – and even worse German spies. There is limited criticism of Stalin, but the victorious outcome is assured, and the dedication of ordinary soldiers never questioned.

In terms of style and presentation, one of the problems for all national cinemas in depicting war on screen is the authenticity of combat scenes, for they demand great investments of time and money (especially for special effects). Soviet films would not shy from showing Nazi atrocities, including the killing of women and children in films such as *Zoia* (1944) and *The Rainbow* (1943), but special effects would take second place to the ideology. Until recently, even in the West, directors would baulk at the amount of true-to-life, harrowing, physical detail that can be shown to the viewer. On-screen gore is generally restricted or sanitised in order for the film to be accepted by the broad cinema-going public, who may expect to be shocked by scenes of combat, violent death and bloody wounds, but who will be repelled by gloating excess. Hollywood's treatment of the Second World War is a case in point: in the 1940s and 1950s dozens of battle scenes registered barely a drop of blood. The Vietnam War brought home to a generation that *real* combat is very different from *reel* war. As the writer and journalist Michael Herr remarked: 'I can't help thinking of the kids who got wiped out by seventeen years of war movies before coming to Vietnam to get wiped out for good.'[1] Furthermore, without the explicit depiction of the carnage of war in such Vietnam movies as Oliver Stone's *Platoon* (1986) and Stanley Kubrick's *Full Metal Jacket* (1987), it is doubtful whether the definitive war movie of the 1990s, Steven Spielberg's *Saving Private Ryan* (1998), could have been made. Even Spielberg's film now fades alongside the intense and harrowing combat scenes in Ridley Scott's *Black Hawk Down* (2002).

Film makes of the battle, above all, a spectacle, a visual experience with aesthetic and perhaps moral imperatives – but it is a fiction, a recreation, no matter how realistic and authentic the details. As the years pass, film becomes increasingly self-referential as it mimics established conventions, and the war story can become at best hackneyed, at worst a stereotype. War is portrayed by the victors, from the victors' point of view, for the victorious consumer. As Thomas Doherty concludes wrily: 'No wonder Hollywood's favorite war story has always been its own.'[2]

Conflict as metaphor

A notable feature of the Russian war film in the 1990s is the relative paucity of such richly detailed combat scenes. Military conflict is depicted, not as a struggle to the death between nations, but rather as an all-too-obvious metaphor of post-imperial trauma and social collapse. Even films about daily life in post-Soviet Russia make reference to some area of internal strife. At the beginning of Petr Todorovskii's *Ménage-à-trois* (1998) the hero Sergei flees his home as bombs explode outside in order to travel to Moscow and begin a new life there. Pavel Chukhrai's award-festooned *The Thief* (1997) is set in the 1940s–1950s, but contains an epilogue which dramatically transfers the action to the present or the near future, in which Russia is represented as a ravaged and burning urban landscape, torn apart by internecine conflict. Bakhtier Khudoinazarov's *Moon Daddy* (1999) shows abusive and violent Russian soldiers as an unwanted occupying force in a Central Asian republic. The film is a comedy of sorts about a pregnant girl who, together with her father and brother, are looking for the father of her child, but the presence of sullen Russian troops and military planes flying overhead provide a constant and sinister counterpoint to the light-hearted plot.

The remorseless hitman Danila in Aleksei Balabanov's *The Brother* (1997) has learned his trade in Chechnia, a trade which he puts to devastating use in the course of the film. After he cleans St Petersburg of Chechen and Russian bandits, and helps a damsel in distress, Danila cheerfully sets off for Moscow. The beginning of the sequel, *The Brother 2* (1999), shows that true male friendship is forged through the fire of Chechnia, and the murder of a friend and former comrade-in-arms serves as the pretext for Danila and his brother to wipe out assorted hoodlums in Moscow and Chicago. In *A Tender Age* (2000) Sergei Solov'ev traces back the erosion of childhood innocence to the 'stagnation' years and the crushing of any idealism or moral purity in the killing fields of Chechnia in the 1990s. In Solov'ev's film civil strife characterises Russia's future, its younger generation corrupted and destroyed.

A Tender Age also includes a lament for past glories, delivered by the stammering and increasingly apoplectic Bespal'chikov, a former special services soldier who is the head of military training in a school, played with gleeful abandon by Sergei Garmash: 'It's over. The Third World War, which many people casually called the Cold War, is over. AND WE HAVE BEEN CRAPPED ON! (*My ee prosrali!*). I am leaving because I am no longer needed. Forget everything that I ever told you, because it's too late now.' He then proceeds to smash a pile of bricks, not with his hand, karate-style, but with his forehead, seriously gashing himself – another metaphor for failed ambition and empty posturing. Bespal'chikov later dies a useless death in Chechnia. This whole episode – funny, touching and pathetic at the same time – can be seen as an ironic synecdoche for collective angst, an expression of society's bewilderment at the loss of super-power status, and its economic and political humiliations in the 1990s.

The ten-year engagement of the USSR in Afghanistan received scant attention in the cultural media before the advent of *glasnost'*. Documentaries and films appearing in the late 1980s showed, often in grim detail, the human cost of the war – it was in the post-Soviet period that the emerging post-imperialist trauma could be more fully explored. Vladimir Khotinenko's *The Muslim* (1995) used the conflict as a basis for exploring Russia's relationship with its non-Christian neighbours. Kolia Ivanov is a Russian soldier who has spent eight years in captivity in Afghanistan and has converted to Islam. He returns to his native village to find thoroughgoing drunkenness and corruption, the locals fed on a diet of vodka and foreign sex films, and alienation within his own family. His loutish brother Fed'ka tries to bring him back to Orthodoxy by forcing him to drink vodka and kiss an icon, but Kolia stands firm. Such decency and moderation cannot thrive in this community, and at the end of the film Kolia is killed by a former comrade-in-arms from his Afghan days.

This is a confrontation between Russia and the 'other', non-Christian, world beyond its eastern borders. The hero is a Russian Everyman returning home to his village, for centuries seen as the repository of spirituality and the Russian 'soul', and his own high moral stock is a stark contrast to the degradation and venality all around (with the exception of the Orthodox priest). The film offers a bitter commentary on the moral and spiritual crisis of post-Soviet Russia, shorn of all values and identity, its own traditions and culture seemingly abandoned.

Vadim Abdrashitov's *Time of the Dancer* (1997) is similarly set in the immediate aftermath of a civil conflict. Here the central characters are Cossacks. They observe their own rituals of friendships and comradeship, horsemanship, dancing and swordplay – but against a background of social uncertainty, adultery, and moral and sexual betrayal. The main character is Andrei, often bedecked in his Cossack uniform and riding his horse. He is no longer needed in civilian life, however, and is little more than a figure of fun as he dances in a tourist restaurant for tips. He is even out of place on the dance floor, as he awkwardly bumps into others, just as he is in real life. He is often referred to as 'your Honour' (*blagorodie*), an ironic reflection of how anachronistic he has become. He and his friends, Valerii and Fedor, are weak and introverted individuals, lost without someone or something to fight, and fuelling their self-pity through vodka binges.

In the second part of this (three-hour) film, time has moved on to find that Valerii owns a restaurant frequented by foreigners and rich Russians, Fedor has married the local doctor and keeps bees, and Andrei exchanges his tunic and horse for civilian life and a Muslim wife. Still, the past is never far away, and the former doctor Temur, now a professional killer, returns to kill the man (Fedor, it turns out) who killed his former business partner.

Abdrashitov's film revolves around the clash of past and present where war-ravaged souls try to rebuild their lives. Some can, some can not and some, like Andrei, eventually return to the horse to escape. Death catches up with Fedor. War destroys some lives, and turns others upside down. As the former life-saver Temur comments: 'I never would have thought that I could kill just as well as once I could cure.'

Civil strife, then, is the reflection of an uncertain, crisis-stricken, national psyche numbed by decades of ideology-driven struggle, the trauma of a weak nation bereft of values, spirituality or role in the world. The new Russia seems torn between the certainties of its past and the insecurities of the present, unwillingly forced to adopt an unfamiliar, and unwelcome, identity.

Sergei Bodrov's *A Prisoner of the Mountains* (1996) can be seen in a similar context. It is an updated adaptation of a short story by Lev Tolstoy
written in 1872. The film, like Tolstoy's story, is set in the Caucasus, and
takes place against the background of a Caucasian war. We are encouraged
to believe that it is the war in Chechnia, although nowhere is this made
explicit.[3] Two Russian soldiers, the conscript Ivan Zhilin and the professional soldier Sasha, are captured by rebels and held hostage. Over time,
Zhilin strikes up a tentative relationship with Dina, the daughter of his
captor Abdul-Murat. Bodrov's film updates Tolstoy's text in bringing the
plot closer to the present, so endowing it with a topical social resonance,
and also significantly changes it. In Tolstoy's story the two captured
Russians are officers, while in this film they are ordinary soldiers, one
from the regular army, the other a conscript. Bodrov therefore invites
scrutiny of the moral make-up of the post-Soviet Russian army – and finds
it wanting.

Tolstoy's story shows Russian soldiers as a force for civilisation and
humanity, and the Caucasians as savage and hate-filled. In Bodrov's film the
Russian troops are brutal occupying forces who refer to the locals as 'non-
Russians', 'bitches', 'bastards' and 'bandits', and are themselves hated in
return. One old Caucasian even shoots his own son because he works for
the Russian-backed police. Russian soldiers terrorise the local population.
When prisoners try to flee, they are summarily shot. The officer class feasts
on caviar and is content to trade guns for a bottle of vodka. The army as an
institution is seen as corrupt and time-serving, refusing to help the mother of
Zhilin in trading him for the son of Abdul-Murat, held in Russian captivity.
Instead, they seek only revenge, by sending in helicopter gunships to pound
Abdul-Murat's village into the dust. In the figure of the foul-mouthed, spite-
ful Sasha (played by Oleg Men'shikov) the army has its own arrogant, ruthless killer. Sasha, significantly, has no past: an orphan, he has known only
the army as his family. It is his lack of regard for human life that leads to his
own execution.

Apart from Zhilin, Russian soldiers offer not peace or civilisation, but
brutality and ignorance. Zhilin is an honest Russian boy from the provinces
who does not want to kill anyone. He even fails to fire his rifle in the opening ambush in which he is captured, preferring to cover his ears to block the
sound of gunfire. When imprisoned, he at least tries to understand this alien
culture. He helps repair a watch and makes Dina a wooden model of a bird.
When she tries to free him, he refuses to leave, knowing that she will suffer
at the hands of her father and the rest of the village. Zhilin retains his
humanity in brutal conditions, and Abdul-Murat, supposedly the
uncivilised savage, spares Zhilin's life, showing himself to be nobler and
more humane than the supposedly 'civilised' Russians. A truth that emerges
strongly from this film is that both the Russians and the Caucasians are
victims of war: nobody wins.[4]

A word should be reserved for the style of the film. Caucasian folk music serves as an evocative accompaniment to the majestic mountain scenery, and both diegetic and non-diegetic music foregrounds the opposing themes of war and humanity. The film begins, as it ends, with Russian martial music, especially the popular song *The Farewell of the Slavic Girl* (*Proshchanie slavianki*) that blasts out from the loudspeakers of the helicopter gunships in the closing scenes. Elsewhere there is a wartime ballad and a pre-revolutionary waltz, and even Louis Armstrong's *Go Down Moses*, with its refrain 'Let my people go', an incongruous diegetic device adding poignancy to the captivity of Zhilin and Sasha – but also satirising Russian colonial hegemony.

A companion piece is Aleksandr Rogozhkin's *Checkpoint* (1999), which depicts a group of soldiers stationed somewhere in the North Caucasus (probably also Chechnia), and their troubled relationship with the local population. Their foul-mouthed superiors care little for them and look to further their own careers by manipulating media coverage, as the soldiers are blamed for the death of a young village boy during a routine patrol and the ensuing shoot-out with villagers. The young soldiers are treated by the locals with undisguised contempt. They pay local women for sex (they have no money, so payment is made in cartridges), and do not understand or appreciate the local culture. Nevertheless, these are honest Russian boys, and the director takes pains to individualise them.

Rogozhkin also pays great attention to the minutiae of conscript life, the sheer boredom of routine, and the interrelationships of the soldiers. These soldiers do not know what they are doing here, in an alien landscape and an alien culture. They do display true comradeship, and their close bonds can be judged by the humorous and ironic nicknames they give each other: 'Lawyer', 'Skeleton' (for the fattest of them), 'Boeing', 'Rat', 'Ash', 'Buzz' (*Kaif*), 'Freebie', 'Piss'. Their bored conversations and trivial preoccupations reflect the tedium of being stationed at an isolated post, guarding the road to a Muslim cemetery. The tension, however, is never far away, as an unseen sniper casually lets off shots in their direction, and locals brandish guns and shoot in the air, taunting and humiliating them. The air of menace is intensified as the local scenery is viewed through the telescopic lens of the sniper's rifle.

The locals' contempt for the soldiers eventually becomes deadly serious, as the young female sniper shoots Lawyer in the finale. Both Bodrov and Rogozhkin have made films that question Russia's role in the troubled Caucasus region in the late 1990s, but which also explore hidden tensions in the make-up of the army itself. The army as an institution is corrupt, callous and self-serving – a microcosm of the State that has let so many of its citizens down in the 1990s. The real hero of these films is the young soldier, who is honest and prepared to lay down his life for his country. Although the local population is not viewed with real sympathy – bandits, prostitutes and murderers – *Checkpoint*'s real target is the professional army machine, characterised by cynicism and venality at the very top. An unnamed general (played by Aleksei Buldakov, the 'General' in Rogozhkin's 1995 comedy hit *Peculiarities of the National Hunt*) exhibits them to a group of Canadian journalists in a show of false pride, eager for plaudits. As the soldiers become increasingly beleaguered, they are betrayed by him as he connives in the murder of one of them accused of shooting at the villagers in the original incident.[5]

The contrast between the professional army and the conscripts in these films by Rogozhkin and Bodrov is a metaphorical reflection of a greater dichotomy. The army should be the embodiment of national cohesion, as represented by the best sons of Russia fighting to the death to defend the motherland. Instead, they are sent by an uncaring, untrustworthy, military bureaucracy to fight a faceless enemy. None of these films offers hope via narrative closure, pointing only to continued violence and exploitation. The ultimate victim is Mother Russia herself.[6]

These films of the Yeltsin period are thoughtful and provocative in a time of general instability and uncertainty. They offer a bitter revision of war as depicted in Soviet films. Films about the Great Patriotic War featured a clearly defined enemy who threatened the very existence of the Russian State, and could be defeated only through great will and sacrifice. Therefore, even if a film ended with the death of the hero, the greater struggle would always be victorious in the end. Those certainties are no more. Instead, war films of the 1990s provide a sad commentary on the disempowerment of the State, once a mighty global player, now unable to repress a rebellion by a tiny nation in its own backyard. The Russian body politic is ripping itself apart: it is a country at war with itself, and it is the young soldiers who are the first to die.[7]

The downbeat depiction of armed conflict thus reflects the loss of super-power status, the erosion of national pride and the quandary of 'Russianness' in the post-Soviet world. The collision of Christian and non-Christian value systems exposes a moral and spiritual vacuum in post-impe-rial Russia. But the ordinary soldier, the conscript, retains his pride, dignity and bravery, just as he did in the Soviet Great Patriotic War movie, and this definition is further refined in films made after the Yeltsin era.

For directors such as Rogozhkin and Bodrov the Caucasian problem is handled with grim irony. But Chechnia can also be the stimulus for national spiritual rebirth, as explicitly – and quite reprehensibly – proposed in Aleksandr Nevzorov's *Purgatory* (1998). Nevzorov's cheaply made film communicates his themes in as graphic detail as possible, piling on the horrors of modern warfare and the deprivations of soldiers. It also differs from the films mentioned above in several ways. Firstly, it is amateurishly produced, with a hand-held video camera, little script and generally poor acting. Secondly, the film is nothing short of a racist glorification of holy

Russia. Thirdly, it is based on an actual incident – the battle for Groznyi Central Hospital in January 1995 – and so lays claim to factual accuracy. Fourthly, *Purgatory* was shown on national terrestrial television in March 1998, only five months after its commercial release, and so undoubtedly reached a much larger audience than any of the films mentioned above.[8]

The gore and the sadism are unrelenting, as Chechen rebels and their foreign (Arab) supporters take great pleasure in killing Russians. Reproducing some of the myths generated by the war – such as that of female snipers merrily mowing down Russian soldiers – it is full of fire, smoke and violent death. These Chechens and their foreign allies (even English-speaking ones) are little more than beasts: they behead Russian prisoners and defile Russian corpses, and even crucify a wounded soldier in the film's harrowing closing scenes. This is more than a battle between Russia and its Muslim enclave: it is also a justification of genocide, where the only answer to the problem is to blast the Chechens into oblivion. Nevzorov's film is an unflinching endorsement of the official vilification of the Chechens as a race that has been a feature of government policy since the late 1990s.[9]

It is more than a deliberately racist film, however, for it is also a crusade of the Christian forces of good against the Islamic forces of evil, a fight to the death of true believers against barbarians. Embattled Russian soldiers light candles, and display great heroism and self-sacrifice in order to win the day for Christendom and civilisation.[10]

After Yeltsin: the empire strikes back

In these films of the 1990s it is unclear whether the greater foe facing Russian soldiers is the perceived non-Christian enemy or the army machine itself. However, with the arrival of Vladimir Putin as president in 2000, the Russian war film finds a new hardness and clarity of focus. As a consequence of the September 1999 apartment bombs in Moscow and other Russian cities, the enemy has been identified and there is a clear determination to defeat him. We should therefore make a distinction between films of the 1990s that present civic strife as a blatant metaphor for lost national prestige and purpose, and the more hard-boiled offerings of the Putin era. Aleksei Balabanov's aptly titled *War* (2002) is important in this respect.

Like Nevzorov's film, *War* is based on actual events: the kidnapping in Chechnia in 1999 of the British aid workers Jon James and Camilla Carr (here called John and Margaret). Like Nevzorov, Balabanov demonises the Chechen foe: 'Chechens are bandits, all of them', says a Russian soldier. Also like Nevzorov, Balabanov suggests that the solution to the Chechen problem is the annihilation of the Chechens as a race. The Russian conscript Ivan is the instrument of this catharsis.

At the beginning of the film we see the Chechens at their merciless worst: using Russian prisoners as slave labour, publicly beheading a Russian soldier and capturing the atrocity on video, then punishing another Russian by cutting off a finger. John and Margaret are being held captive for a ransom of £2 million, and Aslan, the Chechen leader, allows John to return to England to gather the money within two months. The soldier Ivan, who speaks some English, is allowed to leave the camp with him.

John returns to England, but finds no support either from the British Government or from NATO officials, who reject his affirmations that the Chechen nation is collectively criminal. John finds an ally only in Ivan, who accepts his money, and together they travel to Vladikavkaz, on the border with Chechnia. They get help from the Russian FSB, which agrees to smuggle them into Chechnia. From there they are on their own. With an assortment of high-powered weapons and explosives, and a renegade Chechen who agrees to help them, they destroy Aslan's camp and kill most of his men. Margaret is released, along with the wounded Russian captain (Sergei Bodrov Jr, in a totally redundant role) with whom she had been forced to live in a tiny pit dug in the ground. Margaret has been raped, and John takes out his fury on Aslan, killing him in cold blood – there is no room for the Geneva Convention in this war. Russian helicopter gunships then pound the village and rescue our heroes.

Although the film proclaims that war is the only way to resolve this conflict, it also shows that war is a means of national self-definition. Ivan's hospitalised father tells him that 'war makes a man out of a boy', and would offer to go to Chechnia himself if he were fit. Even the initially sensitive and pacifist Englishman John soon realises that the only way to deal with Chechens is to blow them away: he is the only Westerner to understand the real nature of Russia's problem in Chechnia. Heroism in war is legitimised by the chance encounter Ivan and John have on the train to Vladikavkaz with a character called Aleksandr Matrosov, the namesake of the USSR's best-known hero of the Great Patriotic War.

Yet the film is shot through with a bitter irony, as events are related retrospectively by Ivan while he is interviewed by a journalist in his prison cell. After successfully rescuing Margaret, Ivan was arrested and imprisoned for killing Chechen citizens. War is good and necessary, but the soldier on the ground remains a pawn of his government.

Balabanov's film was released in the spring of 2002, coinciding with Andrei Maliukov's *Spetsnaz,* a mini-series shown on nationwide state television (ORT). Hackneyed but undeniably thrilling, it follows the work of a team of elite Russian forces working in Chechnia, fighting a cunning and cruel enemy. Chechens will stop at nothing to attack Russia, even looking at the possibility of acquiring a nuclear device. In the course of these films the *Spetsnaz* track down ruthless terrorists and their foreign allies (one is a UK-trained former SAS officer now working for the Chechens), and even uncover Chechen attempts to destroy the US economy by producing counterfeit dollar bills. Indeed, in the post-September 11, 2001 world order,

Russian and American soldiers are colleagues in rooting out the enemy, who is portrayed as operating not only in Chechnia but in Afghanistan and Libya. Russia is part of the global war on terror, and is actually saving the West from the enemies of civilisation.

War on screen, and beyond

Early Soviet films about the civil war had clearly defined certainties and idealism. Stalinist pictures about the Great Patriotic War were imbued with triumphalist bombast and focused on the Great Leader as a national inspiration. The 'thaw' undertook a reassessment of the victory, pointing to the massive cost in human lives. The best war films of the 'stagnation' period confronted explosive issues such as collaboration and betrayal, and posed uncomfortable questions about the value of ideology and the permanence of political systems. The post-Soviet preoccupation with civil strife, and a new-found resolution to be tough with a ruthless enemy, also reflect the changing political sensibilities of a country and a state still grappling with the realities of the post-Cold War world.

Nevertheless, some continuities with past tradition remain. In particular, the Russian soldier is consistently seen as an embodiment of all that is good in Russia, a repository of the honour and decency missing from the political system. Significantly, Balabanov's soldier–killers are from the provinces, not the Westernised metropolitan centres. The soldier's capacity for self-sacrifice in the name of Russia is never questioned, nor is his ability to perform magnificent feats of heroism. In films of the 1990s the soldier may be the victim of Russia's disempowered State, but in films since 2000 the State is side-stepped in favour of massive fire-power. Ivan who defeated the Nazis can also defeat the new threat to global security. *War*, indeed, shows the influence of Hollywood in its debt to the *Rambo* or *Missing in Action* films of the 1980s, themselves reflecting Reaganite power politics and the need for at least a mythic victory after actual defeat. Nikolai Stambula's *Forced March* (2003), another *Rambo*-esque adventure in Chechnia, did not provoke the same agitated response as did *War* on its release, but reinforces with added ferocity the patriotic–nationalist agenda of Balabanov's earlier film. With a tough new president, though, the gloves come off and payback time is near.

Russian films of the 1990s were obsessed with a 'crisis of masculinity' that reflects the image of an emperor caught without his clothes. The self-doubting male has since 2000 been replaced by testosterone-fuelled competing masculinities, one hell-bent on destroying the other. It is not fortuitous that in *War*, as well as in *Forced March* and the *Spetsnaz* series, female characters are at best peripheral: Margaret's rape serves only as another pretext for blood-letting, grounded as it is in recorded fact. The literary text of *The Prisoner of the Caucasus*, in the poems by Pushkin and Lermontov, and the short story by Tolstoy – the literary foundations of Bodrov's film, and undoubtedly the inspiration behind *Checkpoint* and *War* – explore the emotional relationship of a Russian male with a Caucasian girl, thus offering an erotically charged metaphorical narrative about imperial ambition and conquest. Putin-era films will have none of it.[11] The enemy is at the gates, and has to be destroyed.

The lunatics and the asylum

The exception may, however, prove to be the rule. In 2002 Andrei Konchalovskii's film *The House of Fools* was released. It is undoubtedly the most important cinematic statement on the Chechen war, and is one of the most significant films of the whole post-Soviet period. Based on actual events in 1996, it is set in a lunatic asylum in Chechnia in the midst of war, and in the course of the film the asylum is overrun by both Chechen and Russian troops. This gives the viewer an opportunity to compare the behaviour of the two sets of soldiers. The heroine, Zhanna Timofeeva, fantasises that she is love with the Canadian rock star Bryan Adams (who makes several appearances in her dreams/fantasies), and her visions of peace and harmony are starkly juxtaposed with the unfeeling callousness of the real world.

The relative order of the asylum is interrupted by the arrival of Chechen soldiers, but these are not the ruthless, sadistic bandits we have come to expect from previous films, but rather are respectful, cultured, deeply religious men with an obvious sense of grievance: no rapes, no torture, no beheadings here. The real madness of the outside world intervenes with the arrival of the Russian troops pursuing them, their commanding officer (Evgenii Mironov) continuously on the verge of a nervous breakdown, and Russian troops firing on each other in the panic and uncertainty of combat.

Konchalovskii's film is a remake of Milos Forman's *One Flew Over the Cuckoo's Nest* (1975), updated and transferred to strife-torn modern Russia, where the inmates of an asylum represent more order and sanity than the world that reigns outside their walls. Russian troops sell back to the Chechens corpses of their fallen comrades ($2,000 per cadaver), and Chechens sell Russian soldiers dope. A superbly jarring effect is achieved when Zhanna sits in the grounds of the asylum playing her accordion, as a Russian helicopter in slow motion crashes to the earth behind her, an incongruously beautiful juxtaposition of images of war and peace. There is a moment of sad irony when a Russian and a Chechen commander simultaneously realise that they had fought on the same side in Afghanistan years earlier. Akhmed, the last remaining Chechen soldier and Zhanna's intended groom, is by the end of the film himself unhinged and becomes one of the inmates.

Konchalovskii's film is evidently at odds with the prevailing post-1999 mood of confrontation and engagement with a demonised enemy, but, like Forman's film, it encourages us to see the world from the point of view of its victims: those who have no power, and whose words and protestations go unheard. War is madness, and only the lunatics seem to know any semblance of order, routine and normality.

Filmography

Apocalypse Now!, dir. Francis Ford Coppola, 1979
The Ascent (Voskhozhdenie), dir. Larisa Shepit'ko, 1976
Ballad of a Soldier (Ballada o soldate), dir. Grigorii Chukhrai, 1960
Black Hawk Down, dir. Ridley Scott, 2002
The Brother (Brat), dir. Aleksei Balabanov, 1997
The Brother 2 (Brat 2), dir. Aleksei Balabanov, 2000
Chapaev, dir. Georgii and Sergei Vasil'ev, 1934
Checkpoint (Blokpost), dir. Aleksandr Rogozhkin, 1999
The Fall of Berlin (Padenie Berlina), dir. Mikhail Chiaureli, 1949
Forced March (Marsh-brosok), dir. Nikolai Stambula, 2003
Full Metal Jacket, dir. Stanley Kubrick, 1987
The House of Fools (Dom durakov), dir. Andrei Konchalovskii, 2002
In August 1944 (V avguste 44-ogo), dir. Mikhail Ptashuk, 2000
Kotovskii, dir. Aleksandr Faintsimmer, 1942
Ménage-à-trois (Retro vtroem), dir. Petr Todorovskii, 1998
Missing in Action, dir. Joseph Zito, 1984
Missing in Action 2: The Beginning, dir. Lance Hool, 1985
Moon Daddy (Lunnyi papa), dir. Bakhtier Khudoinazarov, 1999
The Muslim (Musul'manin), dir. Vladimir Khotinenko, 1995
One Flew Over the Cuckoo's Nest, dir. Milos Forman, 1975
Peculiarities of the National Hunt (Osobennosti natsional'noi okhoty), dir. Aleksandr Rogozhkin, 1995
Platoon, dir. Oliver Stone, 1986
Prisoner of the Mountains (Kavkazskii plennik), dir. Sergei Bodrov Sr., 1996
Purgatory (Chistilishche), dir. Aleksandr Nevzorov, 1997
The Rainbow (Raduga), dir. Mark Donskoi, 1943
Rambo: First Blood Part Two, dir. George Pan Cosmatos, 1985
Rambo III, dir. Peter MacDonald, 1988
Saving Private Ryan, dir. Steven Spielberg, 1998
Shchors, dir. Aleksandr Dovzhenko, 1939
Spetsnaz, dir. Aleksei Maliukov (3 x 52 mins), 2002
The Star (Zvezda), dir. Nikolai Lebedev, 2002
A Tender Age (Nezhnyi vozrast), dir. Sergei Solov'ev, 2000
The Thief (Vor), dir. Pavel Chukhrai, 1997
Time of the Dancer (Vremia tantsora), dir. Vadim Abdrashitov, 1997
Trial on the Road (Proverka na dorogakh), dir. Aleksei German, 1971
War (Voina), dir. Aleksei Balabanov, 2002
Zoia, dir. Leo Arnshtam, 1944

Notes

1 T. Doherty, *Projections of War: Hollywood, American Culture and World War II* (New York: Columbia University Press, 1993), p. 3.
2 *Ibid.*, p. 15.
3 Bodrov said shortly after the film was released that he at first intended to make the film in Bosnia, but was prevented by the war there. The film features dialogue in several Caucasian languages: Dagestani, Chechen, Georgian. See S. Bodrov, 'Ne tol'ko o chechenskoi voine', *Literaturnaia gazeta* (7 August 1996), p. 8.
4 Julian Graffy comments: 'Both Russians and Caucasians are portrayed by Bodrov with sympathetic attention, since none of them is responsible for the tragedy that engulfs them … Even the two opposing commanders are shown as driven to acts of savagery by circumstance and ignorance. The real orchestrators of this tragedy are, eloquently, absent:' 'Soldier, soldier', *Sight and Sound*, March (1998), 35.
5 It is interesting to note that both Rogozhkin and Bodrov refer, not to the conventions of the Soviet war film, but to those of Western cinema, as both films close. In *Prisoner of the Mountains* Zhilin is released by his captors, and as he makes his way back to base encounters a fleet of helicopter gunships blasting out martial music passing overhead, heading in the direction of the village from which he has just come. It is a clear cinematic echo of Coppola's *Apocalypse Now*, when the assault helicopters of General Killgore ('I love the smell of napalm in the morning') attack a Vietcong village to the sounds of Wagner's *Ride of the Valkyries*. In Rogozhkin's film the sniper stalking the conscripts turns out to be the young girl who had to an extent befriended them, a nod to the ending of Kubrick's *Full Metal Jacket*, where the Vietcong sniper sadistically shooting wounded GIs to shreds is revealed to be a teenage girl.
6 Birgit Beumers notes: 'In any war soldiers look first and foremost to the state for motivation in their action: the ultimate responsibility for the war and the placement of soldiers lies with the state. The war in Afghanistan was led by the Soviet state and party apparatus; the Chechen war of 1994–95 was instigated by a state with a democratically elected government and president. This has vast implications for the individual's responsibility: it is no longer a totalitarian system that forces its ideals onto man, but a state that places its men in situations where they need to defend the country against a declared enemy. The relationship between state and soldier is different, based on give and take, on trust in the state's righteousness and the soldier's commitment. This precludes that the soldiers believe in the political and national values harboured by the country they fight for. But in the new Russia, there were none of those: instead, political chaos reigned:' 'Myth-making and myth-taking: lost ideals and the war in contemporary Russian cinema', *Canadian Slavonic Papers*, 42:1–2 (March–June 2000), 177.
7 Birgit Beumers again: 'Film-makers have focused on the life of individuals, young men who have risked their lives not knowing for what. In concentrating on individual stories, neither Bodrov nor Khotinenko create a myth, which would enable a glorification of the war. Both are impartial, and inclined to criticize the Russian army rather than the "enemy"': *ibid*, p. 186.
8 However, Bodrov's film was the most popular Russian film in terms of video sales for 1997: see M. Segida and S. Zemlianukhin (comps), *Fil'my Rossii: Igrovoe kino (1995–2000)* (Moscow: 'Dubl'-D', 2001), p. 46.

9 In 1995 the MOD published a booklet purporting to provide 'facts, documents and eye-witness testimony' of Chechen outrages against Russian citizens in this 'cancerous tumour of Russia'. It reproduces Boris Yeltsin's characterisation of Chechnia as 'a testing area for the training and dissemination into other regions of Russia of a criminal authority': see A. Gorlov (ed.) *Kriminal'nyi rezhim. Chechnia, 1991–1995 gg: Fakty, dokumenty, svidetel'stva* (Moscow: 'Kodeks', 1995), p. 88.

10 Elena Stishova comments on the essential difference between the films of Nevzorov and Rogozhkin: 'A. Nevzorov's hysterical attempt to create in his studio a mythology of the new Caucasian war with the aid of copious amounts of ketchup did not say anything new. Rogozhkin chose the opposite strategy: demythologization ... *Checkpoint,* as a result, apart from its accurate details of everyday life, has its own mathematical constant, due to retain its own place amongst the collection of "national peculiarities". We are waging war, as in totalitarian times, against our own': 'Zapiski s kavkazskoi voiny', *Iskusstvo kino,* 1 (1999), 24.

11 Elena Stishova has also commented on this paradigm: 'If Russian writers of the XIX century tried to humanize Caucasian– Russian relations, and saw in this their mission and a possible psychological exit from the impasse of war, then today we do not observe anything similar. Both Bodrov and Rogozhkin include motifs of mutual cruelty and mutual mistrust between the Russian military and the local population. There can be no question of friendship. *Volens volens* you come to the conclusion that there is no such thing as peace-loving Chechens': 'Tranzit: Visbaden–Pittsburg–Kavkaz. Kavkazskaia tema v rossiiskom kino', *Iskusstvo kino,* 1 (2002), 101.

II

The political and economic interfaces with the military sphere

Back to hell: civilian–military 'audience costs' and Russia's wars in Chechnia

On 18 April 2002 radio-controlled landmines went off in the Leninskii neighbourhood of northern Groznyi – Chechnia's capital – devastating two vehicles carrying riot police officers of the pro-Russian Chechen Government: 17 officers died in the attack and at least 6 more were reported wounded. In the Associated Press photo accompanying the story, covered corpses surrounded by their shocked fellow-servicemen conveyed a feeling of dejected helplessness.[1] The attack served as a reminder that the Chechen pro-independence guerrillas had enough freedom in Groznyi to plant land-mines and that Russian soldiers died daily in the smouldering war.

A few hours after the attack, Russian President Vladimir Putin – unflap-pable and correct as usual – delivered a State of the Nation Address to the joint-session of the Duma in Moscow. In an hour-long speech televised live across Russia, Mr Putin talked for slightly less than one minute about the conflict in Chechnia. Claiming once again that – despite continuing deadly fighting – 'the military stage of the conflict may be considered concluded', the Russian president called on the Chechens to return to normal daily life. He discounted episodes, such as the one which had happened that same day, as disruptions by 'sorties of remaining bandits'. 'Only a year ago we counted how many bandits and terrorists there were – 2,000, 5,000, or 10,000. Today it is no longer important to us how many of them are there. We must know where they are.'[2]

These two events in Groznyi and Moscow encapsulated a major puzzle of civil–military relations in post-Soviet Russia. How is it that democratically elected chiefs of government may use the armed forces in internal conflicts with massive loss of their own military and civilian lives (there were close to 40,000 deaths in Chechnia between 1994 and 2002) and yet remain in power and avoid mass public protest? More specifically, how could a demo-cratic government in Moscow authorise Second World War style military operations in Chechnia that caused greater physical destruction and a larger-scale forced relocation of people than Stalin's mass deportation of

1944 and the 'scorched-earth' decades-long campaigns by Russia's tsarist generals in the nineteenth century? Democratic governance, after all, is supposed to promote restraint, cooperation and compromise, especially on issues that threaten the lives of hundreds of thousands of the State's citizens and affect millions of voters. And by 2002 Russia was arguably an institutional democracy with:

- a competitive multiparty system;
- relatively free and fair presidential (1991, 1996, and 2000) and parliamentary (1993, 1995, and 1999) elections;
- a separation of powers between an executive, a legislature, and a judiciary; and
- a pluralistic media.[3]

Moreover, since the mid-1990s Russian governments have signalled their appreciation of the value of human life – even the lives of the most violent criminals – by suspending the death penalty in line with the norms set by the Council of Europe.

The transitional democracy dilemma: public accountability v. state-building

One might be tempted to explain Russia's massive violence in Chechnia by citing multiple *ad hoc* and context-specific factors (e.g., from Yeltsin's hatred of the Chechen separatist leader Dudaev in the early 1990s to apartment bombs in Moscow in the autumn of 1999).[4] Yet, one could also address the same question as part of a broader problem, namely: under what conditions may chiefs of government in institutional democracies sanction the indiscriminately violent use of military force to resolve internal political conflicts? The obvious benefit of interpreting Russia's policies in Chechnia within this frame of reference is that it would enable an analyst to explain both the seemingly idiosyncratic behaviour of policy-makers, and the conditions that are likely to give rise to or to discourage similar behaviours in Russia or elsewhere in the future.

From this broader comparative perspective, the attacks in Groznyi on the day of Putin's annual address to the Duma in April 2002 highlighted what I call a transitional democracy dilemma. The dilemma arises from simultaneous changes to both a state's political system and its identity, such as in Russia's transformation both from an authoritarian state to a democracy and from an empire to a nation state. With regard to the use of military force in domestic political conflicts, this type of transition creates two imperatives – democratic accountability and state-building.

On the one hand, the very fact of Putin's address to the joint-session of the *Duma* and the Federation Council – regardless of its content – represents a typical democratic requirement for one elected leader to account for his or her policies to other popularly elected leaders. In contrast to the practice in the Soviet and other authoritarian systems of governance, chiefs of government in post-Soviet Russia make decisions not as principals (such as unelected *politburos* or monarchs) but as agents of the principals (the electorate). The eternal spectre of accountability to the electorate is one of the mainstays of the Kantian argument that democratic governments would, on average, be more sensitive to public opposition to war and the use of the military against their own civilian populations than would authoritarian governments.[5]

On the other hand, the guided landmine explosions in Groznyi – easily classifiable as acts of terrorism by Moscow and as acts of freedom-fighting by the Chechens seeking independence – highlighted a threat to the security and territorial integrity of the post-Soviet Russian State. These are the ultimate threats to state-building; and to build a new state (or to avoid the failure of an existing one) policy-makers need the military to suppress internal opposition, extract resources from the population to sustain state bureaucracy, police socio-economic activity, and provide a symbol of national pride and unity.[6]

The two imperatives interact uneasily. Avoiding state failure may be a stronger incentive than democratic accountability, because state failure entails either the immediate loss of power with unpleasant consequences for the incumbents or the incapacitation of governmental authority, rendering political tenure meaningless. Yet, democratic accountability is arguably a more immediate and tangible imperative than fear of state collapse. While the latter is a relatively infrequent occurrence with high odds against it, elections happen routinely and relatively frequently. Especially in the tumultuous politics of transitional states such as Russia, where the very nature of the political system was at stake in the 1996 presidential elections, a defeat at the polls can threaten consequences as severe as a government overthrow. Witness, for instance, campaign promises by communist candidates in Russia to file criminal charges against Yeltsin and his family.[7] Thus, taken separately, neither the democratic accountability imperative nor the state-building imperative would explain the Kremlin's decisions to deploy or to withdraw military force during Moscow's confrontation with Chechnia in the 1990s.

Democratic accountability arguably mattered in Yeltsin's decision to withdraw troops from Chechnia in the summer of 1996 following the presidential election. According to analysts of VTsIOM, Yeltsin's campaign promise to stop military operations in Chechnia played a crucial part in his victory at the polls, helping him to increase his approval rating from a dismal 5 per cent in January 1996 to 20 per cent in May 1996.[8] Valerii Tishkov, Russia's former minister of nationalities and director of the Institute of Ethnology and Anthropology of the Russian Academy of Sciences (*Rossiiskaia Akademiia Nauk* – RAN), reported that another major factor in Yeltsin's decision was the threat of Boris Nemtsov, the popular dynamic governor of Nizhnii Novgorod, who started a campaign to collect one million signatures under an anti-war petition in his province. Yeltsin, according to Tishkov, feared that the petition campaign would galvanise a nationwide anti-war movement during a critical presidential election year. Yeltsin reportedly feared that such a movement would jeopardise the chances for the re-election of incumbents in the same way as the anti-Vietnam War movements had done in the USA. As Tishkov writes, 'that [Nemtsov's petition campaign] sent an extremely alarming and painful signal to the president who was under pressure to avoid any kind of signature collection campaign at the time when he himself needed to collect one million signatures to put his name on the ballot in a presidential campaign.'[9]

Yet, democratic accountability fails to explain why Yeltsin decided to launch a war in December 1994 despite an obvious lack of public support. In September 1994, only 7 per cent of Russian respondents in an authoritative VTsIOM poll supported Russia's use of military force in Chechnia, while 42 per cent said Russia should not get involved at all and 31 per cent favoured Russia's involvement only as a mediator between the warring factions in Chechnia.[10] Similarly, democratic accountability fails to explain military mobilisation for war early in 1999 despite the fact that even the incursion of Basaev's and Khattab's fighters into Dagestan in August 1999 failed to persuade the majority of Russians to support operations in Chechnia. The state-building imperative would explain the mobilisation and the initiation of the military operations, but it fails to explain the withdrawal of the army from Chechnia in 1996 (especially given that Yeltsin had already won the presidential election and could simply renege on his campaign promise). Moreover, if state-building had been the only imperative, then the Kremlin should have shown a greater appreciation of the effects of the massive, brutal and costly military deployments in Chechnia in delaying and jeopardising military reform. An effective reform of the military would have allowed the Russian armed forces to become a more efficient institution for state consolidation and a symbol of national pride.[11]

The Russian wars in Chechnia in the 1990s suggest a different explanation for the interaction between the two imperatives, giving decision-makers the opportunity to exploit the very tension between the needs of democratic accountability and those of state-building. Assuming that political leaders in a transitional democracy are rational actors (in the sense only that they prefer victory to defeat and life to death), one would expect the dual tasks of democratisation and state-building to create incentives for them to make a massive *show* of military force in response to even small *imagined* threats to the State's territorial integrity at times when their political fortune requires them to signal to the electorate a credible commitment to state-building. An important implication of this argument is that the demonstration of a credible commitment to state-building would matter more to such leaders than would the effectiveness of military operations or political strategies. If the use of force backfires (as in the case of the 1994–96 war), the leaders would have an incentive to repeat the show of force and continue to demonstrate a credible commitment to state-building until the avoidance of state failure is no longer perceived as a crucial task. Focusing on perceptions of Russia's political–military leaders and of the public leading into Russia's military campaign in Dagestan and Chechnia in August 1999, I draw out some implications of this dual imperative for the decisions to use military power in domestic political crises.

Public opinion, 1994–99: fear, the State and war

The escape from the transitional democracy dilemma outlined above suggests that decision-makers are sensitive not so much to levels of public support for the use of military force at any given time as to the extent of public fear of state failure, or a governance crisis. Indeed, the majority of the Russian public opposed military operations in Chechnia from 1994 and until the apartment bombs in Buinaksk, Moscow and Volgodonsk in August and September 1999. This shift in public opinion, however, happened too late to account for Moscow's decision, earlier in 1999, to increase mobilisation for war in Chechnia. But other public opinion trends signaled: first, that Russians associated their personal insecurity with the weakness of central government and wished for a stronger government and, second, that they may have associated the weakness of central government with military failure in Chechnia.

On the first point, a study of the VTsIOM polling data indicates that the Soviet-era association of 'the capacity of the state to instill fear' with security as a public good endured throughout the 1990s. The study's author, Lev Gudkov, saw this linkage translate into evaluations of the prime minister, Vladimir Putin. Respondents who approved of Putin saw him as 'decisive, strong-willed and strict in his demands to re-establish order'.[12] The yearning for 'order' came out strongly in a survey of 2,426 Russians conducted by the University of Strathclyde in January 1996, when 77 per cent of respondents claimed to see 'order' as something that was 'more important for Russia' than were other factors.[13] On the second point, Russian decision-makers after the 1994–96 war had opinion data showing as early as January 1995 that the overwhelming majority of Russians attributed the failures of Russian troops in Chechnia to 'inept military command and operational planning' (42 per cent) and to the 'unwillingness of the Russian military to engage in active combat operations that may lead to civilian casualties' (27 per cent).[14] In this context, the decline in Yeltsin's approval rating during the Chechen war cannot be interpreted as evidence of Russian society's opposition to the use of military force in domestic crises.[15] Finally, the leaders could count on a significant increase in Russian public antipathy towards

the Chechens. In open-ended VTsIOM surveys the Chechens were identified
in early 1999 as the ethnic group that evoked the greatest antipathy among
Russian respondents –in sharp contrast to the results of this same survey in
1992, when the Chechens were ranked seventh.[16]

These trends made it less important for Putin – who came to power
pledging to make Russia a strong state – to estimate the extent of public
support for the use of military force in Chechnia at any given time or the
strength of popular belief in the effectiveness of any specific military operation. But Putin could credibly see in these opinion trends an opportunity to
capitalise on the fear of anarchy and to gain popularity through a renewed,
and more intensive, use of military power as a symbol of his commitment to
the consolidation of the State.

Power and state consolidation: the makings of the Putin leadership

But why would Putin need to seek such an opportunity and, more importantly,
why would he believe that Russia faced the threat of state failure? Putin's autobiography, *In the First Person,* offers critical insights that are reflected in his
later statements and policies. Putin's service as a KGB foreign intelligence
officer in East Germany became a springboard into St Petersburg politics and
from there to Moscow, where he served as the FSB chief prior to being
appointed prime minister by Yeltsin in August 1999. But it appears that Putin
found it hard to get over parting with the KGB – something he had to do by
default after the collapse of the USSR. According to Putin's family friend
Sergei Roldugin: 'Putin talked with pain and indignation about [the KGB]
abandoning its entire intelligence network in Germany. "One cannot do such
things! How could they?" he said ... He was very disappointed.'[17] In his autobiography Putin talks fondly about his brief meeting with Henry Kissinger in
St Petersburg, during which both agreed that Gorbachev should not have
ended Soviet military and political domination of East and Central Europe:
'Kissinger was right. We would have avoided many problems, if we had not
run away from there so precipitously.'[18]

Putin saw post-Soviet Russia's problems with centre–periphery relations
– from the *de facto* secession of Chechnia by 1997 to the 'asymmetric feder-
alism' that gave provincial leaders opportunities to gain power at the
expense of the Federal Government – as part of the same trend that started
with the dissolution of the KGB spy network in Germany:

> Trust me, even back in 1990–1991 I knew for a fact ... that with these kinds
> of social attitudes toward the army and the security services, especially after
> the Soviet collapse, Russia itself would soon be on the brink of disintegration
> ... After all, what is the essence of today's situation in the North Caucasus
> and in Chechnia? This situation is an extension of the collapse of the Soviet
> Union. It is clear to me that someone would have to stop that sooner or later.

Yes, for a while I hoped that with economic growth and the development of democratic institutions that this process of disintegration would come to a halt. But life showed that this hope was in vain ... And so this is how I evaluated the situation in August [1999] when the bandits [Basaev's and Khattab's fighters] attacked Dagestan – if we did not stop it immediately, Russia would cease to exist in its present shape. At stake was stopping the disintegration of the country.[19]

Not only does this message resonate with the widespread public regret over the collapse of the Soviet Union among Russians in the 1990s, but it clearly implies that the Government needs to strengthen the army and the security services in order to prevent the disintegration of the State. In his autobiography, which was mass-published in Russia shortly before the March 2000 presidential election, Putin portrays himself as precisely the tough leader capable of dealing with the domino effects of Chechen secession and giving back power to the centre. But in order to do that he would need to overcome a formidable challenge:

I never doubted for a second – and anyone who has elementary political literacy would understand – that Chechnia would not be satisfied with gaining independence. Their leaders would use this independence as a bridgehead for continuing attacks on Russia.

They started the aggression. They amassed forces and attacked a neighboring territory. Was it done to defend the independence of Chechnia? Of course, it was not. Their goal was to annex the adjacent territories. If Dagestan got swept up in these events, that would have been it. The entire [northern] Caucasus would secede, it is clear. Dagestan, then Ingushetiia, and then the wave would spread up the Volga river, to Tatarstan and Bashkortostan. And that would be a strike at the country's heartland.[20]

From that point Putin needed to make just one short logical step to argue that this partial secessionist challenge posed a grave military threat to Russia that could hurt thousands of Russian civilians:

The problem is that if the conflict spread [beyond Chechnia] we would not have enough armed forces to deal with it. We would have had to call up the reservists and send them into battle. A truly large-scale war would begin. Otherwise we would have to agree to a partition of the country. We would have immediately seen discontented leaders of some regions and *krais* [territorial units] who would say, 'We don't want to live in this kind of Russia, but we want to be independent.' And there goes the neighborhood.[21]

Put succinctly, Putin's arguments boil down to this: the cost of not intervening with massive military force in Chechnia would have been greater than

the cost of the intervention in the autumn of 1999, whatever the consequences of the latter. Curiously, the articulation in Putin's autobiography of
these positions on Chechnia is a manifestation of a political leader successfully merging the accountability and state-building imperatives. After all,
these views – regardless of the extent to which they reflected Putin's actual
views of the situation – were published in the run-up to a presidential
campaign that decided Yeltsin's succession and Putin's political future.

Putin's fears had some plausible bases in real-world developments. After
the Soviet collapse that emotionally traumatised Putin, he had witnessed:

- the 1991–93 'parade of sovereignties' across eighty-nine constituent
  units of the RF;
- the conclusion of separate power-sharing treaties between Moscow and
  more than half of those units;
- the failure of the Federal Government to remove from office regional
  governors who violated state laws; and
- a military withdrawal from Chechnia followed by a peace treaty that
  allowed for the possibility that Chechnia would officially secede by
  2001.

Along the Volga River, the leaders of Tatarstan held a referendum that gave
support to their claim of sovereignty. The Tatarstan Government opened a
foreign ministry and placed its own representatives in key Russian
embassies abroad. Further east, a Urals Republic was proclaimed and the
idea of a local currency, the 'Urals franc', was floated in Sverdlovsk region,
the former home of Russia's president, Boris Yeltsin. Oil-rich Tiumen', in
western Siberia, exchanged 'embassies' with Ukraine. Diamond-rich Sakha-
Yakutiia – an autonomous republic the size of India in the Russian far east –
negotiated trade deals with De Beers, the international diamond distributor,
and even attempted to coin its own currency featuring the governor's profile
instead of Russia's two-headed eagle.[22]

In the wake of the financial and currency 'meltdown' and a traumatic
devaluation of the rouble in August 1998, independent observers with no
stake in the country's future pointed to a serious threat of 'federal collapse'
in Russia. A UK scholar, Graeme Herd, writing in the *Journal of Peace
Research* – one of the world's top international relations journals – argued
that Russia's regions were assuming increasing control over federal agencies, including the military, creating alliances with powerful businesses,
setting up their own communication networks, and developing foreign relations independently of Moscow:

> The 1998 'August Meltdown' disrupted the balance between centripetal and
> centrifugal forces within the federation by dramatically weakening the
> centre's power. As a consequence, the federal system of governance is

disintegrating not by design, but by default ... As the centre is largely unable to combat the crisis, Russia will either become a very weak federation dominated by large regional blocs, or a confederation.[23]

On 11 September 1998 the newly nominated prime minister, Evgenii Primakov, started his speech at the parliamentary confirmation hearings by saying: 'The new government must first and foremost pay special attention to preserving Russia as a single state. Today this is a lot more than a theoretical or a hypothetical issue. We are facing a serious threat of the disintegration of our country.'[24] Following Primakov, Russian politicians of every political hue – from fascists in the south to the mayor of Moscow, Iurii Luzhkov, and the former deputy-prime minister, Boris Nemtsov – proposed a wholesale administrative redivision of Russia and argued for harsh court penalties against the mutinous governors. The Russian political arena in late 1998 was strikingly different from what it had been in the 1994–96 period, when actors such as Nemtsov proposed drastic measures (a nationwide petition) to stop the war in Chechnia. *The Economist* reported that the economic and currency crisis signalled 'the beginning of Russia's dissolution', as regional bosses were declaring their own 'state of emergency', issuing surrogate currencies and closing their borders to trade with other regions. The article asked: 'Could Russia break up, as the Soviet Union did seven years ago?'[25] Putin presented himself first as prime minister in August 1999 and then as a presidential candidate in early 2000 as uniquely suited to take decisive measures to prevent Russia's collapse.

Incursions and explosions: 'focusing events' in the frame of revenge

Persistent public fears and a sense of humiliation in Chechnia (linked with the humiliation that resulted from the Soviet collapse, the loss of superpower status, and the economic decline of the early 1990s) did not necessarily predicate the 'return to hell'[26] in Chechnia in the autumn of 1999. Putin's appreciation of those fears and his own assessments of the threat of Russian disintegration certainly increased the viability of the war option in Chechnia and help to explain Russia's continuing military mobilisation in the north Caucasus throughout 1999, but they cannot explain either the timing or the intensity of Russian military operations. After the 1994–96 war the Russian Government considered three major military options in Chechnia that it could have plausibly pursued at any time prior to or after 1999. In addition to large military operations, those options included a partitioning of Chechnia with a concentration of Russian troops in the northern half of the republic (which has a flat terrain and has historically been populated by ethnic Russians), and a blockading of Chechnia with a massive troop deployment along its periphery.[27] The partition option continued to enjoy considerable elite and public support even after the war had been launched, suggesting that a sizeable conflict was not necessarily predicated on Putin's determination to consolidate the State and the public's fear of anarchy. As is frequently the case in public policy-making, major decisions – such as a large military campaign on one's own territory – required a 'push' in the form of a 'focusing event like a crisis or disaster that comes along to call attention to the problem, a powerful symbol that catches on'.[28]

The series of apartment bombings in Buinaksk (Dagestan), Moscow and Volgodonsk that claimed close to 300 lives and left hundreds more injured and homeless was precisely such an event. Regardless of whether, as Boris Berezovskii and others have argued, the explosions were the result of Moscow's policies and were masterminded by the FSB, it is important to note that they were preceded by a series of other major acts of violence in the north Caucasus and in Moscow that *could* have served as similar focusing events, but did not. For example, while conducting research in Russia in May 1999, I watched television news of armed attacks on Russian checkpoints along the border between Chechnia and Dagestan, with heavy exchange of fire and casualties. And in late July 1999 several detachments of fighters (*boeviki*) under the command of the radical Islamist leaders Basaev and Khattab crossed the border into Dagestan, took over several villages in the Botlikh area and announced a campaign to create an independent Islamic Republic of Chechnia and Dagestan. In a diary published as part of his memoirs about the Chechen wars, the then-commander of the North Caucasus Military District, (two-star) Gennadii Troshev portrays this invasion as posing a grave threat to Moscow's power in Dagestan:

3 August 1999, 17:30
Received a cipher cable from Moscow. It says the [rebels] elected a presidium of 'The Caucasus House for the Liberation of Chechnia and Dagestan' (chaired by Udugov and the Basaev and Khachilaev brothers) and approved a plan for staging a revolt in Makhachkala [Dagestan's capital].[29] They plan to start the revolt sometime between 5 August and 8 August [1999]. According to the plan, the city will be divided into zones, with Chechen field commanders and Dagestani *Wahhabis* in charge of each zone. The fighters intend to take hostages in the most crowded locations and then give the Government of Dagestan an ultimatum demanding their resignation. Six hundred of their fighters have been moved from the Chechen village of Kinkhi to Botlikh in Dagestan, pending infiltration of Makhachkala and its suburbs. The fighters intend to increase decoy manoeuvres along the Chechen–Dagestani border as well as to carry out individual subversive acts at various locations, including an oil transit depot at Izerbash.[30]

To comprehend the magnitude of public repercussions to these developments one has to imagine how the public in England would react to an attack by 600 Irish Republican Army (IRA) fighters on British Army positions in Northern Ireland, or how the public in Spain would react to an attack by 600 ETA (Basque nationalist) separatists on Spanish Army's positions around the Basque region. Moreover, if a plausible argument could be made that the Russian public was primed for massive outbursts of anger and calls for revenge when the apartment buildings exploded, the same argument would be plausible regarding the Chechen incursion into Dagestan. By that time the Russian public had been exposed to several years of news reports about kidnappings, murders, bomb scares and explosions in downtown Moscow, and even the discovery of a crude nuclear device that the Chechen fighters intended to detonate in one of Moscow's parks. In December 1998, the Russian public was exposed to gruesome television footage of the severed heads of Darren Hickey, Rudolf Petschi and Peter Kennedy of the UK and their New Zealand colleague Stanley Shaw. The heads were found on a roadside in Chechnia, the victims having been starved, beaten and tortured prior to decapitation.[31] Finally, one should not necessarily assume *ex ante* that apartment bombings would generate massive support for a large military invasion of Chechnya. The 1990s saw several large apartment buildings throughout Russia explode due to malfunctioning gas-supply systems and the mishandling of gas stoves by residents. A terrorist bomb attack in November 1996 that devastated a nine-storey apartment building in the town of Kaspiisk in Dagestan killing 22 people, including 7 children, failed to spark revenge protests. Such bombings failed to generate even a fraction of the mass calls for revenge that the apartment bombings would in 1999.

None of these prior developments – not even the Islamist incursion into Dagestan – became a 'focusing event' in the sense that the apartment bombings did in 1999. Hence, it was not the brutality, the suddenness, the abnormality or the 'tipping-point' effect of the September 1999 explosions that made them a policy-relevant 'focusing event'. A cautiously pacifistic politician in Putin's place could even have used the post-explosion polls to argue that renewed military operations in Chechnia would encounter serious public opposition. In September and October 1999, VTsIOM found that 52 per cent of Russian respondents to its surveys believed that the Russian Government would be unable to protect them from Chechen terrorist acts, whereas 85 per cent of respondents believed such acts would occur in response to the Russian air strikes on Chechnia that were then taking place.[32]

Rather, it was the way that policy-makers, starting with Putin, publicly interpreted these developments that gave them their political significance. They first linked these explosions to Chechen independence fighters and then adopted the position that any means of revenge would be appropriate and no military measure too tough. While in Moscow in September 1999, I watched a television report of Putin's press conference at which, in response to the apartment bombings, he made the pledge, politely translated into

English as: 'If we find them [terrorists] in the outhouse, we will stick their heads in the bowl.'[33] As I stood in front of the television shocked by this crude statement, my Russian friends were expressing approval of Putin's tough, forthright language. But more importantly, with respect to Putin seeking public support for a Chechen war, this statement and others like it convinced the Russian public that the apartment blasts were the doings of Chechen rebels. In his autobiography Putin reproduced his public interpretations of the blasts that reinforced this belief. According to Putin, it was time for revenge: an eye for an eye and a tooth for a tooth. Above all, it was time to defend Mother Russia:

> Last summer we started a struggle not against Chechen independence, but against aggressive intentions that began to emerge in that territory. We are not attacking. We are defending ourselves. We knocked them out of Dagestan. They came back. We knocked them out again. And they came back. We knocked them out the third time. And when we knocked in their teeth, they blew up buildings in Moscow, Buinaksk and Volgodonsk.[34]

In this representation, the battle for Chechnia was not about politics but about survival of the Russian State, described in the parlance of the fist-fight and implying that there was only one side in this struggle that any sensible Russian could take and that any other position amounted to betrayal.

The apartment explosions therefore became pivotal in the decision to initiate military operations on a large scale in Chechnia because they resonated perfectly with long-term anxieties about state weakness among the Russian public and allowed the political and military leaders seeking to consolidate the State to present those operations as the only and the best option. It was not that the Russian public itself necessarily wanted Moscow to fight a war to the last Chechen, but that it became generally more accepting of a wider range of violent actions in Chechnia. A friend working in Moscow's political advertising sector argued that, following these explosions, the Russian public would support even the use of nuclear weapons in Chechnia.

This packaging of the wars in Chechnia as defensive, just and state-consolidating – seeking a broad remit to go into Chechnia and completely crush the resistance against Moscow's rule – also sent a strong message to political opponents of Putin. In this situation they could only express opposition to Moscow's military operations at the risk of appearing soft on defence of the motherland, insensitive to horrific acts of violence in the heart of Russia and unwilling to build a strong, viable state in Russia. Unsurprisingly, no major Russian politician in the autumn of 1999 took that risk. Putin's approval rating surged from 5 per cent in September to nearly 45 per cent in November 1999. Putin's formidable rivals, the Mayor of Moscow mayor Iurii Luzhkov and former prime minister Evgenii

Primakov, saw their ratings drop and pro-Putin parties won a working majority in the *Duma* in the December 1999 elections. At the same time, Putin no longer needed to fear public protests over his imposition of stricter state control over the media – as became evident in the detention of the Radio Free Europe journalist Andrei Babitskii and, later, in the Kremlin's take-over of the NTV and TV6, independent television channels that were the most critical of Putin's Chechnia policies. In March 2000, Putin convincingly won the presidential election in the first round. Thus he had masterfully showed how a government's use of massive military power within its own state could be put to political advantage in a transitional democracy and how accountability costs could be turned into electoral victories.

Conclusion

In this chapter I have addressed a question central to systematic theoretical and empirical research in the discipline of international relations: 'During a crisis, how do leaders come to revise their beliefs about an opponent so that attack is preferred to holding out concessions?'[35] I have raised this question, however, not in relation to crises between or among states that are assumed to have stable democratic or authoritarian political systems – as is the case with most of the instances discussed in the international relations literature – but in relation to an internal crisis in a nation where political systems and state identity are themselves indeterminate and subject to contestation. Thus, I view the decision to go to war as part of a broader process of civil–military relations in societies facing the challenges of state- and nation-building. The analysis suggests that the theory of 'audience costs'[36] and the Russian case have mutually valuable insights that help us to understand decision-making in domestic political crises which resemble political wars of attrition.

The case of Russia's wars in Chechnia in the 1990s confirms the importance of understanding that crises – such as the one over Chechnia's status – become political 'wars of nerves' because 'they are carried out in front of political audiences evaluating the skill and performance of the leadership'.[37] This appeared to have special significance in Russia's politics of transition, in which institutions have been weak and personal relationships have been paramount. As Eva Busza points out, telephone calls between the president, the prime minister and the defence minister have mattered more in post-Soviet Russia than have laws, bureaucratic procedures and parliamentary debates.[38] After the collapse of the USSR, the Russian leaders learned quickly, as the theory suggests, that in making decisions they were 'an agent acting on behalf of the principals (voters) who have the power to sanction the agent electorally or through the workings of the public opinion'. And, as the approval ratings of all leading Russian politicians plummeted after the withdrawal from Chechnia in late 1996, the 'agents' quickly learned that they risk paying 'added domestic political costs for "engaging national honor" [the military] and subsequently backing down'.[39]

It follows that political leaders in transitional democracies, to the extent that they perceive state-building as a challenge, have the incentive to resort to the use of massive military force in domestic crises when they need to signal to the electorate the credibility of their commitment to consolidating the state and defending national honour. The show and the intensity of its firepower are more important politically than the effectiveness of military operations in resolving the crises. For this reason, the Russian leadership is likely to tune out the argument that Moscow's military operations in Chechnia made the latter into a breeding-ground for precisely the acts of terror and violence that the military campaigns were designed to eradicate in the first place. A credible demonstration that the army can defend national honour and consolidate the State takes precedence over the violence-producing plight of refugees, of victims of the indiscriminate bombardments of cities and villages, of victims of torture in the Russian 'filtration camps' and of victims of beatings, rape and haphazard bullets in 'cleansing' operations (*zachistki*) in the 'national honour'. In short, in a transitional democracy dilemma, the state-building imperative trumps the democratic accountability imperative, prompting the leaders to exploit public fears, frustrations and yearnings for revenge.

The analysis in this chapter also suggests, however, that the political and ideological context in which 'audience costs' are estimated matters decisively. Decision-makers have multiple audiences to take into account and multiple, confusing signals about the political costs of any given policy delivered by messengers whose political agendas diverge. Leaders also do not make policy autonomously, but rather ask how similar actions have affected political leaders in their own country and in other countries in the past. The military itself is treated as an audience in a crisis – especially in a state undergoing political change. Failure to give the military a sense of mission during a crisis may result in a disoriented and frustrated force on which the State would be unable to rely later.

The role of ideology and individual leadership becomes decisive in the audience and signal selection. By interpreting the anti-war petition campaign in Nizhnii Novgorod as a signal that the political consequences for Russia of the wars in Chechnia would resemble the political consequences for the USA of the war in Vietnam, Yeltsin made a decision to withdraw the Russian forces from Chechnia and abided by it even after he was re-elected and had no need to fear the loss of power. By interpreting unrest in the north Caucasus as engendering a domino effect that would lead to a 'Yugoslavisation' of Russia, Putin pushed for a tough military campaign and lamented in his autobiography that he perhaps had not been sufficiently tough. Yet, even after the explosions in the apartment buildings in Moscow, a leader less deeply affected by the collapse of the USSR and its

European spy network than was Putin, would still have had room for manoeuvre with regard to military intervention in Chechnia. At the very least, Putin had the credible option, not of moving troops into the half of Chechnia which is south of the River Terek, but of conducting tightly focused anti-terrorist operations and of categorically prohibiting cleansing (*zachistki*) operations.

The lesson for civil–military relations is that the more acutely the political leaders feel the state-building imperative, the less they need formal, rule-based oversight of the military by democratic institutions within society. Significant military reform, therefore, is unlikely to take place as long as Russia needs a massive military presence in Chechnia.

Notes

1 M. Wines, 'Rebel ambush in Chechnya betrays Putin's rosy view', *New York Times* (19 April 2002), p. A10.

2 *Ibid.*

3 M. McFaul, *Russia's Unfinished Revolution* (Ithaca, NJ: Cornell University Press, 2001).

4 M. Evangelista, *The Chechen Wars: Will Russia Go the Way of the Soviet Union?* (Washington, DC: Brookings Institution, 2002).

5 I. Kant, *Perpetual Peace* (New York: Bobbs-Merrill, 1984); M. Doyle, 'Liberalism and world politics', *American Political Science Review*, 80:4 (1986), 1151–69.

6 See C. Tilley (ed.) *The Formation of National States in Western Europe* (Princeton, NJ: Princeton University Press, 1975) and C. Tilley, *Coercion, Capital and European States, AD990–1990* (Cambridge, MA: Blackwell, 1992).

7 In a December 1998 VTsIOM poll, 49 per cent of respondents supported bringing charges against Yeltsin for 'unlawful activities and abuse of office while in power': see I. Levada, '1989–1999: Desiatiletie vynuzhdennykh povorotov', *Monitoring obshchestvennogo mneniia* 1 (January–February 1999), 12 (Moscow: VTsIOM).

8 V. Nikitina, 'Na krugi svoia', *Monitoring obshchestvennogo mneniia* 4 (November–December 1999), 54 (Moscow: VTsIOM).

9 V. Tishkov, *Ocherki teorii i praktiki etnichnosti* (Moscow: Russkii mir, 1997), p. 494.

10 Nikitina, 'Na krugi svoia', p. 54.

11 See chapter 5, by Pavel Baev, in this volume.

12 L. Gudkov, 'Strakh kak ramka ponimaniia proiskhodiashchego', *Monitoring obshchestvennogo mneniia* 4 (November–December 1999), 48 (Moscow: VTsIOM).

13 In M. Kramer, 'The people choose', *Time* (27 May 1996), p. 56; only 9 per cent in the same survey chose 'democracy' in response to the same question.

14 Nikitina, 'Na krugi svoia', p. 55.

15 In the July 1995 VTsIOM survey 63 per cent of respondents agreed that Yeltsin was unfit to be president due to his policies in Chechnia: see *ibid.*

16 L. Gudkov, 'Kompleks "zhertvy": Osobennosti massovogo vospriiatia rossianami sebia kak etnonatsional'noi obshchnosti', *Monitoring obshchestvennogo mneniia* 3 (May–June 1999), 58 (Moscow: VTsIOM).

17 V. Putin, *Ot pervogo litsa: Razgovory s Vladimirom Putinym* (Moscow: Vagrius, 2000), p. 75.

18 *Ibid.*, p. 74.

19 *Ibid.*, p. 133.

20 *Ibid.*, p. 135.

21 *Ibid.*, p. 136.

22 Foreign Broadcast Information Service (FBIS), Collection: Soviet Union, FBIS–1992–067 (26 June 1992); FBIS–1992–047 (28 July 1992); FBIS–1992–025 (27 March 1992); 'Edward Rossel, Russia's ungovernable governor', *The Economist* (7 November 1998), p. 58.

23 G. Herd, 'Russia: systemic transformation or federal collapse', *Journal of Peace Research* 36:3 (1999), 259.

24 *Voice of Russia*, 1700 UTC 13–09–98. Primakov threatened to apply the 'strictest measures' against regional politicians attempting to 'destroy the vertical chain of subordination, weaken central authority, and ignore the central government'. Signalling the growing political importance of regional leaders, Primakov appointed a number of governors to the Russian Government Presidium, a new body with vast powers.

25 Radio Free Europe–Radio Liberty (RFE–RL), 'Luzhkov, Nemtsov condemn regional separatism', *Newsline*, 2:188, part I (29 September 1998); 'Will Russia hold together?', *The Economist* (12 September 1998), p. 56.

26 The notion here and in the title comes from Chechen graffiti in Groznyi that read: 'Welcome to hell' during the 1994–96 war addressing the Russian troops.

27 Tishkov, *Ocherki teorii i praktiki etnichnosti*, p. 495.

28 J. Kingdon, *Agendas, Alternatives, and Public Policies* (New York: HarperCollins, 1984), pp. 99–100.

29 Movladi Udugov was Chechnia's foreign minister in the Dudaev Government in the early 1990s and formed an Islamist opposition to the Maskhadov Government after 1997 that allied with Shamil Basaev and most other field commanders of the 1994–96 war. The Khachilaev brothers, one of whom was the leader of the Lak ethnonationalist movement in Dagestan, were known to the Russian public as the leaders of the one-day coup in Makhachkala in the spring of 1998. At that time Khachilaev supporters took over the government headquarters building and replaced Dagestan's blue, red, green and yellow flag with a green Islamist flag.

30 G. Troshev, *Moia voina: Chechenskii dnevnik okopnogo generala* (Moscow: Vagrius, 2001), p. 190.

31 M. Warren, 'Russia uses TV to show off body of feared Chechen warlord', *Daily Telegraph* (26 June 2001).

32 Gudkov, 'Kompleks "zhertvy"', p. 48.

33 '*Esli naidem ikh v sortire, budem mochit' v sortire.*'

34 Putin, *Ot pervogo litsa*, p. 137.

35 J. Fearon, 'Domestic political audience and the escalation of international disputes', *American Political Science Review*, 88:3 (1994), 577.

36 See *ibid.*, and K. Schultz, 'Domestic opposition signaling in international crises', *American Political Science Review*, 92:4 (1998), 829–42.

37 Fearon, 'Domestic political audience', p. 580.
38 E. Busza, 'State dysfunctionality, institutional decay, and the Russian military', in Valerie Sperling (ed.) *Building the Russian State: Institutional Crisis and the Quest for Democratic Governance* (Boulder, CO: Westview Press, 2000), p. 120.
39 Fearon, 'Domestic political audience', p. 581.

Military reform and regional politics

Introduction

In the first twelve years of its post-Soviet existence, Russia has undergone an enormous, painful and remarkably incomplete transformation which has consumed and exhausted much social energy and has created as many problems as it has resolved. There was never any blueprint for reform. Indeed the Soviet tradition of planning was so eagerly abandoned that there was very little policy coordination on the key directions, leading to all sorts of unforeseen consequences. Two dimensions of the ongoing transformation are taken up in this chapter: military power and the territorial organisation of political space, both of which have a record of colossal change. The formidable Soviet military machine was split into pieces and much reduced in size, and many of its key parts were broken beyond repair; the efforts invested recently in its reconstruction have fallen far short of the ambitious targets. The strictly centralised State has evolved into a loose and asymmetrical federation, continually balancing on the brink of disintegration, and then was pressed back into an over-centralised political design that fits poorly the logic of economic and social modernisation.

There was very little interaction between state policies in these two directions. Military policy and military reform were essentially left to the 'top brass' to manage with very little political leadership or control. Relations between the centre and the 'subjects' of the RF were, on the contrary, a matter of 'high politics', with complex bureaucratic intrigues and spectacular personal conflicts. However, there probably was a connection between the two trends: as the military structures were shrinking and degenerating, the regional processes were strengthening and maturing. The rapid dismantling of the Soviet military machine opened the way for the development of regional processes, and the growth of regionalism reduced the share of resources available for the centre and thus forced further shrinkage of the armed forces. Re-centralisation and the collection of the oil rent have made it possible for the Kremlin to pump new money into the military structures, which, however, had degenerated too far for any rejuvenation.

With hindsight, it is possible to establish that by the end of the 1990s, both processes had developed serious shortcomings and arrived at dead-ends. The dual tasks of arresting the decline of Russia's military might by advancing a comprehensive military reform and consolidating the integrity of the State by restoring the levers of central control were looming large for the new Russian leadership. President Putin's initial approach to these tasks was marked by boldness and determination. Instead of carefully designing optimal parameters for military structures, he pushed the army into a new Chechen war. Instead of rewarding the regional leaders for their support of his presidential campaign, he advanced legislation aimed at curbing their prerogatives and privileges. He also sought to establish a new level for the management of these tasks, creating seven new federal districts which corresponded quite closely to the military districts.

At the end of Putin's first presidency (which is also the time of this writing), he could claim significant achievements in both directions. However, new challenges related to the US-led global campaign against terrorism have illuminated the scale of the remaining problems and the lack of dynamism in tackling them. Whether Putin's re-centralisation and power-building amount to clear brakes on both trajectories – rising regionalism and declining military capabilities – or merely to temporary setbacks is as yet unclear. This chapter attempts a preliminary assessment, looking also into possible interplays between the two processes in the near future. I start with an examination of the trajectories of military reform and regionalism, then look at their interplay during Putin's first term in power, before evaluating the impact of the global anti-terrorist campaign. The final section offers a provisional risk assessment for Putin's second presidency, outlining three possible scenarios for the mid-term developments.

The trajectory of military reform

The need to reduce, restructure and reconstitute the enormous military machine that had been the core structure of the collapsed Soviet State was one of the most obvious and demanding tasks for the leadership of the new Russian State in early 1992.[1] With hindsight, it is possible to say that this was the best opportunity to set in motion a comprehensive reform not just of the armed forces but of the whole military system.[2] After hesitating for a few months, President Yeltsin decided to let the opportunity slip and to preserve as much as possible from the old system, only emphasising the redeployment from Germany and the Baltic states and unavoidable numerical cuts. This tactically astute move helped him to secure the loyalty of the high command, which stood by him during the September–October 1993 crisis and with a few tank salvos secured his victory over the parliament.[3]

That experience did not make Yeltsin any more attentive to the problems of reforming the military. On the contrary, after 1994 the funding of the armed forces was cut significantly; and, in late 1994, the army was pushed into the protracted and unpopular war in Chechnia, which consumed a disproportionate share of resources, inflicted heavy damage on Russia's military structures and prestige, and effectively blocked any possibility of reform.[4]

Russia's defeat in the first Chechen war created both the necessity and the opportunity to advance a large reform project (in much the same way as had the defeats in the Crimean War of 1854–56 and the Russo-Japanese War of 1904–5). Although the conditions for military reform were far less promising than they had been in early 1992, several sound proposals were advanced by academic experts,[5] while Defence Minister Igor' Rodionov resorted to desperate public relations efforts in order to get Yeltsin's attention. The president's entourage opted for the minimalist and cheapest option – and for a more agreeable defence minister.[6] The reform package approved by the end of 1997 included modest numerical cuts, a few long-debated mergers in the command structures (like the 'hostile take-over' of the Air Defence Forces by the Air Force) and the inevitable reduction in the number of army divisions in order to build up several combat-capable units.[7] The financial crash of August 1998 instantly reduced the resource base available for implementing military reforms and determined the narrow 'nuclear-first' focus of further efforts.[8] Defence Minister Igor' Sergeev placed the emphasis on the modernisation of the Strategic Rocket Forces,[9] seeking to integrate all elements of the strategic deterrent into one command. The plan was blocked by firm bureaucratic resistance championed by Chief of the General Staff Anatolii Kvashnin,[10] but this protracted in-fighting consumed so much time and energy that the whole issue of military reform essentially disappeared from the debates.

The failure to reform the military system had its roots in the deformed pattern of civil–military relations, determined both by the weakness of civil society and by the strength of military's sense of institutional self-preservation. An examination of the sources of the former would go far beyond the scope of this chapter,[11] but an analysis of the latter uncovers a highly unusual evolution of military identity and culture. Facing a systemic collapse, the military sought an easy way out, quickly forging a new identity as a presidential institution, answerable only to the commander-in-chief and relying on his 'special attention'.[12] The crisis of October 1993 firmly sealed that identity: there was simply no other way for the military leadership to justify its actions. A direct consequence of this new military identity was the weakness of parliamentary, and more generally, of democratic control over the military: the top brass was firmly opposed to giving the legislative branch and other 'outsiders' (particularly the media) any opportunity to interfere in its 'domestic' affairs. The military's anti-parliamentary attitude – which did nothing at all to help settle budgetary requests in favour of the armed forces – reflects the fact that the army had used its tanks against the legitimate Parliament and, in principle, could be ordered to do it again.[13]

In cultivating the identity of a *presidential institution* and jealously keeping itself outside of democratic control, the army was also separating and shielding itself from society. While the public, as well as the political elite, accepted with few reservations the guns of October 1993, an event that created a deep antagonism between society and the military as a presidential institution was the first Chechen war. That war also reinforced the transformation of military culture, which featured a peculiar mix of old bureaucratic patterns and new war-fighting skills, of deadly corridor intrigues and battlefield manoeuvring, of high regard for paperwork and low respect for human life. The war added new aggressively self-protective traits to that culture, since the army saw itself as 'betrayed' by society, which in turn was appalled by the brutal prosecution of the conflict, leaving the military in an isolation resembling ostracism. The defeat, while inflicting painful psychological traumas, was not accompanied by any sense of the need for critical self-reflection: the public was largely glad to forget about the war and the army was left alone to lick its wounds.

Overall, the trajectory of military developments from early 1992 to mid-1999 was one of decline and degradation. There were two clear points at which this trend could have been reversed: at the very start and at end of the first Chechen war. Political neglect of the problems accumulating in the armed forces was accentuated by the political abuse of military force, most seriously in Moscow in October 1993 and in Chechnia. Between 1994 and 1999 the state budgets seriously under-financed military structures, further reducing both the incentives and the means by which to implement reform. The military leadership was therefore forced to channel its resources primarily into covering personnel costs, abandoning investment in modernisation. The drastic fall in the procurement of all weapons systems resulted in the disappearance of the domestic market for the defence industry; and many of those elements of the defence industry which survived did so by re-orienting their production towards the export market.[14] Thus, during the second half of the 1990s, the formerly tightly-integrated Soviet military-industrial complex split into two barely connected parts. By the time Putin came to power in the autumn of 1999, the stance of the armed forces had become unsustainable, and further delays in revitalising and restructuring the military would seriously risk its disintegration.

The trajectory of regionalism

The very fact that the USSR had collapsed along its republican borders rendered Russia's federal arrangements *politically* uncertain as well as fragile. While only one 'subject' of the RF instantly opted for a secessionist path (the example was never tempting for others, even without the massive destruction which Chechnia suffered in two wars), the Russian leadership had serious worries about regional interpretations of Yeltsin's casual words: 'Take as much sovereignty as you can swallow.'[15] A new federal treaty was hastily prepared and signed in March 1992 (later made an annexe to the constitution), but it did not limit the political ambitions of regional leaders in any meaningful way. Many of them saw here a golden opportunity to get rid of central control in the confrontation between the president and the Parliament in the spring and summer of 1993, and advocated a 'zero option' (simultaneous resignation of the former and dissolution of the latter). Yeltsin's decision to use military force to resolve that crisis had a strong deterrent effect on the provincial *fronde*: the tank salvos resounding in Moscow resonated in every regional capital.

That forceful reconstitution of central authority was legitimised with the adaptation of the new constitution in December 1993, but gradually the regional leaders began to consolidate their control over their respective domains, taking maximum advantage of privatisation projects advanced by the Government. From this perspective, the main aim of Moscow in the first Chechen war was not to prevent disintegration (as claimed by official propaganda) but to strengthen central control through deterrence, reinforcing the 'tank message'.[16] The result, however, was strictly the opposite: the slow-moving military disaster weakened the centre and created space for a regional self-assertiveness just short of outright separatism, which by then was broadly perceived as troublesome and unnecessary. Yeltsin's re-election campaign in early 1996 involved the desperate 'suzerain' granting all sorts of concessions and special privileges to regional leaders. More importantly, regions began to elect their governors (instead of receiving appointees from Moscow), who from that moment embarked on consolidating their local power bases.[17]

That erosion of the centralised State stood in sharp contrast to the unifying impact of the Chechen war on the military.[18] The requirement to sustain combat operations, for which the armed forces were so ill-prepared, necessitated the mobilisation of all reserves and the deployment of composite units assembled from troops arriving from various military districts. Although the demands of the war were debilitating for the integrity of military structures in the medium term, they generated a strong centralisation impulse in 1995 which lasted perhaps until mid-1996. The practice of rotating combat units relatively quickly – sometimes after just three months of deployment – gave the armed forces across the whole country (except for the Strategic Rocket Forces and the navy, which sent only its marine battalions) a sense of being united by the war. The scale and intensity of the conflict greatly strengthened the war-fighting traits of military culture, including the high value placed on battlefield camaraderie and the low value on human life. The defeat, however, annulled that integrative momentum, uncertain as it was.

The armed forces were left mostly to their own devices, and it is precisely through that neglect that the effects of regionalism began to penetrate. The key agent was certainly the shortage of resources. Many observers started to notice that under-financing had multiple impacts, such as forcing many units to rely on a local draft, abandoning the system of officer rotation, encouraging the development of ties with local suppliers and tempting officers to take second jobs in the local markets. All of these factors encouraged the military to participate in the growth of regional networks.[19] But pauperisation, experienced through unpaid salaries, accumulating utility services' bills and crumpling logistics, was not the only incentive for the military to go 'native'. In addition to failing in its resource distribution function, the 'centre' (which for the military has always had an omnipotent and almost mystical significance) failed to perform its command and control role as well as its quintessential role of providing the armed forces with a purpose for its existence. The military's identity as a presidential institution became almost meaningless as the president lost interest in the armed forces. That identity crisis was aggravated by a crisis of professional culture, since the defeat in Chechnia deeply undermined the war-fighting ethos and 'warrior' style of the military.[20] Yeltsin's choice of a new defence minister confirmed this cultural trend: Marshal Sergeev had made his career in the Strategic Rocket Forces where diligence, efficiency and dedication were cultivated as the core values. Personifying the bureaucratic trait in military culture, Sergeev indeed showed little sympathy towards 'Chechen warriors'.

The combination of starvation, identity crisis and professional cultural conflict strongly pushed the military towards the regions, where dynamic economic processes went hand in hand with political *sovereignisation* and identity-building.[21] The main questions at that time were how fast the army would become enmeshed in regional political processes and how violent those would turn as a result.[22] The main limitations were in fact set by the scale of interests of the regional elites. While often tempted to make some grand gestures,[23] the regional leaders were in practical terms not especially interested in *privatising* expensive but not very usable military units. Their interests were much more focused on 'domesticating' the MVD and other law enforcement structures in their respective domains: the most attractive were the Special Purpose Militia Unit (*Otriad Militsii Osobogo Naznacheniia* – OMON) and the Special Rapid Reaction Unit (*Spetsial'nyi Otriad Bystrogo Reagirovaniia* – SOBR)[24]

The landmark event that reduced the ability of regional leaders to sustain their own 'armies' and forced them to scale down their ambitions for sovereignty was the August 1998 financial meltdown. While the instant reaction in the regions to that catastrophe was self-protective (such as erecting extra trade barriers or introducing their own *ersatz* money), in a matter of a few weeks they all flocked back to Moscow. The regional leaders pursued a coordinated strategy of recovery and gave their support to the new prime minister Evgenii Primakov, who in fact cherished such centralist ideas as doing away altogether with regional elections.[25] While the bankrupt regions had limited means with which to support military structures, the armed forces were also badly hit by the August 1998 crisis, and their deterioration towards complete disintegration continued unchecked and unnoticed.

Overall, the trend of regionalism developed through wide 'pendulum swings' during the 1990s,[26] and was most dangerously in synch with the military dislocation between mid-1997 and mid-1998.

Putin's re-centralisation and power-building

Vladimir Putin arrived at the summit of power in the autumn of 1999 (while Yeltsin was still nominally in charge) with very limited experience of leadership; what he *did* have was a grand vision of 'Great Russia' and two clear ideas: that military power is the key to restoring that 'greatness'; and that total centralised control is the only rational way of organising the State's affairs. While Putin as a political phenomenon remains open to interpretation, that the launching pad for his breathtaking rise was a war skilfully instrumentalised for 'patriotic mobilisation' is fundamentally important.

Putin took a great risk in unleashing the second Chechen war but was fortunate beyond the most optimistic expectations.[27] Russian society rallied behind the 'counter-terrorist operation' and the military did its best to deliver the requisite victories, seeking not only revenge for its humiliating defeat in the first Chechen war but to restore its weakened identity as a 'presidential institution'. The president indeed spared no effort in demonstrating his high regard for the army and his particular affection for military hardware. Apparently, he was sincerely convinced at that time that firm leadership and some extra money (which was indeed found) would suffice to re-invigorate the armed forces and eliminate the need for fundamental reform.[28] He even made an honest attempt to re-connect the parts of the military-industrial complex by persuading the directors of major enterprises that the army was a serious and privileged customer.[29] The top brass, first and foremost the 'Chechen generals', were able in the first half of 2000 to maintain the impression that the structural problems of the armed forces had been miraculously overcome. The moment of truth, however, arrived on 12 August 2000 with the *Kursk* catastrophe.

In the meantime, Putin was making determined efforts to arrest the trend of re-distributing power to the regions. His re-centralisation policy involved:

- tightening control over tax collection and budget allocation;
- nullifying the bi-lateral treaties between the federal centre and the 'subjects';

- cutting regional leaders down to size by denying them seats in the Federation Council; and
- the unrestrained use of the secret services and the prosecution of every regional maverick.[30]

What is particularly interesting for this analysis is that at the very start of his presidency Putin was already opting for the organisation of political space at a new level, decreeing the creation of seven federal districts intended to integrate the management of regional issues and military problems. The borders of these new districts coincided closely with those of military districts (and even more closely with the MVD's districts and most of the new presidential envoys had military or security services' backgrounds.[31] The clear aim was to reverse the tendency of many military units and law enforcement forces to 'go native'. The possibility of losing control over these districts (which, in the medium term, could become functional and semi-autonomous units) was dismissed as negligible.

Moving into the second half of his first term, Putin had to face the undeniable need to reform the armed forces, which had arrived at the familiar deadlock in Chechnia and had all but exhausted the positive momentum of the 'patriotic mobilisation'. He also had to admit that the professional military culture is increasingly defined by the warrior style of the 'Chechen generals' – but he was not comfortable at all with this brutal crowd.[32] Seeking to keep them in check, Putin replaced Defence Minister Sergeev with his most trusted 'lieutenant', Sergei Ivanov (very much a product of bureaucratic culture), and lessened the priority put on strategic nuclear forces through an emphasis on conventional capabilities. The fundamental assumption, however, was still that additional finance (which again was found in the budget, largely due to high oil revenues) would provide for a sufficient build-up of these capabilities, while the fundamental and inevitably painful reform of the armed forces could be postponed, perhaps even into the second presidential term. In the spring of 2003, Putin appeared ready to move beyond the minimalist aims, proclaiming military reform to be a top state priority in his address to the *Duma*.[33] However, six months later, he stepped back to the General Staff line, announcing that the reform of the military was over and that a 'normal build-up and modernisation' would duly continue.[34]

The federal reform, after such a dynamic start, was essentially stalled in 2002–3. On the one hand, there was no particular political need to push it further as the regional leaders showed the requisite loyalty to the Kremlin and eagerly resigned their powers to central control. On the other hand, it proved rather difficult to forge the newly created federal districts into a meaningful level of management, particularly since the distribution of resources continued through the old networks. The presidential envoys quickly established impressive headquarters and staffed them with their protégés, but found it difficult to keep their staff busy insofar as the real lines of control went directly between Moscow and the regional capitals. The intended integration of administrative and security functions also did not take place, the various 'power bureaucracies' jealously guarding their domains; for that matter, the merger of the Volga and the Urals military districts by September 2001 obviously violated the integrity of the seven-units design. Overall, the new structure increasingly appeared redundant and, therefore, was interpreted by experts as a fall-back position in the event that a sharp turn towards authoritarian methods of control were to be ordered by the Kremlin.[35]

Overall, by the start of his second term, Putin's regional reform had run out of steam while his military reform had yet to get off the ground. He had no particular reason to worry about regional developments, though he did have good reason to worry about sustaining economic growth and plenty of reasons to worry about the integrity of military structures. The war in Chechnia was a heavy burden and the quandary of launching a far-reaching military reform while in the middle of a war had no easy answer.

Changing course half-way?

It is, perhaps, necessary to emphasise that the US-led global war against terrorism, with all its heavy resonance and controversial strategy, did not by itself bring about any changes in Russia's policy. It did, however, accelerate the process that was already under way and trigger some decisions that had been maturing in the Kremlin. The autumn of 2001 did not, therefore, mark a mid-term correction of course, but the summer of 2003, probably, was a watershed in Putin's presidency, with a major shift from a security-centred to an economy-first paradigm: while the vision of Russia's 'greatness' persisted, its key content evolved from rebuilding a military super-power to establishing an energy 'powerhouse'.

Putin's strategy of 'economisation', while inconsistent and even paradox-ical in the context of the terrorism-driven 'securitisation' of the global agenda, has been unmistakable. The most crucial negotiations Russia has conducted were not in Brussels with NATO but in Vienna with the Organisation of Petroleum-Exporting Countries (OPEC) and in Geneva with the the World Trade Organisation (WTO). While evidently a part of Putin's own on-the-job learning process, this shift of priorities towards the economy has been taking him deeper and deeper into uncomfortably unfa-miliar territory, where he is dependent on advice and guidance from quarrel-some experts, none of whom he can really trust.[36]

The process has also been rich in internal contradictions, particularly since the expansion of market reforms inevitably involves liberalisation and the relaxing of central control. Such steps remain an anathema for Putin, who is a natural *dirigiste*. The focal point of these contradictions has been the so-called 'Iukos affair', which essentially defined the content and the outcome of the parliamentary elections in December 2003 and the presidential elections in March 2004. This affair (still continuing in the courts at the time of this writing) has signified the growth in the political influence of a narrow circle of Putin's courtiers and a redistribution of the property under their control – and both these trends are running against the course of Russia's modernisation.[37]

This half-hearted 'economisation', with its incompatible goals of growth and control, has had controversial consequences for the military. On the one hand, Putin has shown remarkable restraint towards many 'hard-to-swallow' security challenges made by the USA in its global anti-terrorist campaign, from the withdrawal from the Anti-Ballistic Missile (ABM) Treaty to the decision to advance the 'maximalist' second round of NATO enlargement to the military deployments in Central Asia and Georgia. On the other hand, he has lost interest in the development of doctrine (which was a kind of cottage industry sponsored by the Russian Security Council)[38] and has requested more emphasis on training, at times even pressing for real reforms in the military establishment. The main direction of these reforms has been set towards a gradual transition to a professional army, but it is exactly this design that invites the most determined resistance of the top brass.[39] This resistance has been instigated particularly by the fact that the Government has become reluctant to spend additional resources on the military, seeing more need to invest in basic economic assets as well as in social infrastructure.[40] What has made the reform drive even more uncertain is Putin's inability to find any way out of the Chechen quagmire. The war has become less controversial internationally in the context of anti-terrorist 'crusade', but no less burdensome and demoralising. Putin's intention to gear the reconstituted bureaucratic culture of the armed forces towards fundamental reforms appears seriously misplaced, while the resilience of the warrior culture – and, to an increasing degree, its hostility to any reforms – is constantly reinforced by the ongoing war.

Turning to regional developments and federal reforms, towards the end of Putin's first term we find very little of either. Apparently, this political dimension has been seriously de-prioritised and the regular meetings between the President and his seven 'envoys', all of whom are members of the Security Council, have become pretty much a pro-forma non-event.[41] The presidential administration may have drawn the conclusion that the readiness of most regional leaders to subscribe to every political slogan issued by the Kremlin means that the problem of regional opposition is reduced to an irrelevance. The impressive victory of the central bureaucracy over the regional elites could, however, turn out to be short-lived.[42] A major (perhaps, even *the* major) challenge for Putin's 'new course' is related to the task of creating more space for economic modernisation by significantly reducing the power of bureaucratic control. He is well aware that a key precondition for further reform is a meaningful de-bureaucratisation.[43] If implemented with sufficient consistency, this 'bureaucratic purge' is certain to encounter massive resistance from the overblown apparatus,[44] but that may be only a part of the problem for Putin (even leaving aside his personal difficulties in launching an attack against his own system). Another part of this problem inevitably will be the rapid reassertion of a high political profile on the part of the regional elites, emboldened by the self-made crisis of the central bureaucracy. A plain fact of current political life is that under the guise of servility the regional 'barons' have been continuing to consolidate control over their respective domains, where generally the fusion of economic and administrative power has advanced even further than in Moscow.

While at the beginning of Putin's new attempt at reform the connection between military and regional developments appears to be broken and as such irrelevant, it may be re-established and manifest itself in a range of sharp security challenges for Moscow as early as the second half of this decade.

The challenges ahead

Compiling a list of possible problems for Russia in the next 5–10 years might be an interesting analytical task,[45] but the focus of the present analysis has to remain on the interplay between regional trends and military transformations. The character of this interplay inevitably depends on the general design of state-building adopted and pursued by the Government. For instance, strong regional centres of power and weak military structures engender the risk of the *privatisation* of the army, while the opposite stance would stimulate 'warlordism'. There is no certainty – perhaps there can be none – about these designs, but for the purpose of this analysis three basic scenarios can be identified (without examining the 'drivers' that might force the shift from one to another)

- the advancement of market reform and the continuing rapprochement with the West;
- the reconstitution of a semi-authoritarian regime and essential self-isolation; and
- the combination of reforms and centralism, with ambivalent external orientation.

In the first of these scenarios, a military reform plan centred on a smaller professional army (perhaps numbering some 750,000) is advanced, despite resistance from the military. De-bureaucratisation is also seriously attempted, but the regional elites seize the opportunity to reclaim political power – and that becomes the main source of difficulty. In order to secure their position of power, some regional leaders might seek to take effective control over military instruments, targeting particularly those that are short-listed for scrapping by military planners in Moscow. After acquiring these capabilities, only a few regions might be tempted to use them for a power-play against Moscow, and then only in exceptional circumstances. Such circumstances could, for instance, involve *economic secessionism* when a region concludes that it would be much better off outside of any formal affiliation with Russia. Kaliningrad, drifting westward in the EU gravitation field, and Sakhalin, taking stock of its energy riches, are two possible candidates.[46] More probable are cases of inter-regional conflict with the use of newly acquired military instruments, driven by economic tensions, border disputes or nationalistic agendas. Possible candidates here are Krasnoiarskii *krai* against Tyva, Astrakhan *oblast'* against Kalmykiia or Kamchatka *oblast'* against Koriakskii *okrug*.

The second scenario involves a conscious and determined effort by the Kremlin to roll back democratic reforms and restore a vertically integrated centralised state. However, Putin (or his successor) may discover that the task of rebuilding a functional authoritarian regime is no easier than that of advancing democracy.[47] Quite possibly, the federal centre would be able to sustain the consolidation of control achieved in the first half of Putin's presidency and even strengthen it further, relying increasingly on the administrative levers concentrated in the seven federal districts. One of the main sources of trouble in this scheme could be deeper deterioration of the unreformed military structures, since the lack of resources for maintaining their existence is pretty much guaranteed to continue. The chain of military accidents that is already an habitual feature[48] could not only escalate but trigger full-blown mutinies in such militarised and 'hungry' regions as Murmansk and Kamchatka *oblasti*. The rich history of mutinies in the Russian Navy in the early twentieth century may provide some clues about the dynamics of such crises, but the presence of nuclear weapons – a natural target for the rebels – would increase the risks enormously.[49] An aggressive effort to achieve a military solution in Chechnia would lead to a broad destabilisation of both the north and the south Caucasus: Russian military units in this conflict zone might be increasingly *privatised* by local 'entrepreneurs'. Overall, the sharp change of course towards authoritarianism (however triggered) significantly increases the risks of Russia's implosion, where regional borders might become faultlines.

The third scenario amounts to the implementation of some reforms under strict central control, where political campaigning takes precedence over strategy and bureaucratic compromises are achieved on lowest common denominators. That would most probably suffice to get Putin safely through most of the second term, but towards the end of it many postponed problems might escalate in a multidimensional crisis. In the armed forces, gradual numerical cuts and the professionalising of some units would prevent a rapid deterioration, but the continuing painful pressure from Chechnia would lead to an erosion of integrity. In the regional perspective, the gaps between rich and poor units would widen, with several regions (including Moscow) growing self-confident and many others turning desperate. Of all the federal districts it is only the southern that might become a functional unit due to strengthening security coopera-tion between five *Russian* regions (Krasnodar and Stavropol' *krai*, Astrakhan, Rostov and Volgograd *oblasti*). This 'Alliance of Five' could increasingly take control of the military infrastructure of the North Caucasus Military District and thus acquire the capabilities for conducting its own wars (first of all against Chechnia), as well as its own foreign and security policy *vis-à-vis* Georgia (providing support to South Ossetia and Abkhazia) and even Ukraine (for instance, backing a new separatist drive in Crimea). Another area where serious troubles might accumulate is the far east where the combination of prolonged economic stagnation, political in-fighting coloured by nationalism, and the dislocation of extensive military structures creates an explosive mix. Primor'e and Sakhalin might reinvent the concept of the Far Eastern Republic and advance a solution to the Kurile problem with Japan in order to attract new investments and, more importantly, tacit Western security guarantees *vis-à-vis* China.

These three conflict-rich scenarios are certainly entirely hypothetical but the risks are real, while the Kremlin's ability to address them does not seem very convincing. Putin has resolved the centre–regions quandary only on a superficial level and has declared only an intention to advance military reform. He cannot find any resolution for the Chechen problem, which continues to erode both regional and military structures. In Russia's case, popularity and skilful campaigning are no substitute for a consistent modernisation strategy since both the federal arrangements and the military infrastructure remain too heavily burdened with the heritage of the Soviet era. Moving into the 'late teens' of its new life, Russia can rely neither on the continuity of old centralist patterns nor on the dynamism of new networks. Russia's integrity and even its survival remain uncertain propositions, and its military – under-resourced and overworked as it is – is one of the weakest elements in the chaos of state-building.

Notes

1 Perhaps the most solid research on this topic is W. Odom, *The Collapse of the Soviet Military* (New Haven, CT: Yale University Press, 1998).
2 For more detail see my book *The Russian Army in a Time of Troubles* (London: Sage, 1996).
3 See on that B. Taylor, 'Russian civil–military relations after the October uprising', *Survival*, 36:1 (1994), 3–29.
4 The best analysis of the impact of that war can be found in A. Lieven, *Chechnya: Tombstone of Russian Power* (New Haven, CT: Yale University Press, 1998).

5 See, for instance, A. Arbatov, 'Russia: military reform', in *SIPRI Yearbook 1999: Armaments, Disarmament and International Security* (Oxford: SIPRI–Oxford University Press, 1999), pp. 195–212.

6 The expectations of advancing meaningful reforms were at that point placed not so much on the new defence minister Sergeev, as on Andrei Kokoshin, who found himself in the key position of the secretary of the Security Council. His initiatives and, indeed, political career were cut short by the August 1998 financial melt-down.

7 While hesitant and incomplete, this step made it possible to deploy a relatively powerful grouping against Chechnia in the autumn of 1999; see M. Orr, 'New structures, old thinking', in M. Crutcher (ed.) *The Russian Armed Forces at the Dawn of the Millennium* (Carlisle Barracks, PA: US Army War College, 2000), pp. 159–70.

8 I looked into the available options for reforming Russia's military structures in a report for the Norwegian Defence Research Establishment, although the launch of a new Chechen war was, admittedly, unforeseen: P. Baev, 'Russian military development: muddle through from 1992 to 1998 and beyond', FFI Report 99/01229, Oslo, March 1999).

9 The deployment of the Topol-2M intercontinental ballistic missile (ICBM) was the only satisfactorily financed programme in the armed forces, and its importance was such as to make it a state symbol; see V. Iakovlev, 'New Russia's nuclear-missile philosophy for the XXI century', *Nezavisimaia gazeta* (12 February 1998).

10 The debates around the Joint Strategic Deterrence Command were uncharacter-istically sharp, and the crisis in Kosovo added greater urgency, with the special meeting of Russia's Security Council in late April 1999 devoted to the build-up of the country's nuclear capabilities. The final phase of these debates was the public clash between Sergeev and Kvashnin in July 2000; see A. Gol'ts, 'The last chance of the technocrat', *Itogi*, 30 (28 July 2000).

11 For a systematic and competent analysis see M. McFaul, *Russia's Unfinished Revolution: Political Change from Gorbachev to Putin* (Ithaca, NY: Cornell University Press, 2001).

12 It was certainly Yeltsin himself who carefully steered the military towards this identity. He was fully aware of his low personal prestige with the army but had the gut feeling that he might soon need its loyalty. On this identify formation see S. G. Simonsen, 'Marching to a different drum? Political orientation and nationalism in Russia's armed forces', *Communist Studies and Transition Politics*, 17:1 (2001), 43–64.

13 For a sharp analysis of this problem see chapter 9 ('Presidential or parliamentary armed forces?') of R. Barylski, *The Soldier in Russian Politics: Duty, Dictatorship, and Democracy under Gorbachev and Yeltsin* (New Brunswick, NJ: Transaction Publishers, 1998).

14 See chapter 6 by Julian Cooper in this volume. He has argued incisively that the integrity of the military–industrial complex (MIC), even in the Soviet times, should not be overestimated. See, for instance, his chapter 'The future role of the Russian defence industry', in R. Allison and C. Bluth (eds), *Security Dilemmas in Russia and Eurasia* (London: Royal Institute of International Affairs, 1998), pp. 94–117.

15 For a thorough analysis see part III of R. Sakwa, *Russian Politics and Society*, 2nd edn (London: Routledge, 1996), particularly pp. 183–8.

16 Leonid Smirniagin argued that 'the threat of disintegration in the 1980s and 1990s was due not to the aggrandizement of power by the regions, but to the weakening of central authority. However, the momentum of centrism was sufficient enough to avoid this danger by 1994:' J. Azrael and E. Pain (eds) *Conflict and Consensus in Ethno-Political and Center–Periphery Relations in Russia: Conference Proceedings*. (Santa Monica, CA: RAND Centre for Russian and Eurasian Studies, 1998), p. 3.

17 Examining these developments, Gail Lapidus warned: 'While a healthy dose of decentralisation was initially viewed as an important element of political democratisation, given a long tradition of hyper-centralisation of state power, Russia now faces an uncontrolled and seemingly uncontrollable unravelling of central power:' 'State building and state breakdown in Russia' in A. Brown (ed.) *Contemporary Russian Politics: A Reader* (Oxford: Oxford University Press, 2001), pp. 348–54, quoted from p. 350.

18 See E. Busza, 'State dysfunctionality, institutional decay, and the Russian military' in V. Sperling (ed.) *Building the Russian State* (Boulder, CO: Westview Press, 2000), pp. 113–36.

19 Thus, Martin Nicholson pointed out that 'the penury of the armed forces has made local commanders increasingly dependent on regional elites for pay, food and housing': 'Towards a Russia of the regions', *Adelphi Paper*, no. 330 (London: International Institute for Strategic Studies, 1999); for an earlier diagnosis, see T. Thomas, 'Fault lines and factions in the Russian army', *Orbis*, 39:4 (1995), 531–41.

20 For my more elaborate analysis of this identity crisis, see P. Baev, 'The plight of the Russian military: shallow identity and self-defeating culture', *Armed Forces & Society*, 29:1 (2002), 129–46.

21 On the latter see the chapters by Iurii Perfilev (on regional symbolism) and Nikolai Petrov (on vodka brands) in N. Petrov (ed.) *Regiony Rossii v 1999 g.* (Moscow: Carnegie Centre, 2001).

22 Alexei Arbatov looked into the possible consequences of deliberate as well as spontaneous regionalisation of the armed forces in his excellent article 'Military reform in Russia', *International Security*, 22:4 (1998), 83–134. My own speculations along these lines can be found in P. Baev, 'Why are the Russian power structures falling apart so slowly?', *Perspectives*, 13 (1999–2000), 91–104.

23 Aleksandr Lebed''s proposal to assume responsibility for strategic assets on the territory of Krasnoiarsk *krai* made headlines abroad, but while Iurii Luzhkov's generosity in financing the construction of a new strategic submarine and the housing projects in Sevastopol' attracted less attention, it can also be seen as an example of a regional politician exerting influence over military assets: see P. Baev, 'The Russian armed forces: failed reform attempts and creeping regionalization', in D. Betz and J. Löwenhardt (eds) *Army and State in Postcommunist Europe* (London: Frank Cass, 2001), pp. 23–42.

24 Mark Galeotti argued that these preferences of regional leaders could lead not so much to military warlordism but rather to 'multiple warlordism': 'Kalashnikov confederalism', *Jane's Intelligence Review*, 11:9 (September 1999), 8–9.

25 For a balanced and thought-provoking analysis see G. Herd, 'Russia: systemic transformation or federal collapse?' *Journal of Peace Research*, 36:3 (1999), 259–69 (and the follow-up debate in the January 2001 issue of the same journal).

26 Nikolai Petrov described this 'pendulum' model in detail in his chapter 'The center–regions relations', in N. Petrov (ed.) *Regiony Rossii v 1998* (Moscow: Carnegie Centre, 1999), pp. 57–74.

27 Mikhail Alexseev (chapter 4, this volume) provides an interesting conceptual perspective on this gamble.

28 I examined that blunder in my chapter 'The Russian Army and Chechnya: victory instead of reform?', in S. Cimbala (ed.) *The Russian Military into the Twenty-First Century* (London and Portland: Frank Cass, 2001), pp. 75–95.

29 For a critical analysis of the key speech in Nizhnii Novgorod see V. Shlikov, 'Inescapable complex', *Itogi*, 19 (12 May 2000).

30 For an incisive overview, see V. Gelman, 'The rise and fall of federal reform in Russia', *PONARS Memo*, no. 238 (Washington, DC: CSIS, December 2001).

31 For an insightful analysis of the security elements of this design, see A. Gol'ts, 'Seven jokers in one pack', *Itogi*, 21 (26 May 2000); A. Gol'ts and D. Pinsker, 'The Babylonian vertical', *Itogi*, 35 (15 August 2000).

32 I looked into the nuances of these relations in 'Putin's court: how the military fits in', *PONARS Memo* no. 153 (Washington, DC: Council on Foreign Relations, November 2000); and 'President Putin and his generals', *PONARS Memo* no. 205 (Washington, DC: CSIS, November 2001).

33 I have examined the content of that priority in 'The trajectory of the Russian military: downsizing, degeneration, and defeat', in S. Miller and D. Trenin (eds) *The Russian Military: Power and Policy* (Cambridge, MA: Harvard University Press, 2004).

34 Putin's tactical retreat was tacitly challenged by the extensive and far-reaching proposals in the report by the Council on Foreign and Defence Policy – 'Military build-up and modernization of Russian armed forces' (April 2004), available online: www.svop.ru/live/materials.asp?m_id=9719&r_id=9720.

35 For an informed analysis of the federal districts as structures of a 'police state', see N. Petrov, 'Seven faces of Putin's Russia', *Security Dialogue*, 33:1 (2002), 73–91.

36 Egor Gaidar, one of the few serious economic thinkers in Russia, speaking at a conference in March 2002, noted that the logic of every reform process determined that 'the ability of any government to conduct deep structural reforms is limited and inevitably begins to decrease after a year and a half.': 'Attempts to increase the growth by non-trivial methods are unproductive', *PolitRu*, (22 March 2002), available online: www.polit.ru/documents/47630.html.

37 The literature on the 'Iukos affair' is considerable and growing daily; for a concise analysis see V. Volkov, 'The Iukos affair: Terminating the implicit contract', *PONARS Memo*, no. 307, and B. Taylor, 'Putin's state-building project: issues for the second term', *PONARS Memo*, no. 323, both available online: www.csis.org/ruseura/ponars/policymemos/pm_index.cfm.

38 See on that S. Blank, 'The new turn in Russian defense policy', in Cimbala, *The Russian Military into the Twenty-First Century*, pp. 53–73.

39 For a competent argument in favor of a professional army, see I. Golotiuk, 'Military shrewdness', *PolitRu* (7 March 2003), available online: www.polit.ru/documets/473874.html.

40 Giving a net assessment of the status of Russian armed forces for the US Senate Armed Services Committee, Vice Admiral Thomas R. Wilson, Director of the Defense Intelligence Agency, asserted that 'this level of spending is not enough to fix the Russian military', while 'the process of allocating monies remained extremely erratic and inefficient': 'Global threats and challenges', in *Johnson's Russia List*, no. 6144 (20 March 2002).

41 See N. Petrov, 'Policization versus democratization: 20 months of Putin's "federal" reform', *PONARS Memo*, no. 241 (Washington: CSIS, December 2001).

42 An updated and multiperspective analysis of this problem can be found in A. Aldis and G. Herd (eds) *Russian Regions and Regionalism: Strength Through Weakness?* (London: Curzon, 2002).

43 As Vladimir Ryzhkov, one of very few *Duma* deputies capable of independent analysis, argued: 'Putin's plan to modernize the country by means of a strengthened and disciplined bureaucracy is unrealizable. In fact, it is a contradiction in terms': V. Ryzhkov, 'No modernization without representation', *Moscow Times* (22 March 2002).

44 Advocating such a purge, Goyal argued that 'Putin's biggest problem is the Russian bureaucrats – the *apparat* – the prosecutors, generals and armies of clerks with seals and stamps [who] developed a thick skin through decades of communism and withstood all the irritations of Gorbachev's and Yeltsin's reforms': A. Goyal, 'Putin's perestroika also headed for history', *The Russia Journal* (15–21 March 2002).

45 I indulged myself by engaging in this exercise while preparing a paper entitled 'Russia: super-power turns battleground' for the US DTRA study *All Our Tomorrows* (presented in July 2001), that was later published by the Norwegian Defence Studies Institute: P. Baev, *Russia in 2015: Could the Former Super-Power Turn into a Battle-Ground?* (Oslo: Forsvarsstudier, April 2002).

46 On the problems of Kaliningrad, see J. Baxendale, S. Dewar and D. Gowan (eds) *The EU and Kaliningrad* (London: Federal Trust, 2000); on Sakhalin, see V. Supian and M. Nosov, 'Reintegration of an abandoned fortress: economic security of the Russian far east', in G. Rozman, M. Nosov and K. Watanabe (eds) *Russia and East Asia* (Armonk, NY: M. E. Sharpe, 1999), pp. 69–100.

47 Thus, Stephen Holmes, emphasising the problems of creating an authoritarian regime in Russia 'because the underlying situation remains forbiddingly difficult', warned that Putin is 'fabricating an illusion of power' which brings only 'a simulacrum of societal order': S. Holmes, 'Simulations of power in Putin's Russia', *Current History*, 100:648 (October 2001), 307–12.

48 For an updated record see the section on military accidents in *GraniRu*, online: www.grani.ru/incidents/articles.

49 As Stephen Cohen observed somewhat philosophically: 'For the first time in history, a fully nuclearized nation is in the process of collapse. The result is potentially catastrophic': S. Cohen, 'Russian nuclear roulette', *The Nation* (25 June 2001).

Society–military relations in Russia: the economic dimension

Introduction

Over a period of almost fifteen years, Russia has been undergoing a transition from a highly militarised economy to one with a relatively modest resource commitment to defence. The former was based on almost total state ownership, administrative allocation of physical resources and decision-making processes in relation to the military economy that totally excluded public participation and were concealed from society by an extraordinarily comprehensive regime of secrecy. In the new institutionally weak market economy, priority has shifted away from the military and decision-making has become more open. However, in relation to the military economy it has not been easy to break from practices and attitudes of the Soviet past. Society's access to information on the economic dimension of military power and its ability to influence decisions in this sphere have been contested since the end of the communist system and this contestation remains a feature of life in Russia under President Putin. This chapter provides an analysis of the evolution of the economic dimension of society-military relations in Russia since the collapse of the USSR, but to set the scene it opens with a consideration of the extent to which the economy has been demilitarised since the mid-1980s when Gorbachev came to power.

Taming the 'monster'

In the final years of the USSR it became common to characterise the Soviet military economy as a *molokh* (Gorbachev), or, in one controversial *Moscow News* article, a 'monster'.[1] In Gorbachev's words, 'In the recent Five-Year Plans, military expenditure rose twice as fast as the Gross National Product (GNP). This *Molokh* devoured the fruits of hard labour and mercilessly exploited the industrial plant …'.[2] It was Gorbachev in 1988 who began the process of scaling down the resource commitment to defence. As the performance of the economy deteriorated from 1990, the

pace of downsizing accelerated. The percentage of the State's budget
devoted to defence was reduced and the output of the defence industry, and
its labour force, began to contract. But the real turning point was Egor
Gaidar's decision, with the backing of Yeltsin, in early 1992 to reduce by
two-thirds the spending on weapons procurement for the armed forces.
Thereafter, in circumstances of severe economic decline and a deep budgetary crisis, military spending fell steadily in real terms, dropping to less than
one-third of the 1991 level by 1998. Starved of funding, the vast defence
industry underwent a process of spontaneous contraction. Wages of defence
industry personnel, which in Soviet times were above the industrial average,
fell dramatically. Many workers, especially young people with skills which
could be used in the emerging market economy, left in search of better
prospects. While there was some recovery of military spending and defence
industry output after 1999, the latter almost entirely a product of increased
arms exports, the overall scale of the military economy was very substantially smaller than in Soviet times, as can be seen from table 6.1. It must be
stressed that the data in this table are approximate, but they nevertheless are
considered to provide a reasonably accurate overview of the general trends.
The downsizing would be even more dramatic if evidence of equivalent
accuracy were available for 1985, before Gorbachev's cuts. In Russia at the
start of the twenty-first century, total spending on defence as a share of gross
domestic product (GDP) was about one-quarter of the Soviet level of the
mid-1980s, defence industry employment was one-third of the 1990 level,
and its share of total industrial employment was halved.

With little new recruitment, the workforce of the defence industry has
aged inexorably and further contraction is likely. Major factors here are pay,
prospects and status. Whereas defence industry personnel in Soviet times
saw themselves as an elite, with an average monthly wage in 1985, 5 per
cent higher than the average for industry as a whole, in 2001 the military
sector's wage was only 80 per cent of the industrial average and even less if a
small number of successful export companies are excluded.

In one respect, however, the military sector has maintained its share: it is
still responsible for a very large proportion of the total research and development (R&D) undertaken in the country. In the USSR in 1990 almost 80
per cent of industrial R&D was performed by the defence industry and
almost 70 per cent of this was for military purposes.[3] In Russia in 2001 the
defence industry still employed 54 per cent of the country's scientific personnel.[4] However, overall national spending on R&D has fallen sharply, both in
real terms and as a proportion of GDP, and by 2001 the number of people
engaged in defence sector R&D was only one-third of the 1991 total.

Thus over 10–15 years, through starvation and neglect rather than the
pursuit of any coherent policy, the 'monster' has shrunk and no longer presents a threat to Russia's economic prosperity. There are occasional calls for
a substantial increase in military expenditure, for example, in response to

Table 6.1 The Soviet and Russian military economies

	USSR 1990	RF 1990	RF 2001
Number employed in defence industry[a]	8,270,000	6,075,000	2,040,000
Industry	6,815,000	4,775,000	1,580,000
R&D	1,465,000	1,300,000	460,000
Employment in defence industry as % of total employment in the economy	7.3	8.1	3.0
Defence industrial employment as % of total industrial employment	19.3	20.9	10.8
Average monthly wage in defence industry as % of average wage in industry	97[b]	85[c,d]	78
Average age of defence industry employees		39	58
Output of the defence industry as % of total industrial output	12	no data	6
Inc military output	6		3
Arms exports ($mn)	c.16,000	7,100[d]	3,705
% of total exports	16.5	13.9	3.6
Expenditure on 'national defence'[e,f] as % of GDP	7.1	5.9[d]	3.2
In real terms, 1991 = 100		100	41

[a] Excluding nuclear industry: note: peak, mid-1980s, including nuclear industry, 10,450,000 employed, of whom 5.8 million were working directly in production of weapons and other military equipment; 8.9% of total employment and, with an estimated 8.6 million in industry, 23% of total industrial employment. [b] 1985, 105%. [c] Lowest point, 59%, June 1995. [d] 1991. [e] Including pensions of servicemen. [f] With account of all other military spending, USSR 1990: 12.3%; using same methodology, 1987: 16.6% (source: Julian Cooper, 'The military expenditure of the USSR and Russian Federation, 1987–97', in *SIPRI Yearbook 1998* (Oxford: SIPRI–Oxford University Press,1998), p. 246. Russia on similar basis, 2001: 4.1% (*SIPRI Yearbook 2001*, p. 314). Sources[5]

the war against Iraq in 2003, when the State *Duma* Defence Committee urged an increase in spending on national defence from 2.6 to 3.5 per cent of GDP on the grounds that the conflict brought a threat to Russia's national security, but Putin has resisted such pressure. At a session of the Security Council in February 2003 he declared: 'Our defence outlays must not fall on the people as a burden, obstruct economic growth and the resolution of social problems'.[6]

Civil engagement with the economic dimension of the military and national security

In any democratic society it is important that there should be civilian control over military spending and other economic aspects of national security. For public accountability and good civil–military relations there needs to be transparent and reliable information about the economic dimension of the military. Such openness can be helpful to the military itself in so far as it can promote a better understanding in society of its place and role, helping to overcome public suspicion that the military leadership, or military–industrial complex (MIC), is pursuing its own interests. In a society in transition from an over-militarised economy and an almost total lack of accountability, the development of institutions for democratic control, together with greater transparency, is an essential component of the process of transformation.

There are several dimensions to this process. Central is the issue of the defence budget: the process of its adoption by Parliament; its content; and the level of accountability to tax-payers and society in general. What is required is detailed and reliable information, the possibility of the full involvement of members of Parliament, and the ability of Parliament to investigate actual spending and hold the military or defence industry to account in the event of failure or abuse. However, in most countries there are limits to transparency, especially in relation to new and sensitive R&D programmes, which are often classified. Accountability also has an international dimension. There is now a well-established procedure according to which countries report their military spending to the United Nations (UN), and members of NATO and the OSCE have similar obligations to their own institutions.

It is generally accepted in democratic societies that citizens have a right to know basic economic information pertaining to the defence industry, such as its scale, employment, structure, role in the economy, environmental impact, etc. Clearly there are limits to transparency relating to both national security and commercial interests, and these considerations also apply to information about arms exports, which are often sensitive from a policy point of view. Here there are also issues of international accountability: most developed countries now make returns to the UN register of conventional arms sales, which came into effect from January 1992. Finally, shrouded in almost total secrecy, the USSR had an extraordinarily developed system of mobilisation preparation, i.e. planned measures to increase the scale of military production rapidly in the event of war or other national emergency. At various times during the period since 1945 the USA and other countries also had systems of mobilisation preparation, but on a far more modest scale and with less pervasive secrecy. Given the Soviet experience, this is a dimension of society-military relations that requires consideration: citizens have a right to know if their country possesses a mobilisation system that hampers economic development and holds back living standards.

The Soviet legacy

In the USSR the military economy impinged on the lives of every citizen but hardly anyone had access to information permitting an assessment of its true scale, and the main decisions about its development were taken by a very small number of Communist Party and government leaders in total secrecy. Gorbachev confirmed the extent to which the military burden on the economy was concealed, even from members of the *Politburo*. When Iurii Andropov was general secretary, he 'did not allow us [Ryzhkov, Dolgikh and Gorbachev] to approach the budget and data on military expenditures'.[7] In his memoirs Gorbachev observed: 'All statistics concerning the military–industrial complex were top secret, inaccessible even to the members of the Politburo ... only two or three people had access to data on the military–industrial complex'.[8] Even for him it was a revelation:

> I did not realize the true scale of the militarization of the country until I became General Secretary. Finally, although the leaders of the MIC ... opposed it, we published those data. It turned out that military expenditure was not sixteen per cent of the state budget, as we had been told, but rather forty per cent; and its production was not six per cent but twenty per cent of the gross national product'.[9]

However, Gorbachev has not explained the origin of the 40 per cent and 20 per cent figures, which were not those published when he was in office.

One problem the Gorbachev team found on coming to power was that it was the Communist Party's Central Committee, not the Soviet Government, which had a near monopoly on matters concerned with the military economy and its control. Nikolai Ryzhkov, prime minister for most of the Gorbachev period, has acknowledged that he had no real say in defence industry matters and had to struggle to wrest the Military–Industrial Commission (*voenno–promyshlennaia kommissiia*, or VPK) from the Central Committee structures, bringing it more under the control of the Council of Ministers. In this he was aided by Iurii Masliukov, appointed chair of the VPK in November 1985.[10]

Prior to 1989 the only figure on military spending made available to the public and, it appears, even the *Politburo*, was misinformation. There was no defence budget in the normal sense. The armed forces were funded through separate chapters of the state budget without any attempt to derive a meaningful aggregate figure. The published figure referred only to the operations and maintenance of the *Minoborony*. All spending on arms procurement, for example, was allocated directly to the defence industry. There have been hints that prior to 1988 there was some kind of summary, but this was considered a secret of special state significance available only to the leadership of *Gosplan* and some members of the *Politburo*. The figures could not be printed or copied and were passed to the authorised recipients by hand.[11]

It appears that Gorbachev began to work towards cuts in military spending from the spring of 1987. A former deputy chair of the VPK claims that it was at this time that Iurii Masliukov (chair of the VPK) came from a meeting with Ryzhkov and said that Gorbachev wanted proposals for cutting defence spending from 13 or 14 per cent of GNP to 10 per cent within 3 years.[12] However, it was not until November 1988 that Gorbachev ordered the MOD to prepare specific plans for force reductions, which were revealed the following month in his speech to the UN's General Assembly. Foreign Minister Eduard Shevardnadze appears to have played a significant role in this decision. Frustrated by his inability to obtain reliable information from the military on the scale of the armed forces and their holdings of weapons, in October he sent a memo to Gorbachev claiming that the military was deceiving him. This appears to have strengthened Gorbachev's resolve to take action.[13]

By this time Gorbachev must have seen the consolidated figures for defence spending prepared by Masliukov and others using the broad parameters of UN standards.[14] The 1989 defence budget on this new basis was made public by Gorbachev at the First Congress of People's Deputies of the USSR in May 1989 and shortly after Ryzhkov and then Chief of the General Staff Mikhail Moiseev provided more details.[15] This was a breakthrough, but the new figure, 77.3 billion roubles, immediately provoked controversy, starting a public debate which continued until the fall of the USSR.

This new openness prompted the first ever opinion poll on defence spending in the summer of 1989, undertaken by telephone in Moscow and five other major cities: 'do you consider the (planned) fourteen per cent reduction in military spending sufficient? It revealed a very wide divergence of opinion: yes, sufficient – Kiev 46 per cent, Alma-Ata 45, Moscow 42, Leningrad, 31, Tallinn 16, Tbilisi 10 per cent; no, insufficient – Tallinn 66 per cent, Tbilisi 60, Moscow 33, Leningrad 31, Kiev 29, Alma-Ata 27; against any cuts – Moscow 9 per cent, Tallinn 2, and Tbilisi 1 per cent.[16] These responses foreshadowed the forthcoming fragmentation of the Union.

During the years 1989–91 the range of information about the military economy made available to members of Parliament and the public steadily increased, but the military leadership did not meet this development with enthusiasm. The new figures for military spending were challenged by independent observers and for the first time military specialists found themselves having to respond in public, at times providing additional new information.[17] Another first came in December 1989 when V. N. Bab'ev, head of the central financial directorate of the Ministry of Defence, answered questions on Soviet military spending at a press briefing.[18] Bab'ev later revealed that 'it was like a bolt from the blue' – he was given just an hour's warning that he had to appear at the Ministry of Foreign Affairs (*Ministerstvo inostrannyykh del* – MID) press centre.[19] This was related to another significant event: in December 1989, in connection with the adoption of the federal budget for 1990, the MOD issued an official communication, published in the press, setting out the main headings of the defence budget and adding for the first time quantitative details of the USSR's strategic and conventional stocks of weapons.[20]

At times discussion became acrimonious. Georgii Arbatov, director of the USA–Canada Institute of the Academy of Sciences (*Institut SShA i Kanady*), charged the military with concealing the true scale of military spending, provoking an angry response from Chief of the General Staff Sergei Akhromeev. The legacy of secrecy was such that many independent specialists were simply unable to believe that the authorities were now providing accurate information. They suspected that the military burden was still being substantially understated; indeed, from his memoirs one suspects that even Gorbachev held this view. The problems of measurement were formidable. Many items of military spending were included in non-defence chapters of the budget. The new 'defence budget' referred only to the MOD forces and not the forces of other 'power ministries', in particular those of the MVD and the KGB (Committee of State Security), and any true assessment of the actual military burden was rendered all but impossible by the distorted, administratively fixed prices, in particular the artificially low prices of armaments and other military hardware.

Another legacy of the Soviet past also limited the quality of public debate: expertise on military–economic matters had been a virtual monopoly of the military and the specialist Communist Party and government agencies directly associated with the defence industry, arms exports and other economic aspects of the military effort. This had not always been the case. From 1960 to 1983 the Institute of World Economy and International Relations (*Institut Mirovoi Ekonomiki i Mezhdunarodnykh Otnoshenii* – IMEMO) of the USSR Academy of Sciences had a specialised military–economic research unit, the Department of Technical-Economic Research (*Otdel Tekhnicheskogo Ekonomicheskogo Issledovaniia* – OTEI). At first it maintained close links with the Military Intelligence Directorate (*Glavnoe Razvedyvatel'noe Upravlenie* – GRU), but later lost access to information. By the early 1970s it had a staff of almost 400 and was home to some of the independent specialists prominent in the Gorbachev period, notably Sergei Blagovolin, at one time director of OTEI.[21] According to Vitalii Shlykov, former GRU specialist on mobilisation preparation, IMEMO, the USA–Canada Institute and other academic centres became reluctant to undertake work involving access to secret information, as they knew that it would make difficult, if not impossible, foreign travel and access to foreigners more generally for the staff involved.[22] However, in the late Gorbachev years some independent academic expertise did develop, notable figures being Blagovolin and Kseniia Gonchar of IMEMO, Aleksei Iziumov of the USA–Canada Institute, economists at the Institute of National Economic Forecasting, in particular its director, the late Iurii Iaremenko, and his colleagues Aleksandr Ozhegov and Evgenii Rogovskii, and Aleksei Kireev, an economist working in the structures of the CC CPSU.

The phenomenon of 'export' *glasnost'* emerged – revelations about the military economy made to foreigners, sometimes by military leaders themselves, but not to the Soviet public. Thus, Akhromeev revealed figures on the Soviet defence effort at hearings of the US Congress in 1989 at a time when the same data were classified for Soviet parliamentarians.[23] In May 1989 the USSR supplied some data on the defence industry to the ILO as a limited response to an ILO questionnaire of 1984. However, this new information was not published in the USSR.[24] At times this process operated in another form: in 1990 Richard Cheney, then US defence secretary, spoke in the Kremlin to Soviet parliamentarians and revealed details of the volume of Soviet production of missiles, submarines, etc., then considered secret in the USSR.[25]

On other aspects of the military economy, apart from the defence budget, very little was made public before the end of the USSR. The limited information on the defence industry related mainly to its civilian activities and plans for 'conversion'. Arms exports were shrouded in almost total secrecy until the beginning of 1991, when a few details of their scale were provided for the first time by the then chair of the VPK, Igor Belousov.[26] However, there was a growing suspicion in reform-orientated circles that the large transfers of Soviet arms reported by the US Arms Control and Disarmament Agency and the Stockholm International Peace Research Institute (SIPRI) were misleading, bearing little relation to actual export earnings.[27] This was later confirmed: during the 1980s arms deliveries were $21–2 billion a year, but actual hard currency receipts only $1.8–2.0 billion.[28]

Perhaps the most sensitive and secret of all aspects of the Soviet military economy was the extraordinarily comprehensive system of mobilisation preparation. This system, which had its origins in the 1920s, had an impact on many aspects of the economy and society.[29] Many enterprises of both the defence industry and the civil economy were obliged to maintain substantial spare capacities convertible in the event of national emergency to the production of armaments and other military hardware, together with stocks of raw materials and components. Many defence plants used part of this spare capacity for the production of consumer goods and other civil products. These were often of poor quality as they were not manufactured with the use of appropriate specialised equipment, while civilian enterprises at times produced goods close in design and production technology to military items, e.g. heavy-tracked tractors, compatible with the production of armoured vehicles.[30] The scale of the mobilisation capacities and stocks were, and still are, a matter of the very strictest secrecy. The maintenance of these spare and dual-use capacities raised the cost of production, lowered productivity and had a negative impact on the living standards of Soviet citizens.

The General Staff justified the maintenance of vast mobilisation capacities on the basis of extravagantly overstated estimates of the mobilisation potential of the USA and other NATO countries, estimates produced by analysts of a research institute of the GRU. A former prominent figure in this GRU system, Vitalii Shlykov, a department head of the institute, has provided a vivid account of its methods and of his own attempts, ultimately futile, to reform them.[31] In the late Soviet period the mobilisation system was very rarely mentioned in open publications, and it was Shlykov who first discussed the mobilisation system in detail in January 1991.[32] Later in the year he characterised the Soviet mobilisation preparedness system as a 'sacred cow', the basic principles of which had remained unchanged from the 1930s.[33] Given the stance of the General Staff and the KGB, this initiative of Shlykov was an act of considerable civic courage.

Public accountability

In time the release of additional information led to a larger role for Parliament in considering the draft state budget for defence. This began cautiously. The Committee for Defence and State Security in the autumn of 1989 considered the defence budget for 1990 in some detail and heard addresses by Defence Minister Iazov and Chief of the General Staff Moiseev, but the session was closed and no record taken of its proceedings.[34] In February 1990 Moiseev acknowledged that money for defence was not always used effectively, due in part to weak public oversight of military expenditures which was in turn the result of excessive secrecy. He argued that the situation had now changed. Spending would be considered by the Committee of the Supreme Soviet for Defence and State Security and at full sessions of the Supreme Soviet, and Moiseev undertook that the MOD would report regularly to parliament on its actual spending.[35] This was an overstatement of the reality at that time, but in December 1990 the Committee of the Supreme Soviet for Defence and State Security did examine the draft defence budget for the following year article by article and urged increased spending on R&D. [36] Something approaching genuine budget politics did emerge for the first time with the 1991 draft defence budget. Open discussions took place with the participation of reform-minded economists, for example Sergei Aleksashenko and Evgenii Iasin.[37] Furthermore, the appendix to the draft budget on military spending was published in detail for the first time, including a breakdown of spending on operations and maintenance. [38]

A feature of Soviet life was the resort to *dual* publication, the practice of producing two editions of publications, the one unclassified, the other classified – the latter containing military–economic material excluded from the former. This applied in particular to decrees of the USSR Government: for example, the public at large had access to *Sobranie zakonov*, but a limited number of restricted *Postanovleniia Soveta Ministrov SSSR* were issued monthly 'for official use only'. Here almost all decrees appeared in full, including those covering defence economic matters, and issues were numbered for identification of the small circle of recipients.[39] Within the military–economic community it became the convention to issue reports and other materials with distinctive orange covers, providing instant warning that they were classified. This colour was used for the cover of the first official journal on the economics and conversion of the defence industry made available to a wider audience, *Voprosy ekonomiki i konversii*, issued by the Central Research Institute for the Economics and Conversion of Military Production *(Tsentral'nyi nauchno-issledovatel'skii institut ekonomiki i konversii voennogo proizvodstva* – TsNIIEiK). This journal first appeared in 1989, initially on a restricted basis with very general articles, but over time – especially after 1991 – it became increasingly informative.[40] It is no longer published. There was also a monthly journal, *Konversiia*, on defence industry conversion in the late Soviet years, but again it was not very informative until 1992.

The USSR first supplied data to the UN on military spending for the year 1989, in accordance with the standardised form of reporting adopted by the UN in December 1980. This first report, supplied to the UN by the MID in October 1990, was published in full in the Soviet press.[41] This was a major innovation, as for the first time it provided a breakdown of spending by service (with the exception of the strategic missile forces) and spending on procurement by main types of weapon system. A similar report for 1990 was supplied, but with less publicity, but, unsurprisingly, there was no report for 1991. A second significant form of international transparency, the UN Register of Conventional Arms, recording basic arms exports, was initiated after the collapse of the USSR. Whether the USSR would have provided a report on exports can be a matter of speculation only, but one suspects that any such report would have given a bare minimum of detail.

Under Gorbachev the first hesitant steps were taken in changing the military-society relationship in respect of its economic dimension. While the public and parliamentarians were provided with some new information on military spending, and a nascent budgetary politics emerged, it was still very difficult for anyone in society, even in the top political leadership, to gain even an approximatiion of the real extent to which the economy was militarised. Other aspects of the military economy – arms production and exports and the mobilisation system – were still almost completely opaque, although the final years of the USSR did see the emergence of some new civilian expertise on military–economic issues. In the absence of reliable information and in circumstances of a general mistrust of the authorities, it became common in more radical democratic circles to promote an exaggerated view of the scale of the military economy, presenting it as the *molokh* sucking the life blood from the Soviet economy and society. It is not surprising that when the system collapsed the new regime in Russia did not find it easy to come to terms with this legacy of Soviet communism.

The evolution of military–economic transparency and civilian engagement in the RF

The break up of the USSR was followed by a brief transition period during which responsibility for funding its vast defence effort was uncertain, but by the spring of 1992 it became clear that all the newly independent states were now responsible for their own defence budgets. In the RF there was a general expectation among reformers that military spending would be cut back, but surprisingly little public debate. It is known that some argued for a complete freeze on spending on weapons procurement on the grounds that stocks were more than adequate and that a cessation of budget spending would shock the defence industry into a major downsizing and restructuring. This was the view, for example, of Vitalii Shlykov, then deputy chair of the State Committee for Defence, the predecessor to the Russian MOD created in spring 1992.[42] In the event, First Deputy Prime Minister Egor Gaidar decided in March 1992 to cut military spending severely, with a two-thirds reduction of spending on weapons procurement. The impact of the latter on the defence industry was initially blunted by a very substantial order for arms to be exported – an order that was totally unrealistic and led to the accumulation of stocks of unsold weapons that enterprises had produced without payment, exacerbating the industry's already acute difficulties.

The defence budget and budgetary politics: advances and retreats
Russia's first real defence budget was debated and adopted by Parliament in 1992. It followed the late-Soviet practice of providing details of proposed spending under broad headings:

- operations and maintenance;
- procurement;
- R&D;
- military construction;
- pensions of servicemen;[43]
- spending of the Ministry of Atomic Energy on the development and production of nuclear devices.

However, whereas the 1991 Soviet defence budget had been made available in some detail and had been subject to discussion, as noted above, the first Russian budget was non-transparent and was adopted with very little debate, either in Parliament or more widely in society. This was not an encouraging start. However, the adoption of the 1993 federal budget saw more discussion of the chapter 'national defence', and with it the beginnings of some genuine budgetary politics; it started what was to become an annual process. First the MOD put forward a claim for resources far in excess of the allocation made by the *Minfin* in the draft budget. This allocation was then challenged within

Parliament and in the press, in particular in the military newspaper *Krasnaia zvezda*. In some cases *Minfin* would give way to this lobbying pressure, but only to a very limited extent, leaving the MOD unsatisfied and resentful.[44]

Vital for informed debate and meaningful budgetary politics is the availability of information about the military budget, not simply by broad headings, but with line by line detail within those headings. In this respect, progress in Russia since 1992 has been limited, with both advances and retreats. During the period 1992-97, aggregate budget allocations to procurement, R&D and construction were made public, although even for members of parliament details were sparse or non-existent. For the 1998 federal budget even the summary information about spending on procurement, R&D and construction was classified, and this remained the case with the budget for 2003. In this respect, Russian practice falls far short of that typical of most developed democratic countries. It should also be noted that there is an almost total lack of transparency about additional non-budgetary incomes of the MOD (or of other forces), although occasionally figures are revealed for the MOD's earnings from the sale both of surplus property and of civilian goods produced by military repair factories.

Was more detail made available to deputies of the *Duma*? The author has a copy of the official October 1994 *Minfin* submission to the *Duma* of the draft budget for 1995. The appendix to the chapter on 'national defence' had no more detail than was provided in the version of the draft budget published at that time, making it very difficult to speak of any meaningful parliamentary control. The document does contain some information, however, on the authorised number (*shtat*) of servicemen in the MOD and other forces in 1995. For the 1996 budget there was a change: it is known that the appendix on military spending was enlarged, with ten lines introduced for the item 'maintenance of the armed forces'.[45]

Initially this secrecy did not go without challenge. As early as September 1992, two experienced economists formerly working within the armed forces, Efim Liuboshits and Vitalii Tsymbal, noted that whereas there were many Russian specialists on the US defence budget, including Andrei Kokoshin, former deputy director of the USA–Canada Institute of the Academy of Sciences (and from April 1992 to May 1997 first deputy minister of defence), there was a dearth of specialism on the Russian defence budget. They argued that the defence budget could not be left to the MOD and that it was essential to have independent external monitoring and control. However, they identified a serious obstacle: the lack of relevant expertise in Parliament. In their view all the basic articles of the defence budget should be open, with the exception of expenditures relating to the development and production of fundamentally new weapons, although even these should be overseen by a small group of deputies and experts.[46] However, this sober and informed plea had little impact as Liuboshits acknowledged a year later. He observed that Russian practice differed from that of the majority of developed countries where basic military–economic information was open, allowing control over spending which helped to legitimise military spending in the eyes of taxpayers. At the very minimum, he argued, information should be supplied to the public at the same level of detail as supplied to the UN. Liuboshits revealed that proposals for a new system of forming the defence budget had been formulated by a group including himself, Tsymbal and A. A. Danilevskii, deputy chief of the General Staff, but this work had been curtailed because of a lack of interest on the part of Parliament and the Ministry of Economics.[47]

There is now a standard procedure for handling the defence budget in the Russian Parliament. All deputies are supplied with the draft budget providing information about spending intentions for the chapter on 'national defence' in highly aggregated terms. The draft budget of the MOD and other security agencies is then examined in detail by a special commission comprised of some forty members drawn from a number of *Duma* committees: budget and taxes; defence; security; and industry. This commission was chaired in 2003 by Vladislav Reznik, deputy chair of Committee for the Budget and Taxes.[48] It meets *in camera*, and its members must have the appropriate security clearance. As critics have pointed out, this requirement seriously limits its potential membership. Aleksei Arbatov, deputy chair of the Defence Committee of the *Duma*, has observed that many deputies are unwilling to obtain the security clearance required to gain access to state secrets, as they fear that it may lead to restrictions on their rights to travel abroad and to meet foreigners.[49] However, over time, especially since 2000, this closed commission has been given access to more detailed information on the defence budget. In 2000 members of the 40-member special commission received a document with over 150-line items, including funding allocations to specific programmes for the development of new weapons.[50] In 2002, there were 128 line-items, of which only 18 were declassified and made available to all deputies.[51] This system has a major shortcoming, however: the special commission is dissolved when the budget has been adopted by Parliament, with the consequence that there is no possibility of meaningful parliamentary control over the implementation of the budget.

Which agencies have favoured secrecy and which have pressed for greater transparency? In spite of occasional statements in favour of greater openness, the MOD and the General Staff have had a tendency to favour secrecy. In taking this stance, the MOD has taken advantage of the Law on the State Secret, which makes possible the classification of any data referring to the State's defence order of armaments and military equipment, information on the content and directions of military R&D, and, crucially, data on expenditures of the federal budget connected with maintaining national security, apart from indicators in summary terms.[52] During the 1990s, when funding was severely constrained and the military experienced sequestration of funding on a regular basis, there is no doubt that the MOD favoured secrecy as it gave greater freedom in allocating the limited funding. Indeed, the secrecy was such that even *Minfin* was unable to track the use of the money that was transferred to the armed forces. The money was disbursed to the Main Directorate for the Military Budget and Finances of the MOD, which distributed it according to the MOD's own system of spending categories, which were not the same as those of the official budget classification. This system led to weak financial control, and it is probably no accident that two heads of the directorate were dismissed for alleged financial violations and fraud. It appears to have been the dismissal of the first, Vasilii Vorob'ev, in 1995 that led to moves by *Minfin* to transfer MOD funding to the treasury system, a means of disbursing budget money to all levels of the armed forces, down to the individual unit, fully under the control of *Minfin*. This transfer was realised with considerable delay because of fierce opposition from the military,[53] but eventually took place in the late 1990s.

Minfin has favoured transparency for its own purposes but has not been very supportive of openness in relation to the public or to parliament. In the early years, the position adopted by the MOD made it easy to argue that it was the principal opponent of transparency, allowing *Minfin* to escape attention. However, over time it became apparent that *Minfin* was also complicit in the classification of the defence budget, and for similar reasons. It feared that greater openness would restrict its freedom of action, in particular by promoting more lobbying and pressure for changes in the proposed allocation of limited funding.

A key figure in the drive to transfer military funding to the treasury system was Liubov' Kudelina in her then-role as deputy minister of finance for defence spending. However, Kudelina was not in favour of greater transparency. Interviewed in October 2000, she was asked why as many items of the defence budget as possible were not made open instead of the six budget headings then made public. She responded:

> From the military point of view, I do not think it would be advisable to make our defence spending transparent, which is something we did in the early 1990s. The UN cost estimate that we complete is not the same thing as the detailed classification of military expenditure. Besides, the open military spending would worsen clashes of lobbies, which would complicate the normal work of the budget. I am sure that many items should remain classified. It is a different thing when some comparative analysis should be communicated to society every once in a while showing what the army spends its money on. No more than that.[54]

She went on to express great confidence that the treasury system was an effective means of bringing MOD spending under full control. In the spring of 2001 Kudelina was appointed to the new post of deputy minister of defence for financial and economic matters. In her first interview in the post she stressed that she would be coordinating all the finances of the MOD, to each district, division and unit, including all extra-budgetary funds, and she intended to work towards transparency within the ministry in relation to its own financing.[55]

Over the years it has been the *Duma*'s Committee for Defence, or at least its leadership, that has played an important role in promoting transparency in relation to the defence budget. Andrei Nikolaev, chairperson since April 2000, and his deputy Aleksei Arbatov, a member of the *Iabloko* party, have been tireless advocates of greater openness, arguing that the public as tax-payers have a right to information about the State's spending on the armed forces and that *Duma* deputies need the information in order to exercise meaningful parliamentary control. Reading the draft budget every year, Arbatov has written, one has to conclude that defence funding is not an issue on which deputies should waste their time. He noted that the US defence budget is detailed to 3–4,000 open positions, but in Russia depart-mental spending by the MOD is covered by 128 positions – and, he could have added, this level of detail is not available to the public or to all *Duma* deputies.[56] Nikolaev has often used the argument that the degree of classifi-cation is unreasonable when the Russian government every year supplies far more detailed information on military expenditure to the UN.[57] The posi-tion of the *Duma*'s Defence Committee, he has stated, is for the declassifica-tion of at least those items of expenditure that are reported to the UN and the OSCE.[58]

While the Defence Committee has backed greater openness, this call has not until recently had the consistent support of parties and factions within the *Duma*. However, in the course of debates about the draft budget for 2003, deputies of the Union of Right Forces (*Soiuz Pravykh Sil* – SPS), and *Iabloko*, and other deputies of liberal orientation campaigned for more transparency, and some threatened to vote against the approval of the budget if their demand was not met.[59] This achieved some success: addi-tional information about spending on the maintenance of the armed forces was released by *Minfin* and a declassified appendix about this spending was included in the law on the budget when it was finally published.[60] In the end, 59 spending positions were declassified, about half the total number, compared with only 18, less than 15 per cent, for the 2002 budget.[61] This was significant progress, but, as Arbatov has acknowledged, still leaves much to be done. In particular, Parliament still has almost no information about spending intentions by arm of service, and no possibility of monitor-ing the volume and structure of actual spending during the course of the budget year.

Until the appointment of former Prime Minister Sergei Stepashin as leader of the Accounting Chamber in April 2000, Russia lacked an authori-tative, independent agency with investigative powers able to monitor state finances. Under Stepashin, the Accounting Chamber has undertaken a number of investigations of the financial affairs of the MOD and the armed forces. The chief auditor overseeing federal budget outlays for securing national defence is Aleksandr Piskunov, appointed in 2001. Piskunov, experienced in many aspects of the defence economy, is a former deputy chair of the *Duma* Defence Committee. In that capacity he was an advocate of transparency in relation to the defence budget, arguing that this would give parliamentary deputies a greater sense of responsibility for securing appropriate funding of the armed forces.[62] This remains his position. Interviewed in July 2003 about the work of the Accounting Chamber in the field of defence, Piskunov revealed that a check of spending on 'national defence' from the beginning of the 1990s had revealed irregularities in spending totalling some 2.4 billion roubles. In addition, he had serious concerns about the effectiveness of spending on state orders for arms procurement and R&D. Broad classifications in the defence budget gave too much scope for the diversion of funds, for example, the article 'procurement' included repairs and modernisation, and in reality less than a quarter of the allocated funding was going on the acquisition of new weapons. This led the Accounting Chamber to conclude that it was necessary to transfer to a 'reasonable' (*razumnaia*) degree of transparency and detail of spending on national defence.[63] Specific investigations of the Accounting Chamber have revealed the misuse of budget finance and also inadequate accounting of earnings from the sale of arms and other military goods and services undertaken by the MOD. Reports of these investigations have been published in considerable detail, and in this respect the Accounting Chamber is making a significant contribution to enhancing public awareness of the use of spending on national defence.[64]

Other dimensions of the military economy

The annual order for weapons, military R&D, and supplies of fuel, uniforms, food, etc., for the MOD and other forces is summarised in the state defence order. Under the Law on the State Secret, the volume and structure of the state defence order are classified. However, almost every year some details emerge, often through high-level leaks. As Arbatov and other critics have argued, this is a very unsatisfactory state of affairs, with little scope for parliamentary control. In Arbatov's view, the procedure for elaborating and implementing the state defence order provides no guarantee that the funding is used effectively.[65] This is an aspect of the Russian military economy that clearly requires far-reaching reform, with a transition to a much more transparent system.

In relation to the defence industry, there have been some limited improvements. Here the internet has played a role – for a number of years there has been a dedicated website, the Information Agency for the Military–Industrial Complex TSV–PK *(Teleinformatsionnaia set' voenno–promyshlennogo kompleksa*) with three levels of access and security; however, the open, public, part is clearly only the tip of a substantial iceberg. Compared to Soviet times, more information is now available about the scale, output and employment trends of the defence industry, with open acknowledgement of its previously secret enterprises and R&D organisations, many of which now have their own websites. Prior to March 2004 the defence industry was overseen by five government agencies, each of which had its own website, although these varied in quality and openness of information. The best of them was the Russian Agency for Control Systems (*Rossiiskoe Agentstvo po Sistemam Upravleniia* – RASU), which has overseen the electronics, radio and communications equipment industries. The munitions industry agency had a website with much useful material on the control and destruction of chemical and biological weapons.[66]

In the field of arms exports, there are still many problems, with a considerable degree of secrecy, now often justified in terms of 'commercial secrecy'. The State's arms export agency *Rosoboroneksport* has a website, but it does not carry any economic data. In the absence of reliable official information, there has been much press speculation on the topic of arms exports, with frequent accusations of intrigue around the substantial export earnings accruing to a number of successful exporters. However, a very welcome development has been the emergence of some well-informed independent expertise in relation to the arms trade, on which more below.

The Soviet system of mobilisation preparedness is still basically in place and remains shrouded in almost total secrecy. Vitalii Shlykov is still almost alone in occasionally discussing the issue in print. In late 1991 Shlykov (as deputy chair of the State Committee for Defence) tried to persuade Yeltsin and Gaidar to use the country's mobilisation reserves as a once and for all boost to the economy.[67] The attempt was abruptly curtailed in early 1992 by Egor Gaidar, who favoured the retention of the Soviet system, probably not wishing to antagonise the military at a time when his economic reforms were at a crucial stage. In March 1992, on Gaidar's representation, Yeltsin signed the (secret) order, 'On Mobilisation Preparation of the National Economy of Russia', providing for the retention of the mobilisation assignments set in Soviet times.[68] During the rest of the Yeltsin period there was hardly any discussion of mobilisation preparedness, although in July 1994 there was the presidential order, 'On the Reduction of Mobilisation Capacities and Mobilisation Reserves', which made reference to a forthcoming new mobilisation plan.[69] However, this appears to have been delayed. The issue was discussed by the Defence Council in November 1996, when it was noted that the mobilisation plan then in force was elaborated in 1986 and was 'hopelessly obsolete'. A revised plan had been under elaboration in 1991, it was revealed, but for understandable reasons had not been completed or implemented.[70] This was followed in February 1997 by the new law 'On Mobilisation Preparation and Mobilisation in the

Russian Federation', leading to the formal repeal of the 1992 and 1994 presidential orders later in the year.[71] Details are sparse, but by taking as a base the data for the year 1995 it does appear that mobilisation assignments were somewhat reduced.[72]

Under Putin, the first real signs of change appeared. At the beginning of 2002 the Government apparently decided to reduce the scale of mobilisation capacities in industry, beginning in 2003.[73] But this information became public only after a leak to the newspaper *Vedomosti*.[74] A new mobilisation plan of the economy was being elaborated in 2002, taking the year 2000 as the base year. It has been reported that this new plan will reduce mobilisation capacities retained by enterprises 'by several times'.[75] Since early 2002 there have been more open references in the press to mobilisation plans and capacities: thus in March 2003 it was reported that RASU planned to reduce the volume of reserve capacities at its enterprises. According to the general director of RASU, Gennadii Kozlov, one of the causes of low profitability of production in the industry was the necessity of funding the maintenance of unused and conserved mobilisation capacities. Surplus property associated with mobilisation would be sold and the proceeds invested in the development of production.[76] It does appear that this legacy of the Soviet system is at last beginning to undergo change, but with no meaningful openness and public discussion.

The fulfilment of international obligations: the UN

Since 1992 Russia has been meeting its obligation to supply the UN's Development and Disarmament Agency (DDA) with an annual report on actual military spending, although two years (1998 and 1999) were missed. This may have been a result of the catastrophic impact on spending of the 1998 crisis rather than a deliberate decision to withhold the information. However, in some respects the amount of detail in these reports has declined. For example, since 1995 there has been no information about spending on nuclear weapons, which was included in the first Soviet and Russian reports. Another retreat from openness is the fact that these reports have not been published in Russia, whereas they were in the late Soviet period. However, the reports for 1997, 2000 and 2001 are now accessible, in Russian, on the specialised defence industry website. The existence of these detailed reports has often been cited by critics of excessive secrecy, for example, Andrei Nikolaev and Aleksei Arbatov of the *Duma*'s Defence Committee, who correctly point out that if Russia can supply this level of detail in data to the UN then why not to the Russian public and parliamentarians. Now, however, any interested Russian citizen can access the latest reports as they are available in full on the UN website.[77]

Russia has also supplied an annual return to the UN Register of Conventional Arms for each year since 1992, but in minimal detail. Unlike most countries, including Ukraine, no information is provided on the types of aircraft, tank, etc., delivered, and there are some omissions. In particular, some deliveries to China of air defence systems and other arms are excluded, probably at China's request. Furthermore, Russia has not supplied any returns on holdings of weapons, an option which is open to countries that supply data to the register. These reports are occasionally published in Russia; again, they are openly available on the UN's DDA website. Thus Russian compliance with its obligations to the UN has been somewhat formal and the reluctance to make the reports easily accessible to the Russian public suggests that 'export' *glasnost'* is still practised.

Civilian expertise and engagement in military–economic policy and decision-making

As noted above, in the late Gorbachev period some independent academic expertise on the Soviet military economy began to develop, but the number of specialists involved was small and their work was severely hampered by the paucity of reliable information. With the end of the USSR, some of the experts left academic life to work in government, business or the media (e.g. Rogovskii, Ozhegov and Blagovolin), or went abroad (e.g. Aleksei Iziumov). As for Kseniia Gonchar of IMEMO, she has mainly published abroad as the Russia specialist of the Bonn International Centre for Conversion (BICC).[78] The Central Institute of Economics and Conversion became more open, but was starved of funding. By the mid-1990s there were very few academic specialists left and in general there was a lack of informed elite and public debate of military–economic issues, although a handful of academics, for example Director of the USA–Canada Institute Sergei Rogov, and journalists such as Pavel Felgengauer and Aleksandr Gol'ts continued to provide informed contributions. In recent years there have been some welcome new developments.

In 1997 the Centre for Analysis of Strategy and Technology (CAST) was established as an independent, non-commercial, non-governmental centre for research and an offshoot of the Moscow State Institute of International Relations of the MID. There, a small group of specialists under the directorship of Ruslan Pukhov originally focused on arms exports, but gradually broadened activities to cover the defence industry more generally; its informative publications include the journal *Eksport vooruzheniia*.[79] During its brief life CAST has established a very strong reputation for expertise and appears to have gradually gained the understanding and respect of the defence community. Another centre of expertise is the Institute for the Economics of the Transition Period under former government leader Egor Gaidar. This now has a small military economy group headed by Vitalii Tsymbal, its members, like Tsymbal, mainly former military personnel. The work of this group has focused on military spending, the budget and military reform. The fact that

Tsymbal and his colleagues have military backgrounds probably explains their ability to enter into dialogue with the MOD and other military representatives. For example, participants at a conference on financial and economic aspects of the military held at the institute in December 1997 included the then First Deputy Defence Minister Nikolai Mikhailov, the Secretary of the Defence Council Andrei Kokoshin, presidential administration members, *Duma* deputies, representatives of the CSM and the association Civil Peace, and journalists. The conference was organised on the-joint initiative of Gaidar and the defence minister at the time, Igor Sergeev. However, of all the speakers it was only Efim Liuboshits of the Gaidar Institute who made reference to the unjustified secrecy, which, he argued, was detrimental to the military itself, in so far as it hindered the optimisation of the military economy. He noted that Russia reported data on military spending to the UN and other international bodies, but the Law on the State Secret stated that outlays on armaments could be classified. He urged that the law be amended so that the military budget could be open and transparent.[80]

Vitalii Tsymbal of the Gaidar Institute is vice-president of the Academy for Problems of the Military Economy and Finance, which was founded in 1998. In 2001 it listed 73 members, almost all attached to the MOD and other power ministries, with only 4 as independent academic economists (2 at the Gaidar Institute), itself a graphic illustration of the paucity of civil expertise.[81] The president of the Academy is Professor Sergei Vikulov of the MOD's Military Finance–Economics University. From the Academy's membership one suspects that appropriate security clearance is a prerequisite of membership and this is probably one of the biggest obstacles to the development of independent expertise on military–economic issues. This suspicion is heightened by the fact that some publications of recent years on the defence budget and economic problems of the military are not on open sale, but are 'for official use only'.[82] This is an unwelcome revival of a traditional Soviet practice. Books of a similar character are on open sale in most developed, democratic countries.

The economics of military reform

It is the Gaidar Institute team that has played a key role in what is without doubt the most significant landmark to date in the involvement of independent expertise in military–economic issues in Russia. It was Tsymbal and his colleagues who developed an alternative programme of military reform for Russia, establishing an economic case for transition to all-volunteer armed forces within a period of a few years. This programme was put forward in 2001 and was soon adopted as policy by the SPS, which has organised a number of demonstrations and other public events to promote it.[83] This initiative has been relatively successful: for the first time proposals for reform from outside the MOD and General Staff have been given serious consideration by the government, with some dialogue between the Gaidar Institute economists and the MOD. In addition, *Iabloko* has advanced its own proposals for the professionalisation of the armed forces, with a large role in this being played by Aleksei Arbatov and party leader Grigorii Iavlinskii. Thus by the summer of 2003 there were three rival programmes for transition to volunteer forces: those of the MOD, the Gaidar Institute–SPS and *Iabloko*'s. The MOD's initial programme called for a gradual transition to partial volunteer forces over the period to 2010, retaining two-year service for conscripts and requiring a total spending, mainly on housing, of 154 billion roubles. The Gaidar Institute–SPS programme called for a transition to volunteer forces within three years at a cost of 91 billion roubles, mainly on improved pay, with the retention of a six-month period of conscription in order to create a reserve with basic military training.[84] A modified version of the MOD's programme (to 2008, at a cost of 138 billion roubles, with conscription being reduced to one year) was considered by the Government in April 2003, with SPS leader Boris Nemtsov and others associated with the alternative present for the discussion. Meanwhile, *Iabloko* argued for a complete transition to contract forces, with an end to conscription, but with a scaling-down of the number of servicemen to 800,000. In the event, a modified version of the MOD's programme was adopted, but with a reduced level of funding. However, this could be the first time that independent expertise on an important military–economic issue has had genuine influence on policy.

Obstacles to greater transparency and civilian engagement: legacies, attitudes, interests

Progress has undoubtedly been made in post-communist Russia in opening up the military–economic sphere to greater parliamentary and public scrutiny, but the legacy of excessive secrecy has proved to be very difficult to overcome. There is still a vast gap between the level of transparency associated with military–economic matters in developed Western countries and that in present-day Russia. This is very striking in relation to the defence budget, but also true of most other aspects. Parliamentary control is weak, public knowledge and concern remains limited, and independent civilian expertise, while growing, is hampered by excessive secrecy and the distrust of the military. Actions by the security services, including the arrest of civilian security specialists, such as Igor Sutiagin of the USA–Canada Institute, do little to encourage new entrants into the military–economic field. Those pressing for greater transparency and civilian involvement face not only opposition from within the security establishment, but also a predominant view from society that military–economic matters should be the preserve of military specialists. To make matters worse, apart from a small group of informed specialists, there are very few journalists with relevant skills and interest.

But it is not only the Soviet legacy that hinders progress: various government agencies, in particular the MOD itself, other 'power' ministries, and to some extent *Minfin*, find limited transparency convenient. Secrecy provides a shield from public scrutiny. In circumstances of severely constrained funding over more than a decade, the MOD has become accustomed to the pursuit of a survival strategy that involves the protection of particular influential interests and the diversion of funding from specified purposes. It is almost certainly the case, as Arbatov and others argue, that the limited military spending is being used ineffectively. It is unlikely that the MOD is unique in this respect. The MVD and other security agencies probably have a similar interest in the maintenance of secrecy.

In these conditions the forces pressing for greater transparency face an uphill struggle. The Accounting Chamber has made progress, as has the *Duma* Defence Committee, with backing from some of the liberal democratic forces in parliament. However, it is striking that there has been no pressure from the top political leadership for openness and civilian engagement and control in military–economic affairs. This need was never mentioned by Boris Yeltsin or his successive prime ministers, and this situation is unchanged under Putin. In these circumstances, international engagement and dialogue are of great importance, with a process of education and patient but persistent pressure for change.

Notes

1 *Moskovskie novosti* (*Moscow News – MN*), 8 (1991), pp. 8–9.
2 M. Gorbachev, *Memoirs* (London: Bantam Books, 1997), p. 174.
3 A. Shulunov, 'Sistemnyi krizis "Oboronki"', *Nezavisimoe voennoe obozrenie*, 2 (1998), p. 4.
4 *Source*: http://ia.vpk.ru/sbornik_2001/nauka (accessed 9 April 2003).
5 *Employment*:
    USSR 1990: calculated from total labour force of defence industry, including nuclear industry (*Moscow News*, 7, 1992, p. 7), less nuclear industry (*Izvestiia*, 20 January 1992 and *Ekonomika i organizatsiia promyshlennogo proizovdstva*, 10, 1991, p. 110). (USSR mid-1980s: see V. Kataev, 'MIC: The view from inside', in V. Genin (ed.) *The Anatomy of Russian Defence Conversion* (Walnut Creek, CA: Vega Press, 2001), p. 58.
    RF 1990: same method and source for total employment, less nuclear industry (Minatom RF, *Press-reliz*, May 1992; Conference, *Konversiia i sotrudnichestvo*, Moscow, 1993, p. 99).
    RF 2001: calculated from data of: http://i.vpk.ru/vpkrus/vvedenie/2001 (11 July 2002). and http://i.vpk.ru/vpkrus/kadri (15 November 2001).
    Share of total and industrial employment (total employment data):
    USSR 1990: *Narodnoe khoziaistvo SSSR v 1990g.* (Moscow: Finansy i statistika, 1991), p. 100.
    RF 1990 and 2001: *Rossiiskii statistichecheskii ezhegodnik 2002*, (Moscow: Goskomstat Rossii, 2002), p. 141.

Average monthly wage:
USSR 1989 (and 1985): *Voprosy ekonomiki i konversii*, 4 (1991), p. 95.
RF 1991: *Komsomol'skaia pravda*, 14 April 2003 (June 1995: *Krasnaia zvezda*, 23 September 1995).
RF 2001: http://i.vpk.ru/sbornik/2001/vpk.sostav.rus (9 February 2003).
Average age:
RF 1990 and 2001: http:// i.vpk.ru/vpkrus/kadri (15 November 2001).
Share of industrial output (military output):
USSR 1990: calculated from *Nezavisimaia gazeta*, 9 October 1991, p. 4 and *Narodnoe khoziaistvo SSSR v 1990g*. (Moscow: Finansy i statistika,1991), p. 5. (Military share: *Izvestiia*, 17 October 1991, p. 2).
RF 2001 (also military share): http://i.vpk.ru (9 February 2003).
Arms exports:
USSR 1990: *Delovye liudi*, 3 (March, 1999), p. 32 (1987: *Izvestiia*, 4 June 1994).
RF 1991: *Svobodnaia mysl'*, 8 (1998), p. 61.
RF 2001: www.cast.ru, 3 February 2003.
Expenditure on defence as % GDP:
USSR 1990: *SIPRI Yearbook 1998*, p. 244.
RF 1991 calculated from: Institute of Economy in Transition, *Russian Economy, January–September 1998: Trends and Prospects*, p. 15, and *Rossiiskii statistichecheskii ezhegodnik 1999* (Moscow: Goskomstat RF, 1999), p. 245.
RF 2001 calculated from: www.minfin.ru (4 September 2002) (plus military pensions as budget, *SIPRI Yearbook 2001*, p. 314) and http://www.gks.ru (29 April 2003).
In real terms, 1991 = 100: calculated by author from reported spending on national defence (plus pensions) and GDP, using the GDP deflator (*Goskomstat* data for GDP and deflator).

6 *Sources*: www.mfit.ru/defensive/pub (20 March 2003) and www.strana.ru (26 February 2003).

7 *Pravda* (10 December 1990), as cited by Anders Aslund, *Gorbachev's Struggle for Economic Reform*, 2nd edn (London: Pinter Publishers, 1991), p. 191.

8 Gorbachev, *Memoirs*, pp. 174, 277.

9 *Ibid.*, p. 277.

10 N. Ryzhkov, *Perestroika: istoriia predatel'stv* (Moscow: Novosti, 1992), pp. 104, 112–20.

11 Iu. Masliukov and E. Glubokov, 'Planirovanie i finansiro vanie voenoi promyshlennosti SSSR', in A. Minaev (ed.) *Sovetskaia voennaia moshch' ot Stalina do Gorbacheva* (Moscow: Voennyi parad, 1999), p. 105.

12 Interview with 'X', (April 1994): background paper for M. Ellman and V. Kontorovich, *The Destruction of the Soviet Economic System: An Insider's History* (Armonk, NY: M. E . Sharpe, 1998). I am grateful to Professor Michael Ellman for making available some of the interviews undertaken for this book.

13 V. Genin (general editor), *The Anatomy of Russian Defense Conversion* (Walnut Creek, CA: Vega Press, 2001), pp. 194–203 (account by Oleg Grinevskii, a leading member of the Soviet team of disarmament negotiators).

14 The Masliukov team prepared a retrospective series for defence spending for 1960, 1970, 1980 and 1985 using the new method, but this was not published until 1999 (Masliukov and Glubokov in Minaev, *Sovetskaia voennaia moshch' ot Stalina do Gorbacheva*, p. 105). However, the equivalent series for 1976–90 was published in *Megapolis-Express*, 8 (1991), but this appears to have been leaked information, not officially sanctioned for publication.

15 *Pravda* (31 May 1989; 8 June 1989; and 11 June 1989).

16 *Izvestiia* (4 June 1989).

17 See, e.g., A. Iziumov, 'Voennoi glasnosti ne khvataet', *MN*, 37 (1989) and V. Deinega, 'Oboronnyi byudzhet i ego realizatsiya', *Kommunist vooruzhennykh sil*, 3 (1990), 30–6.

18 *Vestnik ministerstva inostrannykh del SSSR*, 2:60 (31 January 1990), 73.

19 *Soviet Soldier*, 7 (1990), 3.

20 *Krasnaia zvezda* (16 December 1989), p. 5.

21 V. Shlykov, *Voennyi vestnik*, 9 (September 2002), available online: www.mfit. ru/defensive/vestnik/vestnik9.

22 Interview with Vitalii Shlykov, *Problemy prognozirovaniia*, 4 (1996).

23 See 'Polstakana glasnosti', *Izvestiia* (2 November 1990).

24 It was later published in English: ILO, *Disarmament and Employment Programme*, Working Paper no. 16 (Geneva: ILO, March 1990).

25 Hence Arbatov's article, 'Spasibo misteru Cheini …' ('Thank you, Mr Cheney'), *Izvestiia*, 297 (1990).

26 *Pravitel'stvennyi vestnik* (2 January 1991).

27 On the pre-*glasnost'* situation see my 'Soviet arms exports and the conversion of the defence industry', in L. Bozzo (ed.) *Exporting Conflict. International Transfers of Conventional Arms* (Firenze: Cultura Nuova, 1991), pp. 135–42. This volume related to a UN conference on transparency in international arms transfers, held in Florence, in April 1990, attended by the future Russian Foreign Minister Andrei Kozyrev and the future director of the USA–Canada Institute, Sergei Rogov. In conversation with both it became clear that they also knew very little about the scale of Soviet arms exports, although they suspected, as I did, that a large proportion of the transfers were realised without monetary payment.

28 *Svobodnaia mysl'*, 8 (1998), p. 59.

29 On the origins of this system, see the pioneering study, by L. Samuelson, *Plans for Stalin's War Machine: Tukhachevskii and Military–economic Planning, 1925–1941* (Basingstoke: Macmillan–CREES, 2000).

30 It has been claimed by informed Russians that products such as cigarettes and spaghetti were of the same diameter as basic munitions, which could be manufactured using the same technology!

31 V. Shlykov, 'Chto pogubilo Sovetskii Soiuz? Genshtab i ekonomiia', *Voennyi vestnik*, 9 (September 2002), available online: www.mfit.ru/defensive/vestnik/vestnik9.

32 See *Soiuz*, 5 (January 1991), 16.

33 *Ibid.*, 24 (June 1991), 11.

34 *Krasnaia zvezda* (5 October 1989), p. 1.

35 *Izvestiia* (22 February 1990).

36 *Trud* (21 December 1990).

37 *Izvestiia* (30 December 1990).
38 *Nezavisimaia gazeta* (21 January 1991).
39 Information of author, who has three monthly volumes dating from the period 1987–89, 'liberated' from the party's headquarters, *Staraia ploshchad'*, at the time of the collapse of the USSR by an insider who must remain anonymous.
40 Issue no. 1 for 1992 gives a print run (*tirazh*) of 500 copies.
41 *Pravitel'svennyi vestnik*, 45 (November 1990), p. 9.
42 V. Shlykov, 'Economic readjustment within the Russian defence–industrial Complex', *Security Dialogue*, 26:1 (March 1995), 23.
43 The pensions of servicemen were transferred to the 'Social policy' chapter of the budget from 1998.
44 For the extent of the shortfall, see my chapter in *SIPRI Yearbook 1998* (Oxford: SIPRI–Oxford University Press, 1998), p. 247.
45 *Sobranie zakonodatel'stva Rossiiskoi Federatsii*, 1 (1996), article 21, appendix 5.
46 *Nezavisimaia gazeta* (9 July 1992). Liuboshits and Tsymbal were then members of the Centre for International and Military–Political Research of the Russian–American University.
47 *Segodnia* (16 October 1993).
48 Source: http://www.rossud.ru/svodki.htm (accessed 22 April 2003).
49 *Novoe vremia*, 40 (2000), p. 15.
50 *Ibid.*
51 A. Arbatov and P. Romashkin, 'Voennye i politicheskie aspekty oboronnogo biudzheta 2003g.', *Mirovaia ekonomika i mezhdunarodnye otnosheniia*, 6 (2003), 37
52 List of data considered a state secret, presidential order of 24 January 1998, *Sobranie zakonodatel'stva Rossiiskoi Federatsii*, 5 (1998), article 561.
53 See, e.g., the editorial of *Krasnaia zvezda* (18 January 1997), p. 1.
54 *Izvestiia* (27 September 2000).
55 *Krasnaia zvezda* (6 May 2001).
56 *MN*, 37 (2002).
57 *Nezavisimaia gazeta* (15 September 2000).
58 *Vremia novostei* (25 September 2002), p. 2.
59 Source: www.strana.ru (7 October 2002).
60 *Ibid.*, (18 October 2002).
61 Arbatov and Romashkin, 'Voennye i politicheskie aspekty oboronnogo biudzheta 2003g.', p. 37.
62 *Inzhenernaia gazeta*, 103 (October 1995), p. 2.
63 *Izvestiia* (2 July 2003), p. 1.
64 For these reports, see www.ach.gov.ru/results/piskunov.shtml.
65 Arbatov and Romashkin, 'Voennye i politicheskie aspekty oboronnogo biudzheta 2003g.', p. 39.
66 Sources: www.rasu.ru and www.munition.gov.ru, respectively. The defence industry is now overseen by the Federal Agency for Industry; it is too early to assess the openness of its information policy.
67 BBC, *Summary of World Broadcasts*, SU/1372 B/5 (5 May 1992); see also Shlykov, 'Economic readjustment within the Russian defence–industrial

complex', pp.19–34, and my comment, 'Demilitarizing the Russian defence economy: a commentary', *Security Dialogue*, 26:1 (March 1995), 35–40.

68 Shlykov, 'Chto pogubilo Sovetskii Soiuz?'
69 *Sobranie zakonodatel'stva Rossiiskoi Federatsii*, 11 (1994), article 1195; *Rossiiskaia gazeta* (13 July1994).
70 *Segodnia* (21 November 1996); *Krasnaia zvezda* (22 November 1996), p. 1.
71 *Krasnaia zvezda* (1 March 1997), pp. 1–2; *Rossiiskaia gazeta* (15 October 1997), p. 4.
72 Source: http://nvo.ng.ru/armament (25 April 2002).
73 *Ekspert*, 11 (18 March 2002), 8.
74 For 13 March 2002.
75 *Ekspert*, 11 (18 March 2002), 8.
76 Source: http://www.mfit.ru/defensive/publications (25 March 2003).
77 See www.un.org/Depts/dda/military.htm.
78 Producing some excellent reports: see, e.g., Kseniia Gonchar, 'Research and development (R&D) conversion in Russia', *BICC Report*, 10 (May 1997), and 'Russia's defense industry at the turn of the century', *BICC Brief*, 17 (November 2000).
79 See the CAST website: www.cast.ru.
80 Institut ekonomicheskikh problem perekhodnogo perioda, *Finansovo-ekonomicheskie problemy voennogo stroitel'stva i puti ikh resheniia (materialy nauchno-prakticheskoi konferentsii)* (Moscow: 1998), p. 98.
81 See www.iet.ru/ame/list (accessed 31 October 2001). Unfortunately, the list of members has since disappeared from the Academy's website.
82 Examples known to the author are: *Voennyi biudzhet gosudarstva* (Moscow: Voenizdat, 2000); and S. Vikulov (ed.) *Voenno–ekonomicheskii analiz* (Moscow: Voenizdat, 2001). Yet these books have been openly reviewed in the Russian press: see http://nvo.ng.ru/notes/2001–02–23 and http://nvo.ng.ru/notes/2001–06–08. I am grateful to the Moscow office of East View Publications for confirming that these books are not available for sale or through ordinary libraries in Russia.
83 See the following three works by E. Batolkin, E. Liuboshits, E. Khrustalev and V. Tsymbal: 'Reforma sistemy komplektovaniia voennoi organizatsii Rossii riadovym i mladshim komandnym sostavom', *Nauchnye trudy*, 39R (Moscow: Institut Ekonomiki Perekhodnogo Perioda, 2002); *Voennaia reforma: reforma sistemy komplektovaniia voennoi organizatsii Rossii* (St Petersburg: Norma, 2001); and 'Vybor za Prezidentom', *Nezavisimoe voennoe obozrenie*, 46 (14–21 December 2001), p. 4.
84 See http://nvo.ng.ru, (25 April 2002) and www.ng.ru (23 May 2001).

III

Citizenship, identity and the challenges of the society–military relationship

The citizenship dimension of the society–military interface

Russia: towards a post-military society?

The influence of the military sphere on the citizenship identity of Russian citizens, as with any country in which the armed forces and war have played a major role in the historical development of State and society, has been considerable. In the aftermath of the demise of the Soviet Union and with it the decline and fall of military superpower status, would the military influence on citizenship identity also be reduced? Or would the attempts at (re-)militarisation seen during the presidency of Vladimir Putin achieve success? These are important questions for Russian society, and for the development of democracy in Russia, for, as we demonstrate in this chapter (as, indeed, other contributors do so throughout the volume), the reach of the military into Russian society has extended far beyond the direct contact experienced by those who have served in the armed forces as conscripts or regular personnel.

Analysts of Russian society would be forgiven for reacting sceptically to the suggestion that the post-military society thesis,[1] put forward by Martin Shaw with regard to the possible effect on Western societies of the process of demilitarisation that was expected to accompany the end of the Cold War, might be seen to apply to the Russian case. However, as we show in this chapter, if we proceed from the assumption that Russian citizens are (actively and passively) engaged in a constant process of renegotiation of society–military relations, the post-military society notion provides an effective starting point to identify the ways in which the military's influence on society has been reduced, and of the manner in which the State's and the military institutions' attempts to reassert influence have been received and responded to at the societal level. In *The Post-Military Society*, Shaw suggested that the role and influence of the armed forces in the societies of such countries as the UK had already declined considerably in comparison to the experience of the preceding centuries, and would continue to decline in the light of the then forthcoming end of East–West conflict and the reduction in the existential threat to Western societies from *traditional* military threats.

The consequences of moving towards a post-military society are substantial, in political, economic, social and cultural terms:

- it means a decreased influence and presence of the military in the governance of the State;
- it raises questions about the amount of expenditure to be diverted to the military and the MIC; and
- it necessitates a revision of the relationship between individual citizens and their obligations and rights, with regard to what we can see as the *military component of citizenship*.

As we have argued elsewhere,[2] there is a need to provide conceptual elaboration of the post-military society thesis, in order to establish, for instance, just where the starting point for the transition towards a post-military society can be located, and how to measure and evaluate what can at times be contradictory trends in the evolution of society–military relations following the Cold War. Further, as Shaw himself has responded in his work on 'risk-transfer militarism',[3] the sea change in the international security environment following the terrorist attacks on the USA on 11 September 2001 necessitates a revisiting of the concept. However, Shaw's pioneering work stands as a key contribution to the field, opening up avenues of enquiry previously ignored or little studied. The Russian case, moreover, provides a challenging case study in which to test out Shaw's hypotheses, for it is a country where an emphasis on military power and values is still very much present in the political discourse, yet where, too, we can find abundant evidence of the relative decrease in influence of the military in line with changes at both the international and domestic levels:

- Russia's armed forces have contracted in size considerably since 1991, the reduction in numbers having an impact on the extent of visibility and contact between military and society.
- Russia's security concerns – despite lingering debates in Russia and in the West over more traditional issues such as NATO enlargement – have undergone considerable transformation since 1991, as have Russia's policy responses to these concerns, and its readiness to cooperate on the international stage in tackling these issues.
- Despite legitimate concerns over the extent of civilian control of the armed forces, the hard reality is that tight budgetary controls have been exercised over military expenditure by *Minfin*, thereby directing the nature of military reform in Russia.
- A military reform programme has been underway since the start of the 1990s – notwithstanding changes of policy direction, obstacles and resistance to change – in which modernisation, force size reduction and a shift to professional forces are at the core.

- This is taking place against the backdrop of major changes in Russian society, and in the political and economic landscape of the country, in which we can observe a readiness on the part of both society and the media to adopt a critical stance towards the military and a willingness to engage in public debate on the future of the society–military relationship (see the Introduction to this volume).

Mapping the contours of the military component of citizenship

The nature of the changes in Russia's security environment and the process of military reform have been covered extensively elsewhere (see, for example, chapter 5, by Pavel Baev, in this volume). These developments provide part of the broader stage against which we can examine the nature of the citizenship dimension of the society–military relationship, studied by means of the society–military interface (SMI) Model presented in the Introduction. Our examination of the citizenship dimension of society–military relations in Russia therefore can reveal a great deal about the opportunities and the limits inherent in the notion of citizenship in Russia today – the relationship between the individual and the State, and with one of the state's key institutions, the recognition and protection of human rights, the development of civic culture, gender relations, social equality and the socialisation of the young. It can also provide an insight into the way in which Russian citizens can locate themselves within the broader transnational environment, with regard to the development of such notions as global citizenship, something which has central relevance to ideas of transnational armed forces' development, for instance.

In our analysis we address one of the key points embedded in the Introduction to this volume – namely, that any study of policy initiatives must include an evaluation of the way such initiatives are received and responded to at the societal level. We will argue, accordingly, that while attempts made by the political and military authorities to continue to impose their will in the sphere of military service – which some commentators in the West and in Russia have perceived as signs of ongoing militarisation of society and citizenship – do indeed indicate a continued failure to recognise the rights of citizens that should accompany a transition to democracy, they demonstrate also the weakness of the policy agenda and the capacity for implementation of the political and military authorities, with the societal reception undermining the initiatives themselves and the broader legitimacy of the institutions by which they were issued. As a result, Russian society has seen the development of a more evenly shared and democratic pattern of *ownership* in the society–military relationship, opening the way, we argue, for a broader redefinition of social relations in Russia and a deepening of the democratic consolidation.

This process has, however, some considerable way to go, on the basis of current evidence. By focusing on the issue of military service, a key aspect within the military–citizenship nexus, we can identify the extent to which the change seen in the nature of the individual citizen's relations with societal and State institutions in general in post-Soviet Russia (with an increase in pluralism, democratic freedoms and an enhanced appreciation of individual needs) can be contrasted with the tensions inherent in the military sphere, where not only citizenship rights but, frequently, fundamental human rights are ignored or actively denied by the military and State authorities.

Before we move to a detailed examination of the military service question, we need to set the context through a brief overview of the broader contours of the *military component of citizenship*. We define this as an inclusive notion, to be seen as a broad landscape of the multifarious ways in which military-related issues can be said to have a degree of influence on the formation of citizenship identity. These can range from participatory elements (for example, the active involvement of a citizen in or with the military organisation, through, for instance, compulsory military service, military service as professional personnel, both active and reserve, and basic military training in schools), to such intangible, and at times subliminal, factors as the level of popular trust in or distrust of the military organisation, perceptions of a country's standing in international politics, the influence of a country's military past on contemporary citizenship identity, etc.

In the academic literature, the participatory elements have, traditionally, received greater attention. The part that the development of the 'mass army' played in the evolution of the relationship between the citizenry and notions of the nation state, for instance, has received extensive coverage,[4] as have such related questions as the military service aspect of the 'social contract'[5] and notions of obligation and military service (including combat duty),[6] and the relationship between military service issues and questions of citizenship and gender,[7] masculinity, ethnicity,[8] social class, etc. This coverage extends to the impact of mass mobilisation in the era of total war in the twentieth century, the preparation for conflict seen during the Cold War and, from protests against the Vietnam War to the standing down of societies East and West following 1989–91, the growing influence of changes in society at large on the nature of the military organisation.[9] In the case of Russia, scholars have devoted considerable attention to the role played by military service in the linkage between the citizenry and the pre-1917 Russian State,[10] and then the Soviet State,[11] although less attention has been afforded to the process of demobilisation since the late 1980s (hence the need for this discussion).

The non-participatory elements of the military component of citizenship present a more challenging task for the analyst, both with regard to their identification and measurement, and to establishing the extent of their influence on citizenship identity. One relatively *tangible* aspect is that of public attitudes towards the military sphere, as measured through public opinion polls, interviewing, participant observation and other means (although the study of public attitudes holds a host of methodological problems for the researcher, who needs to bear in mind such questions as the salience of military issues for respondents, the degree to which military issues may be taboo, etc.). Other factors are more difficult both to identify and to evaluate with regard to their effect on citizenship identity, by dint of the fact that they are often so deeply embedded in social practices that their relation to military issues may be blurred or even have disappeared altogether. Here we can refer to examples of what Gillis labels 'metaphoric militarisation'[12] (e.g. the use of military terminology to describe everyday practices unrelated to the military sphere), and also what we might term 'banal militarism' (to borrow from Michael Billig's treatment of the everyday nature of embedded nationalism),[13] for example, the presence of military-related symbols, such as statues dedicated to wartime exploits, the wearing of military uniforms by the British royal family, and so on. Further instances of the ways in which the military component of citizenship can be expressed are provided by what Luckham terms the 'armament culture' that developed during the Cold War,[14] the public's tendency to see the use of armed forces as akin to a 'spectator sport', as Michael Mann suggests,[15] and the presence of military-related symbols in the cultural sphere (films, toys, etc.), as studied by Regan and others.[16]

The starting point for some studies of this aspect of militarism and militarisation in the West was clearly an ideologically driven motivation on the part of certain authors to challenge the discourse and the practices associated with the arms race and the East–West conflict seen during the Cold War, a fact that skews the analysis somewhat. However, we do not dwell on this issue here – the key point is that such *banal* features of militarism and militarisation clearly must be counted in to any assessment of the citizenship dimension of the society–military relationship, and that in this evaluation, to echo a comment made in the Introduction to this volume, it is the extent to which such features are actually perceived by citizens as having a military–militaristic connotation that is the most important criterion in judging their impact on citizenship identity.

The SMI in Russia: studying the citizenship dimension

We have established above that the military component of citizenship is a complex mix of observable and unobservable phenomena, ranging from the inclusion in a country's constitution of the obligation of young men to serve in the armed forces as conscripts, government policy and the numbers of conscripts who serve (or evade service), to the items referred to above that belong to the symbolic–metaphorical–attitudinal plane. The latter in particular pose key fundamental problems for the researcher, who must seek to overcome the fact that the military component of citizenship, in this comprehensive sense, has not been adequately studied by the academic community. Further, one needs to be aware that, while there is tacit recognition of discrete issues of the component within political and popular discourse, these issues need to be unravelled from their embedded contexts, and (re-)constructed by the researcher within the framework of analysis required for the study of the military component of citizenship.

Stemming from this stance in examining the military component of citizenship as a complex of observable and unobservable phenomena, we then encounter methodological issues regarding the deployment of the concept. In Webber's research project on societal perceptions of citizenship and security in Russia, Germany and the UK,[17] for instance, a key concern in the conduct of focus group and individual interviews was to design questions which would elicit data to allow us to map the military component of citizenship, while controlling the introduction of bias into the study. In turn, there was a need to recognise that, in the majority of cases, a cognitive gap exists between the ways in which respondents relate to issues surrounding the military component of citizenship. Linked to this is the degree of salience of military- and security- related issues (in the Russian case, in fact, military issues proved to be far more salient than in the case of UK respondents, a finding that feeds into our evaluation of the post-military society hypothesis), and the question of the extent to which military- and security- related issues have been, or still are, regarded as a taboo area by respondents[18] – something that may also serve as a disincentive, or at least an obstacle, to researchers of the subject.

As we have argued elsewhere,[19] opinion polls (the more traditional source of information on public attitudes towards the military and security spheres) may give an interesting starting point for investigation, yet this is ultimately a limited, and therefore insufficient, insight. The value of qualitative studies of the kind employed in the project referred to above, and in the relatively limited number of other studies that draw on qualitative approaches,[20] is that they allow us to delve more deeply into issues. For instance, Eurobarometer polls on such complex issues as the development of European defence and collaboration and the introduction of the Common Foreign and Security Policy (CFSP), issues in which a lack of clarity over aims and definitions is evident even within the policy-making community, can only be judged, as Webber has argued elsewhere, as giving a very limited impression of what the public understands about these issues – cause for concern, given the weight attached to such findings by policy-makers looking to justify their policy positions.[21]

Turning to the Russian case, we can note that the task of the researcher is further complicated by the facts that not only the society–military sphere but Russian society as a whole has been in a state of flux since the late 1980s, and that the military sphere remains very much a contested, emotional and sensitive one (see also the Introduction to the volume). In addition, the legacy of the ideological restrictions on the development of independent social science research that existed in the USSR still weighs heavily over the academic field, both with regard to the lack of data available from the decades preceding the late 1980s and the current state of social science research in Russia, which often suffers from chronic underfunding and the struggle to develop a stronger methodological base (although it should be noted that major advances have been made in the social sciences' field in general in Russia in recent years). These are all factors that should be borne in mind when assessing the existing knowledge in Russia on questions related to the military component of citizenship.[22]

In the Russian case, as with other countries, there is no single comprehensive body of work available on the military component of citizenship in its broad form as laid out in the introduction to this chapter, so we need to develop our analysis by drawing on a diverse range of sources, unravelling those elements pertaining to the subject of our investigation. In addition to the work referred to above on the question of military service in Russia, we can also use, for instance, the large number of works on the subject of SMOs (including chapter 9 of this volume by Valerie Zawilski), the participation of women and specific groups, such as the Cossacks, in military service (see chapters 8 and 10, by Jennifer Mathers and Elisabeth Sieca-Kozlowski, respectively), representation of this subject in the media (see chapter 2, by Bettina Renz) and culture (as in chapter 3, by David Gillespie on films about conflict), and relevant aspects of works on citizenship, civic culture, social movements and political culture in Russia. On the question of 'banal militarism' in Russia, sources are harder to find, as one might expect, although the contributions by such authors as Aleksei Levinson on the 'Aesthetics of violence'[23] and Manfred Sapper on 'Diffused militarism',[24] in addition to that of Forest and Johnson on the symbolic significance of Victory Park in Moscow,[25] provide valuable orientation points. Finally, the mass media coverage itself of relevant issues, and the analysis of opinion poll data and qualitative research conducted by VTsIOM, and now by Iurii Levada's own analytical centre, as well as by FOM and other organisations, mean that there is now a great deal more data available for the analysis of Russian society than ever before.

We will engage with the broader contours of the military component of citizenship in Russia in future publications. In this chapter, we narrow the focus to what should be regarded as the central issue in this nexus – the societal debate over compulsory military service.

Military service – the front line of the SMI

At the abstract–symbolic level of attitudinal expression, opinion polls conducted by VTsIOM, FOM and other organisations since the start of the post-Soviet period in Russia have consistently indicated a relatively strong level of trust in the armed forces which, as an institution, often ranks second or third in trust ratings.[26] Polls have also shown stable support for Russia's need of a strong and effective military capacity, for the importance of treating military reform as a priority, and a recognition of the symbolic value of military achievements (in particular the victory in the Great Patriotic War) for current-day notions of what it means to be a Russian citizen. Within this abstract level a complex bundle of factors can be said to influence respondents' attitudes, including:

- the historical (collective) memory of the role played by the military in the USSR and Russia, with regard to the existential imperatives of protection from invasion and repulsion of invaders, and the victory culture associated with the Great Patriotic War;[27]
- the complicated interrelationship between pride and shame in citizens' attitudes with regard to the armed forces, for instance, tensions caused by reflecting on Russia's opposition between victory and defeat culture, which are held simultaneously, as well as questions surrounding the legitimacy of the use of Soviet and Russian armed forces in such cases as Czechoslovakia (1968); Afghanistan (1979–89); Chechnia (1994–);[28]
- the symbolic importance of the military sphere in Russia's self-image and international standing; and
- respondents' dissatisfaction with other societal–political institutions.[29]

If we were to take these results at face value, we might proceed to a hypothesis that the broad level of trust in, support for and perception of need for the armed forces, combined with the relatively high degree of salience and knowledge of military-related issues among Russian citizens, might be used by the military institution as a societal base from which to proceed with the programme of reform with which it has been tasked, and even the various combat-related missions it has conducted since 1991[30] (in contrast to the more specific case of support for or opposition to the use of armed force to resolve the crises in Chechnia, which saw much greater fluctuation in public opinion polls[31]).

However, we need to investigate the nature of any such consensus. In the qualitative enquiries conducted during Webber's research project, for instance, in which such abstract–symbolic attitudes were examined in more depth, it would often be found that respondents would resort to the use of official-sounding rhetorical statements on these issues, apparently unwilling or unable to engage with these issues on a personal and critical plane. This can be traced to several possible explanations: the ongoing legacy of the taboo nature of the subject and the restricted debate of the Soviet years; the ongoing tendency to preserve the public/private divide with regard to the expression of opinions;[32] residual effects of the internalisation of Soviet (and to a lesser extent, post-Soviet) socialisation and indoctrination on issues relating to military values; and also, we would contest, the degree of salience and knowledge of the subject among respondents (it will require further empirical investigation to examine the nature and weighting of these factors).

Further, any discussion of the potential for consensus must take into account the attitudes of the younger generation – a key group, given that young people are in the vanguard of society's interaction with the military (including the conscript pool, with regard to young men), and among whom, one can expect, the value changes in post-Soviet society are likely to be most pronounced. As the leading Russian sociologist and pollster Iurii Levada notes with regard to the findings of polls conducted from the start of the 1990s on, there has been a constant discrepancy between the view of the younger generation and that of older respondents on issues relating to the military sphere, with younger respondents indicating the lower level of trust in the military institution.[33] This fact provided one of the starting points for Webber's research project, which focused on the perceptions of people aged 15–30. From that project's findings we can note that the responses indicated a greater salience of military issues among Russian young people than among their peers in Germany or the UK. Within the Russian context, however, while the generally positive nature of the responses of general population samples in opinion polls towards the military sphere did resonate among the project respondents to some extent, a gap *can* be observed between the views of young people and older respondents in Russia (when compared with additional research conducted by Webber among respondents aged over 30).

This gap becomes even more visible when the questions (both in the research project and in Russian opinion polls) turn from the abstract–symbolic plane to the discrete–personal level. Polls, for instance, have shown time and again that the vast majority of respondents would not want their male relatives to serve in the Russian armed forces, for a variety of reasons indicated by secondary questioning – the risk of falling victim to abuse; likelihood of being sent to conflict zone; poor living conditions in the military, etc.[34] (It should be noted also that for respondents with no close relative in this category this question was hypothetical – which we contest, renders the high majority scores recorded even more compelling.) Within these results, younger respondents have consistently been more vocal in their opposition to military service than older respondents. The results appear to indicate that the respondents place the needs of the individual above the demands of the State and its military institution – a significant point with regard to notions of the individual in post-Soviet Russia (continuing, as we demonstrate below, a trend begun in the late Soviet period), and something that feeds into broader discussions of the relationship between the individual and societal institutions, and the extent of the individual citizen's ability to pursue his or her 'lifestyle choices'[35] and negotiate the 'risks'[36] found in the encounters with state institutions. These factors serve to explain the views of younger respondents in polls and interviews on military-related issues.

With regard to citizenship issues in particular, while this tension in societal attitudes towards the military sphere constitutes a source of a potential rift between the Russian citizenry and the military institution, whether or not a rift will develop (and what the implications of this might be) would depend on the responses of the actors involved in the SMI to these issues. In the Soviet period the number of those able to play an active and visible role in the debate over military service was very limited, of course, restricted in the official/public sphere to personnel of the CPSU and the State's institutions, until the societal changes brought by *perestroika* and *glasnost'*, when the mass media, the general public and dedicated groups such as the SMOs, engaged in what became a lively and emotional debate on military service, a subject with broad symbolic significance given the centrality of the military institution to the Soviet State. In the post-Soviet period the number and diversity of actors has increased further with, for instance, Russian political parties and political figures, the *Duma*, foreign NGOs, the foreign mass media, academic researchers, the judicial system and others all taking part, at times very actively, in the debate.

Given this opening up of the debate, and the concurrent developments in Russian society (the drawing back of the State's influence in such areas as the upbringing of the young) and in the military sphere itself (the ostensible commitment to military reform and a shift to professional armed forces), we might have assumed that the debate, and the practices embedded in the SMI, would become more democratic and that the State and the military institution would need to be prepared to give ground on this question (something, indeed, which military organisations across Europe have faced in recent years, as the dividends of the demobilisation brought by the end of the Cold War have mixed with trends towards greater empowerment of the individual).[37] Would this prove to be the case? We address this question by examining the way in which the debate on military service has unfolded in the 1990s and beyond. First, however, we give a brief review of the functions that compulsory military service has been supposed to perform in Russian and Soviet society.

Problems of conscription – why do Russian young men seek to evade military service?

The functions that compulsory military service has performed, or has been supposed to perform, from Tsarist through to post-Soviet times, have been covered quite extensively elsewhere (as indicated on p. 162). In addition to the military institution's function of filling the ranks of the mass army, in wartime and peacetime, its conscription system also served the citizenship-related function of a social unifier – strengthening the patriotic bond between the individual and the nation state, and contributing to the development of 'Soviet man' and the attempts to tie individuals to the communist ideology. It was a key institution of socialisation for the male citizenry, a route to social mobility for some (with regard to educational and vocational opportunities, as well as geographical relocation, and a factor contributing to the rural exodus). In addition, the forging of masculine identity was a strong sub-element within the conscription system.

The question of how effectively the conscription system met these diverse aims is discussed elsewhere (with regard to such issues as the level of military preparedness of the Soviet armed forces,[38] the degree of national unity that the system engendered, and the linkage between the conscription system and the development of independence movements in the late 1980s). Here we narrow down our attention to the specific legacy of the system with regard to citizenship identity in the RF, where the relationship between the individual and the institution is fundamentally important. We can state with confidence that the individual has traditionally been far removed from the central concerns of the military institution, from the Tsarist practices of selecting conscripts to serve for twenty-five years, through the 'cannon-fodder' approach to the lives of Soviet and Russian personnel employed until very recently at least by the political and military leadership of the country during times of conflict, to the treatment of the conscripts on combat and non-combat duties in contemporary Russia.

Conscript abuse and the dedovshchina *phenomenon*

The problem of conscript abuse, and the spread and worsening of such dysfunctional practices as *dedovshchina* (for a brief definition of this phenomenon see the Introduction to this volume), have been covered extensively, if at times superficially, in the Russian mass media (and, to a lesser extent, that of the West), and has received somewhat minor treatment in the academic literature. The subject was first given attention by Soviet military sociologists in the mid-1970s, while investigating the consequences of the reform of military service introduced in 1967. Interviewed by Webber in 1997, one of those sociologists, Colonel Iurii Deriugin (then retired), stated that he had taken his report, detailing the worrying signs that the problem was expanding, to the Soviet General Staff – but had seen it dismissed out of hand; Deringin was told to desist from this research, since such a problem 'could not exist in the glorious Red Army that had been victorious in the struggle against the Fascist invader [Nazi Germany]'.[39] The phenomenon was also given coverage in the 1980s by some Western analysts,[40] at times using data gathered from Jewish émigrés from the USSR who had served in the military as conscripts,[41] while later in the 1980s the *glasnost'* period made it possible for non-military sociologists in the USSR to contribute to the public scrutiny of the previously hidden problem through the publication of academic works, albeit under restrictions imposed by the authorities for the conduct of research.[42] In the post-Soviet period, the scope for research has widened, contributions being made by Russian sociologists and social psychologists working directly on this issue,[43] by journalists and NGO workers,[44] and tangential inputs from those working on the SMOs and other topics. The media attention has also continued, although remaining for the most part superficial and shying away from fundamental questions about the problem's persistence. Among the coverage was a revealing documentary by the UK's Channel 4, shown as *Soldat* in 2001, in which the programme makers gained access to Russian army barracks and with hidden camera shot (fairly mild) instances of conscript abuse.

There is no consensus over the starting point of *dedovshchina* – some place it at the end of the Great Patriotic War, others as a result of the 1967 reforms, still others contend that it is merely a continuation of the problem of abuse seen during Tsarist times – or over why it began and developed in the way it has. There is also no agreement in the literature over the scale of the problem, either during the Soviet period or today: some see the problem as having got out of control during the early 1980s on, with increasing instances of inter-ethnic violence in the barracks fuelling the issue; in the post-Soviet period, the military authorities and the SMOs continually provide wildly varying figures on the number of abuse-related deaths occurring annually in the armed forces (figures presented have tended to range from several hundred to up to 5,000, respectively, from these actors). The fact is that neither the military institution nor the State's authorities have ever conducted an adequate enquiry into the problem – a shocking dereliction of responsibility, which makes it impossible to provide any firm verdict on the extent of the problem. Informed speculation can tell us that the problem has been less prevalent, traditionally, in those military environments where lives depend on technological understanding and skill (e.g. submarines) or on close interpersonal cooperation (e.g. border forces), and more prevalent in environments where conscripts are engaged in menial duties, often little related to military preparation. The scale of the problem, while hard to define, is perhaps not the key point here – rather, it is that the problem exists in a sufficiently extreme form and on a sufficiently large scale according to anecdotal evidence, to label it a mass phenomenon.

With regard to the definition of *dedovshchina*, this, again, is a contested and grey area. It can mean relatively *harmless* humiliation practices (e.g. informal initiation ceremonies, with no lasting side-effects, of the kind seen in just about any military organisation) or low-level physical abuse (light beatings which have no permanent effect), again, a common feature of the experience of the barracks life of junior personnel in many military organisations.[45] In interviews conducted by Webber with older respondents who served in the 1950s and 1960s, this level of *dedovshchina* was more often than not what was described. It increasingly came to acquire a more grotesque form later in the 1970s and after, however, in which the degree of abuse has frequently been extreme, with severe cases of psychological and physical torture commonplace, in addition to homosexual rape – an issue which is rarely discussed in media and academic coverage of the problem.[46] In this abuse, the usual pattern is that the more senior conscripts (those who are in their third or fourth six-month period of service, and from whom a good proportion of the NCO cohort is drawn) will mete out punishment to the junior conscripts. The role of the unit's officers is often unclear – *dedovshchina* is an informal system, but it is tolerated, and sometimes encouraged, by the formal system represented by the officers.

The results of the abuse can be devastating for the victims: the disputed figures on deaths give only one aspect of the consequences, with suicide a frequent consequence (and murder covered up as suicide by the military authorities also often reported). Another outcome reported in the Russian media is the breakdown of the victims of abuse, although reports tend to cover only those cases in which victims desert their unit – often having taken 'vengeance' on their tormentors by shooting them. Perhaps the most telling example of the problem is the case of the conscript who deserted his unit in 1994, and then spent the next *seven* years hiding away in isolation in the middle of a forest, terrified of the consequences should he be found and brought to military justice.[47] It can be difficult to describe the abuse and its full effect to Western audiences – in a briefing to UK military officers, Webber was asked by an apparently shocked colonel why a conscript who had subsequently been murdered had not written to his commanding officer. Webber replied, drawing on knowledge of such cases gleaned from many hundreds of interviews and studies, that such a letter would have probably brought about the young man's death even more quickly; moreover, it can be difficult for younger Russians to explain to the older generation just how serious a problem *dedovshchina* has become.

This reply reflected the sad reality of military service for many thousands of young Russian men[48] – that their rights as citizens are virtually suspended while they perform duty as conscripts, an ironic state of affairs, given that in the official rhetoric to this day the emphasis is on the benefits accruing to conscripts, who will become 'real men' by performing their sacred duty as 'defenders of the motherland or fatherland' (*zashchitniki rodiny* or *zashchitniki otechestva*).

Grey labour and military service

Linked to the question of citizenship and military service, and the rights of the individual, is the use of conscripts to undertake 'grey labour' – illegal or semi-legal employment (according to the definition of campaign groups such as the European Council of Conscripts Organisations or, indeed, the ILO – which can include labour conducted at the behest of the State (e.g. working in the fields to collect the harvest) or 'private' work for individual military commanders (perhaps building a *dacha*, or country cottage, for a general, or selling products at the local market for their base commander).[49] This is a blurred issue, because conscripts are not supposed to be employed in such activities, yet such work may allow them to avoid the conditions present in the barracks while supplementing the pitiful income they are entitled to as conscripts. However, this represents another case of the individual's rights being suspended, and can in extreme cases lead to terrible consequences. In 1986, for instance, soldiers from the reserves (those who were already working in other employment) were called up without warning and, after being intimidated, sent to Chernobyl to shovel the nuclear rubble left by the nuclear power station explosion – without even rudimentary protection. Many (if not all) have subsequently died of radiation sickness; according to the family of one such conscript, no compensation was provided by the State with regard to healthcare, loss of earnings, etc.[50]

The social conditions of military service

These conditions, indeed, can at times be quite intolerable, and conscripts have been known to die of starvation through being isolated on a military base in the middle of nowhere with no supplies, or, as in the case mentioned in the Introduction to this volume, dying of the effects of exposure to cold while in transit to their military base because of neglect by the military authorities – a case we return to when examining the societal response to these problems. In this context we should bear in mind that in the post-Soviet period many families in rural areas have tried to persuade their sons to go to serve as conscripts, believing that the conditions of service life will be better than those in their impoverished villages. For these conscripts, and for their more urban peers from unskilled backgrounds who face few opportunities of a stable career, military service is still seen as a path towards upward social mobility and an escape route from the problems faced in their home towns and villages – a telling statement about those problems, given all that is known in Russian society about the severe nature of conditions of conscript service.

Poor living conditions are often intertwined with the abuse of conscripts, both by their fellow conscripts and by officers, as this extract from a Human Rights Watch report details:

> In many units, conscripts were systematically undernourished. Fed mainly on watery cabbage soup and porridge, many conscripts received meat, fresh vegetables, or fruit during their service only if sent by their families. Frequently, conscripts were given too little time to eat and could not finish meals. Few conscripts received adequate medical care in their units. Many had problems gaining access to military doctors, and care was often inadequate and not timely. Numerous conscripts told Human Rights Watch that fellow soldiers threatened them with abuse if they sought medical help. Conscripts being treated in sick bays and military hospitals were not spared from hazing [abuse].[51]

Social problems are further exacerbated by the composition of the conscript cohort, which reflects the range of social problems present in broader society. The fact that during the 1990s and beyond an ever-increasing proportion of those in the eligible age-group for conscription received exemptions from service has meant that it is often those in the lowest socio-economic groups who are conscripted. Within this group, an increasing number of conscripts have entered service with existing problems of alcohol, substance and drug addiction, as well as a history of involvement in criminal activity.[52] The military organisation has been simply unable to cope with this influx of social problems – it is reported, for instance, that in nearly all units now there are 'risk groups' to which no weapons are issued, for fear of the consequences.[53] We can suggest that the increasingly undemocratic nature of the call-up (by 2004 some 90 per cent[54] of the conscription age cohort were able to receive exemptions because of, for instance, engagement in full-time education, poor health, having to care for elderly relatives – according to any one of a total of twenty-four categories for exemption[55]) must also contribute to the problem of abuse, since a proportion of those who are conscripted are likely to experience frustration and resentment because they have to serve in such conditions, while the vast majority of their peers are exempted.

Meanwhile, in what is often a war of words between the military institution and the SMOs and others who call for change in the system of conscription, it is often the case that the military will blame society for the problems that exist in the services, while proponents of change blame the military institution. In fact, of course, there are many who realise (outside of this polarised debate) that the military reflects the nature of problems to be found in civilian society, with conscripts acting as what Juergen Kuhlmann calls 'symptom carriers' by bringing their values (whatever their nature) into the military organisation with them. During their term of service, of course, the conscripts undergo further socialisation, and then will carry the 'symptoms' acquired in the military back into their civilian lives after completion of service. In a functioning military organisation, the process of socialisation is given enormous priority, with recruits undergoing an intensive programme of training in which the military's core values, ethos and approach to discipline will be transmitted.

However, in the dysfunctional setting of the fragmented Russian military organisation, in which discipline is applied only patchily, and where the institution and the officers corps at times seems to have capitulated,[56] the military unit can be seen to act as an incubator for the brutal behaviour seen among conscripts. The responsibility for running the barracks lies with the military institution, and here it can be seen to have failed in its duty, for all too often the junior officers (and even mid-ranking officers) make little attempt to tackle the abuse, but turn a blind eye to it, cover it up, or participate in it to some degree. Meanwhile, the military institution itself has proved bereft of ideas, capacity or willingness to address the problem by restructuring the conscript corps (e.g. by separating younger from older conscripts), by seeking to improve social conditions, or – most fundamentally, by paying due attention to the human and citizenship rights of their conscripts.

The outcomes of the problems of conscription

The consequences are considerable and wide-ranging, and surely must be considered as intolerable in a country which aspires to democratic norms. Those who are conscripted (some 700,000 or fewer young men at any one time) can be considered a minority – and any country should be judged, in part, on the way it treats its minorities. The outcomes can be summarised as follows:

- *Fatalities*: SMOs have consistently claimed that the number of fatalities among conscripts exceeds that provided by the MOD. The latter openly admitted during the 1990s that around three conscripts die each day of the year (thus just over 1,000 deaths per year)[57] while the SMOs have at times estimated the total to be closer to 5,000 per year. In the absence of accurate and open figures, there is no way to verify the number of cases, or to extrapolate how many fatalities are the result of accidents or are not related to abuse. The problem is further complicated by the tendency of military commanders to disguise abuse-related deaths as cases of suicide. However, from all available evidence it is clear that cases of murder and manslaughter are frequent in the military, and that all too often these cases are not investigated and the criminals go free.
- *Suicide*: the point above should not be taken to mean that the problem of suicide is not also acute (in fact, it is a major problem, both among conscript and professional military personnel). In 2004 the Mother's Right Foundation (*Fond Pravo materi*) reported a rapid increase among soldiers in the rate of 'death as a result of illness' from 8 per cent in 2003 to 22 per cent in 2004. The Foundation argues that in many such cases the real cause of 'death as a result of illness' is suicide. According to the Foundation, the principal catalysts for suicides among conscripts are '*dedovshchina*, lack of discipline, and the use of soldiers as free labour by their commanders'.[58]
- '*Desertion*': annually, some 5,000 soldiers flee their military units. According to the chief military prosecutor's office, the reasons behind this are *dedovshchina* and the hardships of military service, as well as personal issues, such as illness in the family or a birth of child (this last point relates to the restrictions placed on home visits for conscripts during their period in service). Between 1994 and 2004 almost 50,000 conscripts have fled military bases. This total, as one Russian commentator pointed out, would, if combined with the approximately 30,000

young men who evade military service every year, make up the personnel of a large military *okrug*.[59]

- *Permanent injuries and health problems*: there are no reliable or adequate statistics provided by either the military institution or the healthcare and social welfare systems, on the long-term physical and psychological injuries sustained by conscripts during their service. (We can suggest that one explanation for the dearth of information on this topic is the reluctance of the authorities to be held responsible for disability payments and pensions, as has also been the case with regard to the veterans of the Afghanistan and Chechen wars, for instance.) However, on the evidence of interviews conducted in Webber's research project, and from a mass of other evidence that can be gleaned from media coverage, it is clear that the experience of military service has in very many cases a long-lasting and problematical effect on the young men and, by extension, on their interpersonal relations, career development, etc.

- *Inculcation of a culture of violence*: again, there is no reliable statistical information openly available, to our knowledge, on the extent to which former conscripts subsequently engage in criminal and/or anti-social behaviour when they return to civilian society. However, given the 'incubator' effect of military service in fostering a propensity for violent behaviour, and given the ongoing societal concern over the criminalisation of Russia, this should be seen by investigators as a priority issue. (Within this the experience of those conscripts and soldiers who have been in combat zones such as Chechnia is of particular consideration.[60])

The increasingly dysfunctional aspects of compulsory military service in post-Soviet Russia, embedded in a military organisation that sought to retain the culture and practices of the Soviet period, has led to what we can view as a substantial clash between the demands of the State and its military institution, on the one hand, and the growing awareness and ability of individual citizens to insist that their rights and needs are given the attention they are due, on the other. In the following sections we contrast the responses made at various levels in Russian society, highlighting the fragmentation apparent within the governmental and military institutional positions, and demonstrating how attempts made by the military institution at a 'remilitarisation' of Russian youth have been met with strong societal resistance, including rejection and defeat.

The official line on military service

The state-level and military institutional rhetoric on conscription has hardly changed since Soviet times: young men are still exhorted to do their patriotic duty (a call often accompanied by the assertion that by doing so they will become 'real men'). A link to the notion of citizenship is conspicuous by its absence in such rhetoric – instead, the assumption seems to be that the State has the right to dictate its will without challenge. The implication is that these young men belong to the military organisation and thus cannot lay claim to their full rights as citizens. When reference to citizenship is made, it is usually in terms that relate to the obligations of the citizenry to the State ('fulfilling the honourable duty of a Russian citizen'[61]), rather than any discussion of the notion of a 'social contract' or the benefits that will accrue to the individual. Frequently military authorities criticise those young men who do turn up for service for being in poor health (which is a reflection of worsening socio-economic conditions[62]), while those who seek to evade service are castigated for their failure to demonstrate patriotism and loyalty to the nation.[63] At the same time, those who run away from their units after enduring abuse are labelled 'deserters' and treated as criminals when they are found (a process with which the mass media often seems happy to comply),[64] while those who perpetrated the abuse are often not investigated, as the practice of 'upward accountability' leads base commanders to cover up the crimes, preferring to report to their superiors that there are no problems, rather than calling for a criminal investigation.[65]

An example of the way in which the post-Soviet Russian military institution, supported by other State institutions such as the police and the courts, has assumed that it has a claim on the lives of conscripts and the ability to deny them their rights as citizens is provided by such practices as the 'raids' that have been undertaken during the draft periods (twice annually), in order to round up young men. In one case, for instance, the Conscription Commission (*Prizyvnaia kommissiia*) in St Petersburg saw fit to descend on a group of young men celebrating their graduation from high school in an apartment (having just turned 18, the minimum age for conscription) and take them off in a military van to start their service without any opportunity to appeal.[66] In some recorded cases, the Conscription Commission, accompanied by police officers, conducted raids in public places such as night clubs or metro stations, or conscripts' homes. As a result, some young men who were entitled to deferral from military service on the basis of poor health or having the status of student, would find themselves sent off for conscript service with no opportunity to protest until after their arrival at the military unit.[67] According to the CSM, during the 2003 autumn draft campaign in Moscow some 60 per cent of conscripts were drafted as a result either of raids on conscripts' homes or of violations of the right of students for the exemption of military service.[68] Whether they have been rounded up through raids or have reported for duty willingly, conscripts tend to find that their individual rights are neglected from the start: the Channel 4 documentary referred to earlier recorded a quite extraordinary yet frequently observed scene in which the new 'recruits' (still in their civilian clothes) were locked in a public transport trolleybus, waiting to be taken off to the military unit to begin their service, and not allowed out of the bus to say last farewells to relatives.

Such behaviour on the part of the military institution displays the characteristics associated with an authoritarian State, rather than a liberal democracy, and these patterns of behaviour continue at the time of writing. As Aleksandr Gol'ts, the respected Russian journalist on military affairs, noted in February 2004 regarding Putin's reaction to the claim made by the minister of defence of the RF, Sergei Ivanov, that the most difficult stages of military reform had been completed (a very much contested claim): 'The Russian president implicitly endorsed the preservation of the model of the armed forces in which the complete absence of the rights of those who end up in its ranks is guaranteed'.[69] There are some within the Russian administration who still seek to control society, rather than accepting the changes that have taken place, working with society, and seeking to respond to its needs. Much of the rhetoric is still very much couched in terms of society and individuals belonging to the State, as we can observe in attempts during Putin's first and second terms in office to (re-)militarise and delay the process of demobilisation, through the following policies.

Renewed emphasis on conscription – call up of reserve officers

By 2003–4, the military's enormous cumulative problems with regard to the recruitment of both conscripts and professional personnel (there were problems with shortfalls in the intake and with the retention of *kontraktniki* – enlisted personnel and non-commissioned officers – and of junior officers) led the military institution to adopt a more desperate stance on the call-up of conscripts and reserve officers. With regard to the intake of conscripts, for instance, by 2004 the extent of exemptions from compulsory military service meant that only 10.3 per cent of all young men of conscription age could be drafted,[70] while of those who were not eligible for exemption, a considerable proportion chose to evade service (on an annual basis, some 30,000 young men have done so, which equates to 8–10 per cent of the total number of those who were due to be drafted[71]). As for *kontraktniki*, the armed forces have been able to recruit and retain enough personnel to maintain a figure of 120–30,000 personnel (in 2004 the figure stood at 133,000), but, as Jennifer Mathers demonstrates in chapter 8 of this volume, a great proportion of the *kontraktniki* are actually female personnel (in 2004 this figure was almost 90,000), which did not resolve the issue of the undermanning of combat units, since women are deployed in these only in very limited numbers.[72] Furthermore, the military has tended to be unhappy with the quality of those it has managed to recruit to professional service, resulting in a high drop-out rate, while the much-publicised experiment with forming a fully professionally manned division (the 76th Airborne Division, based in Pskov) has run into a number of problems.[73] The key issue in retention is the inability of the military to provide a salary adequate to the needs of the recruits, as well as appropriate living conditions, while some recruits also complain that they are treated in the same way as conscripts.[74] As a result of the combined problems in the conscription and professional recruitment systems, the forecast for 2010 is that the Russian armed forces will be 50 per cent short of its sergeant and private soldiers' cadres.[75]

This has already left the Russian armed forces very much 'top-heavy', with almost 400,000 officers,[76] which gives an impractical officer – NCO/enlisted personnel ratio of almost 1:2. However, there is also a crisis in the recruitment and retention of junior officers: one-third of the graduates of military education institutions resign in their first year of military service[77] (a reflection, in part, of the fact that a proportion had entered the institutes in order to avoid having to do military service as conscripts[78]).

Out of desperation, therefore, the military has agitated strongly for the number of exemptions from military service to be reduced,[79] for a concerted effort to be made with the State to ensure that conscripts are brought in, and for junior reserve officers to be recalled to military service (in 2004 there were plans to call up 15,000 reserve officers, for instance[80]). There were further plans to reduce by one-third (from the number of 226 as it stood in 2004) the number of so-called 'military faculties', located in civilian universities, in order to limit the possibility for students to use these as a route to avoid having to do conscript service by taking advantage instead of the status that the training they do in such faculties (during their regular university studies) gives them as officers in the reserves.[81]

Alternative service
According to article 59 of the constitution of the RF, published in 1993, it is the right of an individual citizen to declare that they would prefer not to perform military service, but instead perform service in the civilian sector. In practice, as recorded by human rights organisations and campaign groups, in the majority of attempts by citizens to invoke this right problems have been encountered, as the military and judicial authorities have been reluctant to allow the principle of alternative service to become established. In cases reported by the Anti-Military Radical Association (*Anti-Militaristskaia Radikal'naia Assotsiatsiia* – ARA), for instance, judges were recorded as saying that they felt bound to apply the Law on Military Service, rather than the constitution (despite the fact that the latter has higher status), and a good proportion of those who have applied for alternative service have ended up either serving a prison sentence or, indeed, have been sent off to serve in military units.[82] The societal pressure to introduce a law on alternative service, which attracted support also from the political party SPS and the regional authorities in the city of Nizhnii Novgorod (the home base of Boris Nemtsov, a high-profile SPS leader), where an experimental scheme was established as a local initiative, eventually overcame the *Duma*'s years of neglect of this matter with the adoption of a law in June

2003. However, the military institution seemed bent on refusing to accept the principles involved in setting up alternative service provision and has made ludicrous demands with regard to its implementation, insisting that the length of service should be forty-two months (nearly twice as long as that for military service), a fact that has received a negative assessment both among human rights activists and among some military officials themselves.[83]

The return of basic military training to the secondary schools

The Soviet programme of NVP was discussed in the Introduction to this volume (pp. 18–20). Notwithstanding the fact that, as scholars such as Friedrich Kuebart showed,[84] the system proved ineffective even in the late Soviet period (despite the backdrop of increased East–West tension, and in the context of tighter central control by the CPSU over its institutions), it was reintroduced as an optional subject in schools as one of the first policy initiatives made by acting President Putin in 1999,[85] under the new title 'Foundation of Military Service' (*Osnovy voennoi sluzhby* – OVS), although several titles have been used, and most people still refer to it as NVP. This represented something of a victory for those in the military establishment who had argued for the return of NVP since it had been removed from the classrooms by educational reformers even before the end of the USSR,[86] and brought some hope to those who had been calling for the 'development of the military consciousness of youth'.[87] The introduction of the programme was met, understandably, with concern by a number of Russian[88] and foreign observers[89], who (following the pattern seen in coverage of the issue in the 1970s and 1980s) raised the spectre of the militarisation of youth. However, as Webber predicted at the time, the attempt at reintroduction encountered considerable difficulties, lacking both material resources and general acceptance by parents and teachers,[90] and generally was seen to have had only very patchy implementation by 2003.

Undeterred, the military institution sought to resolve the issue in 2003 by making the programme compulsory, despite the fact that this would contradict the Law on Education[91] – a move which again prompted alarm among observers. Supporters of the programme like to point out that the military training of youth also occurs in such democracies as the USA and the UK,[92] and that it therefore should not be regarded as an infringement of democratic rights. However, while it is true that such schemes do exist in these countries (for the most part on a voluntary basis, although the UK's Conservative Government did propose in 1997 an initiative to encourage all British teenagers to do 'basic military training' in the military cadet forces, which, it was suggested, should be expanded to cover all schools in the country[93]), and leaving aside the issue of whether or not the military institution and its values should be seen as an appropriate means of inculcating good citizenship values, the point in the Russian case is that this system is being *imposed* on the schools and the pupils, against the backdrop of all of the problems associated with military service in Russia. Given all of this, could the programme be made to work?

Patriotic education programme

The attempt to return military training to the schools forms part of a broader programme aimed at the 'Patriotic Education of the Citizens of the Russian Federation, 2001–2005'.[94] The programme and its accompanying concept and other documentation are strangely reminiscent of the kind of policy initiative launched by the CPSU during the heydays of the Soviet period in its language (e.g. in the similarities with the kind of clichéd phrases used then to refer to the 'building of communism'), its blatant disregard for the realities of contemporary society and its top–down dictatorial approach to the relationship between the State and the citizenry. Given all of this, it is not surprising that, as we write in mid 2004, just a year before the end of the programme, it appears to be falling short of its ambitious and unrealistic aims. These aims include 'the formation of patriotic feelings and conscious-ness of [Russian] citizens on the basis of historical values and Russia's inter-national role, the retention and development of a feeling of pride for one's country'; and 'the development of the personality of the citizen (*vospitanie lichnosti grazhdanina*) as a patriot of the Motherland who is able to defend the state interests of the country', aims which are supposed to be achieved through the creation of a legislative basis for patriotic education, and the development of tools for its implementation through state institutions, and, notably, the activities of the State in promoting 'patriotic propaganda' in the mass media.

The final results predicted for the programme include:

- 'Ensuring the spiritual and moral unity of society, a reduction in the level of ideological confrontation, the restoration of the true spiritual values of the Russian (*rossiiskii*) people, the strengthening of unity and friend-ship among the peoples of the Russian Federation';
- 'Ensuring that society is interested in the development of the national economy and on this basis the reduction of social tensions, and the provision of support for societal and economic stability'; and
- 'In the sphere of the country's defence capacity – the eagerness of youth (*stremlenie molodezhi*) to serve in the armed forces, the preparedness of citizens to defend the Fatherland, the retention and development of [the Fatherland's] glorious traditions in warfare and labour'. (This compo-nent of military–patriotic education is seen as a key element within the programme as a whole.)

If we locate this discussion in the context of the citizenship component of the SMI, we can see that the State is attempting to impose a framework on the citizenry in which it is able to make demands on the citizens and appears to expect that they will dutifully oblige – a stance which is completely out of touch with the nature of Russian society today. Yet again we emphasise that any evaluation of this and the other attempts outlined here must be conducted with regard to the way it has been received and responded to in Russian society. While some have expressed alarm and concern at the introduction of this programme[95] (understandably, perhaps, given its anti-democratic tone), we can state, using the evidence referred to above and in the following sections, that this programme has not and could not meet its aims, due to the way it was designed and presented to the public.

As was argued in the Introduction, the present-day discourse on patriotism in Russia, with regard to the military sphere in particular, can be seen as having the value of an 'empty signifier.'[96] At the abstract–symbolic level it may resonate to a certain extent, as our analysis shows, among respondents in Webber's research project, and to respondents of opinion polls and focus groups run by FOM and other organisations. In Webber's project, for instance, the majority of respondents expressed general agreement with the thought that patriotism is a positive value and has a central place in the contemporary Russian military, while in a January 2004 poll run by FOM the vast majority of respondents declared themselves to be in favour of patriotic education (in questions which targeted this issue as a separate item), and the majority also stated that they felt that insufficient attention was being paid to the issue by the education system and the media.[97] However, the use of the term in abstract, slogan-like, terms means that those who engage with it at the state or societal levels can bring more or less whatever meaning they like to the term (patriotism as defined most commonly in the phrase 'love for the Motherland' can be interpreted in many ways, for instance, even those which are contradictory), thus rendering its meaning shallow and vague. At the discrete–personal level, when respondents are asked to position patriotism among a larger set of personal and societal priorities, or when asked open-endedly to list their own priorities, patriotism is seen to come low down among the priorities identified: surveys demonstrate that it is rated much lower than other societal values (such as personal well-being, justice, stability, and so on), receiving only a 3 per cent rating in a poll conducted in 2002, for instance.[98] This allows us to contextualise the results of such opinion polls as FOM's poll of January 2004, referred to above, the results of which also allow an insight into the expected outcomes of the 'Programme on Patriotic Education'. That the majority of respondents felt that the education system and the mass media were not doing enough to promote patriotism serves as something of a verdict on the programme's impact in those areas, given that this poll was conducted in the third year of its operation.

The introduction of this programme reflects the desire (one might say obsession) among some in the Russian elites to search for a national unifier, a cause around which they could seek to unite what they perceive to be a disunited nation, a quest that has been going on since at least the end of the USSR (some would say for centuries). It is an elusive yet attractive idea to those who see in it an easy solution to Russia's problems, and it also provides a way to shift the blame for the fact that problems are not being solved (the State can blame unpatriotic attitudes among the populace, while citizens can blame other citizens for being insufficiently patriotic). In the end, however, Russian citizens are not that easily duped. Moreover, there is an understanding among some of the populace of the manipulation of the notion of patriotism by the elites, as this respondent stated in an FOM focus group: 'Patriotism is very convenient for the purpose of manipulation. Let a person [instead] be responsible for himself and give him freedom. You find patriotism where there is freedom and *glasnost'*, where there are laws that apply to everybody'.[99]

Given this, should such initiatives as this programme be seen as aberrations, therefore, which are ultimately of limited interest as they will have limited effect? Or do they indeed provide cause for concern with regard to the development of democratic notions of citizenship in Russia? The answer lies in the nature of the societal response to these issues.

The societal mediation of official demands

This approach on the part of the State would seem to fit with the claims of those who see Russia under Putin as taking an authoritarian turn, with the military and other elements of the 'power structures' said to be gaining (or regaining) greater influence over the way the country is run. However, as was demonstrated in the Introduction to this volume, such claims need to be approached with caution and engaged with critically. While there is no doubting the fact that attempts have been made by those within Russia's institutions who would cling to the practices of the Soviet era, it is essential that we study not just the launching of these attempts, but that we also conduct a rational and informed evaluation of their *outcomes*.

Russian society has changed enormously since the Soviet times, and attempts to control information, manage democratic processes and manipulate public opinion come up against the hard reality that even in a situation where the State has tried to influence the mass media through various heavy-handed tactics, policies still need to achieve a degree of resonance with the citizenry. The weight of knowledge held about the ways in which public opinion is formed and how it can be measured[100] means that we can say with confidence that it is naive to believe (although this is implicit in the analyses of many observers of Russian politics and society both in Russia and the West) that Russian public opinion can be *manufactured* according to the whim of the Presidential Administration or other actors, or that public opinion is not a factor in policy-making processes.[101] Indeed, within the policy-making structures in Russia there are those who understand very well the need to have a sophisticated understanding of public opinion and that it can be ignored only at the policy-maker's peril, as confirmed in our interviews with former senior members of the Presidential Administration and its policy advisors. At critical junctures, such as the reaction to the sinking of the *Kursk*, as Webber has argued elsewhere,[102] or the impact of public opinion on the conduct of the first Chechen war, or Putin's position on the Iraq crisis in 2003, the response of Russia's citizens has mediated the attempts made by the State and its institutions, and has demonstrated that it can actually force them to be heavily modified or even withdrawn.

Such events show that the State should not assume that it will be able simply to impose its will on its citizens, but that policy outcomes will be the result of a complex process of renegotiation within the societal sphere. Such practices of renegotiation have always been present, of course, even in the darkest years of Stalinism,[103] with hidden renegotiation taking place constantly beneath the surface of individuals' interaction with institutions, and at times in the public arena, when Soviet citizens sought to take advantage of the limited and rudimentary democratic possibilities embedded in the Soviet system in order to influence change at the local level, as more subtle Western analysts of Soviet society were able to appreciate.[104] Now, in post-Soviet Russia, the space for them to operate is immeasurably greater, given the changes that have taken place in Russia. While attempts at what we might term 'partial authoritarian' rule (i.e. policies that influence only specific aspects of the societal domain) can achieve limited success in the short term (e.g. there is limited capacity among the population to counter directly such actions as raids to round up conscripts), in the long-term such measures will be diluted because they have to compete with a more diverse and pluralistic set of societal dynamics. As we argue below with reference to case examples, such flawed attempts can only serve to undermine the legitimacy of the State and its policies, particularly in cases when citizens not only see that state policies can be challenged, but also should and need to be challenged in order to safeguard individual and citizenship rights.

Part of the authoritarian legacy in the post-Soviet democratic Russia, therefore, revolves around the dual failure on the part of the State (repeating the mistakes made by the Soviet regime), firstly, to regard as legitimate and, secondly, to come to terms with the fact that its citizens act on their beliefs and values, which are formed independently of (albeit still affected by) the attempts of the State to dictate their content. And it needs to be recognised that these values are now not the same as they were during the late Soviet period – particularly in the case of the younger generation, many of whom have only a dim memory, if they have any memory at all, of what it meant to live in the USSR. In most aspects of their lives today, young people are much more free from proscriptive attempts to shape their attitudes and behaviour (some would say too free, as the Soviet State's attempts at controlling the process of socialisation have been removed but only partially replaced by a more democratic pattern of pastoral care in the schools, for instance) than was their parents' generation – something that makes it more of a clash of cultural values when young men are confronted with the unreformed (yet also dysfunctional) culture of the Soviet/Russian military institution. In the post-Soviet era, young people have become accustomed to expressing their individuality, to making their own decisions and, often, to assuming the trappings of adulthood at an earlier stage than had been the case in Russia.[105] As Aleksandr Asmolov, a former first deputy minister of education of the RF, succinctly and powerfully puts it:

> We need to recognise that in Russia for a good number of years now an unprecedented, in terms of its scale, process of the privatisation of consciousness has taken place. One of the key features of this process is the separation of the individual from the State (*ot vlasti*). It is becoming more difficult to programme social automatons and robots. They can still be turned into a crowd. But with every year that passes the mechanisms that were tested under socialism of turning people into a crowd have an ever diminishing effect. The right to pursue one's own life-choice has become more and more precious for people.[106]

With reference to attitudes to notions of *obligation* and *duty* – central to the issue of military service – we can also note considerable transformation in recent years in Russia,[107] as the Soviet social contract has been renegotiated. While Russian citizens are still prone to state that their obligations outweigh their rights, this reflects the fact that in the official discourse their attention is often drawn to their obligations, while practices on the ground have increasingly seen the balance shift towards citizens pushing back the boundaries and becoming more assertive in establishing their rights (although again in the context of a dysfunctional pattern, in which lip-service is paid to obligations and the free-for-all acquisition of rights that is sometimes seen can result in the infringement of the rights of others).

If we refer to the issue of attitudes to patriotism and its place in military service, we can again see a dichotomy between views expressed at the level of abstraction and those expressed with regard to the location of patriotism within a broader range of values. In Webber's research project, military officers aged 18–30 displayed a strong conviction that patriotism is a core value within the identity of an officer, a view which also found resonance in the enlisted personnel and civilian groups. However, in two separate studies of the values of military cadets training to be officers conducted by military sociologists in 2003, patriotism was placed lower than certain other values such as the family and personal well-being.[108] These findings should not be seen as contradictory trends. Instead, it should be regarded as understandable that the provision of freedom for the individual to express individual priorities should provide such results, which correlate quite closely with the kinds of results seen among these respondents' professional peers in Western military academies. Further, the military institution should recognise that there is no contradiction between the expression of individual priorities and the sentiment of patriotism – the two can co-exist. It is the problem of the military institution, as we have shown, that it chooses to pay insufficient attention to individual needs and continues to demand unquestioning and undivided loyalty. For there is no direct link between being patriotic and wishing to serve in the military – many respondents in Webber's research have indicated that they consider themselves to be patriotic, but that they did not wish to serve in the Russian military, particularly given its current condition.

Finally, we can also observe a shift in the nature of the expression of societal attitudes to the value of human life. The public now has the opportunity to more openly express its empathy for and interest in the cases of, for instance, the victims of crime or of armed conflicts, and while such practices of expression remain somewhat limited if compared to stable democracies where such practices have been developed over many decades, there are signs of similar patterns in Russia: for instance, the public and media reaction to the case of the conscripts who died as a result of pneumonia after enduring freezing conditions in transit to their military base in Magadan *oblast'* in 2003,[109] or the public outrage in 2004 over the death by suffocation of a schoolboy made to run with a gasmask on during an exercise related to his basic military training at school.[110]

It is in the light of these developments that we should now examine the ways in which the citizenry has engaged with the State's demands in relation to the citizenship dimension of the society–military relationship, for it is in its practices that we can observe the implications of a society's attitudes and values.

The development of civic and citizenship self-empowerment in the SMI

The aim here is to identify trends, highlighting the ways in which citizens' engagement has evolved from the late Soviet period, and demonstrating the growing assertiveness and adeptness of the citizenry as Russia began to display signs of what we can regard as characteristics of a *post-military* society. In this section we draw heavily on the findings of Webber's research project and the extensive findings of interviews and observation conducted by him since the late 1980s.

Hidden social protest and expression of opposition to the system
If we return first to the 1970s, when the problem of *dedovshchina* in its post-1967 form was identified, we can tentatively suggest that the process of the renegotiation of citizenship rights on the part of conscripts acquired a new momentum, expressed in a range of ways. First, the breakdown of discipline in

the barracks illustrated by *dedovshchina* can be interpreted as a form of social protest, in which conscripts challenged the legitimacy of the conscription system and, by extension, the Soviet system itself. However, that protest and the ways in which young men and their families and friends sought to avoid military service or deal with its consequences remained hidden for the most part, with opposition to the system and the expression of individual rights performed in the *private* sphere, while in the *public* sphere a semblance of conformity with the demands of the system was maintained.

The system of conscription forced – to a limited extent it still does – young men, and by extension their families, into facing a moral dilemma: should they do as they were commanded and report to the military commissariat in order to be sent to do what is ostensibly their patriotic duty or should their allegiance be primarily to themselves, to avoiding the possibility that they would encounter abuse or other problems while on service? This was a dilemma that faced and occupied the attention of many families with sons. Those who sought to evade conscription needed to renegotiate their status as citizens. If they evaded service by hiding away from society (and the authorities), they had to forego their rights as citizens – the right to hold a passport (without which they would not officially be entitled to work, education, housing, etc.). If they evaded by subterfuge, – by obtaining (usually through payment of a bribe) a false medical certificate asserting that their health was too poor for military service, then they would have to be prepared to lie in order to safeguard their individual interests. This silent clash between individual rights and the demands of the State more often than not involved the potential conscripts' families – with some parents beginning to collect medical 'evidence' of their sons' ill-health and thus prospective exemption from service from a very early age. The desire to avoid service also led to many early marriages and subsequent births, as fathers of the young were entitled to exemption from service. Others would ask acquaintances to inflict physical injury on them, in order to receive an exemption – an extreme act, though one also practised by some young Americans seeking to avoid being sent to the war in Vietnam. That, however, was to avoid going to *war* – in the Soviet/Russian case, it was usually to avoid *peacetime* duty in a base somewhere in the USSR/RF.

Similarly, we can observe the ways in which Soviet school students engaged with their lessons in basic military training. The first reaction of almost all of those interviewed by Webber, when asked to reflect on their NVP experience in the Soviet period, was either to smile mischievously or to laugh openly, and then to recount the various ways in which they had mocked their *voenruk* (*voennyi rukovoditel'*), or military instructor (who would be a retired military officer or NCO). For many, the NVP sessions provided a chance of a break from the hard grind of studying involved in the demanding Soviet curriculum, and the *voenruk* often proved a soft touch on discipline in comparison with their teachers. As one ex-NVP pupil stated: 'The Major would shout "March!", and we would take this as a cue to run off in all directions!'[111] These views and experiences are echoed by the following account by Sergei Rodchenko, a sergeant in the reserves, given in an interview with *Rossiiskaia gazeta*:

> In our village school ... the NVP teacher was different every year. A young guy would come back from the army – and he would come to us as a PT instructor and *voenruk* ... As far as I remember, in spring and autumn we marched around in the mud, and in winter we examined some dusty posters about nuclear war – and that was it. A complete waste of time. It was during these lessons that I understood that the army is a madhouse (*durdom*). And that's how it later turned out to be.[112]

While on one level such practices can be seen as little more than childish high-jinks in the absence of competent classroom control on the part of the military instructors, they should also be seen as a form of quiet protest against the system – the school, the military institution and the Soviet system itself – as pupils demonstrated their flippant, almost unconscious, rejection of attempts to militarise them, and along with this contributed to the growing tide of societal dissatisfaction with and demands for change in the political system of the USSR.

Returning to the issue of military service itself, in contrast to the (at times frenetic) activities of young men and their families in the private sphere to cope with the issue of conscription, Soviet citizens tended until the late 1980s at least to be extremely reluctant to openly challenge the Soviet military institution. In the case of one family coping with the extreme physical and psychological injuries sustained by a young man as a result of both *dedovshchina* and neglect and abuse by the military unit's officers in 1991, injuries which would scar him for the rest of his life, the initial bravery of the mother in travelling to the military base to take on the authorities (and be verbally and psychologically abused by the base commander and chief medical officer) to bring her son back home was then replaced by resigned fatalism, as the family preferred to just 'be grateful that their son was alive and back with them' than to seek justice and bring the perpetrators to trial. And this was understandable, for taking on the Soviet military institution as individuals was a risky proposition, one likely to lead to further problems of intimidation and worse. Even though the SMOs were operating actively and very publicly by this time, therefore, the option of engaging with them was one that was not so readily contemplated by citizens as it would later become, with citizens still preferring, or perhaps more accurately feeling that they had no real choice other than, to deal with their individual problems through their own efforts or through their local social networks,[113] which were and remain a key component of the survival strategies of Soviet and now Russian citizens in allowing them to cope with the demands of economic and social conditions.[114] Yet in most cases, such networks could be ultimately of little value, with regard to problems encountered in the military sphere.

Unconscious social movement

Among Russian citizens the degree of pessimism and sense of disempowerment and lack of influence in the military sphere continued well into the post-Soviet period and remains residually today, despite the evidence provided in preceding sections and below. In 1999–2001, for instance, Webber asked respondents to give their views on the extent to which they perceived themselves to have a degree of influence on Russian defence policy. In almost all cases, the answer was wholly negative, and the sanity of the researcher was questioned for posing such a question. A small number of respondents did suggest that they had a very limited amount of influence through voting once every four years, yet almost all respondents stated, in response to secondary questioning that, although it was considered important that the public should be able to air its views on military issues, they could not see how such opportunities could be developed.

These viewpoints reflect the generally limited – and self-limiting – stance on citizenship empowerment and self-empowerment often found in Russia, so that citizens are often reluctant to adopt an active stance, a legacy of the enforced passivity of the Soviet era and the division of the private and public spheres, and also of a latent feeling that initiatives will be handed down from above rather than emerge through agitation at the grassroots level. This assumed lack of empowerment can, however, limit citizens' ability to appreciate the level of influence that they have already achieved. For instance, we can point to the mass evasion of military service seen in recent years and its clear effects on defence policy and the military institution in Russia, as outlined above. These effects are the results of the combined actions of individuals, having made their decision to evade independently, yet *en masse* they have produced a powerful societal response to the policies of the State. This can thus be regarded as an instance (drawing on the work of Beck and other sociologists)[115] of an unconscious social movement, a mass coincidence of attitudes and actions in relation to a discrete issue of societal concern. Despite citizens' residual lack of confidence about the extent of their influence, therefore, it does exist – and we can note that during the post-Soviet period the degree of awareness of this fact, and of the potential brought by (self-)empowerment, was substantial and, moreover, was increasingly within reach of a growing number of citizens.

Development of civic culture in the sphere of the SMI

The development of civil society in Russia,[116] and in this the role of social movements,[117] the mass media, international organisations and actors,[118] has been well documented elsewhere (compensating for the relative neglect of the specific issue of citizenship). Within the society–military sphere, the subject of the SMOs has, as mentioned earlier, been afforded a considerable amount of attention in Russia and in the West, with particular attention paid to their impact on notions of social action, gender relations and citizenship.[119] Relevant to our discussion here are the ways in which the various SMOs have provided an alternative voice in the public sphere on young men's citizenship and human rights (as well as those of their families) with regard to military service and the means by which to activate those rights. This has been achieved, for example, through:

- the provision of information;
- running public consultations;
- the establishment of a country-wide network of committees;
- acting as advocates of conscripts and their families;
- providing medical examination facilities;
- legal assistance to conscripts;
- interacting with the military and state authorities; and
- the active presence of the soldiers' mothers in the mass media.

In addition to the highly visible activities of the SMOs, a considerable number of other NGOs (both Russian and foreign) have also been involved in this process of activating civic awareness and responses to the military service issue. For instance, Sergei Sorokin has been helping conscripts for twelve years by exploiting the discrepancy in legislation regarding alternative service.[120] The list of groups active in this sphere include: the ARA, the Law-Based Society, the Moscow Anti-Call-Up Point, the Union of Defenders of Rights and Freedoms, Human Rights in Russia and the major Russian human rights group Memorial.[121] Furthermore, and contrary to the suggestion made by some analysts that the attempts made by the Russian authorities to impose control over the mass media have been effectively implemented and have resulted in an uncritical media forum, it should be noted that critical articles on military service related issues are frequently published (as can be seen from the works cited in this chapter), and that the press in particular provides information on how to contact support groups and the legal rights of citizens with regard to military service, especially during the conscription (call-up) periods.

With regard to the judicial system, the practice of the prosecution service and the judges of refusing to grant alternative service provision, referred to earlier, has been frequently challenged, with the ARA, for instance, providing legal assistance to those seeking to apply for alternative service. In a number of high-profile cases, this support was instrumental in helping the defendant to overturn the verdict of the court by appeal.[122] In Nizhnii Novgorod, the initiative of the local authorities to allow an experimental system of alternative service was sparked by grassroots activists:

They established in several court proceedings that they had a right as citizens not to serve in the army – and criminal cases were not opened up against them. Judges were not able to show that the activists' demands were illegal. Finally in 2001, Nizhnii Novgorod Mayor Iurii Lebedev declared that during the fall conscription campaign, young men in Nizhnii Novgorod would be given an opportunity to serve alternative rather than military service. Public opinion surveys conducted in the region showed that the majority of residents approved of the idea.[123]

Further successes in appeals against the illegal actions of the Conscription Commission have been gained in cases of students being conscripted.[124] On a related issue, according to a Russian commentator, the call-ups of the autumn of 2000 and the spring of 2001 were unprecedented in terms of the number of raids aimed at conscripting as many men as possible without due regard to their right for exemption. The enormous numbers of legal complaints and appeals sent to courts and prosecutor's officers following these raids forced military commissions to scale down such practices, although they have not been dropped completely, and some human rights activists expect them to increase again.[125]

The level of public concern over military conscription has also made it a potential source of linkage between the citizenry and political elites: the centre-right party SPS played heavily on the need for professionalisation of the armed forces, with senior politicians such as Boris Nemtsov making regular references to this issue in speeches. In light of the demise in the political fortunes of the SPS at the 2003 *Duma* elections, and the prospect that military reform and the related questions of military service would not receive the critical attention they deserve, the UCSM of Russia declared that it was considering setting up a political party of its own in order to fight future elections.[126]

The result of such activities has been an activation of citizenship self-empowerment in this sphere, as citizens have become increasingly familiar with and prepared to use the tools available to uphold their rights. Over the fourteen years from 1989 to 2003, for instance, UCSM state that over 100,000 citizens have turned to SMOs for advice and assistance. Furthermore, the evidence of an ever-growing number of cases in which individual citizens and support groups have been successful in establishing and upholding individual rights has served as a powerful message to both the Russian population and, indeed, the military and state institutions.

However, as the CSM states 'Our experience demonstrates that one of the biggest problems of Russian society is the inability of citizens to protect their rights'[127] – evidence of the perceived need to continue to develop the process of citizenship self-empowerment. Indeed, this is shown by the nature of the debate, as we have demonstrated above, with one important consideration revolving around the fact that the 10 per cent of young men eligible for military service come predominantly from disadvantaged groups from rural locations and the working classes, who are least likely, in principle, to be aware of their rights and the means by which they can go about protecting them. Nevertheless, as the experience of support organisations shows, societal understanding of these matters is now much more widespread and informed than even a few years ago, and they do receive frequent appeals for assistance from such social groups.

Societal–State partisan warfare during the conscription periods

Despite all of this progress, however, it should be borne in mind that the strength of the position of those within the military and state institutions who would retain the Soviet system and approaches discussed in preceding sections with regard to conscription (notwithstanding all of the changes that have taken place in society and, indeed, the rationale underlying military reform), and the ongoing problems relating to the conditions of service, means that the society–military relationship in the sphere of military service is still very much prone to conflict, as the following statement shows:

> The draft period is always a war, in which the interests of the 'warring parties' were established long ago … Judgements about the danger [of being in] the modern Russian army and its 'inhuman face' have become commonplace. Notwithstanding all of the efforts of the Ministry of Defence to absolve itself of these accusations and raise the prestige of military service (both professional and conscript), the number of those wishing to perform the mythical duty to their Motherland and undergo the ruthless school of life [of military service] is not getting any larger.[128]

This is not a healthy state of affairs, either for Russian society or for the military institution. We can nevertheless identify prospects for the improvement and potential resolution of this situation by examining the nature and extent of fragmentation in the institutional environment.

A fragmented institutional scene

By 'fragmentation' within institutional positions and responses on the question of military service we refer to the ostensible element of discord, sometimes relatively small, at other times extremely striking, with what to date has been the dominant discourse of the military institution and the State on this subject. We comment below on the possible outcomes of this fragmentation, following a brief survey of select examples:

Presidential level

As was noted in the Introduction to the volume, at key junctures both Boris Yeltsin and Vladimir Putin have responded to (or tapped into) societal concerns over military service. Ahead of the 1996 presidential elections, for instance, with his opinion poll ratings at a critically low level, Yeltsin made an electoral pledge that the transition to fully professional armed forces would be complete by 2000, a pledge that certainly captured the attention of the younger voters and the parents of young males, but was subsequently forgotten by the Yeltsin administration soon after his re-election.[129] Yeltsin's efforts to conclude the first Chechen war prior to the elections can also be seen as relevant here. Meanwhile, Putin has on a number of occasions (e.g. during his meetings and phone-ins with the populace) sought to assure the public that professionalisation will lead to the solution of the problem of brutality among personnel.[130] Putin has also been careful not to use the same kind of Soviet-era rhetoric on military service found in the 'Programme on Patriotic Education', for instance, or to join with members of the General Staff in admonishing young men for not doing their 'patriotic duty' by not undertaking military service.

Governmental level
Within governmental structures we also see a lack of complete solidarity with the position of the MoD and the General Staff, and on occasion outright opposition to (or a dismissal of) their position, for example, the disagreement between Sergei Ivanov, minster of defence of the RF, and the presidential administration over the implications for the MoD of the Government's programme of administrative reform,[131] or the way in which officials at the Ministry of Economic Development and Trade brushed aside the statement of Colonel General Vladeslav Putilin, a deputy minister of that ministry and formerly a deputy head of the General Staff of the Armed Forces, in which he suggested that all schoolboys should be made to serve in the armed forces immediately on graduation from school (and that students should lose their exemption from service). According to *Kommersant Daily*, officials stated that Putilin had been speaking in a private capacity and that no one in the Government was taking such views seriously.[132] Putilin's views actually reflected those put forward by the former Minister of Education Vladimir Filippov (he had recently lost his position during Putin's mass dismissal of his incumbent ministers before the presidential elections of 2004), who suggested that entrance to higher education should include the requirement that young men had already served as conscripts, thus over-turning the right to exemption currently held by students. This is a contro-versial suggestion, and the response of the media and society echoed that seen in the late 1980s when the SMOs had emerged with the aim of campaigning for the reversal of a similar policy move to remove students' exemptions from service. Institutional fragmentation is again apparent here, as *Kommersant*'s journalist discovered when she called the MOD, and found that it would make no comment, claiming to answer only for its own words. Meanwhile, Filippov had to publicly modify his statement following

a storm of protest – although his assurance that the policy would not be introduced before 2008 of course failed to placate the public entirely.[133]

The position of the education system itself is interesting, given the role that it is supposed to play in delivering the basic military training, in promoting patriotic values and, indeed, in helping to prepare young men for military service. As in many countries, the use of the school as a forum for developing young people's civic awareness is a contested issue, with many societal institutions seeking to gain influence – as we can see in the case of the military institution's attempts to re-introduce military training in schools in Russia. The NVP system, however, as we mentioned above, was ineffectual even in the late Soviet period. In the post-Soviet period, this attempt has been mediated by developments in the school system in Russia since 1992, the year the minister of education, Eduard Dneprov, introduced the Law on Education (building on efforts begun at the grassroots level in the mid-1980s), in which the needs of the individual student were supposed to be placed at the centre of the educational process, along with parallel processes of reducing (or even removing) the influence of the State and ideology from the schools through the policy of *razgosudarstvlenie* (de-statisation).[134] As Webber has demonstrated elsewhere,[135] the reform aims embedded in the 1992 Law on Education have undergone considerable modification themselves, not least because of the difficulties schools have faced in effecting change in the context of chronic underfunding and staff shortages, while the tone of the Ministry of Education itself changed from the mid-1990s on, with some influential figures seeking to rein in the more radical policies of Dneprov and his team. However, the hasty decentralisation that Dneprov oversaw has meant that regions, cities and individual schools have developed their own stances on the content and delivery of the curriculum, and the process of 'humanisation' of education (of making it more student-centred) has gathered momentum, driven also by societal changes. While the schools have had to respond to the calls from the State to deliver military training, and also to the demands of the Orthodox Church that the secular stance adopted in the 1992 Law on Education be given up to allow religious education to be delivered in schools, neither of these attempts have produced the results the respective institutions had hoped for. Hence this rather indignant but quite revealing statement of the Minister of Defence, Ivanov:

> It is not a secret that the system of basic military training [in the schools] withered away over the last 10 years in the process of the so-called anti-militarisation of the secondary school. It is all too obvious what this has led to: for many young men being conscripted has become just as severe an ordeal as flying to the moon.[136]

Meanwhile, the school sector itself has slowly but with increasing momentum been engaging in the delivery of a citizenship education element (*grazh-*

danovedenie), which, when it is working well, gives a more rounded and balanced platform from which students can engage with the notions of civic responsibilities and rights.[137]

Federal–regional differences

At the regional level, we can observe significant differences from the official federal line in such cases as the Republic of Tatarstan (which suspended all conscription to the Russian military on 15 September 1999, following the deaths of a number of conscripts from the republic in the troubled region of Dagestan), and the regional authorities in Nizhnii Novgorod (which, as was mentioned earlier, was the site for an experiment with alternative service from 2001).

The military institution

It is within the military establishment itself that we see the most interesting and potentially most significant elements of fragmentation with regard to the military service issue. The post-Soviet period has seen constant tensions and, occasionally, open warfare between the various elements of the 'power *bloc*', as the MOD, the MVD, the FSB, the Border Forces and the other forces now present in the Russian system have been vying for political influence and patronage, and most importantly for a larger share of the limited financial resources available. These conflicts, and the high-profile case within the armed forces of the feud between the MOD and the General Staff, have been extensively reported elsewhere. These latent tensions have spilled over into the debate on military service, which has also seen considerable internal dispute, both open and hidden, within the various military forces.

If we take the armed forces themselves, for instance, we can refer to the early signs of discord and internal debate signified by the activities of the former military officer Vladimir Lopatin, who lobbied for the transition to professional armed forces after election as a deputy to the Congress of People's Deputies in 1989, and who claimed to be reflecting the kinds of opinions held by junior and mid-ranking officers in the armed forces. The Soviet military institution reacted angrily to the actions of Lopatin and others, but it gave a portent of much more wide-ranging and emotive debates to come in the post-Soviet period, as other former military officers entered politics and contributed to the debate on military reform from a range of perspectives (all major parties across the political spectrum include high-profile former military officers), with further contributions made while social movements such as the All-Russian Movement in Support of the Army, the Defence Industry and Military Science (*Vse-Rossiiskoe Dvizhenie v Podderzhku Armii, Voennoi Promyshlennosti i Voennoi Nauki*), established by General Lev Rokhlin in 1997 and subsequently transformed into an electoral bloc under the leadership of Viktor Iliukhin, chair of the *Duma* Committee on Security.

These politicians and movements have played a leading role in the societal debate on the military sphere in post-Soviet Russia, but we can also observe that an active contribution has also been played by some serving personnel from within the military – a situation which does not meet with the approval of those who support the non-involvement of the military in politics, but which, we would contend, have actually acted as a kind of safety-valve for the release of a certain amount of the tensions that have built up within the military organisation. At one international seminar in Moscow, for instance, Webber observed a colonel from the MVD forces openly criticising a very senior Russian politician, who was present, for being a 'hawk' and opposing democratic reform of the armed forces – surely a scene unlikely to be encountered in the stable environment of either an established democracy or an established authoritarian regime. A second example is afforded by the well-known case of an army officer serving in the Leningrad Military District whose apartment became known in the 1990s as a 'safe house' for conscripts running away from the problems of brutality they had encountered in their military units. The military authorities tolerated his open insubordination towards the military organisation – which would inevitably have led to severe disciplinary measures against him in a functioning democratic or authoritarian military organisation – perhaps in a resigned acceptance that they could not deal with such problems effectively themselves.

In a twist to this examination of institutional fragmentation, we can refer to the practice of those military commanders who have 'contracted out' the initiative to tackle problems of conscript abuse in their bases to the local SMOs. This can be seen, at one level, as an example of fragmentation of the institution and its inability to cope with the situation by itself: we would contend, however, that it can be regarded in a more positive and optimistic light as an example of rudimentary partnership between the military and civilian society.[138] For there are many within the military – as any professional soldier might expect – who wish to rid the institution of the awful problems of brutality and social deprivation faced by its personnel, and who seek to do what they can, within the confines of the organisation, about this issue. Such personnel recognise the damage done to the military institution and its reputation by these problems, and are all too aware (as revealed in interviews with Webber) of the need to make military service a far more attractive proposition to young Russian citizens. At a conference organised by the Soldiers' Mothers of St Petersburg in December 1999 on the issue of human rights in the armed forces, the military participants (who included senior officers up to the rank of full general) agreed that it is essential that human rights issues are tackled effectively. Putting such sentiments into action, against the backdrop of decades, if not centuries, of neglect is not easy, as the participants demonstrated by their comments – but surely it was significant that this conference was even taking place, in that setting, with foreign participants present, and with an agenda which stated quite clearly that the relationship between society and the military needs to be based on mutual respect and democratic values.

Conclusions

This has been a wide-ranging and detailed discussion of the nature of the citizenship dimension of the SMI in Russia. The scope of our discussion was dictated by the importance of engaging with a conceptual starting point – the post-military society notion – that itself needs further elaboration (which we intend to do in forthcoming publications on the basis of our application of the notion to the Russian case study); the novelty of the introduction of the SMI model and the location of our study of the military component of citizenship within it; and, consequently, the need to engage with the complex empirical detail of this case study at a depth which has not previously been explored.

Testing the post-military society hypothesis
This investigation, then, has made a valuable contribution to the development of our understanding of the 'post-military society' notion, by testing it out in a case study of the RF – which still displays, on the surface at least, strong signs of the ongoing influence of the military on society. As we have demonstrated, trends in Russia nevertheless can be seen to indicate a momentum towards a post-military condition, through, for example, societal reactions to attempts to retain a level of militarisation that is felt to be unacceptable in the light of the extent of change at the societal and international levels. We have shown that attempts at promoting militarism and at (re-)militarisation of society have not resonated with the citizenry, and cannot, therefore, achieve their aims. Instead, the societal reaction has indicated a reduction of the perceived legitimacy of the State in this sphere, while the stubborn resistance of the military institution to effect change has led to a pattern of dysfunctional relations with society. We can suggest, therefore, that the post-military society notion is both useful and valid as an analytical tool, one which can also be applied on a broad comparative basis to allow for analysis of trends internationally.

Redefining the boundaries and horizons of citizenship
We have demonstrated the evolution of Russian citizens' awareness of their rights as citizens, and their ability and preparedness to engage in self-empowerment in order to assert those rights at the SMI. By applying the SIM model to the discrete question of citizenship, we have been able to reveal the complex process of renegotiation of the relationship between the individual citizen and the State institution, and the ways in which the development of a stronger civic culture has contributed to this process. Further

research will be required to develop this analysis, in order to investigate the long-term implications of the trends we have mapped. For instance, it is likely that a redefinition of the gender dimension of citizenship can follow the reshaping of the military component of citizenship.

Towards a functional society–military relationship in Russia?

The dysfunctional and conflictual relations obtaining between the societal sphere and the military institution revolve principally, then, around what are seen by the citizenry as unreasonable demands on them by the State with regard to military service, in the context of the State's ongoing failure to provide appropriate conditions of service. It is unlikely that this conflict will be resolved until the State both modifies its demands and responds to the need to improve conditions – although, as we write in 2004, it seems likely that the plans to professionalise will again be stalled and introduced only on a mixed basis, while professionalisation itself is unlikely to prove a panacea that will rid the military of the scourge of *dedovshchina*. In order to resolve these issues, and encourage the public to accept its share of responsibility for tackling the military's social problems, the State and its military institution will need to work hard to repair the relationship with society.

The Russian situation provides an interesting instance of the notion of the 'gap' between civilian and military spheres. In such cases as the USA[139] or France, some have raised concerns that this 'gap' can emerge as a result of decreased involvement of the population in military service (following a transition to an all-volunteer force), concerns that are sometimes accompanied by the argument that a reduction in the influence of the military in society can actually lead to the isolation or alienation of the military from society and its values (one of the arguments historically used for the retention of conscription in Germany since 1945). The problem of the 'gap' can itself be placed within the parameters of the post-military society notion, one of the potentially negative consequences of the move towards a post-military condition. In the Russian case, we demonstrated that at the abstract–symbolic level there is strong residual support (for a range of reasons) among Russian citizens for the military institution, support that should have been capitalised on by the military in order to forge a more balanced relationship. However, at the discrete–personal level a gap does indeed exist, within a dysfunctional relationship in which the legitimacy of the military institution is severely challenged.

The presence of this gap sets a major challenge for Russia's policy-makers and the military institution – but it is one they must tackle effectively if they are to make the prospect of service in the military an attractive one for Russia's young citizens. Meanwhile, for Russian society the establishment of a more democratic pattern of relations between the citizenry and the military institution must also be a priority in the consolidation of democracy in that country.

The linkage between the citizenry and policy-making

Finally, we have demonstrated that the clash between societal attitudes and State policy with regard to conscription and military service in Russia has resulted in an ongoing policy failure over conscription, due to draft evasion on a mass scale, and that attempts at introducing even more drastic measures and policies on the part of the military (such as raids to round up conscripts during draft periods), and on the part of the political leadership (the introduction of the patriotic education programme), which were aimed at counteracting societal resistance, have not led to a resolution of these failures. Further, the battle over conscription has had a huge knock-on effect on Russian defence policy *per se*, forcing defence officials and policy-makers to reconsider their efforts in the field of military reform. This reinforces our argument, made here and in the Introduction, that any study of policy-making and policy implementation in Russia must embed the societal dimension firmly within the analysis.

Notes

1 M. Shaw, *Post-Military Society: Militarism, Demilitarization and War at the End of the Twentieth Century* (London: Polity Press, 1991).

2 S. Webber and A. Zilberman, 'Military aspects of citizenship in Russia', in B. Nygren and Y. Fedorov (eds) *Russian Military Reform and Russia's New Security Environment* (Stockholm: National Defence College, 2004), pp. 127–37.

3 M. Shaw 'Risk-transfer militarism and the legitimacy of war after Iraq', online: www.theglobalsite.ac.uk (2004).

4 See, e.g., R. Brubaker, *Citizenship and Nationhood in France and Germany* (Cambridge, MA: Harvard University Press, 1994); B. Posen, 'Nationalism, the mass army, and military power', *International Security*, 18:2 (1993), 80–124.

5 On the case of liberal democracies, for instance, see A. Carter, 'Liberalism and the obligation to military service', *Political Studies*, 46:1 (1998), pp. 68–81.

6 See, e.g., M. Walzer, *Obligations: Essays on Disobedience, War and Citizenship* (Cambridge, MA: Harvard University Press, 1970).

7 See, e.g., C. Enloe, *Does Khaki Become You? The Militarisation of Women's Lives* (London: Pluto Press, 1983); N. Gullace, 'White feathers and wounded men: patriotism and the memory of the Great War', *Journal of British Studies*, 36:2 (1997), 178–206.

8 See, e.g., C. Dandeker and D. Mason, 'The British armed services and the participation of minority ethnic communities: from equal opportunities to diversity?' *Sociological Review*, 49:2 (2001), 219–35.

9 See, e.g., J. Kuhlmann and J. Callaghan (eds) *Military and Society in 21st Century Europe* (New Brunswick: Transaction Publishers, 2000); C. Moskos, J. Williams and D. Segal (eds) *The Postmodern Military: Armed Forces After the Cold War* (Oxford: Oxford University Press, 2000).

10 See, e.g., B. Menning, *Bayonets Before Bullets: The Imperial Russian Army, 1861–1914* (Bloomington: Indiana University Press, 1992); J. Sanborn, *Drafting the Russian Nation: Military Conscription, Total War and Mass Politics,*

1905–1925 (Dekalb: Northern Illinois University Press, 2003); S. Smith, 'Citizenship and the Russian nation during World War I: a comment', *Slavic Review*, 59:2 (2000), 316–29.

11 See, e.g., M. Evangelista, 'Stalin's postwar army reappraised', *International Security*, 7:3 (1982–83), 110–38; O. Figes, 'The Red Army and mass mobilization during the Russian Civil War, 1918–1920', *Past & Present*, 129 (1990), 168–211; N. Gross, 'Youth and the army in the USSR in the 1980s', *Soviet Studies*, 42:3 (1990), 481–98; M. von Hagen, 'Civil–Military relations and the evolution of the Soviet socialist State', *Slavic Review*, 50:2 (1991), 268–76; E. Jones, 'Manning the Soviet military', *International Security*, 7:1. (1982), 105–31.

12 J. Gillis, 'Introduction', in J. Gillis (ed.) *The Militarization of the Western World* (New Brunswick, NJ: Rutgers University Press, 1989), p. 9.

13 M. Billig, *Banal Nationalism* (London: Sage, 1995).

14 R. Luckham, 'Of arms and culture', *Current Research on Peace and Violence*, 7:1 (1984), 1–64.

15 M. Mann, 'The roots and contradictions of contemporary militarism', *New Left Review*, 162 (1987), 35–50.

16 P. Regan, *Organizing Societies for War: The Process and Consequences of Societal Militarization* (Westport, CT: Greenwood Press, 1994).

17 Economic and Social Research Council (ESRC) project no. L 134 25 1045: 'Youth perceptions of security and citizenship in Russia, Germany and the United Kingdom'; project team: Dr S. Webber and Dr K. Longhurst, 1998–2002. The project included focus-group and one-to-one interviews conducted with general population samples, military personnel (officers, enlisted personnel, conscripts), the respondents being aged 15–30; observation of campaign groups, and military training programmes; and elite and expert interviews. In the Russian case study the greater part of the fieldwork was facilitated by the Region (research centre) at Ul'ianovsk State University.

18 S. Webber, 'Public attitudes toward the armed forces in Russia: do they count?', in S. Cimbala (ed.) *The Russian Military into the Twenty-First Century* (London: Frank Cass, 2001), pp. 153–78.

19 A. Zilberman and S. Webber, 'Public attitudes toward NATO membership in aspirant countries', in M. Vlachova (ed.) *The Public Image of Defence and the Military in Central and Eastern Europe* (Geneva and Belgrade: DCAF and CCMR, 2003), pp. 47–68. For a multifaceted analysis and critique of the use of public opinion polling data, see J. Lewis, *Constructing Public Opinion: How Political Elites Do What They Like and Why We Seem to Go Along With It* (New York: Columbia University Press, 2001).

20 E.g. D. Foyle, *Counting the Public In: Presidents, Public Opinion and Foreign Policy* (New York: Columbia University Press, 1999), a study that includes embedded qualitative content analysis of case studies; R. Smoke (ed.) *Perceptions of Security: Public Opinion and Expert Assessments in Europe's New Democracies* (Manchester: Manchester University Press, 1996), the contributions to whch draw on focus-group and other findings.

21 S. Webber, 'Public opinion and European defence: UK attitudes', in A. Flahaut and P. Manigart (eds) *Public Opinion and European Defence: Convergence or Divergence?* (Brussels: Ministry of Defence, 2001), pp. 39–59.

22 This helps to explain the ongoing proportionately large contribution of Western researchers, relative to that of Russian researchers, in the study of post-Soviet Russian society and its sub-components, such as society–military relations, although this is now balancing out, as can be seen from the backgrounds of the contributors to this volume and, indeed, this chapter.

23 A. Levinson, 'Ob estetike nasiliia: Armiia i obshchestvo v SSSR/Rossii za poslednie 10 let', *Neprikosnovennyi zapas*, 2 (1999), online: www.nz-online.ru.

24 M. Sapper, 'Diffuznaia voinstvennost' v Rossii: Nasledie militarizovannogo sot-sializma?', *Neprikosnovennyi zapas*, 1 (1999), 10–21.

25 B. Forest and J. Johnson, 'Unravelling the threads of history: Soviet-era monu-ments and post-Soviet national identity in Moscow', *Annals of the Association of American Geographers*, 92:3 (2002), 524–47.

26 In order to trace the dynamic, see the data supplied on the websites of FOM (www.fom.ru), the analytical centre headed by Iurii Levada (www.levada.ru), and the VTsIOM journal, *Monitoring obshchestvennogo mneniia: Ekonomicheskie i sotsial'nye peremeny*.

27 Although as the eminent Russian sociologist Boris Grushin points out, in 1963 the war featured much lower in the collective public consciousness, as indicated in a survey conducted among the readership of the newspaper *Komsomol'skaia pravda*, in which 6,425 respondents participated. We can note that it was later, during the Brezhnev period (1964–82), that the status of the Great Patriotic War was raised by an increased emphasis in the mass media and other sources, including mythologising of events and exploits: B. Grushin, *Chetyre zhizni Rossii: V zerkale oprosov obshchestvennogo mneniia. Epokha Khrushcheva* (Moscow: Progress-Traditsiia, 2001), pp. 403–4. The Great Patriotic War was named by only 2.7 per cent of respondents when asked to name the most impor-tant event of the twentieth century (compared with 39.2 per cent of respondents who named the Great October Socialist Revolution). The results might be said to reflect the readership profile of *Komsomol'skaia pravda*: 97 per cent of respon-dents were aged under 30, and the majority were urban dwellers.

28 This can be compared with the similarly complex and contested set of attitudes that exist in many, if not all countries, with regard to the use of armed forces: e.g. compare the Russian case with that of UK citizens' attitudes towards the armed forces' role in Northern Ireland during the troubles from the 1960s to the 1990s, the Falklands war of 1982, the Iraq conflict of 2003-date.

29 For an earlier discussion of this, see Webber, 'Public attitudes toward the armed forces in Russia', pp. 162–3.

30 Despite a dip in the level of trust in the military institution during the first Chechen war (1994–96), which can be linked to the public's opposition to the war, this recovered subsequently to its former level, and was not unduly affected by (indeed, was at times seen to be stronger during) the second Chechen war, 1999–2003. See the VTsIOM journal *Monitoring obshch-estvennogo mneniia: Ekonomicheskie i sotsial'nye peremeny* for coverage of this issue from 1992.

31 See, e.g., B. Doktorov, A. Oslon and E. Petrenko, *Epokha El'tsina: mneniia rossiian* (Moscow: Fond Obshchestvennogo Mneniia, 2002), pp. 128–61.

32 On the question of the public–private divide, see I. Oswald and V. Voronkov, 'The "public–private" sphere in Soviet and post-Soviet society', *European*

Societies, 6:1 (2004), 97–117; E. Zdravomyslova and V. Voronkov, 'The informal public in Soviet society: double morality at work', *Social Research*, March 2002.

33 Iu. Levada, 'Mekhanizmy i funktsii obshchestvennogo doveriia', *Monitoring obshchestvennogo mneniia: Ekonomicheskie i sotsial'nye peremeny*, 3 (2001), 7–9.

34 See, e.g., 'Press vypusk no. 21: Rossiiane ne khotiat, chtoby ikh rodstvenniki sluzhili v armii', 20 February (2004), online: www.levada.ru.

35 From the introduction and use of this concept by A. Giddens, *Modernity and Self-Identity. Self and Society in the Late Modern Age* (Cambridge: Polity Press, 1991), p. 182.

36 From the use of this term by Ulrich Beck in *Risk Society: Towards a New Modernity* (London: Sage, 1992).

37 See, e.g., C. Dandeker, 'The military in democratic societies', in Kuhlmann and Callaghan, *Military and Society in 21st Century Europe*, pp. 27–44.

38 A. Cockburn, *The Threat: Inside the Soviet Military Machine* (London: Random House, 1984).

39 See, e.g., Iu. Deriugin, 'Dedovshchina: sotsial'no-psikhologicheskii analiz iavleniia', *Psikhologicheskii zhurnal*, 11:1 (1990).

40 Gross, 'Youth and the army in the USSR in the 1980s'.

41 Cockburn, *The Threat: Inside the Soviet Military Machine*.

42 S. Belanovskii (ed.) *Dedovshchina v armii: sbornik sotsiologicheskikh dokumentov* (Moscow: Institut ekonomicheskogo prognozirovaniia, 1991).

43 See, e.g., K. Bannikov, *Antropologiia ekstremal'nykh grupp: dominantnye otnosheniia sredi voennosluzhashchikh srochnoi sluzhby* (Moscow: Institut etnologii i antropologii RAN, 2002).

44 See, e.g., A. Kostinskii, 'Ocherki dedovshchiny', *Indeks*, 19: (2003), online: www.index.org/ru; V. Marchenko, *Takaia armiia: narusheniia prav cheloveka v vooruzhennykh silakh* (Moscow: Norma, 1995).

45 For an examination of the nature of conscript service, see J. van Bladel, 'Russian soldiers in the barracks: a portrait of a subculture', in A. Aldis and R. McDermott (eds) *Russian Military Reform, 1992–2002* (London: Frank Cass, 2003), pp. 60–72. Van Bladel has recently completed a PhD thesis on the issue of military service in Russia.

46 For a brief discussion, see O. Kharkhordin, *The Collective and the Individual in Russia* (Berkeley: University of California Press, 1999), p. 312.

47 Story recounted to Webber in interview with former conscript, 2002.

48 According to the chief military prosecutor's office, for instance, in the first quarter of 2004, some 1,600 soldiers felt victims of *dedovshchina*: S. Ishcheiko, 'Neboevye poteri', *Trud* (15 May 2004), p. 1.

49 V. Mirolevich, '"Komandirshchina" – eto vam ne "dedovshchina" s "ustavshchinoi"'!', *Russkii kur'er* (28 April 2004), p. 12.

50 Information acquired by Webber through interviews with the family of one of the participants in this operation.

51 Human Rights Watch, 'Annual Report on Human Rights Situation: 2002', online: www.hrw.org/wr2k3/europe11.html.

52 Iu. Tret'iakov, 'Lopata vmesto avtomata', *Trud* (12 March 2004), p. 3.

53 *Ibid.*

54 O. Falichev, 'Rodinoi mobilizovannye, ili uroki prizyva 2003 goda', *Krasnaia zvezda* (26 February 2004), p. 1.

55 M. Vinogradov and D. Litovkin, '"Zato potom prizovem na polnyi srok"', *Izvestiia* (26 March 2004), online: www.izvestia.ru.

56 In the Channel 4 documentary *Soldat*, a telling episode saw a major being openly mocked by conscripts as he attempted to investigate a problem of brutality in the barracks.

57 Ishcheiko, 'Neboevye poteri'.

58 L. Rak, 'Na mamu posledniaia nadezhda', *Trud* (25 February 2004), p. 2.

59 M. Falaleev, 'Diviziia v begakh, *Komsomol'skaia pravda* (25 February 2004), p 10.

60 For discussion of the experience of veterans of the Afghanistan campaign, see M. Galeotti, *Afghanistan: The Soviet Union's Last War* (London: Frank Cass, 2002).

61 V. Denisov, 'Kto otkliknulsia na prizyv?' *Krasnaia zvezda* (17 September 2003), p. 5.

62 *Ibid.*; A Sharov, 'Ofitsial'nyi chetverg: Sergei Ivanov vzialsia za prizyv', *Rossiiskaia gazeta* (15 January 2004), p 9; A Badanov, 'Otsluzhit' za togo parnia', *Novye izvestiia* (6 May 2004), p. 7.

63 Sharov, 'Ofitsial'nyi chetverg'.

64 Falaleev, 'Diviziia v begakh'; Iu. Volgin, 'V begakh–tri batal'ona', *Trud* (19 May 2004), p. 2.

65 Rak, 'Na mamu posledniaia nadezhda'.

66 From an interview conducted by Webber with the St Petersburg SMO, December 1999.

67 A. Kolesnichenko, 'Al'ternativa "psikhushke"', *Novye izvestiia* (20 January 2004), p. 2; See also E. Butorina, 'Aspiranty pod ruzh'em. Voenkomaty nachali prizyvat' v armiiu uchashchikhsia vuzov', *Vremia novostei* (20 May 2004), p. 3; A. Kolesnichenko, 'Po doroge znanii', *Novye izvestiia* (12 January 2004), p. 2; A. Kolesnichenko and S. Anisimov, 'Novyi prizyv po starym pravilam', *ibid.* (31 March 2004), p. 2; A. Trofimov, 'Glavnaia tema. Rodina-mat' prizovet.', *Profil'* (29 March 2004), p. 15.

68 Kolesnichenko, 'Al'ternativa "psikhushke"'.

69 A. Gol'ts, 'Materiinskaia sluzhba', *Ezhenedel'nyi zhurnal* (9 February 2004), p. 18.

70 O. Falichev, 'Rodinoi mobilizovannye, ili uroki prizyva 2003 goda', *Krasnaia zvezda* (26 February 2004), p. 1.

71 Falaleev, 'Diviziia v begakh'; Volgin, 'V begakh–tri batal'ona'. The military institution often refers not to the number of those who are drafted but to the total cohort of those of conscription age (i.e. some 1.5 million young men) when referring to the number of evaders, with the apparent aim of making the extent of evasion seem less severe (since in this case the rate of evasion can be expressed as 1.5 per cent. See, e.g., Denisov, 'Kto otkliknulsia na prizyv?' (this article refers to the Moscow Military District).

72 V. Baranets, 'Kakuiu armiiu sozdaet Putin?', *Komsomol'skaia pravda* (10 March 2004), p. 8.

73 J. Boyle, 'Bricks and mortar key to Russia's new model army', *The Citizen* (2 October 2002), online: www.thecitizen.ru; Iu. Gavrilov, 'Karaul: Kontrakt po-russki', *Moskovskii komsomolets* (19 February 2004), p. 4.

74 S. Babaeva, A. Lebedev and D. Litovkin, 'Vozmozhno li obeshchannoe s 2008 goda sokrashchenie sroka sluzhby?', *Izvestiia* (9 February 2004), online: www.izvestia.ru.

75 Falichev, 'Rodinoi mobilizovannye, ili uroki prizyva 2003 goda'.

76 V. Baranets, 'Kakuiu armiiu sozdaet Putin?'

77 D. Barabash and N.Gafutulin, 'Zoloto pogon ne dolzhno prevratit'sia v med", *Krasnaia zvezda* (6 May 2004), p. 1.

78 A. Degtiarev and E. Litvinenko, 'Voennaia sotsiologiia: desiat' let spustia. Kursanty vuzov: Zhiznennye strategii i innovatsionnyi potentsial', *Sotsiologicheskie issledovaniia*, 12 (2003), 69–75.

79 Babaeva, Lebedev and Litovkin, 'Vozmozhno li obeshchannoe s 2008 goda sokrashchenie sroka sluzhby?'; Falichev, 'Rodinoi mobilizovannye, ili uroki prizyva 2003 goda'.

80 'Non-stop: 15000 ofitserov zapasa', *Moskovskii komsomolets* (15 May 2004), online: www.mn.ru.

81 I. Egorov and E. Babkova, 'Sluzhit' kak vse', *Gazeta* (27 April 2004), p. 1.

82 Details of these and other cases, and the long history of the alternative service issue, are provided on the ARA website: www.ara.ru.

83 V Nikulin, 'Gosudarstvo. Armiia. Zakon bez al'ternativy', *Ogonek* (16 February 2002), pp. 27–9.

84 F. Kuebart, 'Patriotische Wehrerziehung in der Sowjetunion', in H. Adomeit, H.-H. Hoehmann and G. Wagenlehner (eds) *Die Sowjetunion als Militärmacht* (Stuttgart: Kohlhammer, 1987), pp. 90–114. For further discussion of the Soviet NVP programme, see: H. Balzer, *Effects of Soviet Education Reform on the Military* (McLean: SAIC, 1985); E. Jones, *Red Army and Society* (Boston, MA: Allen & Unwyn, 1985), pp. 63–70; J. Muckle, *A Guide to the Soviet Curriculum* (London: Macmillan, 1988), pp. 168–70; W. Odom, 'The "militarization" of Soviet society', *Problems of Communism*, 25:5 (1976), 41–4; W. Rosslyn, 'Peace education in the Soviet Union', in G. Avis (ed.) *The Making of the Soviet Citizen* (London: Croom Helm, 1987), pp. 175–8.

85 Postanovlenie Pravitel'stva RF no. 1441 'O podgotovke grazhdan RF k voennoi sluzhbe', signed on 31 December 1999.

86 The decision was taken in Postanovlenie no. 253 of the RSFSR Government in May 1991.

87 L. Peven', 'Gotovnost' k voennoi sluzhbe: Problemy formirovaniia oboronnogo soznaniia rossiiskoi molodezhi', *Sotsiologicheskie issledovaniia*, 5 (1997), 21.

88 E.g. 'Narisuite v tetradke avtomat', *Uchitel'skaia gazeta*, 3 (2000), online: www.ug.ru:8100/00.03/index.htm.

89 E.g. G. Chazan, 'Putin to restart military training for schoolboys', *Electronic Telegraph*, 1724 (13 February 2000).

90 S. Webber, 'The return of *Nachal'naia voennaia podgotovka*: a military coup in Russia's schools?' paper delivered at the conference 'Post-Soviet education', Indiana University, Bloomington, 16–18 June 2000, available online: www.crees.bham.ac.uk/staff/webber/index.htm.

91 In the spring of 2004, the chair of the *Duma* Defence Committee stated that he was confident that corrections would be made to the Law on Education to facilitate this on a legal basis: V. Mukhin, 'Vsekh shkol'nikov postaviat pod ruzh'e:

V etom godu doprizyvnaia podgotovka stanet obiazatel'noi distsiplinoi', *Nezavisimaia gazeta* (22 April 2004), p. 2.

92 See, e.g., S. Sumbaev, 'V grazhdanine – sila gosudarstva', *Krasnaia zvezda* (27 February 2004), p. 3.

93 R. Sylvester, 'A cadet corps in every school', *Electronic Telegraph*, 608 (23 January 1997). The principal aims of this initiative were 'to promote discipline and patriotism among the young'. Not too different, then, from the declared aims of basic military training in the Russian context (and, moreover, rifle shooting was to be part of the scheme). But few write about the creeping militarisation of British youth, or the intrusion of military values and the military establishment in civilian life! However, the Russian context is, of course, still far removed from that of the UK or of other stable democracies, especially those that do not maintain a system of compulsory military service.

94 Postanovlenie Pravitel'stva Rossiiskoi Federatsii ot 16.02.2001 no. 122, 'O gosudarstvennoi programme "Patrioticheskoe vospitanie grazhdan Rossiiskoi Federatsii na 2001–2005 gody"'.

95 See, e.g., discussion of the issue by Valerie Sperling: 'The last refuge of a scoundrel: patriotism, militarism and the Russian national idea', *Nations and Nationalism*, 9:2 (2003), 235–53.

96 An empty signifier holds a vague or varying meaning, thus reducing the degree of congruence among its interpreters. See, for example, the application of this concept to the presentation of Marxist–Leninist ideology in the USSR in R. Walker, 'Marxism–Leninism as discourse: the politics of the empty signifier and the double bind', *British Journal of Political Science*, 19:2 (1989), 161–89.

97 FOM survey 'Patrioticheskoe vospitanie', 15 January 2004, online: www.fom.ru.

98 I. Klimov, 'Patrioticheskie osnovaniia sovremennoi rossiiskoi identichnosti', 19 June 2002, online: www.fom.ru.

99 *Ibid.*

100 See, e.g., I. Crespi, *Public Opinion Polls and Democracy* (Boulder, CO: Westview Press, 1989); I. Crespi, *The Public Opinion Process: How the People Speak* (Mahwah: Lawrence Erlbaum Associates, 1997); Lewis, *Constructing Public Opinion.*

101 This is not to say, of course, that the practice of employing bias in questioning and the use of targeted opinion polls for the purpose of providing 'evidence' to support policy initiatives does not take place in Russia. It does, on a regular basis – much as it does in just about any country where opinion polls are used. The point is that the analyst should be able to identify such usage, and be able to set the findings of such polls in the broader context through triangulation with other data.

102 S. Webber and J. van Bladel, 'Russia's past or future?' *The World Today*, 56:10 (2000), 4–7.

103 S. Fitzpatrick, *Everyday Stalinism: Ordinary Life in Extraordinary Times – Soviet Russia in the 1930s* (Oxford: Oxford University Press, 2001).

104 T. Friedgut, 'Citizens and Soviets: can Ivan Ivanovich fight City Hall?', *Comparative Politics*, 10:4 (1978), 461–77; J. Oliver, 'Citizen demands and the Soviet political system', *American Political Science Review*, 63:2 (1969), 465–75.

105 On the changing nature of being young in Russia, see e.g., F. Markowitz, *Coming of Age in Post-Soviet Russia* (Urbana: University of Illinois Press, 2000).

106 A. Asmolov, 'Privatizatsiia soznaniia', *Moskovskie novosti* (13 October 1998), online: www.mn.ru.

107 A. Chandler, 'State building and social obligations in post-communist systems: assessing change in Russia and Ukraine', *Canadian Slavonic Papers*, 38:1–2 (1996), 1–21.

108 Degtiarev and Litvinenko, 'Voennaia sotsiologiia: desiat' let spustia'; P. Demin, 'Voennaia sotsiologiia: desiat' let spustia: O prestizhe voennogo obrazovaniia', *Sotsiologicheskie issledovaniia*, 12 (2003), 66–9.

109 Iu. Taratuta and O. Guseva, 'Rassledovanie: FSB proigrala spor Minoborony: Komanduiushchii pogranotriada otvetit za zamerzshikh novobrantsev', *Kommersant Daily* (9 February 2004), p. 7.

110 Iu. Taratuta, 'Mobilizatsiia: Uchebnaia trevoga,' *Kommersant Daily* (20 April 2004), p. 8.

111 Interview conducted by Webber, Iaroslavl', 1992.

112 Untitled and undated article *Rossiiskaia gazeta* (2000), online: www.rg.msk.ru/Anons/0212/66.htm.

113 On the nature of networks, see, e.g., R. Alapuro, 'Reflections on social networks and collective action in Russia', in S. Webber and I. Liikanen (eds) *Education and Civic Culture in Post-Communist Countries* (London: Palgrave, 2001), pp. 13–27.

114 S. Bridger and F. Pine (eds) *Surviving Post-Socialism: Local Strategies and Regional Responses in Eastern Europe and the Former Soviet Union* (London: Routledge, 1997).

115 See, e.g., Beck, *Risk Society*.

116 M. Weigle, *Russia's Liberal Project: State–Society Relations in the Transition from Communism* (Philadelphia: Penn State University Press, 2000).

117 See, e.g., I. Liikanen, 'Education and political capital and the breakthrough of voluntary association in Russian Karelia', in Webber and Liikanen (eds) *Education and Civic Culture in Post-Communist Countries*, pp. 28–41.

118 S. Henderson, *Building Democracy in Contemporary Russia: Western Support for Grassroots Organizations* (Ithaca, NY: Cornell University Press, 2003).

119 See, e.g., A. Caiazza, *Mothers and Soldiers: Gender, Citizenship and Civil Society in Contemporary Russia* (London: Routledge, 2002).

120 A. Torgashev, 'Antiprizyv', *Novye izvestiia* (5 April 2004), p. 1.

121 A. Trofimov, 'Glavnaia tema: Rodina-mat' prizovet', *Profil'* (29 March 2004), pp. 12–15.

122 See www.ara.ru for details.

123 O. Rodin, 'Nizhnii Novgorod gives conscientious objectors an alternative to the army', *RFE/RL Russian Federation Report* (30 January 2002), online: www.rferl.org.

124 Butorina, 'Aspiranty pod ruzh'em; Kolesnichenko, 'Po doroge znanii'; Kolesnichenko and Anisimov, 'Novyi prizyv po starym pravilam'; Trofimov, 'Glavnaia tema. Rodina-mat' prizovet', p. 15.

125 Trofimov, 'Glavnaia tema', pp. 12–15.

126 I. Romancheva. 'Soldatskikh materei prizvali v politiku', *Nezavisimaia gazeta* (5 February 2004), p. 2.

127 Phrase included on the home page of the organization: www.ucsmr.ru.

128 Trofimov, 'Glavnaia tema', p. 12.

129 An account of this event is provided by Aleksandr Oslon, the director of FOM, who was at that time a member of Yeltsin's election team, in Doktorov, Oslon and Petrenko, *Epokha El'tsina,* pp. 370–1.

130 'Putin schitaet, chto professionalizatsiia armii pomozhet razreshit' problemu dedovshchiny', online: www.strana.ru (18 December 2003).

131 V. Mukhin, 'Sergei Ivanov idet naperekor Fradkovu', *Nezavisimaia gazeta* (6 April 2004), p. 1.

132 A. Kachurovskaia, 'Voennaia reforma. V 2008 godu shkol'niki stanut soldatami', *Kommersant Daily* (2 April 2004), p. 7.

133 A. Zver'ev, 'V armiiu – s 16 let?' *Novye izvestiia* (19 March 2004), p. 1.

134 For details of this policy, see: E. Dneprov, 'Alternativa', in B. Eklof and E. Dneprov (eds) *Democracy in the Russian School: The Reform Movement in Education since 1984* (Boulder, CO: Westview Press, 1993), pp. 142–3; and S. Webber, *School, Reform and Society in the New Russia* (London: Macmillan, 1999), pp. 35–7 and 191–2.

135 Webber, *School, Reform and Society in the New Russia.*

136 A. Sharov, 'Ofitsial'nyi chetverg: Sergei Ivanov vzialsia za prizyv', *Rossiiskaia gazeta* (5 January 2004), p. 9.

137 See, e.g., J. Vaillant, 'Civic education for Russia: an outsider's view', in Webber and Liikanen (eds) *Education and Civic Culture in Post-Communist Countries,* pp. 260–72.

138 Details of such cases were recounted to Webber in interviews with SMO representatives.

139 O. Holsti, 'A widening gap between the U.S. military and civilian society? Some evidence, 1976–96', *International Security,* 23:3 (1998–99), 5–42.

Women, society and the military: Women soldiers in post-Soviet Russia

> History demonstrates that the number of women in the armed forces increases when society is in extreme conditions. The current situation in Russia exactly corresponds to that definition ... In such a situation it is completely intolerable to ignore the desire of many Russian girls and officers' wives to serve in the armed forces. The benefits from this are reciprocal: the army gets the necessary specialists and the women, who today have difficulty in finding work, get jobs.[1]

Russia's society and its armed forces are indeed in 'extreme conditions': both are suffering from a crisis of identity and undergoing a painful and lengthy period of transition, the end-point of which for each one remains unclear. Since the collapse of the USSR, the prestige and status of the Russian military have occupied a low point difficult to imagine during much of the period of Communist Party rule, including the deterioration of its effectiveness as a fighting force and a serious crisis of personnel recruitment and retention. But while fewer and fewer young men have been willing to comply with conscription orders, a considerable number of young women have demonstrated their willingness to join the military. Ever since contract service was introduced – in an effort to fill some of the gaps created by shortfalls in conscription – women have made up a significant proportion of the new volunteers. At the beginning of the twenty-first century there are approximately 100,000 women soldiers in the Russian armed forces, which means that women make up about 10 per cent of the total personnel in the Russian military.[2]

The sight of women in the uniforms of their countries' militaries has become almost commonplace, especially in the developed countries of North America, Western Europe and the Asia–Pacific region. Since the 1970s legal restrictions on women's military service have been removed; barriers to the retention and promotion of women soldiers have been lowered; and women have entered many national militaries in substantial numbers. In those countries where there is a significant female presence in the armed forces, the proportion of women soldiers typically ranges from approximately 5 per cent (in countries such as Denmark, Norway, China and the United Kingdom) to about 14 per cent (in countries such as Australia, New Zealand and the USA).[3] Although very few countries *require* women to undergo military service, in most other respects women in the armed forces are, at least in theory, given the same responsibilities as their male counterparts and are offered the same opportunities. The major exception to this last point is the persistence of restrictions prohibiting women from service in some or all posts with a 'combat' designation, and even this restriction has been lifted in some countries, for example Canada, New Zealand, Norway and Sweden.[4]

The influx of women to the ranks of national militaries around the world has sparked a wealth of literature, including: the work of historians who seek to uncover the participation of women in militaries and wars of the past;[5] memoirs of individual women soldiers;[6] case studies focusing on the circumstances of women's military service in particular countries;[7] and conceptual analyses.[8] Amid this burgeoning body of scholarship, however, very little has been written about Russia's women soldiers.[9] This may be due in part to the newness of the phenomenon – little more than a decade has passed since women began to enter the country's armed forces in large numbers – as well as to the difficulty of gaining access to basic information about the subject, which is seldom addressed directly or at length even in those Russian publications which concern themselves exclusively with military topics. Although some Russian sociologists have begun to study this phenomenon and press reports about servicewomen are treating the subject with greater seriousness, the amount of data and analysis available about women soldiers in Russia pales in comparison to the abundance of information and opinion published about every aspect of women's military service in many Western countries.

As a result, the phenomenon of Russia's women soldiers remains an under-researched subject. This chapter seeks to draw together the information which is available and subject it to analysis using three Western frameworks which have been applied to other cases of women's military service:

- the concept of the 'postmodern military';
- the liberal feminist perspective; and
- the anti-militarist feminist perspective.

One of the main purposes of this exercise is to determine how usefully Western concepts and frameworks can be applied to the Russian case, and what insights, if any, they can provide about the relationship between the military and society in post-Soviet Russia. A second, but no less important, aim is to make some judgements about the position and direction of women's military service in Russia, and in particular whether Russia is coming into line with Western practices with respect to the integration of women within its armed forces. If this is the case, it could indicate a movement towards greater equality between men and women in Russian society as a whole.

Russia's women soldiers: sign of a postmodern military?

Unlike the other two frameworks used in this chapter, the postmodern military model is not exclusively or even primarily concerned with understanding women's military service as such. Instead it is a broad model which was developed to explain significant changes to the composition, missions and operations of the armed forces of Western developed democracies after the end of the Cold War. However, the model does contend that militaries of the post-Cold War period are becoming androgynous in their makeup and ethos, and are characterised by the *full integration* of women (in contrast to earlier periods when women were excluded from military service, confined to separate corps or partially integrated).[10] It is this contention and the way in which scholars have applied this aspect of the model in examining women soldiers in other countries which are employed here.

The emphasis in the postmodern military approach to women soldiers lies in the examination of the quantifiable data on the subject – chiefly:

- the extent of any restrictions on the roles which women may perform in the military;
- the range of military roles occupied by women;
- the number and proportion of women soldiers; and
- whether women soldiers are trained separately and serve separately from their male counterparts.

Those countries (such as the USA, Canada, Australia and New Zealand) with the fewest restrictions and the highest proportion of women in the ranks are judged to have the most fully integrated militaries, while the militaries of those which fall down in one or more of these categories (such as Italy and Germany) are described as being only partially integrated.[11] Qualitative measures of women's military service are also considered among the criteria for full gender integration, chiefly the women soldiers' comparative prospects for promotion and the incidence of reported sexual harassment, together with the seriousness with which allegations are investigated and wrongdoers punished. There is an implicit assumption of *progress* incorporated within this model: militaries move through well-defined stages from *modern* (associated with the rise of the nation state and the introduction of the citizen–soldier) through *late modern* (when military professionalism is more strongly developed among officers) to *postmodern*.[12] In this sense, the full integration of women within military service is regarded both as stage in the development of a national military and also as part of a global phenomenon. Finally, among those who apply the postmodern military model there is a clear acknowledgement of the importance of the relationship between attitudes in a society regarding the appropriate roles for men and women and the extent of opportunities available for women in that society's armed forces. More specifically, a factor repeatedly emphasised is that social attitudes favouring greater gender equality provide an impetus for expanding the roles open to women soldiers.

If we examine the case of Russia's women soldiers using a postmodern military framework, we find that Russia performs rather well in terms of the facts and figures. Although estimates vary somewhat, the number of women serving in the Russian armed forces has been consistently around 100,000 since the early 1990s, while the percentage of women soldiers as a proportion of the total forces has increased as the overall size of the Russian military has diminished, and stands at approximately 10 per cent in the early years of the twenty-first century.[13] Women are not subject to conscription but may volunteer under the contract service system provided they are aged 19–40, unmarried and childless.[14] In Russia women soldiers serve in mixed-sex units in almost every branch of the armed forces, in every region of the country, and they carry out a range of duties.[15] In theory women soldiers have the same rights and privileges (including wages, material benefits and pension entitlements) as their male counterparts serving on contracts,[16] and women soldiers are subject to the same disciplinary procedures as the men.[17] Although women soldiers tend to be concentrated in certain categories of work, the civilian equivalents of which are similarly female-dominated (for example, communications, clerical work and medicine), they can also be found in units of the airborne forces and in the *spetsnaz* (special forces).[18]

Although the opportunities for women in the Russian military appear to be wide-ranging, there are restrictions on the roles women soldiers can occupy and the duties they can perform. For example, women soldiers are not issued with personal arms; nor are they permitted to perform guard duty on any facility other than all-female barracks.[19] In addition, the legal provisions governing maternity and the family which apply to civilian women in Russia also apply to women soldiers.[20] The Russian labour code includes protective legislation which bans the employment of women in hundreds of occupations on the grounds that these jobs involve duties which are dangerous to pregnant women or which might endanger the reproductive health of women of child-bearing age. In addition, employers are legally limited in the terms of employment which they must offer to the mothers of young children (defined as 14 years and under): for example, employers must not require them to do heavy manual labour, to work overtime or at night.[21] And while women with young children (together with those who are married) are technically ineligible for contract service, in practice exceptions to this rule are made for the wives (and widows) of servicemen. A study of Russian servicewomen in 6 regions of the country conducted in 1999 by Russian sociologists indicates that the majority (65 per cent) of women soldiers surveyed are married and almost three-quarters have children.[22] This suggests that many of Russia's women soldiers are subject to limitations on their terms of employment as indicated above, although the MOD is reportedly considering reducing or eliminating the link between specific military duties and gender.[23] Women are not permitted to serve in *combat* positions,[24] and women in the navy do not serve on submarines or surface ships, with the exception of hospital vessels.[25]

The evidence relating to the quality of women soldiers' experience in the Russian armed forces also presents a mixed picture. Although the criteria for promotion are formally the same for men and women, only a very small number of Russian women have entered the officer corps, and most of those are clustered in the lower ranks.[26] Only 2.9 per cent of women soldiers in Russia are commissioned officers. The highest rank women have attained in the Russian military is that of colonel, and fewer than twenty women have reached this position.[27] To some extent this may simply reflect the short period of time in which women have been enlisted in substantial numbers, although there *are* indications that women soldiers face systematic discrimination which greatly reduces their chances of promotion in comparison with their male colleagues with similar qualifications.[28] About 30 per cent of the women soldiers surveyed in the 1999 study (cited above) believed their promotion prospects to have been damaged through sex discrimination, and it is apparently common for superior officers to pass over women eligible for promotion, especially if they have children, in the belief that 'family concerns would prevent them from carrying out their official duties'.[29] Moreover women soldiers' prospects for promotion are seriously limited by a key difference in the regulations governing women's and men's military service. According to the Federal Law on Military Obligations and Military Service (article 49, part 2), the compulsory retirement age for a woman in the military is 45 years, while the retirement age for a man varies according to his rank – and it would be very difficult, if not impossible, for an officer to attain the highest rank (general) before reaching the age of forty-five.[30]

Information on the number of allegations of sexual harassment in the armed forces is limited, but press reports suggest that the Russian military is not free from this problem.[31] An article in the newspaper *Nezavismoe voen-noe obozrenie (Independent Military Review)* reports that in 1997 incidents of sexual violence towards women soldiers were recorded in the Urals and Leningrad military districts and in the Pacific Fleet and that the rights of servicewomen were violated more than 2,000 times in 1998. The author points out that such figures reflect only *reported* incidents and cites the results of an anonymous questionnaire indicating that in 1997 21 per cent of servicewomen in the Northern Fleet experienced some kind of sexual harassment from their male colleagues.[32]

In addition to the kinds of quantitative and qualitative information presented above about women's roles, opportunities and experiences within the military, the postmodern military model indicates that we should also take social attitudes, especially attitudes to the appropriate roles for men and women, into consideration when judging how closely the conditions in a national military approach those described by the model. In other words, those societies which place a high value on equality of opportunity between men and women and encourage women to enter traditionally male occupations (including the armed forces) tend to have national militaries which are in the forefront of the movement towards gender integration.

Social attitudes in Russia since the collapse of the USSR have regarded traditional, rather conservative, gender roles as those which are most appropriate for men and women. During a period of deep economic uncertainty, underemployment and the fear of unemployment, women and girls are being encouraged to focus on the domestic sphere of husband, home and children rather than compete with men in higher education and the workplace.[33] At the same time, many Russian women have rejected the very notion of 'equality', which is associated with the Soviet woman's 'double burden': doing a man's job at work as well as a woman's domestic chores and childcare at home.[34] Indeed, the experience of the Soviet period has left many Russian women very sceptical of the Western feminist notion that paid employment can lead to personal emancipation.[35] They prefer instead to emphasise their femininity in every way possible: through their personal appearance (clothing, makeup, hairstyles) as well as in their relationships with men (valuing chivalrous gestures from men such as hand-kissing and door-opening) and in their choice of occupation (where possible, full-time wife and mother). Indeed sociological studies undertaken in Russia during the mid-1990s indicate that most Russian women accepted gendered divisions of labour in the workplace and in the home.[36] The embryonic women's movement in Russia, therefore, has great difficulty in attracting the support of women for campaigns for 'equality' or 'equal opportunities' between the sexes.

How these attitudes about the roles appropriate to men and to women relate to military service can be seen in the results of two opinion polls conducted in Russia. The first, published in 1998, asked different categories of young people (both civilians and service personnel) about their views on the future of the Russian Army. Responses showed a strong association between military service and the formation of a socio-cultural identity as *male*, with 46.4 per cent of all officers and almost half of all servicewomen polled agreeing that 'the only real men are those who have served in the army'.[37] Significantly fewer of those polled (14 per cent of officers, 23 per cent of conscripts and 18.2 per cent of civilian men of conscription age) believed that the army was not a place for women, although none of the officers polled (and only a minority of those in other categories, including women) agreed with the statement 'men and women should have equal rights to serve in the army'.[38] A survey published in 2003 indicated that popular views on women's military service were very evenly divided in Russia: 41 per cent of those polled said their position on the issue was neutral, while 30 per cent felt positively and 28 per cent felt negatively.[39]

Finally, although there is a civil society organisation (Union of Navy Women) which works with a political movement (Women of Russia) to campaign for improved living and working conditions for military women, its primary focus is on women as part of military families rather than on servicewomen.[40]

We can see, then, that there is little support from Russian society for greater opportunities and more equal treatment for women in the armed forces – one of those spheres which can be most clearly identified as traditionally male. This suggests that changes in the military are actually running *ahead* of changes in social attitudes regarding gender and gender integration in the workplace. This is an unusual finding in relation to the postmodern military model, and suggests two contrasting future scenarios. One is that the armed forces will lead Russian society in this respect and act as a catalyst for social change in the direction of greater gender equality. The other is that the gap between social attitudes and women's military service will instead be closed by the marginalisation and eventual exclusion of women from the armed forces at some point in the future when the problems of recruiting and retaining male soldiers have eased. The second framework I apply to the case of Russia's women soldiers, that of the liberal feminist perspective, more directly addresses some of the implications of this gap between social attitudes and women's military service.

The liberal feminist perspective: equality of opportunity for all citizens

What is referred to in this chapter as *the* liberal feminist perspective is not a single view. Feminism is a wide-ranging body of thought encompassing views positioned along a broad political and social spectrum. It is possible, however, to group together a number of feminist perspectives which share certain key features. These include:

- a belief in the traditional liberal values of individual choice and freedom;
- a rejection of the notion of essentialist differences between men and women (that is, explaining the differences between men and women by referring to the existence of unchangeable biological, physiological, psychological or other such factors); and
- an emphasis on providing women with rights and opportunities which are equal to those available to men.[41]

Some feminists who subscribe to these terms would also go further and advocate practices which favour women's recruitment and advancement over those of men (sometimes referred to as 'affirmative action' or 'positive discrimination'), while others would want to set limits on the equal opportunities agenda, for example by continuing or reintroducing restrictions on women's service in combat zones or their occupation of posts designated as 'combat'.[42] Broadly speaking, however, the liberal feminist perspective used here focuses on the importance of creating and maintaining a level playing field to permit individual women to be judged against objective standards. This perspective assumes that, in such conditions, most women would perform as well as most men. It also views it as important for women to be more fully represented in the various institutions which make decisions about society. Such a move is believed to benefit both women and society as a whole. In addition, it is assumed that women are able to change such institutions from within, once a critical mass of them have gained entry or attained leadership positions.[43] In general this perspective favours gradual and limited social change rather than a fundamental restructuring of social relations. Many of the feminists who adopt this perspective believe that it is important for women to play a full role in their national armed forces. Military service for some, if not all, of those women who are eligible is regarded as a responsibility as much as a right, in order to ensure that women throughout the society are regarded as full citizens. According to this point of view, if women are never permitted to risk their lives in defence of their country, then it will always be more difficult for them to enjoy, as a right, the full benefits of equality in civilian life.[44]

The liberal feminist perspective on women in the military has a number of features in common with the postmodern military model. Both by implication include the notion of progress in that greater opportunities for women in the military are seen as being related to greater opportunities and equality of women in the society. Both imply that a move in the direction of increased gender integration in a national military is a positive step. Both use a mixture of quantitative and qualitative indicators to measure the success or otherwise of gender integration in a particular case. The postmodern military model is perhaps the more passive of the two, however, in that it suggests that gender relations in the military merely *reflect* those which exist in society. The liberal feminist perspective advocates the use of political, legal and social campaigns by women's groups in order to ensure that gender relations move in the right direction. Furthermore, liberal feminists who focus their attention on women in the military are keenly aware that progress in this area is reversible: a number of them have warned of the phenomenon of 'cultural amnesia' concerning women's military service. This refers to the tendency of national militaries to regard women as a labour pool to be tapped during times of war or when there is a severe shortage of male recruits. When women are needed to fill the ranks, the history of women's military service and performance in previous wars is remembered and even celebrated in order to convince society that women are capable of making a contribution to the armed forces. Once the war is over or the personnel shortage has passed and *normality* is resumed, women are quickly demobilised. The achievements – even the existence – of women soldiers are often forgotten, making it difficult for women to maintain and extend any gains (towards greater equality in society as well as in the armed forces) which were made during the former periods.[45]

So what do we find when we look at the case of Russia's women soldiers from a liberal feminist perspective? To begin with, both the overall number (approximately 100,000) and the proportion (about 10 per cent) of women in the Russian armed forces would be regarded as a positive sign, indicating that a substantial number of Russian women are willing and able to enter such a traditionally male environment. The proportion of women soldiers in Russia is also comparable with that in the US military at roughly the same point in its development: that is, approximately fifteen years after women began to enter the armed forces in large numbers.[46] The discussions of women soldiers in the Russian military press increasingly feature some reference to the extensive history of women's involvement in wars and in militaries, as well as the contemporary practice of many national militaries in employing women soldiers, to demonstrate the normality of women's military service.[47] There are numerous indications in Russian military press reports that women soldiers are performing their duties competently and efficiently. In most cases the work of women soldiers is given unqualified praise,[48] although on some occasions the praise is given rather grudgingly – for example, the author of one such article remarked that 'women are capable of carrying out *some* of the same duties as men in such areas as medical and support services'.[49] This evidence that Russian women soldiers are coping well with their professional responsibilities and that they are receiving at least some recognition and approval on this basis from their male colleagues and superiors would also be regarded as a positive sign, as well as an affirmation of the liberal feminist tenet that most women need only the opportunity to prove themselves against fair and objective criteria in order to succeed.

In most other respects, though, a liberal feminist analysis of women in the Russian military reveals cause for serious concern. The legal restrictions on the terms of women's employment in the armed forces would be regarded as very negative features, and, even though their intention is to protect women's health, the effect of such regulations is to diminish the equality of the opportunities available to women. When mothers (rather than all parents) are given reduced working hours or when other special considerations permit them to perform domestic duties, the traditional division of labour within the family becomes institutionalised, and in the long term this only increases the domestic burden on women. As we have already

seen in the discussion of the postmodern military model, many Russian officers are reluctant to recommend the women in their units for promotion
because the officers are concerned about the impact which the domestic
demands on women's time will have on their abilities to perform their
professional responsibilities. In other words, Russia's protective labour
legislation actively harms the career prospects of its women soldiers.

These legal restrictions on women's working conditions are also problematical from a liberal feminist perspective because they contribute to the
perception among male soldiers that women in the military have an easy
time. Moreover, they create resentment among the men who are given a
disproportionate share of the heavy labour, the tedious guard duty and the
undesirable night shifts because their female colleagues are not permitted to
do all parts of a soldier's job.[50] In this respect, male soldiers in mixed-gender
units are required to work harder and longer than their counterparts in all-
male units.

The indications of sex discrimination and the sexual harassment of
women soldiers in Russia would, of course, be regarded as serious deficien-
cies when measuring the country's progress towards greater gender equality.
But perhaps more worrying still from a liberal feminist perspective is the
absence from society at large of support for equality of opportunity and the
advancement of women. Whereas the postmodern military model finds
puzzling and anomalous the gap between the apparent advances of women
in the Russian military into traditionally male preserves and the retreat of
women in Russian society back into the domestic sphere, the liberal feminist
perspective would identify this gap as a cause for grave concern. With the
exception of the Union of Navy Women mentioned above, very little interest
in the position and prospects of Russia's women soldiers appears to be
expressed by civil society organisations, including women's groups. The
mainstream civilian media pays little attention to this topic and there is no
Russian equivalent to the American DACOWITS, the Defense Advisory
Committee on Women in the Services, which was created by the US
Congress in 1951 to act as an advisor to the Pentagon and which became a
leading advocate for expanding women's roles in the US armed forces.[51] In
fact, there appears to be no organisation with significant moral authority or
political power in Russia which is willing to take up the cause of the rights
of women soldiers and to work to keep it at the forefront of society's and the
Government's attention. Without such support for the women soldiers and
pressure on the MOD on their behalf, a liberal feminist would probably
conclude, the advancement of their position is likely to be very slow and
subject to reversal, especially if the trends in the Russian military's recruitment and retention of young men begin to be reversed, and women are no
longer needed to make up the numbers to the same extent.

Further evidence of the fragility of women soldiers' position is provided
by the indications that Russia's MOD is making little effort actively to

recruit women and indeed regards them very much as a second choice. In the early 1990s the MOD daily newspaper *Krasnaia zvezda* (*Red Star*) published a series of full-page advertisements encouraging applications for contract service which included the slogan: 'The Air Defence Forces: The Service for Real Men'.[52] By contrast, the major attempt to increase applications from women was a beauty competition for servicewomen sponsored by the MOD, which judged contestants on their ability to cook and sing as well as on their shooting skills.[53] The most valuable potential contract soldiers are identified as those who serve first as conscripts and then choose to extend their term of duties on a contract basis.[54] Women are necessarily excluded from this profile of the ideal contract soldier because they are not conscripted. Articles in the military press and statements by military officials which focus on issues of the recruitment and retention of personnel and contract service rarely refer to the participation of women in the armed forces, in spite of the fact that women make up a substantial proportion of contract soldiers (according to some estimates it is as high as 50 per cent).[55] Instead discussions about the viability of a volunteer force focus on whether the MOD can afford to provide the salary levels and working conditions necessary to attract young men, especially those with families, into military service. Indeed, the author of one such piece remarked on the importance of ensuring that there are local job opportunities for the *wives* of Russia's contract soldiers, indicating that women are not the primary target of recruiting efforts.[56] This message was made more explicit in the caption of a photograph showing women soldiers in an artillery battalion, which emphasised that the conditions of contract service should be such as to attract members of the strong sex, not the weak sex.[57]

While an analysis of Russia's women soldiers from the liberal feminist perspective suggests that Russia has some way to go to catch up with, for example, the USA and Canada, which are relatively more advanced in the gender integration of their militaries, the literature on women's military service in those countries indicates that, even there, things are not as they should be. There have been numerous sexual harassment scandals in the US armed forces,[58] including allegations that women soldiers were raped by their male colleagues or superiors during the 2003 war against Iraq.[59] Canada, which in most respects appears to have equality of opportunity in its military, has a very high rate of attrition among its military women.[60] There are also worrying suggestions that lip service on the part of officials to the language and legislation of equal opportunities is creating a form of *virtual* gender equality in the armed forces of these more 'advanced' countries, one which exists only on paper.[61] Some scholars question whether women can change male-dominated institutions, such as the armed forces, through the means advocated by liberal feminists (a critical mass both of women members and of women in leadership positions), or whether the women themselves become changed by their organisational environments in order to fit in with the dominant male culture.[62] Other scholars question whether military service can be a stepping-stone towards the greater equality of women in a society, pointing out that in the USA the entry of large numbers of women into the armed forces was a consequence rather than a cause of the women's rights movement in that country.[63] Such research on the experience of women in military service raises doubts about whether an equal opportunities' agenda in a country's national military is sufficient to give women meaningful equality in the armed forces, let alone whether it can promote the kinds of social changes advocated by liberal feminism. It is on these very points that anti-militarist feminism takes up the debate, and it is to this framework that I now turn in search of further insights to the case of Russia's women soldiers.

The anti-militarist feminist perspective: feminine soldiers in a man's army

As was the case with the liberal feminist perspective, there is no *single* anti-militarist feminist perspective, rather a number of broadly compatible anti-militarist feminist views are grouped together here to indicate that Russia's women soldiers would be perceived from a different point on the spectrum than that occupied by liberal feminists. Although some strands of anti-militarist feminist thought embrace an essentialist view of femininity (regarding women as inherently peace-loving and therefore unsuited to violence and the conduct of war), the anti-militarist perspective presented here focuses on the creation of gender identities and the role played by militaries in this process.

Anti-militarist feminists regard militaries as very dangerous institutions – dangerous not only in the obvious sense that they have the means and the authority to use force against an enemy, but because they pose a threat to their own societies, which they have the responsibility to protect. In this view, militaries create and sustain a culture of 'virulent masculinism' which glorifies violence, depends on the oppression of women and is closely related to (and helps to maintain) the patriarchal structure of their societies.[64] Anti-militarist feminists therefore believe that 'women have the most to gain by cutting back the military's role in society'.[65] Far from regarding women's military service as a sign of progress for individual women and for society, this feminist position sees the entry of women to the armed forces as a retrograde step. In sharp contrast to the liberal feminist perspective, an anti-militarist feminist would argue that women's military service *cannot* be a mechanism for greater equality between men and women in society because militaries depend for their very existence on a rigid segregation of gender roles, both within the armed forces and in society.

According to this analysis, the military plays a crucial role in creating and sustaining ideal types of masculinity. Traditionally, being a soldier was regarded as a man's work, because only men were believed to possess those characteristics essential for warfare such as physical strength and courage. Women, by contrast, were associated with such characteristics as nurturing and supporting, and were regarded as essentially defenceless and in need of (male) protection.[66] Even when women are permitted to enter the military (chiefly when there is a shortage of men willing and able to serve), there remains an important element of military service from which women are barred. That element, most frequently defined as service in combat, is also regarded as the epitome of military service – and thus of masculinity. Cynthia Enloe argues:

> Women – because they are *women*, not because they are nurses or wives or clerical workers – cannot qualify for entrance into the inner sanctum, combat. Furthermore, to *allow* women entrance into the essential core of the military would throw into confusion *all* men's certainty about their male identity and thus about their claims to privilege in the social order ... Women may serve the military, but they can never be permitted to *be* the military.[67]

This analysis of military service also provides an explanation of the concentration of the vast majority of women soldiers in sectors regarded as traditionally female, sectors which are also dominated by women in civilian society, namely medicine, administration and communications. This creation of women's work within the military, like the preservation of combat as men's work, helps to sustain the notion that women and men are fundamentally different from each other.[68] Furthermore, militaries need to reinforce these gender differences by encouraging women soldiers to continue to exhibit feminine characteristics even while in uniform. Thus from the military's perspective the ideal woman soldier is a conventionally pretty heterosexual who smiles a great deal, especially at men.[69]

If we apply this feminist anti-militarist analysis of militaries and women's roles in them to the case of Russia's women soldiers, we find that our attention is drawn to several features to which the other two frameworks gave little consideration. Although both the postmodern military model and the liberal feminist perspective would place considerable emphasis on the proportion of women soldiers in the Russian armed forces, an anti-militarist feminist would regard this as of less importance than the kinds of jobs women soldiers perform and the ways in which women soldiers are depicted, especially by the MOD and the institutions (such as the military press) under its control or influence. An analysis using this perspective would find the concentration of women soldiers into certain feminised sectors as entirely predictable and as contributing crucially to the maintenance of clearly defined gender roles in the armed forces and in society. Furthermore, the adoption by the military sector of legal restrictions on women's working conditions designed for the civilian economy would be seen as reinforcing the essential differences between men and women. The application of those regulations to women in military service ensures that women will not be permitted to do all parts of a soldier's job and raises questions about the propriety of women's presence in the armed forces. If women soldiers have to be protected from certain tasks which a soldier is expected to perform (such as guard duty or night shifts), how can they possibly protect others?

If we turn to the depiction of women soldiers in Russia's military press, we find a great deal to support the anti-militarist feminist analysis of the military's concern with encouraging femininity in women soldiers. The attributes of Russia's women soldiers which are identified for praise tend to be those usually associated with women, such as attentiveness and accuracy.[70] Similarly, women soldiers are also described as being more observant, efficient and conscientious than their male counterparts, as well as being noted for their 'benevolence in personal relations'.[71] The presence of women in a unit is said to bring cleanliness, cosiness and order.[72] Servicewomen are rarely credited with courage, decisiveness, physical strength, strength of character or the ability to lead others. The gap between those qualities associated with men and those attributed to women is most obvious when the characteristics of male and female soldiers are overtly contrasted. For example, the caption to a photograph of a group of men and women soldiers of an artillery battalion pointed out that, although such a place might be considered a man's preserve, alongside equipment requiring 'muscular' strength there are other technologies, such as electronics and communications equipment, which require a woman's delicate handling and a woman's meticulousness, punctuality and accuracy.[73]

It is very striking that articles in Russian military newspapers and journals referring to women soldiers often describe the armed forces as having become 'feminised'.[74] This is a considerable exaggeration if based solely on the numbers and proportion of servicewomen (after all, if 10 per cent of Russia's soldiers are women, 90 per cent are men), but it makes more sense as an indication that a threat is perceived to the essentially masculine identity of the armed forces and to the men who serve in it. Perhaps as a means of countering this perceived threat to the essence of the military, the Russian military press sometimes expresses surprise at their presence in the ranks, asking, for example, 'Can't they find husbands?'[75] Women soldiers are often described as belonging to the 'weak sex', although the authors of these comments usually qualify their use of the phrase by remarking that the women pictured, interviewed or referred to on *this* occasion should not be described in this way.[76] Women soldiers are also often praised especially for their *feminine* qualities. The photograph of one servicewoman in *Krasnaia zvezda* is accompanied by a caption which describes her as 'fragile' and asks how she manages to preserve her elegance even while packing a parachute.[77] An article in the military press described Russia's women soldiers as 'heroines' and 'flowers', but while the author dwelt extensively on servicewomen's beauty and their smiles, he said nothing about how well they performed their duties or why they should be regarded as heroic.[78]

An examination of the depiction of women soldiers in photographs published in the military press provides another means of assessing whether traditional notions of femininity are being reinforced or challenged. Here the messages are more mixed. On the one hand, it is easy to find photographs of conventionally pretty young women soldiers, with carefully styled hair, makeup and jewellery, smiling at the camera and holding flowers.[79] There is an annual blizzard of such images in the Russian military press on 8 March (International Women's Day), the day on which military publications are most likely to devote attention to issues related to women's military service. However, many of the photographs show women soldiers in a more ordinary professional light, which can be likened to the usual depiction of their male colleagues. In these photographs the servicewomen look away from the camera, have serious expressions, and are apparently focused on carrying out the task at hand without the aid of makeup, jewellery or flowers.[80]

In concluding this discussion of the applicability of the feminist anti-militarist framework to the case of Russia's women soldiers, it is worth pointing out that the early years of the twenty-first century have seen articles in the Russian military press call for greater efforts in the education and training of servicewomen, to improve their integration within the armed forces. However, the areas identified for attention are women's psychology and physiology, in particular the effects of military service on their physical and emotional health.[81] In other words, this analysis emphasises the need for further attention to those characteristics which are peculiar to women rather than a reconsideration of the institutional and cultural barriers which might prevent their fuller integration within the armed forces.

Conclusions

In many respects the conclusions of this discussion are tentative, in part because it is simply too early to make a definitive judgement on which way women's military service in Russia will develop and also because of the need for further detailed investigation of this topic, notwithstanding the greater interest in it which Russian scholars and analysts are beginning to exhibit. We can say, however, that the application of these three Western frameworks does provide important insights which improves our understanding of Russia's women soldiers. The postmodern military model highlights gender integration within the Russian armed forces as part of an international, perhaps even global, phenomenon, but one which is closely tied to social attitudes within the country. According to this model, the participation of women soldiers in the Russian military is indicative of the development of the military as an institution. The liberal feminist perspective also emphasises the significance of social norms in relation to the opportunities for women in the Russian military while raising the possibility that a critical mass of women soldiers (and especially of women officers) could lead to greater gender equality both in the institution and in Russian society. In addition, this perspective alerts us to a potential link between citizenship and military service, suggesting that the presence of women soldiers is a necessary step in the development of a more equitable society for Russia. At the same time, however, the liberal feminist perspective warns that the advances of women in military service can be reversed. The anti-militarist feminist perspective, by contrast, argues that it is a mistake to view Russian women's military service as a means of changing either Russia's armed forces or its society. Instead the military should be seen as a key focus for the formation and reinforcement of gender identities and relationships in Russian society. In this view, both Russia's military and its society have too great a stake in maintaining existing norms of the appropriate roles for men and women to permit women soldiers to challenge them. Instead the Russian military will carefully define a suitably feminine dimension for women's military service and ensure that women soldiers are not permitted to step outside those boundaries.

While these Western frameworks help to highlight certain features of women's military service in Russia, none of them places much emphasis on understanding the motivations and experiences of the women soldiers them-selves, which must be important aspects of the puzzle under discussion. According to surveys conducted by Russian sociologists, as well as anec-dotal evidence, the need for employment and a steady income is the most important reason why the overwhelming majority of women soldiers enter the armed forces.[82] Women have been disproportionately affected by the unemployment and under-employment which have accompanied the shift to a market economy in Russia.[83] Moreover, many of Russia's women soldiers are married to officers who desperately need a second income for their fami-lies but the women have little chance of finding a job in the civilian economy in the remote areas where their husbands are stationed. This suggests that many of the women who have entered the Russian armed forces since the early 1990s have done so for short-term and pragmatic reasons rather than because they aspire to a career in the military. The short-term and pragmatic nature of the women's motives appear to be matched by the short-term and pragmatic nature of the MOD's motives in allowing large numbers of women to enter the armed forces: namely the pressing need to make up the shortfall in (male) personnel. If the women soldiers, the military and society all regard women's military service as a temporary phenomenon taking place in 'extreme conditions' (see the epigraph to this chapter), then it is much easier for women's participation in the military to be limited, and subsequently eliminated when life returns to 'normal'. The presence of women in the Russian military appears fragile and reversible, with little to challenge the mutually reinforcing attitudes of individual women, society and the armed forces about the appropriate roles for men and women. This suggests that Russia may not, in fact, be heading for the full integration of women within the armed forces and that any advances beyond the currently, limited extent of gender integration are not likely to be accomplished quickly or easily. The real test will come when (and if) the armed forces manages to regain the ground that they have lost in terms of prestige and status in Russian society. What will happen if officers once again command relatively high wages and enjoy the respect of ordinary citizens, if young men once again are willing to serve in the military in large numbers? In other words, if women are no longer needed to fill the gaps, will they still be welcome in the armed forces? Although much of the analysis presented above suggests that they will not, much will depend on the progress Russia makes in the meantime towards an all-volunteer force, as well as on how long the present military crisis persists.

Notes

1 T. Ermolaeva and V. Georgiev, 'Neprikosnovennyi zapas ili poslednii rezerv?', *Nezavismoe voennoe obozrenie*, 8 (4–10 March 1999).
2 The term 'military' is used in this chapter to refer to those forces under the control of the MOD. Women also serve in substantial and increasing numbers in the forces of other ministries and departments of the RF.
3 Women's Research and Education Institute, *Women in the Military: Where They Stand*, 3rd edn (Washington, DC: WREI, 2000), p. 29.
4 *Ibid.*, p. 30.
5 See, e.g.: B. Howell Granger, *On Final Approach: The Women Airforce Service Pilots of World War II* (Scottsdale: Falconer, 1991); R. Hall, *Patriots in Disguise: Women Warriors of the Civil War* (New York: Paragon House, 1993); S. Berger Gluck, *Rosie the Riveter Revisited: Women, the War, and Social Change* (Boston, MA: Twayne, 1987); M. Collins Weitz, *Sisters in the Resistance: How Women Fought to Free France 1940–1945* (New York: John Wiley, 1995); F. C. G. Page, *Following the Drum: Women in Wellington's Wars* (London: Andre Deutsch, 1986).
6 See, e.g., M. Cummings, *Hornet's Nest: The Experiences of One of the Navy's First Female Fighter Pilots* (Lincoln, MA: Writer's Showcase, 1999).
7 See, e.g., G. DeGroot and C. Peniston-Bird (eds) *A Soldier and a Woman: Sexual Integration in the Military* (Harlow: Pearson Education Limited, 2000); E. Addis, V. Russo and L. Sebesta (eds) *Women Soldiers: Images and Realities* (London: Macmillan, 1994); R. Howes and M. Stevenson (eds) *Women and the Use of Military Force* (Boulder, CO, and London: Lynne Rienner, 1993).
8 See, e.g.: J. Elshtain, *Women and War* (New York: Basic Books, 1987); M. Herbert, *Camouflage Isn't Only For Combat: Gender, Sexuality and Women in the Military* (New York and London: New York University Press, 1998); J. Goldstein, *War and Gender* (Cambridge and New York: Cambridge University

Press, 2001); I. Skjelsbaek and D. Smith (eds) *Gender, Peace and Conflict* (London: Sage, 2001).

9 Among the few works published in the West on this topic are: D. Herspring, 'Women in the Russian military: a reluctant marriage', *Minerva: Quarterly Report on Women and the Military* 15:2 (1997), 42–59; J. Mathers, 'Women in the Russian armed forces: a marriage of convenience?' *Minerva: Quarterly Report on Women and the Military* 18:3–4 (2000), 129–43.

10 C. Moskos, J. Williams and D. Segal (eds) *The Postmodern Military: Armed Forces after the Cold War* (New York and Oxford: Oxford University Press, 2000), chapters 1 and 2.

11 *Ibid.*: see the coverage of women in the military about the following countries: USA (pp. 22–3); UK (pp. 40–2); France (pp. 64–5); Germany (pp. 91–2); Netherlands (pp. 111–12); Denmark (pp. 130–1); Italy (pp. 141–2); Canada (pp. 165–8); Australia and New Zealand (pp. 195–8); Switzerland (p. 217); Israel (pp. 234–5); South Africa (pp. 253–5).

12 *Ibid.*, pp. 1–2.

13 For a recent estimate by an international source, see International Institute for Strategic Studies, *The Military Balance 2003–2004* (London: Oxford University Press for the IISS, 2003), p. 89. For earlier estimates by Russian sources see: 'Zhenshchinam forma k litsu', *Krasnaia zvezda* (10 December 1992); General-Major A. Avilov, 'Budut li v Rossiiskoi armii zhenshchiny-generaly?', *ibid.* (10 April 1993); V. Georgiev, 'Sotsial'nyi portret zashchitnitsy otechestva', *Nezavismoe voennoe obozrenie*, 9 (6–12 March 1998); General-Colonel V. Zherebtsov, 'Voennaia sluzhba po kontraktu – segodniashniaia deistvitel'nost", *Voennaia mysl'*, 4 (July–August 1999).

14 'Zhenshchinam forma k litsu' *Krasnia zvezda* (10 December 1992).

15 Avilov, 'Budut li v Rossiiskoi armii zhenshchiny-generaly?'

16 P. Altunin, 'Zhenshchina na voennoi sluzhbe', *Krasnaia zvezda* (10 March 1993).

17 Georgiev, 'Sotsial'nyi portret zashchitnitsi otechestva'.

18 Zherebtsov, 'Voennaia sluzhba po kontraktu', p. 6.

19 Major V. Shlikov, 'A "amazonki" stuchat na mashinakh', *Krasnaia zvezda* (3 January 1992).

20 Zherebtsov, 'Voennaia sluzhba po kontraktu', p. 6.

21 V. Sperling, *Organizing Women in Contemporary Russia: Engendering Transition* (Cambridge: Cambridge University Press, 1999), pp. 91–2.

22 A. Smirnov, 'Women in the Russian Army', *Russian Social Science Review* 43:4 (July–August) 2002, translated and reproduced on the Post-Soviet Armies Newsletter website: www.perso.club-internet.fr/kozlowsk/women.html.

23 D. Strugovets, 'Obet bezbrachiia v mechtakh Minoborony', *Nezavismoe voennoe obozrenie*, 35 (3 October 2003).

24 'Kuda Spetsnazu bez Viktorii?' *Krasnaia zvezda* (6 March 1994).

25 A. M. Shelepov and V. V. Peshkov, 'Iz istorii voennoi meditsiny zhenshchiny na voennoi sluzhbe v Rossiiskoi Armii', *Voenno-meditsinskii zhurnal*, 3 (31 March 2003), 76–7.

26 Georgiev, 'Sotsial'nyi portret zashchitnitsi otechestva'; S. Rikov, 'Slabyi pol v sil'noi armii', *Nezavismoe voennoe obozrenie*, 8 (3–16 March 2000).

27 Smirnov, 'Women in the Russian Army'; 'Znai nashikh! Zhenskoe muzhestvo', *Zakavkazskie voennye vedomosty*, 18 (19 March 2003).

28 Ermolaeva and Georgiev, 'Neprikosnovennyi zapas ili poslednii rezerv?'
29 Smirnov, 'Women in the Russian Army'.
30 *Ibid.*
31 Marina Dobrovol'skaia, the chair of the Union of Navy Women, a civil society organisation concerned with protecting the rights of women connected with the Russian Navy, described sexual harassment as a very serious, but also very hidden, problem: N. Azhgikhina, 'Nemuzhskie problemy vooruzhennykh sil', *Nezavismoe voennoe obozrenie*, 16 (26 April – 16 May 1997).
32 Rikov, 'Slabyi pol v sil'noi armii'.
33 E. Dmitrieva, 'Orientations, re-orientations or disorientation? Expectations of the future among Russian school-leavers', in H. Pilkington (ed) *Gender, Generation and Identity in Contemporary Russia* (London and New York: Routledge, 1996), pp. 75–6.
34 Sperling, *Organizing Women in Contemporary Russia*, p. 17.
35 J. Siklova, 'Why we resist Western-style feminism', *Transitions*, 5:1 (January 1998), 32.
36 E. Chinyaeva, 'An identity of one's own', *Transitions*, 5:1 (January 1998), 39.
37 Lieutenant Colonel D. Pozhidaev, 'Molodezh' Budushchem', *Armeiskii sbornik* (March 1998), 22.
38 *Ibid.*
39 'Put' i zhenshchiny sluzhat', *Ural'skye voennye vesti*, 99 (23 November 2003).
40 Azhgikhina, 'Nemuzhskie problemy vooruzhennykh sil'; E. Ustinovich, 'Zhenshchina i armiia: voprosy komplektovaniia', *Voennaia mysl'*, 8 (2003), 55; N. Mikirtumova, 'Rossiiskii soiuz zhenshchin VMF. Iustitsiia v litse polkovnika Mironkinoi', *Flag Rodiny*, 77 (24 April 2003).
41 B. Carroll and B. Welling Hall, 'Feminist perspectives on women and the use of force', in Howes and Stevenson (eds) *Women and the Use of Military Force*, p. 18.
42 I. Feinman, *Citizenship Rites: Feminist Soldiers and Feminist anti-militarists* (New York and London: New York University Press, 2000), pp. 31–40.
43 C. Enloe, *Does Khaki Become You? The Militarization of Women's Lives* (London: Pandora Press, 1988), p. xviii.
44 Feinman, *Citizenship Rites*, p. 1.
45 M. Wechsler Segal, 'Women in the armed forces', in Howes and Stevenson (eds) *Women and the Use of Military Force*, pp. 82–4. For other discussions of this phenomenon, see: R. Roach Pierson, '"Did your mother wear army boots?" Feminist theory and women's relation to war, peace and revolution', in S. MacDonald, P. Holden and S. Ardener (eds) *Images of Women in Peace and War: Cross-Cultural and Historical Perspectives* (London: Macmillan, 1987), pp. 222–3; and M. R. Higonnet and P. Higonnet, 'The double helix', in M. Randolph Higonnet, J. Jenson, S. Michel and M. Collins Weitz (eds) *Behind the Lines: Gender and the Two World Wars* (New Haven, CT, and London: Yale University Press, 1987), pp. 31–47.
46 Segal, 'Women in the armed forces', p. 85.
47 See, e.g.: A. Sinikchiiants, 'Geroi i podvigi, voennye damy', *Krasnyi voin*, 17 (8 March 2003); 'Novye Amazonki', *Zakavkazskye voennye vedomosti*, 16 (8 March 2003); Shelepov and Peshkov, 'Iz istorii voennoi meditsiny'.
48 See, e.g., the following *Krasnaia zvezda* articles 'Rabotat' s nimi legko' (21 September 1994); I. Sergeev, 'Verna ruka, glaza prekrasny' (10 November 1994);

O. Riseva, 'Zhenshchina v armii zhdet rytsarskogo k sebe otnosheniia' (6 March 1993); Colonel Leonid Pozdiv, '"Zhenskii batal'on" spetsnaza' (4 February 1994); Major M. Lisovskii, 'Na boevom dezhurstve – tol'ko zhenshchiny?' (9 June 1992); Colonel L. Pozdeev, 'Desantnik Oksana' (11 February 1994); and see Ermolaeva and Georgiev, 'Neprikosnovennyi zapas ili poslednii rezerv?'; A. Kasatov, '"I devushka nasha v soldatskoi shineli ... "', *Nezavismoe voennoe obozrenie*, 36 (26 September–2 October 1997).

49 Rikov, 'Slabyi pol v sil'noi armii' (emphasis added).

50 Smirnov, 'Women in the Russian Army'.

51 Feinman, *Citizenship Rites*, p. 98.

52 'Voiska PVO: dlia nastoiashchiikh muzhchin', *Krasnaia zvezda* (11 June 1993).

53 The incongruity of this competition attracted the attention of Western journalists: see 'Russia's glamour brigade aims high', *Times* (8 March 2003).

54 Zherebtsov, 'Voennaia sluzhba po kontraktu – segodniashniaia deistvitel'nost'', p. 5.

55 Ermolaeva and Georgiev, 'Neprikosnovennyi zapas ili poslednii rezerv?'

56 General-Major (retired) V. Fedorov, Colonel O. Kobyzev and Colonel V. Baiborodin, 'Ob etapakh i variantakh perekhoda vooruzhennykh sil na dobrovol'nyi sposob komplektovaniia', *Voennaia mysl'*, 2 (2002), p. 16.

57 'Sudaryni v tankovykh shlemakh', Krasnaia zvezda (17 August 1994).

58 See, e.g., L. Meola, 'Sexual harassment in the army', in L. Weinstein and C. White (eds) *Wives and Warriors: Women and the Military in the United States and Canada* (Westport, CT, and London: Bergin & Garvey, 1997), pp. 145–9.

59 M. Moffeit and A. Herdy, 'Female GIs reporting rape by US soldiers', *Denver Post* (24 January 2004), online: http://fairuse.1accesshost.com/news1/charlotte1.html.

60 K. Davis, 'Understanding women's exit from the Canadian forces: implications for integration?', in Weinstein and White (eds) *Wives and Warriors*, pp. 179–98.

61 F. D'Amico, 'Policing the US military's race and gender lines', in Weinstein and White, *Wives and Warriors*, pp. 199–234.

62 J. Bystydzienksi, 'Women in groups and organizations: implications for the use of force', in Howes and Stevens, *Women and the Use of Military Force*, pp. 44–5, 51.

63 Feinman, *Citizenship Rites*, p. 41.

64 *Ibid.*, pp. 1, 11.

65 Enloe, *Does Khaki Become You?*, p. xvii.

66 W. Chapkis, 'Sexuality and militarism', in E. Isaksson (ed.) *Women and the Military System* (New York: St. Martin's Press, 1988), p. 11.

67 Enloe, *Does Khaki Become You?*, p. 15 (emphasis in original).

68 Chapkis, 'Sexuality and militarism', p. 11.

69 Enloe, *Does Khaki Become You?*, p. 141.

70 M. Timofeev, 'Obnaruzhit', opovestit', navesti', *Nezavismoe voennoe obozrenie*, 2 (19–25 January 2001).

71 Colonel V. Laktiushin, 'Stroite vzvod, madam', *Krasnaia zvezda* (20 March 1992).

72 Lisovskii, 'Na boevom dezhurstve – tol'ko zhenshchiny?'

73 'Rabotat' s nimi legko'.

74 See, e.g.: Rikov, 'Slabyi pol v sil'noi armii'; Ermolaeva and Georgiev, 'Neprikosnovennyi zapas ili poslednii rezerv?'; Lisovskii, 'No boevom dezhurstve – tol'ko zhenshchiny?'

75 *Armeiskii sbornik*, 3 (2001), caption for photographs facing p. 33.

76 See, e.g.: *ibid.*; A. Monakhov and O. Veshchii, 'Za milykh dam! Etot sil'nyi slabyi pol', *Strazh Baltiki*, 38 (6 March 2003).

77 'Ot takoi ulybki stanet mir dobrei', *Krasnaia zvezda* (15 November 1994).

78 Lieutenant-Colonel N. Chepurnykh, 'V ognom stroiu: zhenshchina srodni stikham', *Voennyi zheleznodorozhnik*, 25 (16 June 2003).

79 See, e.g.: 'Obitaemyi ostrov', *Krasnaia zvezda* (8 July 1992); 'Na Kunashire umeiut tsenit' obaianie', *ibid.* (25 October 1994); *Armeiskii sbornik* (March 2000), front cover; 'Nashi "Amazonki"', *ibid.* (6 March 2004).

80 See, e.g.: "V ekipazhe – tol'ko devushki', *Krasnaia zvezda* (19 May 1994); 'Voiska Postoiannoi Gotovnosti', *Krasnaia zvezda* (7 April 1995); 'Zhenshchiny v Rossiiskoi armii', *Nezavismoe voennoe obozrenie*, 11 (22 March–8 April 1997); *Armeiskii sbornik*, 10 (2001), inside front cover.

81 Shelepov and Peshkov, 'Iz istorii voennoi meditsiny zhenshchiny na voennoi sluzhbe v Rossiiskoi armii', p. 77.

82 For the results of Russian sociological surveys on women soldiers' motivations for joining the armed forces, see: O. Ryseva, 'Zhenshchina v armii zhdet rytsarskogo k sebe otnosheniia', *Krasnaia zvezda* (6 March 1993); Ermolaeva and Georgiev, 'Neprikosnovennyi zapas ili poslednii rezerv?' For anecdotal evidence see: E. Ustinivich, 'Zhenshchina i armiia: voprosy komplektovaniia', *Voennaia mysl'*, 8 (2003); Kasatov, '"I devushka nasha v soldatskoi shineli …"'; Lieutenant-Colonel O. Shastun, 'Ot chistogo serdtsa: Zhenshchiny v stroiu', *Na boevom postu*, 85 (25 October 2003).

83 Sperling, *Organizing Women in Contemporary Russia*, pp. 43–4, 56–7, 146–58; Pilkington, *Gender, Generation and Identity in Contemporary Russia*, especially the chapters by E. Dmitrieva and S. Bridger and R. Kay.

Saving Russia's sons: the Soldiers' Mothers and the Russian–Chechen wars

And looking into the face of that one dead man we see two dead, the man and the life of the woman who gave him birth; the life she wrought is his life! And looking into his dead face, someone asks a woman, what does a woman know about war? What, what, friends in the face of a crime like that, what does man know about war! (Anna Howard Shaw, January, 1915)

Introduction

In 1989, during the last days of the Soviet–Afghanistan War, 300 women formed the CSM. Led by Maria Kirbassova,[1] the CSM lobbied the Soviet Government for the return of 180,000 young men from the battlefront in Afghanistan and regions in the Soviet republics. During their anti-military campaign the activists became more aware of the inhumane conditions of the Soviet armed forces and subsequently the CSM expanded its protest agenda to include reform of the organisation of the Soviet military. Its demands included:

- exemption from the draft for students in higher education;
- an end to mandatory conscription and *dedovshchina*;
- reduction in the length of military service; and
- the right to alternative service.[2]

Soviet General Secretary Mikhail Gorbachev responded to one of the CSM's demands for reform by signing a decree in 1990 to demobilise the army's construction battalions in which younger recruits had been treated abusively by older conscripts. The CSM's concern over the high level of physical and psychological abuse that Soviet soldiers experienced led it to establish a rehabilitation centre for soldiers leaving the Soviet Army for health reasons; in addition, it set up seminars on human rights and administered legal advice to conscripts and their parents. Eventually, in 1992, the post-Soviet Russian Government passed a law that gave new recruits into the Russian Army the right to alternative service.

In November 1994, the focus of the CSM shifted from writing petitions and lobbying the Russian Government on military reform to organising and staging regular demonstrations opposing Russia's war in Chechnia.[3] The CSM actively questioned Russia's use of military force to control the land-locked area of Chechnia, an important centre for rail and road transport, and a strategic site for the pipelines which carry oil and gas to Russia from the Caspian Sea region. According to CSM spokesperson Valentina Mel'nikova, 'when the Chechen war erupted in 1994, the offices of the Committee of CSM received approximately 100 telephone calls and 200 letters per day from people seeking information about the war'.[4]

The CSM is one of the few grassroots NGOs in Moscow and is part of the nascent Russian civil society.[5] The CSM was created and organised by women who framed their political activities within a politicised *motherist* identity; its membership is imbued with a highly developed *maternal* social consciousness, one that has been reinforced by agents of socialisation in both the Soviet and post-Soviet periods in Russia. The CSM is not a feminist organisation which seeks to advance strategic gender interests and reform the infrastructure of the patriarchal Russian State; it is rather a *feminine* organisation, which advances practical gender-related interests.[6] In this chapter, the social and political origins of the motherist identity of the CSM are discussed in relation to the role it has played in influencing public opinion during the Russian–Chechen wars.

The motherist identity

The 'frame analysis' approach to social movements was developed by social scientists in the 1980s. The notion of *framing* is based on Irving Goffman's idea that individuals develop a schema of interpretation which helps them to locate, perceive, identify and label occurrences within their life spaces and the world around them. Essentially interpretative frameworks enable individuals to

- identify what is happening/has happened to them;
- locate the source of their problems; and
- develop an approach to address those problems.

The frames of everyday life are dynamic, not static, in that actors engage in shaping and reconstructing their individual frames. In a similar manner, during all stages in the development of a social movement, collective action frames are shaped as beliefs and values are mobilised and placed in the larger political context of the social and historical conditions of the state in question. This larger umbrella frame is referred to as a 'master frame', and it may include a political paradigm, such as Marxism, or it may be a religious ideology which encompasses both the public and private spheres of a person's life. A master frame which is designated a maternal frame, or a motherist identity, is in fact an ideological framework, the value and belief systems of which guide the actions and behaviour of a woman. As such, a maternal frame is an extension into the public sphere of a woman's private role as a mother.[7] Through various forms of religious traditionalism and nationalism, their social characteristics have been defined and redefined to identify women as caretakers of the family, the community and the nation state. Thus, the role of motherhood is socially constructed by a social system of power and domination.[8]

In Russia, the ideas of a traditional patriarchal society have been and are filtered through Soviet and Russian political, social and religious ideologies. Women are viewed by men, and by themselves, as narrators of family histories, as kin-keepers and keepers of the hearth, their gender roles learned from Soviet and 'old' Russian primary and secondary agents of socialisation. During the Soviet period, these agents of socialisation included the education system, the Pioneers (Scouts), the *Komsomol* and the media. Soviet institutions acted in tandem with a system of Russian values which were acquired from the family, religious ideologies, and classical Russian art and literature. This Soviet–Russian duality of ideas has created a complex of stereotypes that Russian women have incorporated into their daily lives. The dual image of 'suffering mother' and 'strong woman' nevertheless reinforces the notion that the ideal Russian woman is a 'mother' and a caregiver.

Women in Soviet Russia were subjected to actively pro-natalist policies[9] which coercively promoted gender roles and particular cultural forms of motherhood.[10] During the 1950s Stalin's Government introduced the pro-natalist and pro-Russian nationalist idea of the 'Heroic Mother' as part of the effort to replace the millions of Russian lives lost during the Second World War. To be awarded the prestigious title 'Heroic Mother', a Russian woman had to give birth to at least nine children, and for her maternal efforts she was awarded a medal by Stalin and her picture was printed in the Soviet daily newspaper *Pravda*.

Mary Buckley points out that in the 1960s and 1970s 'the Soviet writings on the family had not tried to restructure the family and socialise housework but to boost the birth rate and strengthen the nuclear family'.[11] The Soviet pedagogical approach built on the pro-natalist policies of the 1950s, applying a more *scientific* understanding of gender roles: social scientists located the foundation of sex differences in the maternal function, while Soviet psychologists explained that girls are inclined towards nurturing activities – looking after people, nursing and exercising compassion – making them naturally suited to be mothers.[12] The 'feeling of motherhood' was, according to the prominent Soviet psychologist Boris Riabinin, 'above all a feeling of responsibility towards society and the child, a responsibility which can be transferred to nobody else. Nobody.'[13] A Russian woman in the Soviet period was expected to be both an exemplary mother and a 'strong woman'. Vera Dunham describes the strong woman as a heroine of Soviet–Russian fiction:

> The heroine, in contrast to the hero, shows consistently fullness of character: *tsel'nost*. She has a multifaceted character of wide range, encompassing positive qualities such as selflessness, endurance, generosity, ability to adjust to stress, ability to solve immediate problems ... Moreover in contrast to a man, woman represents strength which is derived from an ability to relate actively to the family, to the collective and to society.[14]

However, regardless of whether she was a 'strong woman' or a *Stakhanovite* (super worker),[15] maternal cares and the double-duty day prevented most Soviet women from receiving political promotions to managerial levels in factories and to administrative positions on collective farms. Women who lived in other Soviet *bloc* countries such as Yugoslavia and Poland experienced similar forms of gender discrimination.[16] Women living and working on collective farms in the Soviet period were governed by what Cynthia Cockburn describes as 'a modernised form of collective male dominance'.[17]

In Russian society in the 1990s, a collective male dominance muted the voice of women in the formal political arena. In general Russian women are oppressed by the patriarchal power structures of their society. In common with the Mothers of the Plaza de Mayo of Argentina and the Mothers' Front of Sri Lanka, during periods of civil unrest Russian women who were desperately seeking social justice for their families politicised their social roles as mothers, and that, in turn, enabled them to collectively enter the arena of political dissent.

The arena of political dissent

The feeling of maternal responsibility, a key factor in a Russian woman's identity, found expression during the Soviet period in the hundreds of examples of *samizdat* (literally, 'self-publishing' – dissident writings) which were signed by mothers protesting the political or religious persecution of their sons. The discourse of this unofficial information network has been recorded and preserved in the *Arkhiv samizdata* (AS), located in Berlin and containing 6,525 *samizdat* documents, dated from December 1963 to December 1991, the underground writings of anti-Soviet cultural, social and religious activists. These documents are of political, social and historical importance and constitute the only forum in which Russian women had a voice during the Soviet period.[18]

Even though *samizdat* gave women the opportunity to write about social problems that concerned them either collectively or as individual women, the overwhelming majority of Russian women chose to write about the problems that their male kin were experiencing. Of a systematic, 10 per cent sample of the 1,250 *samizdat* archived documents written during the decade 1964–74, 36 per cent of the documents written by women to the Soviet authorities or to the general public were letters seeking information about the conditions of their sons' and husbands' incarceration;[19] an additional 13 per cent of the documents written by women are about the incarceration or persecution of males who were not family members.

It is difficult to measure the actual impact that the underground writings of dissidents had on the Russian population in general, although anecdotal evidence can provide an impression. Elena Vilenskaia, the co-chairperson of the SMO in St Petersburg,[20] is a school teacher whose political values are those of her parents who had been dissidents, or 'kitchen democrats', during the 1960s. She recalls hearing about the persecution of the eight Russian university students who gathered in Moscow's Red Square to protest the invasion of Czechoslovakia by the Soviet Army in 1968:[21]

> I clearly remember all the conversations of the adults in my kitchen. How young women and men were expelled from universities, and moved from prisons to mental hospitals. I understood that the rest of the world was living a different life. And when in 1989 political activity got a boost from the elections in the USSR's Supreme Soviet – I immediately got involved.[22]

Vilenskaia met the woman who became her SMO co-chairperson, Ella Poliakova, in 1989 at one of St Petersburg's courts, where the latter was on trial for organising an unsanctioned public meeting for the People's Front, which had been established to support the Baltic State Independence Movement. Poliakova was the woman named in 1990 by Leningrad Military District Colonel General Sergei Seleznev as his greatest enemy: Seleznev had asked in a meeting with local officers: 'Why do we not raise the people against Poliakova?'[23]

Vilenskaia and Poliakova set up the SMO in St Petersburg in 1991. Zoia Kulakova, a poet and retired teacher who became a member of the SMO, said that she came to the organisation in St Petersburg to personally thank Poliakova for helping her to get her physically disabled son exempted from military service. She said:

> When I came to the SMO and learned about the scale of the problems that these women were dealing with I felt ashamed. I was shocked with what I learned. I was killed morally. All my life I had been dealing with children in kindergartens, schools and orphanages ... I, who told these children all my life about the high standards of patriotism, who taught poems about the

Motherland – I felt everything turn upside down in me. Now I believe that there is no one in the world from whom our country should be protected apart from our own bandits.[24]

Among those bandits are former president Boris Yeltsin and local military commanders who, Kulakova claims, have killed thousands of Russian children in wars that they started.

The legacy of the humanitarian caretaker role that Russian women are playing in post-Soviet Russia is also reflected in the documents in the AS: 19 per cent of women's *samizdat* during the Soviet period were concerned with problems of suffering in relation to issues of social justice and civil rights, and humanitarian issues on a global scale, while no more than 10 per cent of the documents written by men focus on those issues. Conversely, only 5 per cent of the documents written by women are actually about Russian women, either collectively or as individuals.[25]

The supportive role of Russian women during the Soviet period did not diminish during the 1980s, and during the *perestroika* years of Mikhail Gorbachev's Government, Russian women wrote repeatedly to anyone who was willing to listen – and people did listen. In a patriarchal society such as Russia, what greater punishment of a mother could there be than to take her child from her? Though men rarely wrote about women's problems, this is a gender-related issue that was recognised by men, individually and collectively, as the greatest punishment for any woman. Subsequently, mothers were supported in their search for justice for their sons. It was in this way that Russian mothers entered the arena of dissent, which enabled them to express their fear and sadness over the suffering of their sons.

The data yielded by this archival investigation suggests that the construction of gender differences that has historically relegated women to a status subordinate to that of men serves also to reinforce male power at the national level. Thus 'the nation' is synonymous with male needs, male frustrations and male aspirations. As Anne McClintock points out, 'excluded from direct action as national citisens, women are subsumed symbolically into the national body politic as its boundary and metaphoric limit'.[26] Thus, Russian women during the Soviet period accepted their prevailing feminine role as *mothers*, and they asserted their rights according to this role in the form of *political* motherhood.

Political motherhood displays a woman's familial commitment through her protest against the conscription of her son(s) or the disappearance of her children. Sara Ruddick describes political mothers as women who

... often come together out of shared pain: they appeal to mothers and others who are living in relative safety, by making their pain visible. To cite a paradagmatic example, the Madres [of Argentina] literally paraded their suffering by wearing photographs of their lost children around their necks.[27]

Thus, the selfless nature of maternal suffering is characterised by a woman's preoccupation not with herself but with another person's suffering, which leads the observer to identify with the suffering mother and to extend some aid to her and her cause.

In addition to using the symbol of the *suffering mother* to elicit support for their cause, a philosophy of non-violent public protest was endorsed by the Madres of Argentina. Diana Taylor argues that 'the Mothers of the Plaza de Mayo realised that only by being visible could they be politically effective. Only by being visible could they stay alive'.[28] This commitment to non-violent protest enabled the Madres and other motherist groups such as the Mothers Against Silence of Israel[29] and the Mothers' Front of Sri Lanka to mobilise broad support for their cause without having to directly confront the dominant male discourse or the military forces of the government in power.

Ironically, women who had been excluded from the political realms of power precisely because of their subordinate status as women/mothers were able to enter dangerous zones of conflict due to the politicisation and mobilisation of their motherist identity. During the height of Russia's campaign against Chechnia in 1995, Russian television showed images of the CSM braving bombs and artillery to pull their sons out of what they believed to be a pointless war. The CSM in Moscow was evicted from its offices, members were thrown off trains, lied to and confronted by both Russian and Chechen soldiers, and yet the CSM continued to campaign for the end of the war. Members marched to the front lines of Groznyi in Chechnia, where they demanded entrance into prisons and scoured the countryside in search of their sons; some freed their sons from prison, some found their sons already dead, and some found – nothing.[30]

The CSM received tremendous public support for organising the Mothers' March for Life and Compassion in March 1995, which received extensive coverage from both the Russian and international media. Wherever members went in Chechnia 'they were given emotional welcomes in war-devastated towns and villages, and bore witness to the horrific abuses of war'.[31] In September 1995 the CSM was awarded the Sean McBride Peace Prize and the Right Livelihood Prize (also called the Alternative Nobel Prize). The CSM's campaign was actively supported in Germany where 50,000 signatures in favour of its nomination by the International Peace Bureau (IPB)[32] and German women parliamentarians were collected in 1996. IPB president, Maj-Britt Theorin, said:

> The CSM are the most outstanding – but far from the only – example of an active citizen peacemaking in the world today. These women have dared to challenge the militarism of a male dominated society; they are citizens who are determined to have a say in or defy the decisions made by their military bureaucracy and they have risked their own lives in direct confrontations with a violent system.[33]

Similarities exist between the activism of the SMOs and the mother activism in the early stages of the *intifada* in Palestine: Rena Hammami explains that in direct confrontations with soldiers, mother activism was in many ways more successful than women's activism. Soldiers were in shock when these old traditional mothers in peasant dress physically grabbed them and struggled with them ... It became very clear, at least in the beginning stages of the intifada, that older women were much less likely to be beaten and were more successful in getting a person out of harm's way than were young women.[34]

Members of the SMOs, who were generally middle-aged women, received similar reactions from the Russian and Chechen soldiers, who were perplexed by the actions of the women: for the Russian soldiers, the de-sexed 'mothers' were less politically threatening than younger female political activists might have been. Subsequently, these women, who as *mothers* hold some moral authority in Russian society, entered the war zone, mourned with Russian and Chechen women and their families, searched for their sons and buried the dead.

Actually entering the Russian–Chechen war zone was an act of courage which engendered the collective sympathy both of the international community, and of the Russian public itself. Eventually it was largely public opinion, guided by the Russian media, that forced the Russian Government to end its military campaign in Chechnia. In August 1996 a five-year Peace Accord was negotiated which left Chechnia's status as an independent nation undetermined: Chechens considered theirs to be an independent nation while Russians still viewed Chechnia as part of the RF. Due to the lack of economic and humanitarian aid to the region from Russia and the world community, Chechens were living in a lawless society; the inter-war period of 1996–99 was characterised by political corruption, violent confrontations between Russians and Chechens, daily kidnappings, escalating incidences of domestic violence, and food and housing shortages among displaced persons.

During this tumultuous interwar period the SMOs continued their anti-military activities, which included:

- collecting statements from Russians opposed to war and military aggression;
- searching for missing soldiers and civilians from the Russian–Chechen war of 1994–96;
- establishing physical and psychological rehabilitation centres for soldiers and their families;
- providing legal counselling for soldiers and their families; and
- organising conferences, peace rallies and demonstrations.

In November 1997, the CSM and the Novocherkassk NGO Women of the Rostov Region organised the 'Women for Life Without War and

Violence International Conference', in which representatives from all the former Soviet republics discussed the common problems that women experience as victims and refugees of war. A Chechen woman, Khadijad Gateva, was named Woman–Mother of the Year, because she had adopted forty-seven children who were orphaned by the war.[35]

After a turbulent three-year period of political, economic and social strife in Chechnia, the tentative Peace Accord between Chechnia and Russia was terminated in October 1999 and the Russian–Chechen War was renewed.[36] While the Russian media was instrumental in informing the public about the activities of the CSM during the 1994–96 conflict, in 1999 the Russian media generated a fervour of nationalistic hatred against the Chechen people. The Institute for War and Peace Reporting in January 2000 claimed that the media had fuelled a new barrage of public outrage:

> Chechen fighters staged ruthless sorties in Dagestan, [Russian] civilians were taken hostage in Chechnya … and 300 people died in the terrorist bomb attacks in Moscow and Volgodonsk. The nation was consumed with a thirst for revenge – aggravated by a failure of foreign policy in the Balkans.[37]

The Commission on International Religious Freedom (CIRF), which was established in 1998 to monitor religious freedom throughout the world, has accused the Russian Government of using anti-Muslim propaganda in the war against the separatist Republic of Chechnia.[38] Exclusionary tactics and negative images of the Chechen 'other', coupled with fears of rising Russophobia in the Caucasus, reinforced the perception in Russian society that the renewed war against the Chechens was justified. Conversely, in the summer of 2000 Boris Kargalitskii reported in *Izvestiia* that almost 70 per cent of the Russians polled had changed their views about the conflict, which they now oppose – in sharp contrast to the 40 per cent of Russians polled who described themselves as opponents of the war in November 1999. However, if the belief that the geopolitical differentiation represented by the Caucasus, which symbolises the 'great divide' between the 'Christian north' and the 'Muslim south', is maintained by the Russian Government and supported by the Russian press, then peace in the new millennium in the Caspian Sea region is unlikely.

The key role of the Russian and international media in supporting the CSM's campaign during the 1994–96 conflict was absent during the second Chechen war. The SMOs have been marginalised in Russian society, and though they have held demonstrations and publicly protested against the second war, there has been little public interest in or support for their cause. The Russian public's fascination with the soldiers' mothers and its admiration for their courage has diminished. Undaunted, the CSM continues to negotiate within a maternal framework that broadly embraces a human rights perspective. The group's anti-war perspective challenges the lack of democracy within the Russian military forces[39] and it rejects wars based on nationalist, political or territorial claims and contests the use of military force at the global level. Liubov Kuznetsova summarises the CSM's doctrine which, she says, is extremely simple: 'our philosophy is a Mother's philosophy – that our children should be healthy and happy. For this we need peace.'[40]

Notes

1 In 1988, Kirbassova's son was attending university and was drafted into the Soviet Army. When Kirbassova requested that her son be transferred to a unit that was relevant to his education, she was ridiculed by the commander. When the Russian journal *Tretii sektor* reported that Kirbassova's son was suicidal the commander said: 'So what? If he hangs himself we'll look into the matter': see A. Caizza, 'Russia meets its matriarchs', *Transitions*, 5:1 (1998), 59.

2 Ibid., 59; M. Lfgren, 'Russia: mothers for peace oppose sons in war' *Inter-Press Service Journal* (7 March 1996), online: www.ips.org.

3 The area of Chechnia is 6,000 square miles; the Chechens are an indigenous people of the North Caucasus who speak a distinctive Caucasian language and make a living primarily as shepherds and farmers. In pre-war Chechnia 70 per cent of the 1,084,000 Chechens lived in rural areas; 260,000 people living in Chechnia are of Russian descent and 25,000 are Ingush. The Sunni branch of the Muslim religion plays an important part in their society where an ancient clan structure and patriarchal traditions are practised.

4 E. Borisova, 'Soldiers' Mothers lead the way', *St Petersburg Press* (7 February 1996).

5 The CSM is financially supported by donations from countries such as Norway, Switzerland, Germany and international NGOs.

6 S. Alvarez, *Engendering Democracy in Brazil: Women's Movements in Transition* (Princeton, NJ: Princeton University Press, 1990), pp. 24–5. Alvarez makes an important distinction between feminist and feminine organisations. 'Whereas feminist organizations focus on issues specific to the female condition (i.e., reproductive rights), feminine groups mobilize women around gender-related issues and concerns.' The cost of living, for example, is one issue. Cynthia Cockburn points out: 'For a start not all women's activism is feminist. Movements of women defining themselves as mothers, for instance may be constructing the identity biologically, not questioning the ideology of the patriarchal family. Or they may be constructing it socially, as primary caretaker': C. Cockburn, *The Space Between Us* (London: Zed Books, 1999), p. 43.

7 R. Noonan, 'Women against the State: political opportunities and collective action frames in Chile's transition to democracy', in D. McAdam and D. Snow (eds) *Social Movements: Readings on Their Emergence, Mobilization, and Dynamics* (Los Angeles, CA: Roxbury Publishing Company, 1997), pp. 257–9.

8 A. Jetter, A. Orleck and D. Taylor (eds) *The Politics of Motherhood: Activist Voices from Left to Right* (Lebanon, IN: University Press of New England, 1997), p. 4.

9　Pro-natalism has been described as the encouragement of all births considered important to the well-being of a family and an individual woman. Alena Heitlinger has outlined ten major pro-natalist policies in advanced industrialised countries which include: family founding loans; birth grants; child allowances; tax exemptions for children; guaranteed income for mothers (parents) working outside the home; maternity/family leaves and flexible schedules; subsidised housing and recreational facilities for children; pronatalist propaganda and educational programmes; restrictions on abortions and contraceptives and the creation of a more socially 'friendly' environment for children: A. Heitlinger, *Women's Equality, Demography, and Public Policies: A Comparative Perspective* (New York: St. Martin's Press, 1993), p. 129.

10　*Ibid.*, p. 123.

11　M. Buckley, 'Soviet interpretations of the woman question', in B. Holland (ed.) *Soviet Sisterhood: British Feminists on Women in the USSR* (London: Billings & Sons, 1985), p. 45.

12　L. Attwood, 'The new Soviet man and woman: Soviet views on psychological sex differences', in Holland, *Soviet Sisterhood*, p. 66.

13　B. Riabinin, 'Esli u zhenshchiny detei …', *Sem'ia i shkola*, 1 (1967), 6–9, quoted in L. Attwood, *The New Soviet Man and Woman: Sex-Role Socialization in the USSR* (London: Billings & Sons, 1990), p. 140.

14　V. Dunham, 'The strong woman motif', in C. Black (ed.) *The Transformation of Russian Society* (Cambridge, MA: Harvard University Press, 1969), p. 460.

15　In a Soviet mine in the 1930s in the Ural region of Russia, an industrious worker named Stakhanov became famous for his daily output of work which surpassed that of the average worker. He was recognised by the Soviet State as a 'Labour Hero' and he was used as a role model for all workers in the USSR. Even though they had little administrative or decision-making power on collective farms, it was women who received the majority of Stakhanovite awards on collective farms throughout the Soviet period.

16　M. Morokvasic, 'Being a woman in Yugoslavia: past, present and institutional equality', in M. Godout (ed.) *Women of the Mediterranean* (London: Zed Books, 1986), cited in Cockburn, *The Space Between Us*, p. 158; and Y. Cohen, *Women and Counter-Power* (Montreal: Black Rose Books, 1989), pp. 48–9. Although women made up more than half of the membership of the Polish workers' union Solidarity, women were rarely elected to office, and no women signed the Gdansk or Szczecin Accords; and in 1981, in the First National Solidarity Congress elections, only 7 per cent of the delegates elected were women: see: Cohen, *Women and Counter-Power*, p. 40.

17　Cockburn, *The Space Between Us*, p. 108.

18　The AS is a resource base published under the title *Sobranie dokumentov samizdata* until 1977, at which time the archive was renamed *Materialy samizdata*. As a rule, poetry, novels and other works of *belles-lettres* are not included as integral to the AS, which contains primarily documents of social, political, economic or historical significance concerning Soviet–Russian society. Approximately 13 per cent of the archival documents are written solely by women.

19　In my examination of these documents I found that in the decade of 1964–74: 74 per cent (925) of the documents were about political problems and 26 per cent (325) were about religious issues.

20 Similar to the CSM in Moscow, which was established in 1989, the SMO was registered in St Petersburg in 1991 as a public organisation the aim of which was to educate draftees and their relatives on the law and to help mothers get their sons exempted from military service. At the time of the Chechen war in 1994, the SMO of St. Petersburg, along with the CSM of Moscow, took a leading role against Russian military aggression in the region.

21 This event is considered to have been the beginning of the democratic movement in the USSR. Many intellectuals responded to the inhumane treatment of the protestors by the Soviet Government and they wrote about this and other human rights violations in the underground press.

22 Borisova, 'Soldiers' Mothers lead the way'.

23 *Ibid.*

24 *Ibid.*

25 In contrast to this, only 1.5 per cent of the documents written by men are about their female relatives, and 0.4 per cent of the documents are about women in general. That the greater number of documents written by women are about humanitarian issues may be explained in terms of what Carol Gilligan describes as a different approach to social issues: she claims that females and males respond differently to hypothetical problems and that females project 'an "ethic" of care and think of things in terms of relationships, responsibility, caring, context and communication'. See C. Gilligan, *In a Different Voice: Psychological Theory and Women's Development* (Cambridge: Harvard University Press, 1982), quoted in J. Vickers, *Women and War* (London: Zed Books, 1993), p. 129.

26 A. McClintock, 'Family feuds: gender, nationalism and the family', *Feminist Review,* 44 (1993), 62.

27 S. Ruddick, '"Maternal" politics', in Jetter, Orleck and Taylor, *The Politics of Motherhood*, p. 375. In his contribution to this collection, D. Taylor wrote: 'On any given Thursday at 3:30, hundreds of women meet in the square to demand justice for human rights violations committed by the brutal military dictatorship that abducted, tortured and permanently "disappeared" 30, 000 Argentinians between 1976 and 1983, a period that came to be known as the "Dirty War". The Plaza, facing the presidential palace, lies in the heart of Buenos Aires' financial and district … [the women] gather around the microphone and loudspeakers from which they and their leader Hebe de Bonafini, broadcast their accusations to the country's president. *Where are our children? We want them back alive! Why did their torturers and murderers get away with murder? When will justice be done?* Until these issues are resolved, the women claim, the Dirty War will not be over. Nor will their demonstrations.' See D. Taylor, 'Making a spectacle: The Mothers of the Plaza de Mayo', in *ibid.*, p. 182.

28 Taylor, *ibid.*, p. 187.

29 Simona Sharoni maintains, despite the insistence of members of the group Parents Against Silence that the group included men, that the media and public insisted on calling the group 'Mothers Against Silence': S. Sharoni, 'Motherhood and the politics of women's resistance: Israeli women organizing for peace', in *ibid.*, p. 153.

30 Caizza, 'Russia Meets its Matriarchs', p. 58.

31 Lfgren, 'Russia: mothers for peace oppose sons in war'.

32 The IPB is the world's oldest and most comprehensive peace network, comprising 19 international and 140 national/local member organisations of all types in over 40 countries. It was established in 1892, in Bern, and it was awarded the Nobel Peace Prize in 1910 (thus earning the right to make nominations). Thirteen of its officers have been awarded the Nobel Peace Prize individually over the years. The current president of the IPB is Dr Maj-Britt Theorin, MEP, the former Swedish ambassador for disarmament.

33 Theorin quoted in Lfgren, 'Russia: mothers for peace oppose sons in war'.

34 R. Hammami, 'Palestinian motherhood and political activism on the West Bank and Gaza Strip', in Jetter *et al.*, *The Politics of Motherhood*, p. 167.

35 Some of the orphaned children were rejected by their families because the mothers had been victims of rape during the war. A number of the mothers of the now-orphaned children had, for various social and psychological reasons, committed suicide, and it is suspected that other Chechen women died as victims of honour killings at the hands of their husbands' families.

36 In January 1999 Russian President Boris Yeltsin planned to visit Groznyi, the capital of Chechnia. When the separatist region's leaders made it clear that they were ready to welcome Yeltsin only as a *foreign* leader, the Russian Government cancelled the state visit to the region and subsequently broke off diplomatic relations with the leaders of the Chechen region.

37 L. Lurie, 'The Russian media turns', *Institute for War and Peace Reporting, Caucasus Reporting Service*, no. 14 (14 January 2000), online: www.iwpr.net/index.pl?archive/cau/cau_200001_14_03.eng.txt.

38 American Federated Press (1 May 2000), cited in *Johnson's Russia List*, online: www.cdi.org/russia/johnson/default.cfm.

39 The CSM contests a revision by the *Duma* to the 1990 Alternative Service Law for conscripts which extends the period of alternative service for army recruits from 2 to 4 years.

40 Borisova, 'Soldiers' Mothers lead the way'.

The integration of the Cossacks within the Russian Army: political and military implications

Translated from the French by Paul Leahy

Introduction

Perestroika and *glasnost'* provided an opportunity for the Cossacks to demand their re-integration within the Russian armed forces, one which they were eager to seize. This chapter considers why the Cossacks made such a demand and under what circumstances it was taken up by the authorities, as well as discussing the significance of this development in the broader context of Russian society.

After the collapse of the USSR, Russia was a multicultural society in which the army was haemorrhaging men and conscripts were refusing to serve; in other words, individuals were refusing to act as citizens, choosing instead to serve their own interests. Faced with circumstances in which the State could no longer guarantee basic rights for its citizens and there was a risk that the country itself would disintegrate, the Russian Government needed to promote national cohesion but was faced with two possible ways of achieving this goal: basing social consolidation on the reality of its multicultural society or exploiting nationalist and patriotic sentiments. The Government chose the latter: encouraging a sense of common national identity by boosting Russian nationalism, promoting patriotism and mobilising people on the basis of ethnic identity rather than citizenship.

The Cossacks constituted an ideal tool for this societal project, for they represented a form of Russian military nationalism distinct from cultural nationalism or the nationalism of the minority. They had a desire to serve in the army at a time when so many soldiers and recruits of an age to serve were concocting a wide range of strategies to leave or evade it; they seemed to present a source of enormous human potential, and they were the incarnation of military values that were fast disappearing. In this chapter I consider whether the Government viewed the Cossacks as an offshoot of the army – one capable of constituting an interface between the army and society so as to promote military values – or whether they were seen, rather, as an instrument of socialisation that the army could no longer provide due to

its lack of credibility. I ask also whether the Cossacks were seen as comple-
menting the armed forces or were indeed regarded as potential replacements
for a military which was by then in a condition of decay.

Boris Yeltsin's decrees on the Cossacks – biased towards the creation of
an elite caste within the Russian State, a group legitimised by central
government that could proclaim itself an agent of the State[1] – tell us a great
deal about the degree of democratisation of Russian society, particularly
since this group was to be placed under the direct control of the president
and was to reinforce the feudal structure of the Russian Army by creating
parallel or rival structures. The integration of the Cossacks within the
armed forces could, therefore, be interpreted as a complex instance of ethnic
manipulation within the military, one used to legitimise a policy of
'Russification'. The Russian Government's ambivalence about ethnicity and
nationalism is evident in the concept of national security embodied in
Presidential Decree 1300 of 17 December 1997. This decree highlights the
increase in nationalism and localism within the RF, deeming it 'ethnocentric
and chauvinistic', and pays tribute to the multi-ethnic nature of Russia,
while promoting 'the preservation and reinforcement of Russian national
values'. Of course, in the context of the ethnic mobilisation process
observed among citizens of the RF – symptomatic of which were the establishment of inter-regional institutions and ethnic paramilitary groups – the
creation of Cossack units could become a dangerous weapon.

This chapter, therefore, seeks to use the Cossacks as a guide to Russian
governmental policy: Moscow's treatment of the Cossacks is here regarded
as a kind of weathervane for the societal project promoted since the collapse
of the USSR and as a marker for the democratisation of Russian society.

The historical background

Since 1990 the Cossacks have been 'returning' to Russia. A brief historical
summary will help to explain both that statement and the increasing importance of the Cossack phenomenon. Cossacks are linguistically and ethni-
cally Russian (although this has sometimes involved mixed marriages with
Turks and Tartars), despite having as an ethnic group applied for non-
Russian status, wishing to see 'Cossack' on their passports instead of
'Russian'.[2] They were the embodiment of an inherited tradition, one that in
the seventeenth and eighteenth centuries had guaranteed them salaries, land
and privileges from the tsar, under whose direct authority they came. The
role they performed was that of guarding the frontiers and organising
support in battles against the country's enemies.[3] The 1980s saw the renaissance of Cossack culture, and in Russia today there are 6.5 million 'self-
proclaimed' Cossacks. They are particularly numerous in the Don, Terek
and Kuban' regions of southern Russia but they are also to be found in
Siberia and the Russian Far East, and 2 million of them live outside the

borders of Russia, in Kazakhstan, Ukraine, Moldova, Georgia, etc. The phenomenon of the Cossack revival, originally a cultural one, has gradually taken on political and military dimensions over which the authorities have often lost control.

Thus, the assertion of a cultural identity has essentially taken the form of a desire for re-integration within the Russian Army: the Cossacks wish once more to fulfil their historical role guarding the frontiers and protecting Russians abroad. Alongside this demand for re-integration within the army, from 1990 onwards we have seen the formation of illegal regiments and militia that act outside of the control of the State: voluntary Cossack patrols walked the streets of certain towns, playing a part in maintaining order,[4] combating hooliganism and drunken behaviour, assisting tax inspectors and public prosecutors, and so on.[5] The involvement of armed Cossacks in conflicts outside of Russia also was becoming more frequent.

Phases in Cossack policy

As mentioned previously, well before they were given any official status, unofficial short-term alliances could be observed between the authorities and the Cossacks. As early as 1991 former Defence Minister Iazov, who took part in the 1991 coup attempt against Gorbachev, had approved in principle the creation of Cossack units integrated with the Soviet armed forces. Iazov went as far as to state that 'Cossacks would take a different oath [omitting reference to the CPSU], but in terms of command and control they would be subordinated to the Soviet Army'.[6] In 1991 in the Siberian region of Baikal, Cossacks patrolled the streets with the army and the MVD's troops. These were Cossack volunteers who had acted on their own initiative to create squads but had received training from officers of the local MVD.[7] In 1992, a military college in Vladikavkaz served as a training school for Cossack officers.[8] In January of that year, Cossack *atamans* (Cossacks elected to lead military units or villages) attended the All-Army Conference alongside Russian generals. Finally, Cossack volunteers were armed, paid by the Russian armed forces and shipped off to Moldova.[9]

The actual order that Cossacks were to become part of the army (an order put into effect during Boris Yeltsin's leadership) was, however, the culmination of a series of arbitrary and unconstitutional decisions. That order stemmed from two major phenomena: the proliferation of armed forces within the territory of the RF; and the personal seizure of power by Boris Yeltsin, which began in 1991 when he took direct control over a certain number of those forces. It was reportedly in this context that the suggestion was made to Yeltsin that he should use the Cossacks as his Presidential Guard.[10]

No doubt the decision to integrate the Cossacks within the army went hand in hand with an over-valuation of the Cossack movement against the background of an army in decline, its image and prestige dismantled by *glasnost'*. It also reflected a desire to use enthusiastic troops who would serve as a vehicle for the transmission of patriotic and warlike values in order to bolster an army plagued by desertion and the avoidance of conscription. Furthermore, Cossacks were declaring themselves ready to join the army without pay at a time when surveys carried out within the army indicated that most officers were ready to quit.

The official rehabilitation of the Cossacks took place in 1992 by means of Presidential Decree No. 632[11] and then through the project to re-establish Cossack regiments within the army (each Cossack region was to have its own Cossack military unit and the Cossacks were to serve as border guards), against the background of the implosion of the armed forces in Russia. The granting of autonomous status to the MVD's forces, the emergence of new forces, such as the Presidential Guard, and the Cossack renewal were all examples of the proliferation of armed institutions in Russia, which in turn was symptomatic of the mistrust that the civil authorities felt towards the military. Many of these forces came directly under the control of the civil authorities and could act against any army uprising. Decree 341 of 13 March 1993 – 'On the reform of the military structures, frontier and interior forces in the northern Caucasus region of the Russian Federation and state support of the Cossacks' – laid the groundwork for such options. This presidential decree, bolstering military structures in the northern Caucasus and lending support to Cossack units, allowed the Cossacks to take part in measures to enforce law and order.

In June 1994 a Cossack Affairs Council (CAC) was created within the Russian Government. At the end of that year, a law was enacted which guaranteed the twelve Cossack regions, united under an *Ataman* Council directly subordinate to the Russian president, the status of 'Archipelago-State'. These measures indicate the reversion to practices dating back to the tsarist period: the Russian federal authorities (and, from 1990, the Russian local authorities) were arranging to employ the services of the Cossacks to deal with matters of internal or external security. The very composition of the Cossack Affairs Council allowed one to anticipate the possible integration of the Cossacks with most security structures as the deputy defence minister, the deputy minister of the interior, the assistant director of the Federal Intelligence Service, the assistant secretaries of the Security Council and the commander-in-chief of the Federal Border Service all sat on that committee.

One factor accelerating the integration of the Cossacks within the structures of the State was the presence of Nikolai Egorov in the Government. Having served as minister for the nationalities in 1994, on 25 August 1995 this man of Cossack descent became the president's national and regional policy assistant. Cossack policy was immediately speeded up and reinforced; the Cossacks also became an electoral factor that the president's team was able to manipulate. Shortly before the 1996 presidential elections, a Directorate-General for Cossack Troops was created for Cossack enlistment and for coordinating the renaissance of the Cossack movement which came under the direct control of the presidential authorities. The allegiance of the Cossacks to the Russian president was further reinforced by the regulation that the rank of general (the highest Cossack rank) could be granted only by the president[12] and that Cossacks who enlisted (like other members of the armed forces) were not permitted to belong to any political party.

Limitations on the integration of Cossacks within the army

Official estimates of the number of Cossacks who could be incorporated into the army give us a better indication of the numbers that officials hoped to recruit than they do of the reality. In 1995 Secretary of the Russian Security Council Oleg Lobov suggested a figure of 5 million men. In 1996 the authorities revised this figure downwards, putting potential troop figures at 3.5 million. These figures were probably based on the erroneous assumption that those provinces corresponding to the territories where the Cossacks were based at the beginning of the twentieth century were entirely populated by Cossacks. The authorities were therefore to base their policy on the Cossacks upon this overestimation.[13]

In 1992, a survey indicated 18–27 per cent of Slavs (Russians and Ukrainians) within the territory of Krasnodar[14] considered themselves to be of Cossack descent.[15] In reality, there is no direct connection between being of Cossack descent and being a modern-day Cossack. The variability and volatility of the Cossack identity is striking: in 1993 the authors of a survey on Cossack identity reported that 'the given number of Cossacks in a village or a district cannot be established with precision – it depends upon the situation. If the economic and political situation deteriorates, there will be many more as being a Cossack represents a form of social protest rather than an ethnic affirmation.' In response to the question of how many Cossacks were living in the Tempiurskii District in 1993, the *ataman* replied: '[T]wo hundred or two thousand, that depends upon the situation. If national relations deteriorate, there will be a lot of Cossacks.'[16] In fact, opinion polls and the membership of Cossack associations, which would provide an indication of the social base of the Cossacks and of the movement's potential, produce very varied data. However, one might estimate that the actual figures would be close to those of 1916, when a Cossack population of 4.5 million produced 285,000 Cossack men under arms.[17]

But what is the state of Cossack enlistment in the armed forces today? In no way do rumours of mass enlistment during the Kosovo war or widespread Cossack imagery in the press (ever partial to a man in a *cherkessa*, the Cossack uniform, sabre by his side) reflect the number of men actually joining the army. Although there are major obstacles to obtaining up-to-date figures, the data available for the period 1994–98 testify to a more moderate level of Cossack enlistment in the army, supporting the thesis that the official figures cited above represent a substantial overestimation. In addition, due to a lack of men, there are currently no units composed solely of Cossacks, as was anticipated in the presidential decrees. In 1997 there were 32 mixed military units, in which the Cossacks accounted for only 30–49 per cent of the troops.[18] The Cossacks thus represent just a few thousand men within the Russian armed forces, a situation that was not about to change. In 1998, the military press counted around the same number of military units (about thirty[19]), thus confirming the limitations to Cossack fervour to join the army.

Table 10.1 Number of Cossacks joining the army, 1994–96

Enlistments	Entrants
Autumn 1994	4,924
Spring 1996	2,387
Autumn 1996	2,646

Source: I. Modnikova, *Social Problems of the Russian Military* (Alexandria, VA: Center for Naval Analyses, January 1997).

The first Cossacks joined MOD and Federal Border Service units, their duties involving the protection of borders and oil pipelines. An experiment was initiated in 1996, and introduced by presidential decree that same year, using Cossack troops to patrol the Russian–Mongolian[20] and Russian–Ukrainian[21] frontiers. The overall record thus far (as assessed at a meeting between Andrei Nikolaev, head of the Federal Border Service, and managers of the President of the Russian Federation's Directorate-General for Cossack Troops) is positive, but the integration of Cossacks with frontier troops seems to be suffering due to funding problems and a lack of legislation.[22] Then, at the initiative of the Federal Border Service, the first 'Cossack' border post was set up in the Kurgan region, 12 kilometres from the border between Russia and Kazakhstan. The post was intended to block the trafficking of arms and drugs, but it elicited a sharp response from the Kazakh authorities.[23] Gradually the Cossack soldiers were integrated with different border posts, notably along the frontier with Georgia in December 2000.[24]

Since 1999 the media have repeated rumours about the creation of a few official Cossack units (in theory composed solely of Cossacks),[25] but mostly this has involved only sub-units comprising Cossacks serving on a contractual basis, as with the special unit of the 205th Infantry Division, described by the Glasnost Foundation as a 'Cossack unit'.[26] The navy, too, is opening itself to the use of Cossacks: from August 1997 a Cossack battalion was established within a naval infantry division (400–500 men) belonging to the Pacific Fleet, together with a forward posting in Malibovaia composed of Ussuri Cossacks.[27] By January 2000 they were talking about creating a regiment (around 2,500 men)[28] composed of Ussuri Cossacks[29]. Overall, however, the formation of fully Cossack units has been held back, if not halted, by the growing opposition of army staff headquarters, whose enthusiasm for the idea cooled somewhat after a Mutual Protection Treaty was signed in the summer of 1994 between Chechen's President Dudaev and *Ataman* Kozitsin. The Volgograd *oblast'* (in the Don region) was the first to pay the price for this mistrustfulness on the part of the army: staff headquarters' representatives demanded that a halt be called to the formation of military sub-divisions in the *oblast'* on the grounds that it breached the Russian constitution. Similarly, joint GAI (*Gosudarstvennaia avtomobil'-naia inspektsiia* – State Motor Vehicle Inspectorate) and Cossack highway patrol posts were closed down in the *oblast'*.

However, the Cossack integration process has gradually spread to other so-called 'forces' ministries. Such an expansion was to be expected, as presaged by the composition of the president's CAC, created in June 1994: all the forces ministries are represented on the CAC as permanent members. The MVD was the first, in January 1999, to establish a Cossack regiment, deployed on the border between the Stavropol' Territory and Chechnia.[30] Customs and the protection of oil and gas pipelines have also become areas in which the Cossacks are playing a part.

Risks and challenges for the armed forces and for Russia

The integration of the Cossacks within the army involves many risks, both for the armed forces as an institution and for Russia as a country.

The poisoning of inter-ethnic relations

The continuing creation of Cossack units can serve only to poison inter-ethnic relations in the army and the Federation: why should other ethnic groups, such as the Adighe, not claim that they are also entitled to their own military units as the Cossacks have been given this option? As early as 1997 the peoples of the Caucasus were threatening to assemble their own army. This was at a time when the Cossacks were calling for the legalisation of their armed militia in the northern Caucasus, arguing that the MOD and the MVD were unable to defend Russian citizens in Chechnia and in countries just across the border.[31]

The grouping of soldiers by ethnic minority is a practice known in the army as *zemliachestvo* (the grouping of soldiers from the same ethnic origin or region). Soldiers can thus call upon regional solidarity when they feel themselves to have been badly treated or threatened, and, in this way, disputes between individuals have often developed into large-scale fights ending in deaths and revolts. The presence of these men, who declare themselves to be 'more Russian than the Russians', could provoke tensions among those very Russians with whom they serve. The Cossacks' status within the armed forces could also remain hazy in the eyes of other military personnel, leading to further problems and confusion. It is not clear whether the Cossacks would be incorporated on an equal footing, have similar career opportunities and be allocated to different branches according to common criteria. Furthermore, the incorporation of the Cossacks – a privileged caste whose status has been legitimised by the central authorities – breaches the fundamental principle of military organisation as the nation's training ground: that of uniformity.

Breaking the chain of command

Another concern relates to the question of exercising authority over men who possess their own Cossack hierarchy with its own ranks and rules. In this context questions are posed about the nature of this new chain of command, and whether Cossack soldiers, once they have joined the army, will obey their commanders or their *ataman*.[32] These questions are far from purely theoretical, as there has already been cause for one case of insubordination to be brought – a matter that arose not in the army itself but in the Federal Border Troops Service in the summer of 1997. At that time, under the leadership of their *atamans* and with the complicity of the governor of the region (Nazdratenko), Ussuri Cossack army units within the Federal Border Troops Service on the Chinese border opposed the implementation of frontier agreements signed between Russia and China. These agreements provided for the return by Russia to China of 207 square kilometres of land near Lake Khasan and an access point to the Sea of Japan via the River Tuman,[33] but the Cossack units' action contributed to the treaties' cancellation.[34] Clearly, then, this represents an instance in which the Federal Border Troops Service, led at the time by General Andrei Nikolaev, lost control over its own forces. The support that Pavel Maslov (a general attached to the forces of the MVD)[35] provided to the Ussuri *ataman* in this initiative shows the real risks of a crumbling of the chain of command, as well as of creating a form of autonomy over decisions at different hierarchical levels in the different armed forces.

Illegal militias and the risk of Cossack mafia penetration of the armed forces

In addition to the potential problems identified above which are posed by the use of Cossack soldiers in the Russian armed forces, the integration of Cossacks within the army could, in fact, encourage the creation and growth of illegal militias. The series of concessions granted by the Government to the Cossacks since 1991 (that is, the Cossacks' rehabilitation and integration, the restoration of certain privileges, and so on) have contributed greatly to the undermining of law and order in Russia. The Cossack movement and one of its components – illegal militias, which existed even before the idea of integration within the army took on a concrete form – have seen these developments as giving a green light to their existence and activities.

The Cossack movement has been infiltrated by mafia groups, and the risk that the army will be so similarly affected as a result of the integration of Cossack soldiers should not be dismissed. The potential for mafia infiltration of the military should be seen in connection with one of the most dangerous problems facing Russia: the illegal trade in weapons. Today, 'illegal arms trading is another serious factor affecting the general situation. Almost 54,000 light weapons are officially missing.'[36] This statistic relates principally to weapons disappearing from units rather than from the factories where they are manufactured. How could one not fear, when issuing weapons to Cossack soldiers, that they will be transferred to *voiska* (Cossack regiments) or *stanitsy* (Cossack village communities)?

The atomisation and regionalisation of the armed forces

Rejected by the Russian Army, which has disclaimed Boris Yeltsin's campaign promises to the Cossacks, and meeting opposition from the finance and economics ministers to the establishment of a Cossack support programme, the Cossacks are increasingly turning their attention to the regions. This situation does not appear to pose any problems to the Cossacks, for whom loyalty to the central authorities has never been essential. In making this switch, the Cossacks represent the incarnation of this tension between two poles (the legitimacy of the State and regionalism) that have divided the RF for many years. Without hesitation, local authorities are calling on the services of the Cossacks, yet in the past the latter have shown that they have no respect for authority of any kind. In 1992, for example, the Cossacks imposed constraints on the government of the *Krai* of Krasnodar after a local authority representative opposed the Cossacks' call for the expulsion of the Armenians (depending on the circumstances, the Cossacks' targets can range from Turks to Jews to Armenians). The town hall was surrounded and its telephone lines cut; two armoured vehicles supported the blockade.[37]

One may perceive a certain convergence of interests between central government and regional élites over the Cossack question, the former seeking to win votes and the latter seeking to neutralise the Cossack leaders as competitors. The devolution of power to the regions and power-sharing arrangements negotiated between the regions have meant that governors and heads of local authorities have had to deal with the Cossack phenomenon directly, so that the Cossacks have become, in effect, a regional problem. For example, Cossacks enlisted with the army receive a salary from the State, but the wages of those enlisted in other forces, such as the Border

Service, are paid by the authorities of the local *oblast'* in which they are serving.[38] This has led to a situation in which local authorities have called on the services of the Cossacks and established illegal militias in order to conduct their own foreign or ethnic policy, thereby creating their own legal space.[39] The case of Krasnodar is particularly instructive: in early 1996 the *Krai* negotiated and signed a power-sharing agreement that gave it the right to regulate immigration within the region, to pass its own Land Act and to rehabilitate the Kuban' Cossacks. The authorities in Krasnodar consequently saw this as an invitation to assemble a genuine regional militia, which has the power to maintain order.

Might the support of the regional authorities for the Cossacks generate political mobilisation? The evidence suggests that this is a strong possibility. The relationship between the Cossacks and the local authorities is emerging as a source of local opposition to the Government of the RF. Instances of joint-action taken by official bodies and Cossacks against the central authorities have been recorded, as we have seen in the case of the Ussuri Cossacks.

The Putin effect

Putin's presidency has raised numerous questions concerning the relationship between the authorities and the Cossacks: would Putin commit himself to a militarisation of society against the background of a restoration of nationalist discourse? Would he too be tempted to play the Cossack card? It has to be said that Putin's accession to the Russian presidency led to the country being taken in hand once more. In response to the danger that the country and the army would fragment, Putin re-established a strong state. The appointment of seven special envoys to the regions on 13 May 2000[40] presaged the restoration of a greater centralised power as the sole source of authority in many areas, particularly in the military domain.

Putin seems to be adopting a cautious approach to the Cossacks. Officially, no Cossacks have been sent to Chechnia, although some Cossack presence has been observed during both Chechen campaigns. During the first campaign there was an unofficial short-term collaboration, while during the second campaign the only Cossacks apparently fighting in Chechnia have been contract soldiers who enlisted as individuals. Yet, it cannot have escaped notice that during his first visit as president to the regions of the RF, Putin made sure that he was photographed with some Cossacks.

From the Cossacks' point of view, Putin's leadership seems to have fanned their hopes of a return to the glorious era of Cossack collaboration with the authorities. The establishment of a new Cossack structure is evidence of this:[41] the representatives of Russian Cossack organisations and troops have announced the creation of a military–economic structure – the

Cossack reserve troops of Russia. This announcement was made by the *atamans* of the troops of Kuban', the Upper Don, Tersk, Amur-Ussuri and the Cossack Union of Podmoskov'e, and there are apparently 100,000 Cossacks who wish to become Putin's soldiers. Does Putin share this desire? He seems to be in favour of integrating the Cossacks with border control structures, principally in the northern Caucasus and the far east.[42] He is also in favour of such integration with police forces but, as of 2001, seemed to be encountering resistance from the MVD.

Locally, the integration process is forging ahead: in February 2002, within Krasnodar *krai*, the police (represented by the head of the police department for the *krai*) and the Terek Cossacks (under the command of the *ataman* of the Terek Cossacks Brigade, Vassilii Bondarev[43]) formed mixed units designed to ensure public order in the region.[44] On 8 February 2002, a meeting was staged in Nizhnii–Novgorod between regional and federal government representatives and the *atamans* for the Cossack communities of the Federal Region of the Volga. The presidential representative for the region, Sergei Kirienko, and representatives of the Interior, Defence, Emergency Situations and Agriculture Ministries took part in the meeting, together with the tax police. Among the subjects under discussion were the laws governing government relations with the Cossacks.[45] No further information about this meeting has apparently been published in the Russian national press. Lastly, in May 2002 the Cossacks were used on the shores of the Black Sea and the Caspian Sea in order to maintain order on the same basis as voluntary police auxiliaries.[46] As with these police auxiliaries, it remains the case that such experimental integration of Cossacks with the structures of forces takes place infrequently and on a very localised basis, albeit with considerable media coverage.[47] Thus, Putin seems to want to handle the Cossacks carefully and to pander to their self-regard, as was indicated by the reinforcement of the Presidential Guard with a Cossack cavalry regiment[48] in April 2002.

The Cossacks and the militarisation of youth

In parallel with their integration within the army and other forces, it is remarkable that, ever since the early days of their rehabilitation, the Cossacks should have become involved in the military training of young people. In fact, Decree no. 341 of 13 March 1993 ('On the Reform of the Military Structures, Frontier and Interior Forces in the Northern Caucasus Region of the Russian Federation and State Support of the Cossacks') not only authorised them to take part in law and order enforcement measures but gave them the right to organise the training of young people for military service. Very rapidly training camps, or holiday camps with a military connotation began to spring up in regions traditionally inhabited by Cossacks; there were, for example, the equestrian camps for young people, sponsored by Cossack associations, which had activity programmes very similar to those of military training. Cossack schools also were set up in Cossack regions and mirrored the ethnic schools that opened their doors upon the collapse of the USSR. In 1997, the school that opened in Vladikavkaz in the northern Caucasus was rapidly overwhelmed with applications for enrolment;[49] in Novocherkasak, a Cossack school was re-opened, providing tuition on the history and customs of the Cossacks alongside normal lessons.[50] The Kuban' cadet school offered an education biased towards the military professions and catering for 12–18-year-olds.[51] In Siberia, Alexander Lebed' launched four Cossack cadet corps[52] in Krasnoiarsk and established a Directorate for Cossack Affairs responsible for managing them. By the end of 1999, there were more than thirty cadet corps in Russia, excluding those belonging to the forces' ministries.[53]

There is a wider social and governmental context in which to see this strong Cossack interest in providing education and training for young people which could even be described as a project for the militarisation of youth. This societal project, inspired by Boris Yeltsin, then ratified and implemented by Vladimir Putin, began in November 1997 with the army taking responsibility for thousands of orphaned children or children from single-parent families who had been left to fend for themselves. These initiatives on the part of the army came in the wake of an appeal from the minister of defence to officers of the Russian armed forces, an appeal to the humanist tradition of the armed forces in view of the number of abandoned children in Russian society: it was an appeal for the creation of sports and music clubs, and the sponsorship of orphans by army units.[54] This measure was inspired by the project of Feliks Dzherzhinskii (head of the secret police) who, acting on Lenin's orders in the 1920s, had created an emergency committee responsible for the care of orphans. Many of the children who had been raised under its auspices entered the ranks of the secret police when they reached adulthood. A presidential decree issued in February 2000 gave this tradition a legal status. Units belonging to the MOD and the 'forces' ministries could now officially adopt children from the age of 14 and keep them through to adulthood; children aged 14–16 who had been orphaned or who did not have fathers could be enrolled as cadets within military units.[55]

The re-introduction of military preparation classes (NVP) to secondary schools in the autumn of 1999 constituted another aspect of this project for the militarisation of youth. First set up in 1968, NVP classes in secondary schools fulfilled two functions: socialisation (reinforcing lessons in Soviet patriotism and respect for the armed forces) and military training. They were abolished in 1991 and replaced with lessons in first-aid. While in practice little has been done to implement this measure, the re-introduction of NVP to schools marks a new phase in this societal project. Other measures form part of the same project, such as the (fruitless) attempt to revive the *Komsomol* in

April 2000 through the creation of an Association of Youth Organizations, christened the *Soiuzmol* and modelled upon the *Komsomol*. This represented the first attempt for ten years to create a new mass organisation. Finally, in February 2001 the Government launched a patriotic campaign which finally established the ideological framework sketched out over the previous years. This $6 million campaign seeks to promote patriotism by means of a five-year programme[56] mobilising the army, schools and the media in order to help Russians recover their self-confidence and to contribute to 'the fundamental spiritual values of the Russian people'.[57] According to *Rossiiskaia gazeta*, the official government newspaper, the programme will contribute to 'the consol-idation of society and the restoration of patriotism', while also stimulating 'the interest of young people in military service'.[58] The Russian Orthodox Church is involved in this patriotic project, posing as the official defender of Russian patriotism and, in collaboration with the MOD, organising children's holiday camps, giving its encouragement to the war in Chechnia and bestowing its blessing on the troops.[59] As Françoise Daucé points out: 'the Holy Synod does not forbid the faithful from bearing arms and it encourages the defence of the homeland'.[60] After all, did metropolitan *pitirim* of the Moscow Patriarchate not declare in February 2000 that 'Children should be taught to love the smell of barracks and soldiers' boots'?[61] In this context, it is unsurprising to find the Cossacks serving the needs of the Church by acting as security guards for religious buildings and premises.

There was little protest against the military taking children into its care. Overall, the response of the press and society to this initiative was favourable, as it was to the principle of the integration of the Cossacks within the armed forces (only a few human rights activists and leaders of multi-ethnic republics expressed any objections). The association between the Church and the army met with a similarly favourable response. The internalisation of military values thus remains very strong in Russia. Military culture is barely called into question and still dominates Russian society. Russia continues to give prominence to nationalistic patriotism, and the use to which the Cossacks have been put is evidence of this. Everything is carrying on as if Russia were still a 'nation in arms' preparing itself for a permanent war. What could better embody this preparation for permanent combat than the Cossacks patrolling the streets, authorised by decree to wear a uniform and carry a sabre?

Notes

1 M. Reitman, 'Return of the Cossacks', *Peace Review*, 6:1 (1994), 103–8.

2 M. Bradshaw (ed.) *Geography and Transition in the Post-Soviet Republics* (Chichester: Wiley, 1997).

3 W. Laqueur, *Histoire des droites en russie des centuries noires aux nouveaux extremistes* (Paris: Michalon, 1996).

4 V. Vyzhutovich, 'Saddled up: where are the Kuban's Cossacks galloping off to?' *Izvestiia* (5 July 1992), quoted in *Current Digest of Post-Soviet Press*, 43:27 (5 July 1991).

5 L. Grau, 'The Cossack brotherhood reborn: a political/military force in a realm of chaos', *Low Intensity Conflict and Law Enforcement*, 2:3 (1993), 578–612.

6 D. Herspring, *Russian Civil–Military Relations* (Bloomington and Indianapolis: Indiana University Press, 1996), p. 130.

7 *Komsomol'skaia pravda* (22 March 1991).

8 A. Lieven, *Chechnya, Tombstone of Russian Power* (London: Yale University Press, 1999), p. 229.

9 R. Laba, 'The Cossack movement and the Russian State, 1990–1996', *Low Intensity Conflict and Law Enforcement*, 5:3 (1996), 377–408.

10 J. Ure, *The Cossacks* (London: Constable, 1999).

11 On the Rehabilitation of the Cossacks (15 June 1992): Decree Concerning Measures Allowing for the Extension of the Law on the Rehabilitation of Repressed Peoples', *Vedomosti S"ezda narodnykh deputatov Rossiiskoi Federatsii i Verkhovnogo Soveta Rossiiskoi Federatsii*, 30 (1992), p. 21.

12 Thus, in January 1999, three Cossack generals were appointed by Boris Yeltsin: the *atamans* of the Cossack troops of the Don, the Kuban' and the Terek: 'Yeltsin names three Cossack generals', *RFE–RL Newsline*, available online: www.rfast.org/newsline (5 January 1999).

13 Laba, 'The Cossack movement and the Russian State, 1990–1996', p. 389.

14 In 1989, the population of the *Krai* of Krasnodar was 5 million, if one includes the autonomous Adighe region, comprising 4 million Russians and 180,000 Ukrainians: M. McAuley, *Russia's Politics of Uncertainty* (Cambridge: Cambridge University Press, 1997), p. 113.

15 Cited by G. Derluguian and S. Cipko, 'The politics of identity in a Russian borderland province: The Kuban' neo-Cossack movement, 1989–1996', *Europe–Asia Studies*, 49:8 (1997), 1488.

16 McAuley, *Russia's Politics of Uncertainty*, p. 135.

17 Laba, 'The Cossack movement and the Russian State, 1990–1996', p. 389.

18 I. Modnikova, *Social Problems of the Russian Military* (Alexandria: Center for Naval Analysis, 1997).

19 V. Galaiko, 'Atamanov staviat v stroi', *Nezavisimoe voennoe obozrenie*, 45 (27 November–3 December 1998), p. 8.

20 *Segodnia* (28 June 1997), p. 2.

21 *Nezavisimaia gazeta* (5 February 1997): in February 1997 a detachment of twenty Cossack volunteers was created and they took part in surveillance of the Russian–Ukrainian frontier with the Federal Frontier Service.

22 V. Nosatov, '"Monopolisty" prigranich'ia', *Nezavisimoe voennoe obozrenie*, 23 (28 June–4 July 1997), p. 8: Cossacks coming to serve near the frontiers receive 70 per cent of their accommodation costs and an interest-free loan; their salaries are paid by the authorities of the local *oblast'*, which also supplies fodder for horses and a free hunting and fishing permit.

23 S. Kuzovnikov, 'Cossacks guarding Russian borders', *Moscow News*, 31 (7–13 August 1997).

24 'Cossacks will guard the border with Georgia', *Segodnia* (9 December 2000), p. 4, cited in *WPS* (www.wps.ru), no. 145 (13 December 2000).

25 E.g., on 28 December 2000 *Glasnost' Caucasus* announced the creation of a Cossack unit within the 205th Mechanised Brigade.

26 'President's aide denies official formation of Cossack regiments', *Glasnost Daily* news service, 13 February 2001, from *Russian Military and Security Media Coverage* (Ralph Davis e-mail newsletter, online: davis004@sbcglobal.net).

27 *VladivostokNews Online* (8 August 1997), available: http://vn.vladnews. ru/index.html.

28 *Izvestiia* (11 January 2000), p. 2.

29 A Cossack territory near the Chinese border.

30 I. Belasheva and F. Sterkin, 'Cossacks and robbers', *Vremia MN* (28 January 1999), p. 3, translated by *Current Digest of Post Soviet Press*, 51:4 (1999).

31 *Ibid.*

32 *Ataman* is the title used by Cossack chiefs elected to head military units or villages.

33 E. Busza, 'Yeltsin's latest military reform initiative: operational–strategic commands', *PONARS* 44 (November 1998), available online: www.csis.org/ ruseura/ponars.

34 Laba, 'The Cossack movement and the Russian State, 1990–1996'.

35 *Krasnaia zvezda* (18 December 1999).

36 V. Solov'ev, 'An extremely neglected security issue', *Nezavisimaia gazeta* (12 September 2002), via *What the Papers Say*, online: www.wps.ru/e_index. html.

37 Laba, 'The Cossack movement and the Russian State, 1990–1996', p. 392.

38 V. Nosatov, '"Monopolisty" prigranich'ia: Kazaki gotovy k okhrane vostochnykh rubezhei Rossii', *Nezavisimoe voennoe obozrenie*, 23 (28 June–4 July 1997), p. 8.

39 *Jamestown Monitor* (28 August 1997), online: www.jamestown.org.

40 Putin divided Russia into seven federal districts, modelled on military regions.

41 I. Boulanova, 'Neupravliaemyi kazak opasen', *Nezavisimaia gazeta* (23 March 2000), p. 2.

42 M. Galeotti, 'Securing Russia's borders', *Jane's Intelligence Review* 13:9 (September 2001), p. 11.

43 Bondarev is also head of the *krai*'s security council (here we can see the extent to which the question of Cossack penetration of authorities is a burning issue).

44 'Police, Cossacks join forces in north Caucasus region', *RFE–RL Newsline* (4 February 2002), available online: www.rferl.org/newsline.

45 'One envoy meets with Cossacks', *ibid.* (11 February 2002), available online: www.rferl.org/newsline.

46 *RIA-Novosti* (17 May 2002).

47 A. Le Huérou, 'Questioning "ordinary policing" and local law enforcement in contemporary Russia', *Insight*, 2:3 (15 March 2002), available online: www.psan.org.

48 *Gazeta.ru*, online: http://gazeta.ru (24 April 2002).

49 R. Beeston, 'Warrior spirit of Cossacks invoked in Russia's defence', *Times* (27 November 1999).

50 Ure, *The Cossacks*, p. 232.

51 H. Guirchoun, 'L'ordre cosaque règne à Krasnodar', *Le Nouvel Observateur* (16–22 March 2000).

52 A. Chapovalov, 'Petr Denikin: "Kazakov pora vooruzhat'" *Nezavisimaia gazeta* (27 November 1999), p. 4.
53 P. Sukhanov, 'Sozdan fond podderzhki kadetskikh korpusov', *Nezavisimoe voennoe obozrenie*, 48 (10–16 December 1999), p. 3.
54 *Krasnaia zvezda* (25 November 1997).
55 Associated Press, 'Russia's Putin decries rise in orphan numbers' (19 February 2000), via *Johnson's Russia List*, no. 4146, www.cdi.org/russia/johnson/default.cfm.
56 The document is entitled 'The Patriotic Education of the Citizens of the Russian Federation 2001–2005': see E. Korop and S. Novoprudskii, 'Government thinks up ways to rear patriots', *Izvestiia* (23 February 2001), p. 2.
57 *AFP*, 'Russia's school for patriots' (15 March 2001).
58 *Rossiiskaia gazeta* (15 March 2001).
59 N. Babassian, 'Ne sudite da ne sudimy budete', *Novoe vremia*, 47 (28 November 1999), p. 37.
60 F. Daucé, 'L'institution militaire face à la pluralité religieuse dans l'etat russe', *MOST Journal on Multicultural Societies*, 2:2 (2001), available online: www/unesco.org/most/vl2n2dau.htm.
61 G. Chazan, 'Putin restarts military training for schoolboys', *The Electric Telegraph* (13 February 2000), via *Johnson's Russia List*, no. 4104, online: www.cdi.org/russia/johnson/default.cfm.

Jennifer G. Mathers

Conclusion: Military and society in post-Soviet Russia – Reflections

The task of writing the concluding chapter to an edited volume can be a daunting one. My co-editor and I have made this job even more challenging by bringing together in this book diverse points of view as well as distinctive national and disciplinary perspectives to comment on many aspects of a large and complex subject. The contributors to this volume have provided a wealth of information and analysis focusing on the different levels at which the SMI operates. Rather than attempt a grand synthesis with a neat tying together of all loose ends, it may be more useful to consider a few of the major themes which run through the book. This chapter should be regarded not as a definitive conclusion, but as an essay which indicates how this volume made one reader reflect on the relationship between military and society in post-Soviet Russia.

One of the clearest messages in this book is that practically every aspect of the relationship between society and the military in Russia is contested or under pressure, and that this is a relationship in a constant state of flux. Two images in particular stand out for this reader, and these are the intertwined themes that this concluding essay addresses: one is the military's search for an identity and a role to play in the new Russia; the other is the – sometimes subtle – resistance of Russian society to the continuation of traditional priorities which place the demands of the military above the rights and needs of individuals and communities.

During much of the Soviet period, the armed forces had a relatively straightforward set of tasks to perform: to protect the USSR from external threats to its security and to project force at various points around the globe in support of the foreign policy priorities of the country's political leadership. The military was also assigned a crucial role in the formation of Soviet society, which included instilling in its conscript soldiers (effectively all young men) a sense of loyalty to the Soviet State and the Communist Party, as well as providing them with lessons in Marxist–Leninist ideology. Society had several significant parts to play in this relationship. First and foremost, society provided the military with an endless succession of young men to serve in its ranks and workers in the Soviet defence industry to build weaponry and equipment. In addition, society provided the military with an object to defend as well as an admiring and respectful audience for its achievements. In times of war – particularly in a war for national survival, such as the Second World War was for the USSR – the relationship between military and society more closely resembled a partnership, the two elements working together against a common enemy.

The rapid succession of changes which have occurred since the mid-1980s both in the USSR and in the wider international community, however, have changed every aspect of the military-society relationship. The military's previous tasks are now obsolete: the need to defend the country against attack from another state's armed forces has practically disappeared, as has the Russian State's desire to teach its young men to view the world from a Marxist–Leninist perspective. While the military's old tasks have become obsolete, the specifics of its new responsibilities have been slow to emerge, leaving it perched uncomfortably between the past and the future, its leaders sometimes clinging to past practices, while at other times reaching out for new ways of doing things and of relating to the State and to society. At the same time, society is no longer willing to make the personal and material sacrifices necessary to sustain a large standing army and an extensive defence industry. The memory of the shared victories of the Second World War – jointly suffered for and jointly won by military and society – ensure that many older Russians continue to regard the armed forces with great respect, although, as Stephen Webber and Alina Zilberman make clear in chapter 7, this is not necessarily the case for Russia's younger generations, who exhibit, as they point out, 'a lower level of trust in the military institution'. The power of the memory of the Second World War inevitably diminishes with time, and more recent experiences, such as those in the Chechen conflicts, demonstrate that the Russian military of the twenty-first century is a very different entity from the Soviet military of the 1940s. Moreover, the contemporary Russian military has not shown itself to be very effective in defending the country from those threats which it is most likely to face in the foreseeable future. This makes the gap between the capabilities of the post-Soviet Russian military and those of its Soviet-era predecessor all the more apparent, and indicates the fragility of society's residual respect for the military although, as Webber and Zilberman suggest, few Russian civilians appear to believe that their views can have much effect on the development of their country's armed forces or its defence policy.

This brings us to a point that Stephen Webber made in the Introduction to this volume: it is unrealistic to expect the development of society-military relations in Russia during this turbulent transition to travel in a straight line, moving in an orderly fashion from a closed and authoritarian relationship to a more open and democratic one. Indeed, it is far from clear that the Russian MOD even knows what sort of a journey it wishes to make and where it wants to end up. Russian society, too, is divided about precisely how the military should develop and about what sort of a relationship it should have with military. This means that we should not be surprised by the contradictory trends we have seen in society-military relations over the better part of two decades since the introduction of *perestroika* and *glasnost'* marked the beginnings of this period of transition, and that we should expect similarly inconsistent trends to arise in the years to come.

Most of the contributors to this volume comment on the persistence of pre-*perestroika* Soviet-style attitudes and practices on the part of the military, both collectively and by individual officials of the MOD. Lev Gudkov (chapter 1) presents this tendency more strongly than do the rest of the book's contributors and his discussion can even give the impression that little of significance has changed in the relationship between society and the military in Russia. I suggest, though, that we view Gudkov's chapter as a warning rather than as a prediction – reminding us of the long tradition in Russia of the military dictating to society and of the enormous difficulties which have to be overcome in order to break with that tradition. It is not necessarily a vision of Russia's future because society is increasingly challenging the military's *right* to occupy so dominant a position in so many ways, large and small. This constant interplay between competing rights, demands and obligations in turn contributes to the military's confusion about its identity and future role, and also acts to subvert any assumptions that military officials may have about their ability to reinstate the *status quo ante*.

The core element of the military's traditional social role – shaping the next generation of citizens, chiefly through the transmission of key values – is one to which military leaders cling tenaciously, as Stephen Webber and Alina Zilberman's chapter indicates. The Russian military appears to feel a strong affinity with the notion of military service as a rite of passage into full citizenship, even though Russia's military leaders might not use the term 'citizenship' or even recognise some of the most important implications of that concept. Nevertheless the socialisation function of military service remains a key component of the argument in favour of conscription, in spite of its manifest failures. It is fascinating (and disturbing) to contemplate, though, the nature of those values which are in fact being transmitted to conscripted soldiers through their experiences of military service. Although some Russian military officials have a tendency to blame society for what they regard as declining standards of behaviour in young people, the evidence presented in Webber and Zilberman's chapter clearly demonstrates that the experience of military service for many Russian conscripts is a brutalising one. In the worst cases, a conscript's basic human rights are not respected and he will learn to fear and hate those in positions of authority, who often exercise power over him in an arbitrary way. The irony is that the Russian military may indeed be socialising the next generation of young men (or, at least, those who do not manage to evade military service), but by exposing them to its own practices and attitudes it may be contributing to the very anti-social behaviours which it professes to deplore.

As I argue in chapter 8 on women soldiers, one aspect of socialisation which military service seems to contribute to very effectively is the formation and maintenance of gender roles in Russian society. The experience of being a soldier is closely connected in the public perception to the process of becoming a 'real man'. In spite of the enormous difficulties which the MOD faces in recruiting and retaining sufficient male personnel to carry out its essential functions, there are few signs that restrictions on women's participation in the armed forces will be relaxed or that the MOD would welcome further increases in the female proportion of its soldiers. Instead there is a strong resistance to any weakening of the bond between military service and masculinity, and military leaders are expending great efforts to reshape the terms of contract service to make them more attractive to men while in effect ignoring the substantial labour pool of educated and underemployed women. It is ironic, then, that this particular challenge to the traditions and practices of military service – the presence on a large scale of women in the ranks – is in part a result of the way that the military treats its (male) officers. Many of the women volunteering for contract service are the wives and daughters of officers whose salaries are woefully inadequate as the sole means of support of their families.

While the military appears keen to function as a source of social values and certainly takes steps to protect its association with *masculine* values, Elisabeth Sieca-Kozlowski's contribution on the Cossacks (chapter 10) provides a further twist on this aspect of the relationship between society and the military. The fact that Cossack groups are permitted to operate youth training programmes, especially those with strong military overtones to their activities, suggests a recognition by civilian and military authorities alike that the armed forces need some help in this respect. Could it be that the Russian military has moved so far away from its traditional values that it needs the aid of a community of civilians – albeit a deeply militarised one – in the effort to reinstate those values and to instil them in the next generation?

Although the strength of the Russian military's hold on its traditional values may be questionable, Julian Cooper's and Bettina Renz's contributions on the defence economy and on the military's relationship with the media (chapters 2 and 6) both demonstrate that it is particularly tenacious in its attempts to retain its traditional privileges. Cooper draws our attention to the persistence in Russia of official attitudes to secrecy and restrictions on access to defence-related information which were honed during the Soviet period. While this is a disappointing feature, it is not particularly surprising or necessarily even alarming. As Webber points out in the Introduction, the governments of states around the world share the desire to restrict access to information significant for national security, and many (including those in the West) find creative ways to expand that category.

More worrying is Cooper's view that 'those pressing for greater transparency and civilian involvement face not only opposition from within the security establishment, but a predominant view from society that military-economic matters should be the preserve of military specialists'. This raises the possibility that civil society in Russia is not overly concerned about the State's failure to provide even fairly basic information about defence spending and the defence economy. This is clearly an issue where further research is needed, but it is important to note that this apparent lack of public concern comes at time when defence spending in Russia is low and the defence industry is on its knees. As Cooper says, 'the "monster" has shrunk and no longer presents a threat to Russia's economic prosperity'. If the public in Russia is indeed uninterested in this issue, then perhaps it is less concerned about monitoring the detailed operation of an MIC whose size and significance now reflect more accurately the priorities of society. It may also be the case that Russian society has learned through generations of bitter experience to distrust assurances and information which come through official channels, and therefore does not place a great deal of importance on Western-style institutions and processes of civil-military relations. Forms of control and procedures which take place at the elite level are also perhaps more susceptible to manipulation or *management* than those forms which are less formal and less visible. This is not to belittle the potential significance of such institutions and processes for the development of a more democratic and accountable Russia. I do want to suggest, however, that we need to be alert to the possibility that accountability and societal control of the armed forces in Russia will take forms which do not greatly resemble 'civil-military relations' as they are practiced in the West.

The military is similarly seeking to retain its traditional controls over what is reported about defence issues and the armed forces in the media, as Bettina Renz demonstrates, especially now that the clearly defined lines of authority and control over this area, which characterised much of the Soviet period, have broken down. As Renz points out, representatives of the military and of the civilian media have very different views about who should make the decisions on what is reported, reflecting their distinctive views of the roles the media should play in relation to the armed forces. And although Renz discovered among Russian journalists a strong sense of frustration that they are not able to play the full *watchdog* role which they feel is both important and appropriate for the media to adopt in a democratic society, it was also clear from her interviews with military officials that the media's criticisms of the armed forces has placed considerable pressure on those officials. Neither the media nor the military feel able to perform their professional duties as freely as they would wish. Each side feels uncomfortable and unfairly constrained by the actions of the other, but there is a dialogue under way here, which is testing boundaries and establishing some foundations for future media-military relations.

The examples I have discussed thus far have focused on the Russian military's search for its new identity by attempting to cling to elements of its old identity. In chapter 5, Pavel Baev analyses two of the military's attempts to find new roles for itself and to make new connections with the State and society: the creation of a new collective identity for the military as a presidential institution; and the short-term alliances which were formed between military units and local elites in some of Russia's regions. Although neither of these developments proved to be long-lasting, they serve to reinforce the image of a Russian military which is confused and fragmented.

Mikhail Alexseev makes a compelling case in chapter 4 for supposing that even the most senior officials of the State are increasingly taking notice of the views and preferences of society in relation to defence policy issues. Alexseev argues that Vladimir Putin's positions and policies on the second Chechen conflict can be explained as the responses of a leader repelling perceived challenges to the integrity of the State and the honour of the nation, and in doing so addressing himself *to the audience of public opinion*. Alexseev's view of the state–society–military relationship during the second Chechen war places society and social attitudes at the centre, even in the driving seat. This view of the dynamics of this relationship is strikingly different from the impression, one which we are routinely offered through Western media reports, of a Russian society that is powerless to change the government's policies towards Chechnia. If we consider also Valerie Zawilski's discussion (chapter 9) of the activities of the CSM during the first Chechen war, we can see that society has had a profound influence on the direction of both conflicts.

Zawilski's study of the CSM also provides an important reminder of the way that the rights and the fate of the individual seems to resonate with society in Russia today to a much greater extent than in the past. If Julian Cooper suggests that society may remain reluctant to challenge the military's authority on issues of high politics, such as the defence budget, then Zawilski indicates that society *is* willing to take action on behalf of those who are in danger of being consumed by the military machine. The experience of the CSM provides a rare example in Russia of grassroots action which has demonstrable effects on an institution of the State, and we know from the evidence cited by Webber and Zilberman in this volume that some officers have been influenced by the SMOs' views on such issues as human rights and military service. We can see similar evidence in some of the examples provided in Renz's chapter which demonstrates that media coverage of an issue affecting individuals – *dedovshchina* – elicits a remarkably strong response from both society and the military. By way of contrast, Renz quotes a Russian journalist expressing despair at the lack of interest in press coverage of illicit arms deals conducted in the middle of Moscow. Once again, the fate of the individual strikes a chord where issues which are more abstract, or which exist at the level of 'high politics', apparently do not.

David Gillespie provides, in chapter 3, a vivid demonstration of the extent to which cinema can act as a mirror of the condition of a state and its society, but it is even more remarkable that Russian film-makers should so often turn to the genre of the war film for this purpose. If we are tempted to regard society and the military in Russia as growing steadily apart, Gillespie's chapter should act as a corrective. Through the repetition of key themes and images – in particular the predominance of a focus on vulnerable or tragic individuals rather than on large-scale, mass spectacles – the range of relations between society and the military are played out. The prominence which these features are given is itself an indication of the centrality of the SMI in Russia.

Finally, the lessons about Russia's society-military relations which this reader takes away from this volume centre on the importance of attending closely both to developments at the lower levels of this relationship and to indications, often informal and subtle, of societal influence on the military. Although both sides in the society-military equation appear to believe that this relationship is characterised much more by continuity than by change, there are unmistakeable signs of a shift in its balance.

Select bibliography

Adomeit, H., H.-H. Hoehmann and G. Wagenlehner (eds) *Die Sowjetunion als Militärmacht* (Stuttgart: Kohlhammer, 1987).

Aldis, A. and R. McDermott (eds) *Russian Military Reform, 1992–2002* (London: Frank Cass, 2003).

Allison, R. and C. Bluth (eds) *Security Dilemmas in Russia and Eurasia* (London: Royal Institute of International Affairs, 1998).

Altunin, P., 'Zhenshchina na voennoi sluzhbe', *Krasnaia zvezda* (10 March 1993).

Andreski, S., *Military Organization and Society* (London: Routledge & Kegan Paul, 1968).

Arbatov, A., 'Military reform in Russia', *International Security*, 22:4 (1998).

Arbatov, A., 'Russia: military reform', in *SIPRI Yearbook 1999: Armaments, Disarmament and International Security* (Oxford: SIPRI – Oxford University Press, 1999).

Azhgikhina, N., 'Nemuzhskie problemy vooruzhennykh sil', *Nezavismoe voennoe obozrenie*, 16 (26 April–16 May 1997).

Baev, P., *The Russian Army in a Time of Troubles* (London: Sage, 1996).

Baev, P., 'The Russian armed forces: failed reform attempts and creeping regionalization', in D. Betz and J. Löwenhardt (eds) *Army and State in Postcommunist Europe* (London: Frank Cass, 2001), pp. 23–42

Baev, P., 'The Russian Army and Chechnya: victory instead of reform?' in S. Cimbala (ed.), *The Russian Military into the Twenty-First Century* (London: Frank Cass, 2001), pp. 75–95.

Baev, P., *Russia in 2015: Could the Former Super-Power Turn into a Battle-Ground?* (Oslo: Forsvarsstudier, 2002).

Bannikov, K., *Antropologiia ekstremal'nykh grupp: dominantnye otnosheniia sredi voennosluzhashchikh srochnoi sluzhby* (Moscow: Institut etnologii i antropologii RAN, 2002).

Baranets, V., *El'tsin i ego generaly: zapiski polkovnika Genshtaba* (Moscow: Sovershenno sekretno, 1997).

Baranets, V., *Poteriannaia armiia: zapiski polkovnika Genshtaba* (Moscow: Sovershenno sekretno, 1998).

Barylski, R., *The Soldier in Russian Politics: Duty, Dictatorship, and Democracy Under Gorbachev and Yeltsin* (London: Transaction Publishers, 1998).

Batolkin, E., E. Liuboshits, E. Khrustalev and V. Tsymbal, *Voennaia reforma: reforma sistemy komplektovaniia voennoi organizatsii Rossii* (St. Petersburg: Norma, 2001).

Belanovskii, S. (ed.) *Dedovshchina v armii: sbornik sotsiologicheskikh dokumentov* (Moscow: Institut ekonomicheskogo prognozirovaniia, 1991).

Betz, D., *Civil–Military Relations in Russia and Eastern Europe* (London: Routledge Curzon, 2004).

Betz, D. and J. Löwenhardt (eds) *Army and State in Postcommunist Europe* (London: Frank Cass, 2001).

Beumers, B., 'Myth-making and myth-taking: lost ideals and the war in contemporary Russian cinema', *Canadian Slavonic Papers*, 42:1–2 (March–June 2000).

Black, C., (ed.) *The Transformation of Russian Society* (Cambridge, MA: Harvard University Press, 1969).

Blank, S., 'The new turn in Russian defence policy', in S. Cimbala (ed.) *The Russian Military into the Twenty-First Century* (London: Frank Cass, 2001), pp. 53–73.

Busza, E., 'State dysfunctionality, institutional decay, and the Russian military', in V. Sperling (ed.) *Building the Russian State: Institutional Crisis and the Quest for Democratic Governance* (Boulder, CO: Westview Press, 2000).

Caiazza, A. *Mothers and Soldiers: Gender, Citizenship and Civil Society in Contemporary Russia* (London: Routledge, 2002).

Cimbala, S. (ed.) *The Russian Military into the Twenty-First Century* (London: Frank Cass, 2001).

Cockburn, A., *The Threat: Inside the Soviet Military Machine* (London: Random House, 1984).

Colton, T., *Commissars, Commanders, and Civilian Authority: The Structure of Soviet Military Politics* (Cambridge, MA: Harvard University Press, 1979).

Cooper, J., 'Demilitarizing the Russian defence economy: a commentary', *Security Dialogue*, 26:1 (March 1995).

Cooper, J., 'The future role of Russian defence industry', in R. Allison and C. Bluth (eds) *Security Dilemmas in Russia and Eurasia* (London: Royal Institute of International Affairs, 1998), pp. 94–117.

Crutcher, M. (ed.) *The Russian Armed Forces at the Dawn of the Millennium* (Carlisle Barracks, PA: US Army War College, 2000).

Daucé, F., *L'Etat, l'armée et le citoyen en Russie postsoviétique* (Paris: L'Harmattan, 2001).

Deriugin, Iu. and V. Serebriannikov, *Armiia Rossii: sostoianie i perspektivy vykhoda iz krizisa. Sotsial'no–politicheskii srez sovremennogo voennogo sotsiuma* (Moscow: Institut sotsial'no–politicheskikh issledovanii, 1998).

Desch, M., *Civilian Control of the Military: The Changing Security Environment* (London: Johns Hopkins University Press, 1999).

Dobrenkov, V., *Sotsiologiia v Rossii: voennaia sotsiologiia* (Moscow: Mezhdunarodnyi Universitet Biznesa i Upravleniia, 2002).

Elshtain, J. and S. Tobias (eds) *Women, Militarism, and War* (New York: Rowman & Littlefield, 1989).

Enloe, C., *Maneuvers: The International Politics of Militarizing Women's Lives* (Berkeley: University of California Press, 2000).

Ermolaeva, T. and V. Georgiev, 'Neprikosnovennyi zapas ili poslednii rezerv?' *Nezavismoe voennoe obozrenie*, 8 (4–10 March 1999).

Evangelista, M., *The Chechen Wars: Will Russia Go the Way of the Soviet Union?* (Washington, DC: Brookings Institution, 2002).

Feinman, I., *Citizenship Rites: Feminist Soldiers and Feminist Antimilitarists* (New York and London: New York University Press, 2000).

Galeotti, M., *Afghanistan: The Soviet Union's Last War* (London: Frank Cass, 2002).

Genin, V. (ed.) *The Anatomy of Russian Defense Conversion* (Walnut Creek, CA: Vega Press, 2001).

Grushin, B., *Chetyre zhizni Rossii: V zerkale oprosov obshchestvennogo mneniia. Epokha Khrushcheva* (Moscow: Progress-Traditsiia, 2001).

Gudkov, L., *Negativnaia identichnost'* (Moscow: NLO, 2003).

Herspring, D., *Russian Civil–Military Relations* (Bloomington: Indiana University Press, 1996).

Herspring, D., 'Women in the Russian military: a reluctant marriage', *Minerva: Quarterly Report on Women and the Military*, 15:2 (1997).

Holloway, D. 'State, society and the military under Gorbachev', *International Security*, 4:3 (1989/90).

Honneland, G. and A.-K. Jorgensen, *Integration versus Autonomy: Civil-Military Relations on the Kola Peninsula* (London: Ashgate, 1999).

Jones, E., *Red Army and Society: A Sociology of the Soviet Military* (Boston, MA: Allen and Unwin, 1985).

Kokoshin, A., *Armiia i politika: sovetskaia voenno–politicheskaia i voenno–strategicheskaia mysl'*, *1918–1991 gody* (Moscow: Mezhdunarodnye otnosheniia, 1995).

Kolkowicz, R., *The Soviet Military and the Communist Party* (Princeton, NJ: Princeton University Press, 1967).

Kuebart, F., 'Patriotische Wehrerziehung in der Sowjetunion', in H. Adomeit, H.-H. Hoehmann and G. Wagenlehner (eds) *Die Sowjetunion als Militärmacht* (Stuttgart: Kohlhammer, 1987) pp. 90–114.

Kuhlmann, J., and J. Callaghan (eds) *Military and Society in 21st Century Europe* (New Brunswick, NJ: Transaction Publishers, 2000).

Levada, Iu., *Ot mnenii k ponimaniiu* (Moscow: Moskovskaia shkola politicheskikh issledovanii, 2000).

Lieven, A., *Chechnya: Tombstone of Russian Power* (New Haven, CT: Yale University Press, 1998).

Marchenko, V., *Takaia armiia: narusheniia prav cheloveka v vooruzhennykh silakh* (Moscow: Norma, 1995).

Mathers, J., 'Women in the Russian Armed Forces: A Marriage of Convenience?', *Minerva: Quarterly Report on Women and the Military* 18:3–4 (2000).

Mathers, J., 'Reform and the Russian military', in T. Farrell and T. Terriff (eds) *The Sources of Military Change: Culture, Politics, Technology* (Boulder and London: Lynne Rienner, 2002), pp. 161–84.

Mathers, J., 'Outside politics? Civil–military relations during a period of reform', in A. Aldis and R. McDermott (eds) *Russian Military Reform 1992–2002* (London: Frank Cass, 2003), pp. 22–40.

Mathers, J., 'Russia's women soldiers in the twenty-first century', *Minerva: Women and War*, 21:1 (2004).

Mickiewicz, E., *Changing Channels: Television and the Struggle for Power in Russia* (Oxford: Oxford University Press, 1997).

Minaev, A. (ed.) *Sovetskaia voennaia moshch' ot Stalina do Gorbacheva* (Moscow: Voennyi parad, 1999).

Modnikova, I., *Social Problems of the Russian Military* (Alexandria, VA: Center for Naval Analysis, January 1997).

Moskos, C., J. Williams and D. Segal (eds) *The Postmodern Military: Armed Forces After the Cold War* (Oxford: Oxford University Press, 2000).

Nygren, B. and Y. Fedorov (eds) *Russian Military Reform and Russia's New Security Environment* (Stockholm: National Defence College, 2003).

Odom, W., *The Collapse of the Soviet Military* (New Haven, CT: Yale University Press, 1998).

Orr, M., 'New structures, old thinking', in M. Crutcher (ed.), *The Russian Armed Forces at the Dawn of the Millennium* (Carlisle Barracks, PA: US Army War College, 2000), pp. 159–70.

Panfilov, O. and A. Simonov, *Informatsionnaia voina v Chechne: Fakty, dokumenty, svidetel'stva. noiabr' 1994 – sentiabr' 1996* (Moscow: Prava Cheloveka, 1997).

Pogorelyi, M. and I. Safranchuk (eds) *Contemporary Russian Military Journalism: Experience, Problems, Perspectives* (Moscow: Gendalf, 2002).

Politkovskaia, A., *A Dirty War: A Russian Reporter in Chechnya* (London: Harvill Press, 2001).

Putin, V., *Ot pervogo litsa: razgovory s Vladimirom Putinym* (Moscow: Vagrius, 2000).

Rogozhkin, S., and O. Ruban (eds) *Dmitrii Kholodov. Vzryv: Khronika ubiistva zhurnalista* (Moscow: Eksim, 1998).

Sapper, M., 'Diffuznaia voinstvennost", *Neprikosnovennyi zapas*, 1 (1999).

Serebriannikov, V., *Bezopasnost' Rossii i armiia* (Moscow: Institute of Socio-Political Research, 1995).

Shaw, M., *Post-Military Society: Militarism, Demilitarization and War at the End of the Twentieth Century* (London: Polity Press, 1991).

Simonsen, S.,'Marching to a different drum? Political orientations and nationalism in Russia's armed forces', *Journal of Communist Studies and Transition Politics*, 17:1 (2001).

Smirnov, A., 'Women in the Russian army', *Russian Social Science Review*, 43:4 (July–August 2002), translated and reproduced on the *Post-Soviet Armies' Newsletter* website: www.perso.club-internet.fr/kozlowsk/women.html.

Sperling, V. (ed.) *Building the Russian State: Institutional Crisis and the Quest for Democratic Governance* (Boulder, CO: Westview Press, 2000).

Starodubovskaia, I. and V. Mau, *Velikie revoliutsii: ot Kromvella do Putina* (Moscow: Vagrius, 2001).

Stishova, E., 'Zapiski s kavkazskoi voiny', *Iskusstvo kino*, 1 (1999).

Stishova, E., 'Tranzit: Visbaden–Pittsburg–Kavkaz: Kavkazskaia tema v rossiiskom kino', *Iskusstvo kino*, 1 (2002).

Stone, D., *Hammer and Rifle: The Militarization of the Soviet Union, 1926–1933* (Lawrence: University of Kansas Press, 2000).

Taylor, B., *Politics and the Russian Army: Civil–Military Relations, 1689–2000* (Cambridge: Cambridge University Press, 2003).

Thomas, T., 'Fault lines and factions in the Russian army', *Orbis*, 39:4 (1995).

Troshev, G., *Moia voina: Chechenskii dnevnik okopnogo generala* (Moscow: Vagrius, 2001).

Ure, J., *The Cossacks* (London: Constable, 1999).

Ustinovich, E., 'Zhenshchina i armiia: voprosy komplektovaniia', *Voennaia mysl'*, 8 (2003).

Vallance, B., 'Russia's mothers: voices of change', *Minerva: Quarterly Report on Women and the Military*, 18:3–4 (2000).

Van Bladel, J., 'Russian soldiers in the barracks: a portrait of a subculture', in A. Aldis and R. McDermott (eds) *Russian Military Reform, 1992–2002* (London: Frank Cass, 2003), pp. 60–72.

Vikulov, S. (ed.), *Voenno–ekonomicheskii analiz* (Moscow: Voenizdat, 2001).

Vlachova, M. (ed.) *The Public Image of Defence and the Military in Central and Eastern Europe* (Geneva and Belgrade: DCAF and CCMR, 2003).

Wagnsson, C., *Russian Political Language and Public Opinion on the West, NATO and Chechnya: Securitization Theory Reconsidered* (Stockholm: University of Stockholm, 2000).

Webber, S. 'The return of *Nachal'naia Voennaia Podgotovka*: a military coup in Russia's schools?' Paper presented at the conference 'Post-Soviet education', Indiana University, Bloomington, 16–18 June 2000, available online: www.crees.bham.ac.uk/staff/webber/index.htm.

Webber, S., 'Public attitudes toward the armed forces in Russia: do they count?', in S. Cimbala (ed.) *The Russian Military into the Twenty-First Century* (London: Frank Cass, 2001), pp. 153–78.

Webber, S. and I. Liikanen (eds) *Education and Civic Culture in Post-Communist Countries* (London: Palgrave, 2001).

Webber, S. and J. van Bladel, 'Russia's past or future?' *World Today*, 56:10 (2000).

Webber, S. and A. Zilberman, 'Military aspects of citizenship in Russia', in B. Nygren and Y. Fedorov (eds) *Russian Military Reform and Russia's New Security Environment* (Stockholm: National Defence College, 2004), pp. 127–37.

Weigle, M., *Russia's Liberal Project: State–Society Relations in the Transition from Communism* (Philadelphia: Penn State University Press, 2000).

Women's Research and Education Institute, *Women in the Military: Where They Stand*, 3rd edn (Washington, DC: WREI, 2000).

Zaslavsky, V., 'The Soviet system and the Soviet Union: causes of collapse', in K. Barkey and M. von Hagen (eds) *After Empire* (Boulder Westview Press, 1997).

Zaslavsky, V., *Storia del sistema sovietico: L'ascesa, la stabilita, il crollo* (Roma: Carocci, 2001).

Zolotarev, V. A., *Voennaia bezopasnost' gosudarstva Rossiiskogo* (Moscow: Kuchkovo Pole, 2001).

Index

Iraq war (2003) 52, 133, 183, 217
Ivanov, S. 121, 177, 192–3
Iziumov, A. 137, 149

*Kavkazskii plennik see Prisoner of the
    Mountains*
KGB *see Komitet Gosudarstvennoi
    Bezopasnosti*
Khattab, I. 100, 103, 106
Kholodov, D. 18
Khotinenko, V. 82
Khrushchev, N. 18, 40
Khudoinazarov, B. 82, 91
Kirbassova, M. 228
Kireev, A. 137
Kirienko, S. 251
Kokoshin, A. 142, 150
Komitet Gosudarstvennoi Bezopasnosti
    (KGB) 4, 8, 40, 48, 50, 54, 102,
    137, 139
Komitet Soldatskikh Materei see
    Committee of Soldiers' Mothers
Konchalovskii, A. 90–1
Korzhakov, A. 49
Kotovskii 80, 91
Kozlov, G. 148
Kudelina, L. 144–5
Kulakova, Z. 232–3
Kulikov, A. 73
Kursk 5, 74, 120, 183
Kuznetsova, L. 237
Kvashnia, A. 116

Lebedev, I. 190
Lebedev, N. 80, 91
legitimacy 18, 161, 183, 186, 196–7
Liuboshits, E. 142–3, 150
Lobov, O. 245
Lopatin, V. 24, 194
Lunnyi papa see Moon Daddy
Luzhkhov, I. 105, 108

mafia 248–9
Maliukov, A. 88, 91
Marsh-brosok see Forced March
Masliukov, I. 135–6
Maslov, P. 248
Matrosov, A. 88

MChS *see* Ministry for Emergency
    Situations
media 4–6, 9, 13, 17–18, 25, 39, 51,
    61–75, 85, 98, 109, 116, 140,
    142, 147, 161, 165, 168–71,
    175–6, 180–2, 185, 188–9, 192,
    208, 215–17, 219–21, 230,
    234–6, 246–7, 251, 253, 260–2
  censorship 18, 42, 61–2, 72
Mel'nikova, V. 229
Memorial 24, 189
Ménage-à-trois 81, 91
MIC *see* military–industrial complex
MID *see* Ministry of Foreign Affairs
Mikhailov, N. 150
militarisation 1, 8–12, 15–16, 19, 23,
    42, 44, 135, 159, 161, 163, 179,
    196, 250–3
militarism 8–13, 15, 19, 23, 43, 53, 55,
    160, 163, 165, 234
military
  alternative service 23, 178–9,
    189–90, 194, 228–9
  brutality 2, 6, 14, 70, 84–6, 117,
    173, 192, 195, 228, 259
  budget 5, 22, 56, 62, 117, 132,
    142–52, 262
  civilian control 2, 18, 20, 40, 61, 69,
    116–17, 133, 142, 160, 261
  contract service 54–6, 177–8, 207,
    210–11, 217, 250, 260
  corruption 1–2, 17, 62, 69, 84–5
  coup 1, 20, 72
  culture 7, 26, 116–18, 121, 123,
    175, 184, 218
  economy 131–52, 260–1
  expenditure 1, 4–5, 7, 10–11, 21–2,
    46–7, 56, 62, 116–17, 119,
    120–1, 123, 125–6, 131–52, 160,
    261
  General Staff 74, 116, 121, 136–9,
    143, 150, 169, 192, 194
  industry 62, 117, 132–52, 258, 261
  political influence 1–2, 7, 19, 39,
    48–51
  professional 3, 5–7, 21, 23–6, 55–6,
    123–5, 150–1, 160, 177–8,
    190–2, 194, 197